AF771093

Intellectual Property at the Crossroads of Trade

ATRIP INTELLECTUAL PROPERTY

Series Editors: Annette Kur, *Max Planck Institute for Intellectual Property and Competition Law, Germany* and Jan Rosén, *Stockholm University, Sweden*

The ATRIP series presents the fruit of annual meetings held by the International Association for the Advancement of Teaching and Research in Intellectual Property (www.atrip.org). Yielding unique opportunities for IP scholars from a global community to explore together the different facets of one overarching topic, the essence of those meetings is captured in the edited compilation of selected contributions contained in the volumes. Rather than employing a traditional, compartmentalized view of the different areas of IP, the ATRIP series typically applies a horizontal approach, cutting across the usual boundaries of legal categorization, with the aim to uncover hidden commonalities, and accentuate the need for differentiation where that is called for. As ATRIP counts among its members leading IP scholars from all parts of the world, and actively encourages participation of highly talented young researchers, the panel of authors contributing to the volumes does not only guarantee excellence, but also represents a full and vibrant picture of contemporary, high-level IP research in an international setting.

Titles in the series include:

The Structure of Intellectual Property Law
Can One Size Fit All?
Edited by Annette Kur and Vytautas Mizaras

Individualism and Collectiveness in Intellectual Property Law
Edited by Jan Rosén

Intellectual Property at the Crossroads of Trade
Edited by Jan Rosén

Intellectual Property at the Crossroads of Trade

Edited by

Jan Rosén

Professor of Private Law, Stockholm University, Sweden and ATRIP President

ATRIP INTELLECTUAL PROPERTY

Edward Elgar

Cheltenham, UK • Northampton, MA, USA

© The Editor and Contributors Severally 2012

All rights reserved. No part of this publication may be reproduced, stored in a retrieval system or transmitted in any form or by any means, electronic, mechanical or photocopying, recording, or otherwise without the prior permission of the publisher.

Published by
Edward Elgar Publishing Limited
The Lypiatts
15 Lansdown Road
Cheltenham
Glos GL50 2JA
UK

Edward Elgar Publishing, Inc.
William Pratt House
9 Dewey Court
Northampton
Massachusetts 01060
USA

A catalogue record for this book
is available from the British Library

Library of Congress Control Number: 2012940999

MIX
Paper from responsible sources
FSC® C018575

ISBN 978 1 78195 168 2

Typeset by Cambrian Typesetters, Camberley, Surrey
Printed and bound by MPG Books Group, UK

Contents

Contributors

Maciej Barczewski
Dr Maciej Barczewski is Head of Postgraduate Studies in Intellectual Property and High Technology Law, Faculty of Law and Administration at the University of Gdańsk (Poland), and a member of the Polish Bar. Dr Barczewski has also been an Adjunct Professor at IIT Chicago-Kent College of Law and a Visiting Researcher at the Oxford Intellectual Property Research Centre at the Faculty of Law, University of Oxford. He has published four books and over thirty articles in leading law journals, including the *European Intellectual Property Review* and *International Journal of Intellectual Property and Competition Law*.

Dana Beldiman
Dr Dana Beldiman MA, JD, LLM (Int.Prop.) is a professor at Bucerius Law School, Hamburg (Germany), and Director of the Center for Transnational IP, Media and Technology Law and Policy at Bucerius Law School. She is a regular visiting professor at the University of California, Hastings College of Law, San Francisco. Her interest focuses on international and comparative aspects of intellectual property. Dr Beldiman is also a partner with Carroll, Burdick & McDonough LLP, in San Francisco, where she specializes in international intellectual property counselling and international transactions.

Irene Calboli
Dr Irene Calboli is Professor of Law and Director of the Intellectual Property and Technology Program at Marquette University Law School in the United States. She has written on numerous aspects of intellectual property law and her most recent scholarship focuses on trademark law and policy. Before moving to the United States, Dr Calboli was a Research Fellow at the University of Bologna Law School, and has held visiting research positions at King's College London, the University of California at Berkeley, the Max Planck Institute for Intellectual Property Law, and the University Complutense, Madrid (Spain). Most recently, she was the 2011 CIPLIT Visiting Professor of Law at DePaul University College of Law, and during the academic year 2011–12 she was a visiting professor at the Faculty of Law of the National University of Singapore. Dr Calboli holds an LLB and a

Doctorate of Research from the University of Bologna, an LLM from the London School of Economics and Political Science, and a Diploma in Trademarks Law from Queen Mary & Westfield College, London.

Jacques de Werra
Professor Jacques de Werra teaches contract law and intellectual property law at the Law School of the University of Geneva (Switzerland). He holds a doctoral degree from the University of Lausanne (1997), an LLM from Columbia Law School (2001), and has been admitted to the Swiss and New York Bars. He joined the Law School of the University of Geneva in 2006 after having practised in Switzerland and in New York. His teaching and research activities cover intellectual property law, contract law (particularly transfer of technology, licensing and franchising), information technology and internet law, as well as ADR mechanisms for IP disputes. He is the scientific editor for a series of intellectual property titles (www.pi-ip.ch) and organizes an annual international intellectual property law conference at the University of Geneva (www.jdpi.ch).

Josef Drexl
Josef Drexl is Director of the Max Planck Institute for Intellectual Property and Competition Law in Munich and an Honorary Professor of the University of Munich. He also chairs the Managing Board of the Munich Intellectual Property Law Centre, which runs an LLM programme in IP. He is the founding Chair of the Academic Society for Competition Law (ASCOLA). He has acted as visiting professor at Oxford (UK), LUISS Rome and NYU. He regularly teaches at the University of Paris 2. Professor Drexl is an expert in competition law, intellectual property law, consumer law and WTO law.

Christophe Geiger
Christophe Geiger is Associate Professor, Director General and Director of the Research Department of the Centre for International Intellectual Property Studies (CEIPI) at the University of Strasbourg (France), where he teaches intellectual property and competition law. He is also in charge at the CEIPI of the Masters 2 (LLM) on European and International IP Law, co-directs the Masters on Intellectual Property Law and Management (MIPLM) and a joint degree in intellectual property organized in conjunction with the University of Skopje (Macedonia). In addition, he is an affiliated senior researcher at the Max Planck Institute for Intellectual Property, Competition and Tax Law in Munich (Germany), where he was until 2008 in charge of the Department of France and French-Speaking African countries. He specializes in national, European, international and comparative copyright and intellectual property law, has drafted reports for the Council of Europe and the European

Parliament (to which he acts as external adviser) and has published numerous articles on copyright and intellectual property law.

Giuseppe Mazziotti

Giuseppe Mazziotti (PhD, European University Institute, Florence (Italy)) worked as attorney and then as counsel with Nunziante Magrone in Rome from 2007 to 2011. From 2009 to 2011 he was Assistant Professor of Intellectual Property Law at the University of Copenhagen (Denmark). He has published extensively in the fields of intellectual property law, competition law and information technology law. Dr Mazziotti was Visiting Scholar at the University of California, Berkeley (2004–05) and at Columbia Law School, New York (2010–11). He is now Fellow at the Berkman Center for Internet and Society at Harvard Law School and can be reached at giuseppe.mazziotti@gmail.com.

Charles R. McManis

Charles R. McManis is the Thomas and Karole Green Professor of Law and former Director of the Intellectual Property & Technology Law Program at Washington University in St Louis, Missouri. He received his BA degree from Birmingham-Southern College in 1964, and both his MA (in Philosophy) and JD degrees from Duke University in 1972. During 1993 and 1994, Professor McManis was Fulbright Fellow in Korea, where he lectured and undertook research at the International Intellectual Property Training Institute in Taejon. He has served as a consultant for the World Intellectual Property Organization in India, Korea and Oman. Professor McManis' book, *Intellectual Property & Unfair Competition in a Nutshell*, is now in its sixth edition and a seventh is being prepared. He is also co-author of *Licensing Intellectual Property in the Information Age*, the second edition of which was published in 2005 by Carolina Academic Press. He is also the editor of a multi-authored volume, entitled *Biodiversity and the Law: Intellectual Property, Biotechnology and Traditional Knowledge* (Earthscan/James & James, 2007).

John S. Pelletier

John S. Pelletier is a 2012 JD candidate at Washington University School of Law, St Louis, Missouri. He received his Bachelors of Music degree in Music Production & Engineering from Berklee College of Music in Boston, Massachusetts in 2006. Currently, he serves as Executive Editor on the *Washington University Law Review*. John has recently written on the subject of digital sampling and United States copyright law, and his note on this topic, *Sampling the Circuits: The Case for a New Comprehensive Scheme for Determining Copyright Infringement as a Result of Music Sampling*, will be published by the *Washington University Law Review* in 2012.

Irini Stamatoudi
Irini Stamatoudi is currently the Director of the Hellenic Copyright Organization. She holds a law degree from the University of Athens (Greece) and an LLM and PhD from the University of Leicester (UK). She has taught at the Law School of the University of Leicester, on the joint LLM of the University of Turin (Italy), ILO and WIPO and at the Academy of the World Intellectual Property Organization. She is one of the two co-authors of the WIPO Academy specialization course on copyright. She has published eight books and numerous articles in law journals in Greece, the UK, Germany, Switzerland, the Netherlands, the US, Poland and Turkey. She is also a contributor for Greece to P.E. Geller's *International Copyright Laws and Practice*.

Sebastian Sykuna
Dr Sebastian Sykuna is Assistant Professor in the Department of Theory and Philosophy of State and Law, Faculty of Law and Administration at the University of Gdańsk (Poland). His research addresses the theory and philosophy of law and human rights protection. Dr Sykuna has published over thirty articles including: 'Cultural Defence: New Challenges for Criminal Law in Europe' in M. Zirk-Sadowski et al. (eds), *Multicentrism as an Emerging Paradigm in Legal Theory* (Peter Lang Verlag, Frankurt am Main, 2009) (with Jerzy Zajadlo). He is also a member of the Polish Bar.

Paul Torremans
Paul Torremans is Professor of Intellectual Property Law at the School of Law, University of Nottingham (UK). His main research interest is the relationship between intellectual property and private international law and in this context he is a member of CLIP, the European Max-Planck-Group for Conflict of Laws in Intellectual Property. His recent publications include J.J. Fawcett and P.L.C. Torremans, *Intellectual Property and Private International Law* (OUP, 2nd edn, 2011) and P. Torremans, *Holyoak and Torremans Intellectual Property Law* (OUP, 6th edn, 2010).

Guido Westkamp
Professor Dr Guido Westkamp holds a Chair in Intellectual Property and Comparative Law at the Centre for Commercial Law Studies, Queen Mary College, University of London and is Co-Director of the Queen Mary Intellectual Property Research Institute. His main specialisms are in the areas of (comparative) copyright and trade mark law, unfair competition law, antitrust law and media law. He studied law at the Universities of Münster and London (Queen Mary College), and English and Russian Languages in Berlin and Münster.

Foreword

This book is the fruit of the ATRIP congress held in Singapore in 2011 under the common theme of 'IP Law at the Crossroads of Trade'. The 2011 Congress was organized by ATRIP in cooperation with the IP Academy of Singapore and the Faculty of Law at Singapore University, and with the support of the World Intellectual Property Organization (WIPO) and the International Federation of Patent Agents (FICPI). Organizational support to ATRIP is continuously offered by the Max Planck Institute for Intellectual Property and Competition Law.

The International Association for the Advancement of Teaching and Research in Intellectual Property (ATRIP)(www.atrip.org) is a unique community of IP scholars from all parts of the World, who congregate annually to exchange ideas, receive inspiration and gather information in a truly advanced academic atmosphere and environment. The editor was involved in the organization of the congress as President of ATRIP and host of the meeting. It is my wish to express my sincere gratitude to all those persons and institutions without whose support the successful arrangement of the meeting would not have been possible.

The Singapore programme, working under the chapeau of 'IP Law at the Crossroads of Trade', allowed the congress to embrace many fundamental and intrinsic elements of contemporary IP law, with also a certain reference to the region in which the congress was held. Emphasis was placed on goods in transit, exhaustion of rights, bilateral and international agreements, cross-border licensing and trade in goods of cultural heritage. Nevertheless, this book is not merely a compilation of the *per se* very interesting presentations made at the congress, but a selection of essays written specifically for this publication, which naturally connect with the contributors' oral presentations at the Singapore congress.

Accordingly, these contributions are intended to add to a full and rich picture of selected topics. This is why the book has been given a concise structure and theme – or, rather two themes, as the content is divided into two sections. Part I is entitled 'IP Licensing, Exhaustion and Competition Law', in which such distinguished writers as Josef Drexl, Paul Torremans, Guido Westkamp, Irene Calboli, Jacques de Werra, Dana Beldiman and Giuseppe Mazziotti present intrinsic and quite diverse, yet connected, topics. In Part II,

'Aspects of the Anti-Counterfeiting Trade Agreement', excellent scholars such as Christophe Geiger, Charles R. McManis, John S. Pelletier, Irini Stamatoudi, Maciej Barczewski and Sebastian Sykuna cover the very latest developments in the area of that intensely observed anti-counterfeit trade agreement.

It is my belief that this book will find its place on the market to attract a broader array of readers who are interested in topical issues relating to contemporary IP law.

Jan Rosén
ATRIP President

PART I

IP Licensing, Exhaustion and Competition Law

1. EU competition law and parallel trade in pharmaceuticals: lessons to be learned for WTO/TRIPS?

Josef Drexl

1. INTRODUCTION

The principle of European exhaustion is among the most fundamental principles of European intellectual property (IP) law. Its development goes back to the period prior to the adoption of the Single European Act of 1986, when the European Court of Justice (ECJ) promoted market integration by limiting the application of national laws, including IP laws, which created barriers to trade between the Member States. In doing so, the Court relied upon the principle of free movement of goods and former Article 36 EEC Treaty (now Article 36 TFEU) to prevent Member States from applying a principle of national exhaustion.[1]

However, it is to be recalled that even before recognition of the principle of European exhaustion, the ECJ, in its ground-breaking *Consten and Grundig* judgment, had held that parties to a trade mark licensing agreement violate the prohibition on restrictive agreements that is part of European competition law if the licensee is prevented from exporting branded goods to other Member States.[2] Hence, historically, the European competition law prohibition of private restraints on parallel trade preceded, and paved the ground for, the principle of European exhaustion, which, in turn, protects parallel trade against the application of national exhaustion under domestic IP laws.[3]

[1] The first case related to copyright: see Case 78/70 *Deutsche Grammophon* [1971] ECR 487. In later cases the principle was extended to other IP rights: See Case 15/74 *Centrafarm v Sterling Drug* [1974] ECR 1147 (on patents); Case 119/75 *Terrapin v Terranova* [1976] ECR 1039 (on trade marks).

[2] Cases 56 & 58/64 *Consten and Grundig* [1966] ECR 299.

[3] In *Deutsche Grammophon*, the German court referred the case to the ECJ with the question of whether application of the national exhaustion rule under German copyright law violated competition law. The ECJ rephrased the question in the sense of whether German law breached the European principle of free movement of goods: see *Deutsche Grammophon*, above note 1, paras 2–10.

The close link between the exhaustion principle and EU competition law characterized European law from the very beginning. In the EU legal order, the fundamental freedoms, including the principle of free movement of goods, and competition law are complementary legal instruments that pursue the identical goal of establishing and maintaining the internal market. The fundamental freedoms are addressed to Member States and prevent them from applying legal rules that collide with the internal market principle. Competition law, in turn, guarantees that private undertakings do not replace state-initiated barriers to trade by private restraints of competition. This is why territorial restrictions have always been a particular focus of EU competition law.

Since the 1960s and 1970s, when these principles were developed, EU law and EU intellectual property law have moved ahead. The ECJ is no longer the only or principal 'engine of market integration'. The Single European Act has facilitated internal market legislation and, thereby, has laid the foundation for harmonizing IP law in the Member States. In addition, since the 1990s, the European legislature has also created some unitary rights systems, such as the Community Trade Mark system in particular. In this shift from 'negative integration' under the free movement principles to 'positive integration' through legislation, the principle of European exhaustion has also made it to secondary IP law.[4]

European IP legislation has had its impact on how the ECJ views the role of IP in the internal market. Whilst IPRs were largely considered by the Court to be obstacles to free trade in the 1970s and 1980s, the Court now recognizes a positive role of IP with regard to market transparency (trade marks) and enhancing innovation and creativity (patents and copyright) in the internal market. Yet this development did not affect the principle of freedom of parallel trade, which apparently is deeply enshrined in the European legal order.

However, the most recent competition cases on trade in pharmaceuticals seem to be modifying the law on parallel trade within the EU. In three cases, which all involved restraints on parallel trade initiated by GlaxoSmithKline (GSK), the issue arose whether restraints on parallel trade between Member States should always, or practically always, be held to be illegal under EU competition law or whether the argument of innovation should justify a more lenient approach to restraints on parallel trade in pharmaceuticals. While, in

4 See Art. 7 First Council Directive 89/104/EEC to approximate the laws of the Member States relating to trade marks [1989] OJ L 40/1; Art. 15 Directive 98/71/EC of the European Parliament and the Council of 13 October 1998 on the legal protection of designs [1998] OJ L 289/28; Art. 4(2) Directive 2001/29/EC of the European Parliament and the Council of 22 May 2001 on the harmonization of certain aspects of copyright and related rights in the information society [2001] OJ L 167/10.

the first case, the referral was held inadmissible,[5] and the ECJ avoided the innovation argument in the second case,[6] in the last case the ECJ accepted the innovation argument in principle and held that, under former Article 81 EC (now Article 101 TFEU), it can justify a restraint of parallel trade implemented in the framework of a restrictive agreement.[7]

In none of these cases was the ECJ requested to go into reviewing its earlier case law on the European exhaustion principle. Yet, given the complementarity of the two legal instruments, the question may well be asked whether European law on free movement of goods relating to trade marks for pharmaceuticals and pharmaceutical patents needs to be reviewed. This, however, is not the question that will be considered here. Rather, this chapter seeks to investigate whether, from this most recent European development, lessons could be learned for the discussion at the international level, which has most recently become very heated with regard to the seizure of pharmaceuticals in transit in the European Union.

This chapter will dig deeper into the economics of parallel trade (in Section 2) and sketch the recent development of the above-mentioned European case law (Section 3). This chapter will then (in Section 4) turn to reconsider the issue of exhaustion from a global perspective with a particular focus on Article 6 TRIPS and, finally, will address the scenario of pharmaceuticals in transit (Section 5).

2. THE ECONOMICS OF PARALLEL TRADE

In recent years, economic theory on parallel trade has evolved considerably. Most economists would nowadays argue in favour of a more lenient approach towards restraints on parallel trade than was the case in the past. The reasons for this are basically twofold. First, restraints on parallel trade only reduce 'intra-brand' competition between dealers, but may be capable of promoting 'inter-brand' competition between manufacturers. Second, restraints on parallel trade allow for geographical price discrimination. Modern economics

---

[5] Case C-53/03 *Syfait and Others* [2005] ECR I-4609 (however, take account of the most interesting and influential opinion delivered by Advocate General Jacobs).

[6] Joined Cases C-468/06 to C-478/06 *Sot. Lélos kai Sia* [2008] ECR I-7139. See also Josef Drexl, 'Healing with Bananas – How Should Community Competition Law Deal with Restraints on Parallel Trade in Pharmaceuticals?', in Josef Drexl, Reto M. Hilty, Laurence Boy, Christine Godt and Bernard Remiche (eds), *Technology and Competition – Contributions in Honour of Hanns Ullrich* (Larcier 2009) 571.

[7] Joined Cases C-501/06, C-513/06, C-515/06 and C-519/06 P *GlaxoSmithKline v Commission* [2009] ECR I-9291.

argues that price discrimination can be efficient and, therefore, pro-competitive in many instances.

Restraints of parallel trade are restraints that relate to the distribution of goods. Modern economics advocates a lenient approach to such vertical restraints concerning the distribution of goods in general.[8] It is held that a manufacturer who faces fierce competition with other manufacturers (inter-brand competition) will not be able to harm competition by vertically restricting the freedom of dealers to compete. Quite the contrary, it is assumed that such manufacturers will structure their distribution systems in such a way that their ability to compete with other manufacturers will be enhanced. Vertical restraints are therefore held to be efficient and pro-competitive, at least if the manufacturer is not market-dominant. This is why some authors even recommend giving up the ban on vertical market partitioning along the borders of the EU Member States.[9]

The second evolution relates to the evaluation of the link between parallel trade and the manufacturer's ability to price discriminate geographically. Parallel trade makes it harder for manufacturers to charge different prices to consumers in different countries. Therefore, parallel trade serves the interests of consumers in the importing countries, where the ability to pay is higher, by bringing down prices.[10] At the same time, parallel trade puts pressure on manufacturers to raise prices in countries where the buying power is considerably lower in order to reduce the potential of parallel trade. In the EU, parallel trade therefore has a tendency to harmonize the level of consumer prices. It may drive prices down in richer countries and put economic pressure on poorer countries to adjust to higher prices.[11]

Whether parallel trade has overall positive welfare effects is less clear. What is obvious in the first place is that consumers in the exporting countries

---

8 A recent and most prominent manifestation of this is the judgment in *Leegin Creative Leather Products, Inc. v PSKS, Inc. et al.*, 551 U.S. 877 (2007), in which the US Supreme Court switched from *per se* illegality to a rule-of-reason approach on resale price maintenance. For a critical view on this case, see, for instance, Marina Lao, 'Resale Price Maintenance: A Reassessment of its Competitive Harms and Benefits', in Josef Drexl, Warren S. Grimes, Rudolph J.R. Peritz and Edward Swaine (eds), *More Common Ground for International Competition Law?* (Edward Elgar Publishing 2011) 59.

9 See, for instance, Denis Waelbroeck, 'Vertical Agreements: Four Years of Liberalisation by Regulation No. 2790/90 after 40 years of Legal (Block) Exemption', in Hanns Ullrich (ed.), *The Evolution of European Competition Law* (Edward Elgar Publishing 2006) 85, at 99–105.

10 According to Patricia M. Dazon, 'The Economics of Parallel Trade' (1998) 13 *Pharmacoeconomics* 293, 294, parallel trade is exporting low prices.

11 On the pricing of pharmaceuticals in the EU market see, in particular, Dazon, above note 10.

will be harmed, while consumers in the importing countries will benefit. Based on a global welfare analysis, economists therefore argue that positive welfare effects are more likely to arise where two countries are rather heterogeneous in relation to their market size.[12] If parallel trade takes place from a rather small country to a country with a huge number of consumers, the welfare benefits of bringing down prices in the importing country will outweigh the welfare losses in the exporting country.

With regard to competition law, the question is whether the law should prohibit price discrimination in the first place. Indeed, it seems that EU competition law is very critical toward discrimination in general. Discriminatory practices are listed as a competition law violation by both Article 101(1)(d) and Article 102(2)(c) TFEU. Yet modern economics, which is supported on this point by most of today's competition lawyers,[13] does not view price discrimination as *per se* anti-competitive. Territorial price discrimination is no exception to this. Economists advocate a more sophisticated assessment: price discrimination may be efficient in some cases and anti-competitive in others.[14] Most importantly it is held that charging different prices to different groups of consumers may lead to more efficient pricing in areas where producers have to cover high fixed costs like those caused by R&D expenditure in the pharmaceutical industry (so-called Ramsey pricing).[15]

In a competitive market, the reasons for price discrimination may be manifold indeed. Designing tailor-made price policies may serve much better the interests of specific consumer groups. In particular, if manufacturers are able to charge less to consumers in poorer countries, this will facilitate access to the specific goods for poorer consumers. As a consequence, price discrimination leads to cross-subsidization. In the drug market, where originator companies have to recoup high investment in R&D in world markets, price discrimination allows for keeping prices low, yet above the level of variable costs, in poorer countries, while consumers in the richer countries will finance R&D in the interest of patients in the whole world.

---

12 See Frank Müller-Langer, 'An Analysis of the Welfare Effects of Parallel Trade Freedom' [2008] *German Working Papers in Law and Economics*, Paper 9, available at: http://www.bepress.com/cgi/viewcontent.cgi?article=1225&context=gwp (accessed 3 July 2012).

13 See, for instance, Peter Behrens, 'Parallelhandelsbeschränkungen und Konsumentenwohlfahrt – Zur neueren Rechtsprechung von EuG und EuGH' [2008] *Zeitschrift für Wettbewerbsrecht* 20 (commenting on the GSK cases).

14 See, for instance, Femi Alesi, *Federal Antitrust and EC Competition Law* (Ashgate 2008) 374 et seq.; Wolfgang Kerber and Ullrich Schwalbe, 'Ökonomische Grundlagen des Wettbewerbsrechts', in Günter Hirsch, Frank Montag and Franz Jürgen Säcker (eds), *Münchener Kommentar Europäisches und Deutsches Wettbewerbsrecht (Kartellrecht)* (Verlag C.H. Beck 2007) 238, paras 1454 et seq.

15 Dazon, above note 10, 295.

3. EU COMPETITION LAW AND PARALLEL TRADE IN PHARMACEUTICALS

Traditionally, EU law does not distinguish between the legal regimes governing parallel trade in pharmaceuticals and parallel trade in other products. The most obvious manifestation of this is provided by the ECJ judgment in *Merck v Stephar*; in this case the Court confirmed the application of the principle of European exhaustion where the holder of a pharmaceutical patent was denied the ability to rely on the principle of national exhaustion even in a case where the exporting country, at the time when the case arose, did not even provide for the possibility of pharmaceutical patents.[16]

3.1 The Greek and Spanish GlaxoSmithKline Cases

Equal treatment of parallel trade in pharmaceuticals with parallel trade in any other product, however, was questioned by Advocate General Jacobs in his opinion in *Syfait*.[17] Based on three particularities of the pharmaceutical market – namely (i) the high level of regulation of this market in the different Member States, (ii) the importance of R&D expenditure as a competition parameter in the pharmaceutical industry, and (iii) the doubtful beneficial effects on consumers of parallel trade in pharmaceuticals – he held restraints of trade in pharmaceuticals to be capable of justification under former Article 82 EC (now Article 102 TFEU).[18] Yet he also made clear that he considered his conclusions to be 'highly specific to the pharmaceutical industry'.[19]

Advocate General Jacobs' opinion was without any influence on the proceedings concerned. Indeed, he had to provide his opinion on a referral for preliminary judgment initiated by the Greek Competition Commission, which had to decide whether the unilateral refusal of GSK to deliver drugs to Greek wholesalers beyond demand in Greece violated former Article 82 EC (now Article 102 TFEU). This case raised the preliminary question of whether the Greek Competition Commission was to be considered a court or a tribunal of a Member State in the sense of former Article 235 EC (now Article 267 TFEU). This question, against the position of Advocate General Jacobs, was answered in the negative by the ECJ and, therefore, the referral was rejected as inadmissible without the Court addressing the substantive issues of the case.

---

16 Case 187/80 *Merck v Stephar* [1981] ECR 2063 (no patent protection for pharmaceuticals in Italy).

17 AG Jacobs, *Syfait and Others*, above note 5.

18 Ibid., para 100.

19 Ibid.

Yet Advocate General Jacobs' questioning of the illegality of restraints on parallel trade had by then launched an intensive debate on how to deal with parallel trade in the future. Most importantly, in October 2006, two years after Jacobs had rendered his opinion in *Syfait*, it was for the Court of First Instance (CFI, now General Court) to take up some of his ideas in the Spanish GSK case.[20] In Spain, GSK applied a slightly different approach to prevent domestic wholesalers from exporting GSK products to other EU Member States. Instead of simply reducing the volume of sales in Spain, GSK attempted to implement a dual pricing scheme that would have obliged Spanish wholesalers to pay higher prices for such drugs that they resold to customers outside Spain. The question was whether this practice violated the prohibition of restrictive agreements according to former Article 81 EC (now Article 101 TFEU). In order to avoid liability under competition law, GSK decided to apply to the European Commission for an individual exemption.[21] Simultaneously, Spanish wholesalers had brought complaints to the European Commission against GSK for having violated EU competition law. While the Commission denied the individual exemption,[22] the CFI seemed to adopt the earlier position of Advocate General Jacobs by annulling the Commission decision for not having sufficiently reasoned the rejection of GSK's argument according to which the agreement would promote investment by GSK in research and development and, thereby, contribute to technological and economic progress in the sense of former Article 81(3) EC. This was a clear sign that at least the CFI was now willing to accept a more lenient approach to parallel trade in pharmaceuticals.

Later, both the Greek and the Spanish cases made it to the ECJ. After the *Syfait* decision, the Greek GSK case was again referred to the ECJ by the Greek courts, which had to decide on private actions for violation of competition law brought by Greek wholesalers.[23] This time, there was no doubt as to the admissibility of the referral. Most interestingly, the competent Advocate

---

20 Case T-168/01 *GlaxoSmithKline v Commission* [2006] ECR II-2969.

21 When the case developed, the former Implementation Directive 17/62 (First Regulation Implementing Articles 85 and 86 of the Treaty), [1962] OJ No. 13/204, was still applicable. Outside the scope of so-called block exemption regulations, Regulation 17/62 required an individual decision by the European Commission for restrictive agreements to be exempted according to former Art. 81(3) EC (now Art. 101(3) TFEU). This system of the individual exemption was replaced by Council Regulation (EC) No. 1/2003 of 16 December 2002 on the implementation of the rules on competition laid down in Arts 81 and 82 of the Treaty, [2003] OJ L 1/1, which made Art. 81(3) EC directly applicable as of the date of entry into force of the Regulation on 1 May 2004.

22 Commission Decision of 8 May 2001, Cases IV/36.957/F3 *Glaxo Wellcome*, IV/36.997/F3 *Aseprofar and Fedifar*, IV/37.121/F3 *Spain Pharma*, IV/37.138/Fs *BAI*, IV/37.380/F3 *EAEPC* [2001] OJ L 302/1.

23 ECJ, *Sot. Lélos kai Sia*, above note 6.

General Ruiz-Jarabo Colomer explicitly disagreed with his colleague Jacobs, especially on the question of whether the company's need for high income in order to invest in R&D could be accepted as a justification for a restraint of parallel trade.[24] In such circumstances, it would have been most interesting to see how the ECJ reacted to this open conflict between two Advocates General and how it balanced the freedom of parallel trade with the interest in promoting investment in R&D in the pharmaceutical industry. However, the ECJ explicitly left the 'innovation issue' undecided, holding that there is no abuse on the part of a dominant pharmaceutical company in the role of GSK in Greece as long as the company is willing to fulfil orders that are not out of the ordinary.[25]

A year later, in the autumn of 2009, the ECJ finally had to decide on the appeal against the CFI judgment concerning the Spanish GSK case.[26] This time, given the clear statements of the CFI on the recognition of the innovation argument put forward by GSK, the ECJ could not avoid providing its say on how to achieve an appropriate balance between the interest in promoting free parallel trade and the interest in promoting innovation. While the ECJ rejected the test developed by the CFI for identifying a restraint of competition in the sense of former Article 81(1) EC,[27] it confirmed the CFI judgment

---

24 AG Ruiz-Jarabo Colomer, *Sot. Lélos kai Sia*, ibid., para 123 (who explicitly professes 'taking a different view from that taken by Advocate General Jacobs in *Syfait*').

25 ECJ, *Sot. Lélos kai Sia*, ibid., para 70 (the Court's formulation is: 'without it being necessary to examine the arguments raised by GSK AEVE that it is necessary for pharmaceutical companies to limit parallel exports in order to avoid the risk of a reduction in their investments in the research and development of medicines'). In substance, the Court relied upon its earlier decision in *United Brands*, in which it had held that a dominant supplier may not refuse to fulfil ordinary orders: see Case 27/76 *United Brands and United Brands Continentaal v Commission* [1978] ECR 207, para 182. In this regard, the Court seemed to ignore the fact that the *United Brands* case, which related to bananas, was different from the Greek GSK case in so far as *United Brands* did not involve issues of innovation in the first place. For a more extensive critique on that decision, see Drexl, above note 6.

26 ECJ, *GlaxoSmithKline v Commission*, above note 7.

27 The CFI, for the first, and so far only, time had relied upon a consumer-harm approach according to which a showing of consumer harm would be required for an agreement to be considered restrictive in the sense of former Art. 81(1) EC: see CFI, *GlaxoSmithKline v Commission*, above note 20, para 119. This argument was rejected by the ECJ, which defended the earlier case law, according to which former Art. 81(1) EC (now Art. 101(1) TFEU) 'aims to protect not only the interests of competitors or of consumers, but also the structure of the market and, in so doing, competition as such. Consequently, for a finding that an agreement has an anti-competitive object, it is not necessary that final consumers be deprived of the advantages of effective competition in terms of supply or price'. See ECJ, above note 7, para 63 (relying on the previous Case C-8/08 *T-Mobile Netherlands and Others* [2009] ECR I-4529, paras 38 et seq.).

with regard to the standard for an exemption under former Article 81(3) EC (now Article 101(3) TFEU). The ECJ stated that the CFI was correct 'in holding that the Commission's approach may entail ascertaining whether, in the light of the factual arguments and the evidence provided, it seems more likely either that the agreement in question must make it possible to obtain appreciable advantages or that it will not.'[28]

3.2 What is Special About Parallel Trade in Pharmaceuticals? The Argument of Innovation

In the light of the foregoing analysis of the history of the GSK cases, the opinion of Advocate General Jacobs in *Syfait* and the decision of the ECJ in the Spanish GSK case appear as the most important documents for a better understanding of the current EU regime on restraints of parallel trade in pharmaceuticals.

As indicated above,[29] Jacobs relied on three reasons for advocating a special regime for parallel trade in pharmaceuticals. Two of them – namely the level of regulation of pharmaceutical markets in the EU Member States and the lack of economic benefits accruing to consumers from parallel trade – were rejected by the European courts, while the third argument on innovation was finally taken into consideration by the CFI and the ECJ in the Spanish GSK case.

3.2.1 Regulation of pharmaceutical markets in the Member States

With regard to existing regulation in the EU Member States, Advocate General Jacobs had argued that distortions of competition between the Member States did not primarily arise from GSK's unilateral refusal to supply to Greek wholesalers but from 'pervasive and diverse' national regulation of the markets for pharmaceuticals, which led to considerable price differentials between the EU Member States.[30] Under EU medicinal law, the EU Member States are indeed allowed to control prices and to impose a public service duty on pharmaceutical companies to fulfil domestic demand.[31] Jacobs concluded:

---

28 ECJ, above note 7, para 94.

29 At above note 17.

30 AG Jacobs, *Syfait and Others*, above note 5, paras 77 et seq.

31 See Council Directive 89/105/EEC of 21 December 1988 relating to the transparency of measures regulating the prices of medicinal products for human use and their inclusion in the scope of national health insurance systems [1989] OJ L 40/8.

> When pharmaceutical undertakings attempt to block parallel trade, they are not thereby seeking to entrench price differentials of their own making, but rather to avoid the consequences which would follow if the very low prices imposed upon them in some Member States were generalised across the Community.[32]

These arguments were rejected by the ECJ in its decision in *Sot. Lélos kai Sia*, the second ECJ preliminary ruling on the Greek GSK case. In response to the respective arguments advanced by GSK, the Court stressed that national regulation 'does not entirely remove the prices of those products from the law of supply and demand'.[33] It also relied on the arguments of the Commission and Advocate General Ruiz-Jarabo Colomer according to which, even in countries such as Greece, where price controls are strictest, the sales prices are negotiated between the health authorities and the pharmaceutical companies;[34] or, to put it differently, as long as there is some room for free economic action, EU competition law has to be applied against business conduct that may restrict remaining competition.[35]

3.2.2 No benefits for consumers created by parallel trade?

With regard to the benefits of parallel trade, Advocate General Jacobs argued that the special features of the pharmaceutical market made it doubtful that parallel trade would actually bring down prices for the benefit of consumers in the importing countries. Given that the national health care systems will often guarantee fixed prices to pharmacists, he concluded that parallel traders would simply take the advantage of the price differentials and thereby free-ride on the investment of the pharmaceutical companies in R&D and marketing.[36]

In *Sot. Lélos kai Sia*, the ECJ rejected Jacobs' concerns in this regard as well. The Court held that price differentials 'open up in principle an alternative source of supply to buyers of the medicinal products in [the importing] States, which necessarily brings some benefits to the final consumer of those

32 AG Jacobs, *Syfait and Others*, above note 5, para 84.

33 ECJ, *Sot. Lélos kai Sia*, above note 6, para 61.

34 Ibid., para 63.

35 The Court also argued that protecting parallel trade in pharmaceuticals was most important since, in the case of pharmaceuticals protected by patents, parallel trade would be the 'only form of competition which can be envisaged:' ibid., para 64. This, however, is to be criticized, since different drugs, which may all be patent-protected, may well be substitutes for the treatment of the same disease and, therefore, belong to the same market. That IPRs do not confer market dominance as such has long been accepted by the ECJ. See, in particular, Joined Cases C-241 and 242/91 P *RTE and ITP v Commission* ('*Magill*') [1995] ECR I-743, para 46 ('[s]o far as dominant position is concerned, it is remembered at the outset that mere ownership of an intellectual property right cannot confer such a position').

36 AG Jacobs, *Syfait and Others*, above note 5, paras 96–99.

products'.[37] The Court thereby clearly realized that parallel trade in pharmaceuticals will also create price pressure in the importing country. The health care systems will be able to adjust their policies, for instance, with regard to refunding the price of drugs to patients, and large buyers of drugs, such as hospitals, could take parallel trade in pharmaceuticals into account in the framework of their procurement policies.[38]

It was along the same lines that the CFI in its early judgment of the Spanish GSK case had already argued that GSK's dual pricing scheme restricted competition in the sense of former Article 81(1) EC (now Article 101(1) TFEU), after requiring a showing of concrete harm to consumers for an agreement to be restrictive.[39]

3.2.3 Innovation versus parallel trade in pharmaceuticals

This brings us to the most influential innovation argument by Advocate General Jacobs, which was finally held to be relevant by the ECJ for accepting a rather lenient approach to assessing restraints on parallel trade in pharmaceuticals. The Court thereby rejected both the opinion of the Commission in the Spanish GSK case and the opinion of Advocate General Ruiz-Jarabo Colomer in the Greek referral case of *Sot. Lélos kai Sia*.

At the outset, it has to be stressed that the two Advocates General and the courts all agreed to the extent that restraints of parallel trade should not be considered illegal *per se*. Even Ruiz-Jarabo Colomer conceded that former Article 82 EC (Article 102 TFEU) was not suited for holding that any particular conduct, including a restraint on parallel trade, could be considered illegal *per se*.[40] The ECJ confirmed this in *Sot. Lélos kai Sia*, holding that the refusal to supply does not constitute an abuse in the sense of former Article 82 EC so long as the dominant undertaking does not refuse to fulfil ordinary orders.[41] The same holds true for the application of Article 101 TFEU since, from a legal point of view, there is no form of restrictive agreement that, from the outset, would be excluded from the possibility of obtaining an exemption under Article 101(3) TFEU. EU law thereby takes account of the economic insight that price discrimination implemented through a restraint of competition can be pro-competitive.[42]

---

37 ECJ, *Sot. Lélos kai Sia*, above note 6, para 53.

38 Ibid., para 56.

39 CFI, *GlaxoSmithKline v Commission*, above note 20, paras 182–90.

40 AG Ruiz-Jarabo Colomer, *Sot. Lélos kai Sia*, above note 6, para 76 (this is why he then considered the possibility of an economic justification).

41 ECJ, *Sot. Lélos kai Sia*, above note 6, para 71.

42 See above Section 2.

Advocate General Jacobs also relied upon the second economic insight that parallel trade only affects intra-brand competition and, by restricting this form of competition, has the potential to enhance inter-brand competition. In identifying the pro-competitive effects of the restraint of parallel trade, he therefore referred to competition among pharmaceutical companies that do not compete so much by price as by investment in R&D. Accordingly, he argued: 'Innovation is an important parameter of competition in the pharmaceuticals sector. Substantial investment is typically required in the research and development of a new pharmaceutical product.'[43]

However, he presented this idea in the context of a more general debate on the role of innovation in the pharmaceutical sector without putting it in a more analytical scheme for assessing the pro- and anti-competitive effects of restraints on parallel trade. Yet such an analysis is possible. To rephrase Jacobs, it would have to be argued that if pharmaceutical companies are allowed to restrain parallel trade and price discriminate they will be better able to charge a price for the high fixed costs of R&D. The intra-brand reduction of price competition will then be outweighed by the dynamic efficiency gains accruing from the enhanced ability of the pharmaceutical companies to invest in R&D in inter-brand competition for better future products with other pharmaceutical companies.

In order to justify a decision in favour of a restraint on parallel trade, however, Jacobs would also have to explain that pharmaceutical companies would actually reinvest higher profits generated from restraints of parallel trade in R&D. Indeed, this is the point on which both the Commission in the Spanish GSK case and Advocate General Ruiz-Jarabo Colomer most disagreed with Jacobs. The Commission, in rejecting GSK's application for an individual exemption, stated that GSK had failed to demonstrate a causal link between parallel trade and a reduction of GSK's investment in R&D.[44] Similarly, Ruiz-Jarabo Colomer found the harshest words on GSK's allegations on the innovation-reducing effect of parallel trade:

> [A]part from the description of the 'horrors' caused by parallel trade, GSK does not indicate any positive aspect resulting from its restriction of supplies of medicinal products to the wholesalers, except that its profit margins recover, which is irrelevant for the purposes of classifying the conduct as an abuse, or for the purposes of justifying it.[45]

43 AG Jacobs, *Syfait and Others*, above note 5, para 89.
44 Commission Decision, above note 22, paras 154 et seq.
45 AG Ruiz-Jarabo Colomer, *Sot. Lélos kai Sia*, above note 6, para 118.

Ruiz-Jarabo Colomer thereby hinted at the problem that higher profits as a restraint of parallel trade are, first of all, the result of the restrictive effect on price competition, and that making higher profits as such can therefore not be used as an argument for justifying a competition law defence.

However, Jacobs' view could still be supported based on the argument that competitive pressure from other pharmaceutical companies that engage in R&D will guarantee that higher income from restraints of parallel trade will be reinvested in R&D. In the Spanish GSK case, the CFI and the ECJ finally seem to have adopted this view by, first, obliging the Commission to take GSK's innovation argument seriously and, second, by obliging the Commission to assess whether the alleged efficiency gains are more likely to occur than not.[46]

While this may seem a theoretically sound approach, there are yet two problems linked to it. First, competition agencies also have to take into consideration that investment in innovation is not the only form by which originator pharmaceutical companies compete with each other. When patents are about to expire, investment in life-cycle management strategies, including the filing of secondary patents, may turn out to be more successful and profitable in view of maintaining the market position. Originator companies have also started to become more diversified firms; therefore, it cannot be ruled out that higher income from restraints on parallel trade will be invested in mergers with generic companies or the building up of generics departments. Second, the ECJ requires the Commission to make most uncertain predictions about future dynamic processes of innovation. It is not only highly uncertain whether and how much of the higher income will be reinvested in R&D. It is also practically impossible to predict whether enhanced research efforts will be successful, to which forms of innovation such efforts will lead and whether new drugs in the future will provide medical benefits that can outweigh the disadvantage of higher prices arising from restraints on parallel trade for existing drugs.[47]

3.3 Summary of the GlaxoSmithKline Cases

Since the GlaxoSmithKline decisions, EU competition law has reached a more balanced approach to the application of competition law to restraints of

---

46 ECJ, *GlaxoSmithKline v Commission*, above note 7, para 94.

47 On these critical points, see also Drexl, above note 6, 591–94. See also Josef Drexl, 'Real Knowledge is to Know the Extent of One's Own Ignorance: On the Consumer Harm Approach in Innovation-Related Competition Cases' (2010) 76 *Antitrust Law Journal* 677 (highlighting the problem of predicting future effects on dynamic efficiency in innovation-oriented competition cases, including the European GlaxoSmithKline cases).

competition on parallel trade in pharmaceuticals. The argument is that such restraints may enhance the ability of R&D-oriented pharmaceutical companies to compete with each other in innovation. The problem remains that, in individual cases, it will be extremely difficult or even practically impossible to draw the line between pro-competitive restraints that overall enhance innovation on the one hand and anti-competitive conduct on the other.

The question to be asked in the following two sections is whether lessons can be learned from this EU debate for how to deal with trade in pharmaceuticals protected by IPRs (patents and trade marks) at the global level. The article now turns therefore to the issues of international exhaustion and the seizure of transit goods.

4. HOW TO DEAL WITH PARALLEL TRADE IN PHARMACEUTICALS INTERNATIONALLY

Right at the beginning, it has to be pointed out that an analysis from an international perspective has to take into account the fundamental differences between the legal orders of the EU and the World Trade Organization (WTO). With regard to the EU, it is certainly easier to base the analysis and policy recommendations on a global welfare approach, although such an analysis may lead to the conclusion that, with regard to the regulation of trade in pharmaceuticals, some EU Member States will be on the winning side, while others will lose. The EU legal order includes other legal instruments that can guarantee that the negative distributional effects on the losing countries will be balanced out.

In contrast, at the global level, the debate is characterized by a conflict between roughly two groups of states – those that advocate high levels of IP protection in the interests of pharmaceutical companies and in view of maintaining high levels of investment in R&D, on the one hand, and the other and predominantly poorer states that are more interested in keeping prices low in order to facilitate their citizens' access to essential medicines, on the other. Although WTO law is based on the principle of 'mutual advantages' and, therefore, obligations in one field may be balanced by concessions in another field, WTO law does not create a 'social' community of states that would adequately respond to negative distributional effects of its legal regimes.

This difference has to be taken into account in the evaluation of Article 6 TRIPS which, in a somewhat obscure way, stipulates that '[f]or the purposes of dispute settlement under this Agreement, subject to the provisions of Articles 3 and 4 nothing in this Agreement shall be used to address the issue of the exhaustion of intellectual property rights'.

Article 6 TRIPS is the result of a compromise by the WTO Members on the issue of exhaustion.[48] Although exhaustion could be considered to be one of the clearest candidates for being qualified a 'trade-related' aspect of intellectual property rights, during the Uruguay Round negotiations, the Contracting Parties of GATT were not able to reach an agreement on a uniform approach to dealing with exhaustion. Article 6 TRIPS is therefore usually understood in the sense of leaving it to WTO Members to decide whether to implement a principle of national or international exhaustion for the different IP rights regimes.[49]

In the light of the economics of parallel trade,[50] Article 6 TRIPS should not be considered as a rule in need of reform. While it may seem that the authorization of WTO Members to maintain a rule of purely national exhaustion collides with the principle of trade liberalization deeply enshrined in the legal regime of GATT in particular, it is also clear that the interests of individual WTO Members are highly diverse.

The introduction of a principle of international exhaustion as an obligation of WTO law would produce highly unwanted effects in the field of trade in pharmaceuticals in particular.

As indicated above,[51] international exhaustion may make it more difficult for pharmaceutical companies to price discriminate between different countries. Such an effect would contradict the interests of countries that want to support the economic interests of their pharmaceutical companies and the interest in promoting R&D in the pharmaceutical industry, as well as the interests of poorer nations. First, international exhaustion would make it more difficult for pharmaceutical companies to charge a price for the high fixed costs arising from the development of new drugs. Second, international exhaustion would drive prices up in the poorer countries and hamper access to essential drugs even more for the most economically disadvantaged people of the world.

---

48 On the negotiating history, see UNCTAD-ICTSD, *Resource Book on TRIPS and Development* (2005) at 97–104.

49 Ibid., at 105. This interpretation has been confirmed by the Doha Declaration on the TRIPS Agreement and Public Health of 20 November 2001, available at: http://www.wto.org/english/thewto_e/minist_e/min01_e/mindecl_trips_e.htm (accessed 3 July 2012). Para 5(a) of the Declaration reads: 'The effect of the provisions in the TRIPS Agreement that are relevant to the exhaustion of intellectual property rights is to leave each member free to establish its own regime for such exhaustion without challenge, subject to the MFN and national treatment provisions of Articles 3 and 4.'

50 Section 2 above.

51 Ibid.

The only group of people who are harmed by Article 6 TRIPS are consumers in the richer countries, where governments are usually against a principle of international exhaustion for guaranteeing higher returns for pharmaceutical companies, who will be able to rely on their IPRs to prevent parallel imports. These consumers cross-subsidize access to medicines in the poorer countries of the world. Since, however, Article 6 TRIPS leaves the choice between national and international exhaustion to the individual WTO Members, this is not a concern that needs to be addressed at the level of the WTO. It should be left to the political process in the richer countries as potential beneficiaries of parallel imports to balance the current financial interests of their consumers and patients with the interest of the local pharmaceutical industry and the public interest in promoting innovation.[52]

It is to be noted that having a choice between national and international exhaustion has little meaning for poorer countries. Since parallel trade depends on the existence of considerable price differentials, poorer countries can hardly enhance parallel imports by switching to international exhaustion, given the overall low ability to pay in such countries. Rather, poorer countries should have an interest in their richer trading partners applying a principle of national exhaustion that would enable pharmaceutical companies to sell their drugs at lower prices in the poorer countries.[53]

As a matter of clarification, it is also important to understand that these arguments on exhaustion refer only to trade in patented and not in generic drugs, although the latter may be, and regularly are, also protected by trade marks. With regard to generic drugs, there is no argument of innovation that would count against a principle of international exhaustion.

---

[52] The pharmaceutical industry especially tried to rely on Art. 28.1 lit. (a) TRIPS, according to which the patent includes an exclusive right of importation, to argue that WTO Members may not apply a principle of international exhaustion to patents. However, footnote 6 to this provision clarifies that Art. 6 TRIPS will prevail and that Art. 28.1 lit. (a) TRIPS cannot be used to address the issue of exhaustion. Hence, under Art. 6 TRIPS, Members cannot be challenged for having adopted a rule of international patent exhaustion before WTO dispute settlement bodies. See UNCTAD-ICTSD, above note 48, 105 et seq.

[53] In this context, see also the interesting analysis by Patricia Bohn, *Parallelimportregelungen im Patent- und Markenrecht in Lateinamerika* (Nomos 2010) (analysing the policy reasons for having a principle of national or international exhaustion of Latin American countries with regard to patents and trade marks).

5. HOW TO DEAL WITH THE TRANSIT OF PHARMACEUTICALS

Currently the most burning and most intensively discussed issue relating to international trade in pharmaceuticals is whether customs authorities can legally seize pharmaceuticals that are in transit, although patent protection is neither available in the country of origin nor in the country of destination.[54]

This issue arose when, in December 2008, Dutch customs authorities seized drugs in transit from India to Brazil at Schiphol Airport. The seizure was initiated by the pharmaceutical company Merck, which relied upon patent protection in the Netherlands, while the drug did not enjoy any patent protection in India or Brazil.[55] In February 2009, the customs authorities at Schiphol Airport stopped the transit of HIV medicine, produced by the Indian generics company Aurobindo, which was about to be shipped to Nigeria as part of a programme of the Clinton Foundation and UNITAID.[56]

Such transit cases raise legal and moral issues at both the EU and the global WTO levels. As regards EU law, the question is whether the 2003 Border Measure Regulation provides a legal basis for temporary detention or permanent seizure.[57] Article 2(1)(c)(i) of the Regulation requires that the goods seized infringe a patent 'under that Member State's law'. Strictly speaking, however, transit as such does not violate any rights of the patent holder, since the goods are not produced, imported or sold in the country of transit.

---

54 See, for instance, Frederick M. Abbott, 'Seizure of Generic Pharmaceuticals in Transit Based on Allegations of Patent Infringement: A Threat to International Trade, Development and Public Welfare' [2009] *WIPO Journal* 43, No. 1, available at: http://papers.ssrn.com/sol3/papers.cfm?abstract_id=1535521 (accessed 19 July 2011); Shashank P. Kumar, 'Freedom of Transit and Trade in Generic Pharmaceuticals: An Analysis of EU Border Enforcement Law and Implications for the International Intellectual Property Regime' [2009] *European Intellectual Property Review*, available at: http://ssrn.com/abstract=1383067 (accessed 19 July 2011); Marius Schneider, 'Counterfeiting Counter-Fight' (2010) 5 *Journal of Intellectual Property Law & Practice* 285; Xavier Seuba, 'Free Trade of Pharmaceutical Products: The Limits of Intellectual Property Enforcement at the Border', International Center for Trade and Sustainable Development (ICTSD), Issue Paper No. 27 (2010).

55 See Abbott, above note 54, 47.

56 See UNITAID, 'UNITAID Statement on Dutch Confiscation of Medicines Shipment', available at: http://www.unitaid.eu/en/resources/news/158-unitaid-statement-on-gsk-patent-pool-for-neglected-diseases.html (accessed 3 July 2012) (arguing that the drugs were not counterfeit products and did not infringe IP rights).

57 See Council Regulation (EC) No. 1383/2003 of 22 July 2003 concerning customs action taken against goods suspected of infringing certain intellectual property rights and the measures to be taken against goods found to have infringed such rights [2003] OJ L 196/7.

Nevertheless, the Dutch Court of The Hague sustained detention of transit goods by relying upon Recital 8 of the Regulation and applying a so-called manufacturing fiction, according to which the question needs to be asked whether the goods would infringe the patent if they were manufactured in the country of transit.[58] Recital 8 reads as follows:

> Proceedings initiated to determine whether an intellectual property right has been infringed under national law will be conducted with reference to the criteria used to establish whether goods produced in that Member State infringe intellectual property rights.

However, the wording of this Recital does not have to be understood in the sense of a manufacturing fiction. Rather, with regard to patents in particular, Article 2(1)(c)(i) of the Regulation is clear about its character as a pure choice-of-law rule, which provides that infringement has to be assessed according to the domestic patent law of the Member State in which the seizure takes place. Such a rule is needed because EU law does not offer uniform standards for the rights conferred to a patent owner and the concept of patent infringement. It would then be for this national law alone to identify the rights conferred to the patent owner. If that law does not protect against transit, the customs authorities will not be empowered to stop shipment of the goods. Reading Recital 8 as a legal basis for a manufacturing fiction would extend Article 2(1)(c)(i) of the Regulation from a choice-of-law rule to a rule on harmonization of substantive patent law in the Member States, which would fall outside the wording of this provision and the overall purpose of the Regulation.

In the *Nokia* case, the High Court of Justice for England and Wales seemed to be of a similar opinion when it explicitly rejected a reading of Recital 8 as a sufficient legal basis for a 'manufacturing fiction'.[59] The question of how to interpret the Border Measures Regulation, meanwhile, has been decided by the ECJ.[60] The Court concluded that, in line with the view of the English High

---

58 *Sisvel v Sosecal* (Court of The Hague, 18 July 2008). See Jens van den Brink, 'Come Back of the Legal Fiction of the Anti Piracy Regulation', *Kennedy van der Laan Newsletter*, August 2008, available at: http://www.kvdl.nl/KVdL/en-GB/_main/News/Newsletter/Newsletter+August+2008/Anti+Piracy+Regulation_IP/default.htm (accessed 3 July 2012) (with English quotes from the decision).

59 *Nokia Corporation v Her Majesty's Commissioners of Revenue & Customs* [2009] EWHS 1903 (Ch) (decision of 27 July 2009) (dealing with trade mark infringement).

60 Joined Cases C-446/09 and C-495/09 *Koninklijke Philips Electronics* and *Nokia Corporation* [2011] ECR I-0000 (not yet officially reported). The second case was actually referred to the ECJ by the English Court of Appeal, which was asked to decide on the appeal of the cited *Nokia* decision of the Chancery Division of the High Court.

Court, the EU Border Control Regulation does not support a 'manufacturing fiction'.[61] However, the *Nokia* case decided by the ECJ related only to trade marks and not patents. Yet, since the referrals were about the same legal terminology used for trade marks and patents in the Border Measure Regulation, it can be assumed that the expected ECJ judgment will also be relevant for patents.[62]

As to WTO law, the question is whether such border seizure violates the principle of freedom of transit pursuant to Article V GATT 1994, in particular. The seizures effectuated by the Dutch authorities caused India and Brazil to start WTO dispute resolution procedures against the EU and the Netherlands.[63] However, in the framework of their ongoing bilateral trade negotiations directed toward the conclusion of a free-trade agreement, the EU and India now seem to have settled the dispute based on a pledge by the EU to change or clarify its Border Measure Regulation so that pharmaceuticals in transit will no longer be seized by customs authorities in the EU.[64]

The practical problem may therefore disappear in the foreseeable future as a matter of court decisions and legislative reforms in the EU. This, however, does not answer the question of what should be the most appropriate legal regime for dealing with pharmaceuticals in transit. In the light of recent European experience in the field of restraints on parallel trade within the EU, the question could be asked whether the interest in promoting innovation does not argue in favour of seizures of patent-protected pharmaceuticals in transit.

In answering this question, it seems important first to distinguish clearly between the issue of exhaustion and parallel trade, on the one hand, and transit cases on the other. Parallel trade is limited to cases in which the rightholder

---

61 Ibid., paras 69 et seq.

62 Doubts may arise from the fact that trade mark cases are often discussed in the light of the *Rioglass* and the *Montex* decisions, in which the ECJ held that national trade mark laws prohibiting the transit of branded goods may not be applied as a matter of the EU guarantee of free movement of goods and in the light of the Trade Mark Directive, which, for an infringement, requires an 'act in the course of trade': see Case C-115/02 *Rioglass and Transremar* [2003] ECR I-12705; Case C-281/05 *Montex Holdings* [2006] ECR I-10881.

63 *European Union and a Member State* – Seizure of Generic Drugs (EC – Seizure of Generics), Request for Consultations by India (WT/DS408/1, IP/D/28, G/L/921) of 12 May 2010; Request for Consultations by Brazil (WT/DS/409/1, IP/D/29, G/L/922) of 19 May 2010. On these complaints, see Henning Grosse Ruse-Khan, 'A Trade Agreement Creating Barriers to International Trade? ACTA Border Measures and Goods in Transit', (2011) 26 *American University International Law Review* 644, 650–59.

64 See Lynne Taylor, 'EU Pledge to India over Generics Seizures', *Pharma Times Online*, 18 July 2011, available at: http://www.pharmatimes.com/article/10-12-14/EU_pledge_to_India_over_generics_seizures.aspx (accessed 3 July 2012).

has at least consented to the first sale in the country of exportation. In contrast, cases of transit in pharmaceuticals concern generic drugs produced and sold without the consent of the rightholder.

On the other hand, trade in generic drugs and parallel trade share the common feature of generating price competition for the originator drug. Hence, all the pro-innovation arguments developed above in favour of the legality of restraints on parallel trade could also be relied upon for the transit cases. The fact that the rightholders have not even consented to the first sale in the transit cases seems to support the position of the patent holders even more.

Yet the fact that consent by the rightholder is missing in the transit cases should not be taken as an argument to justify seizure of generic pharmaceuticals in transit. Experience with European competition law also teaches us that the appropriate solution has to rely on a balance between the incentives to innovate and the interest in access to medicine at lower prices. This balance can be assessed by EU competition law with reference to the global welfare within the EU, while, as was pointed out above,[65] a global welfare approach would risk harming patients in poorer countries, since the WTO law has no legal and social mechanism in place that would compensate poorer patients for the losses they incur as a result of higher levels of patent protection. This argues in favour of pursuing a balance between the conflicting interests based on the different laws of the WTO Members. This is why, from a legal perspective, transit of pharmaceutical products predominantly presents an issue in which national law should decide on the question of infringement.[66]

To clarify this a bit further, it is helpful to have a closer look at the reasons why patent protection may exist only in the country of transit and not in the countries of origin and destination. In this regard, Abbott identifies at least four different scenarios: (i) the inventor has never sought patent protection; (ii) the patent has expired; (iii) the patent application was rejected for not meeting the criteria of patentability; and (iv) the invention is not deemed to constitute patentable subject matter.[67]

In the first scenario, it is clear that the inventor himself did not deem it economically profitable to even seek patent protection in the respective countries. Accordingly, it may be argued that patent protection in these countries is

---

[65] See above at the beginning of Section 4.

[66] Note that, technically speaking, it would go too far to call this an issue of conflict of laws. Under private international law, states remain free to define the scope of protection under their IP laws.

[67] Abbott, above note 54, 46. With regard to the fourth scenario, Abbott mentions the example of the denial of patent protection for computer software in Europe.

not important enough to raise incentives for innovation significantly. Similarly, there is no economic basis for justifying a seizure of such pharmaceuticals in transit.

In the second scenario, where patent protection has already expired, the inventor has benefited sufficiently from the protection of its patents before they expire according to the law of the countries of origin and destination. Such scenarios may arise, in particular, where the countries of origin and destination do not dispose of any form of patent term extension. In such cases, the invention may still be protected in the EU for some years based on a supplementary protection certificate (SPC) or, in the US, as a result of the patent-term extension rule, while patent protection has expired in other countries. In such instances, domestic legislatures seem to disagree considerably with regard to the appropriate term of protection. Allowing a seizure in the country of transit in this case would export the transit country's balancing of the interests to third countries. Since the interests of the patients in the country of importation in having access to medicine will not be taken into account by the substantive patent law of the transit country, it should be for the country of importation alone to decide on the term of protection.

Similarly, in the third and fourth cases the reasons for lack of protection in the exporting and importing countries are to be explained by differences in the weighing of interests according to different national laws. If some countries deny patent protection because the invention does not meet the patentability requirements or the invention is not considered to be patentable subject-matter, this is so because the grant of a patent would be deemed to lead to overprotection against the public interest of these countries.

In the *Philips* and *Nokia* cases, Advocate General Cruz Villalón seemed to argue in a similar sense. In his Opinion he makes the point that application of a 'manufacturing fiction' would collide with the territoriality principle as a fundamental principle of international IP law.[68]

6. CONCLUSION

European competition law has recently produced considerable new case law on how to deal with restraints on parallel trade in pharmaceuticals between the Member States. The ECJ has thereby recognized that, under certain conditions, the argument of enhancing innovation by higher profits may justify a restraint on parallel trade.

68 AG Cruz Villalón, *Koninklijke Philips Electronics* and *Nokia Corporation*, above note 61, para 65.

However, in accepting the innovation argument, policy makers risk committing a number of fallacies. In competition law, higher profits are first of all a sign of a restraint of competition. The argument in favour of creating incentives for innovation, if driven too far, would risk creating a sectorial exemption from competition law for the originator pharmaceutical industry. Therefore, the innovation argument should not be accepted without a factual basis that justifies the expectation that higher income will indeed be reinvested in R&D. Since there are also other ways to compete with originator pharmaceutical companies than by innovation, the mere existence of competitive pressure by other originator pharmaceutical companies will not guarantee such reinvestment in innovation. Also, the ECJ recognizes that innovation comes with a price for those consumers who depend on affordable access to already existing medicine. For an exemption or a justification under competition law, it therefore requires evidence that the alleged benefits regarding the development of new drugs are more likely to materialize and that these benefits at least outweigh the losses of consumers who have to pay higher prices for existing drugs. A major problem arises from the difficulties in making reliable predictions about future dynamic processes in applying this test defined by the ECJ.

From this EU case law, a few lessons can be learned for the international debate on exhaustion and the seizure of patented goods in transit. As to the exhaustion issue, Article 6 TRIPS applies the correct approach by leaving it to the WTO Members to make a choice between national and international exhaustion. This rule enables the pharmaceutical companies to price discriminate between richer and poorer countries and to recoup high investment in their R&D efforts, while keeping prices low in poorer countries.

With regard to the issue of pharmaceuticals in transit, there is an imminent risk of overstretching the innovation argument supporting strong patent protection if the national laws allow seizure in the transit countries. It is most important in this regard to assess the adequate balance of the interest in innovation with the interest in access to affordable drugs under the law of the country of destination rather than under the law of the transit country. Hence, there is no justification for seizure of pharmaceuticals in transit. The EU should clarify that its Border Measures Regulation does not contain a 'manufacturing fiction', and that trading nations should abstain from entering into bilateral or plurilateral agreements that promote seizure of goods in transit with a view to protecting intellectual property rights.[69]

---

69 On the ambiguous approach of the Anti-Counterfeiting Trade Agreement (ACTA) to seizure of goods in transit, see Grosse Ruse-Khan, above note 63.

2. Cross-border licensing in the absence of a choice of law: is there a way forward?

Paul Torremans

1. INTRODUCTION

The topic of this chapter is 'cross-border licensing'. This could mean that a foreign rightholder grants an intellectual property licence for an intellectual property right it owns in a third state to another, potentially local, licensee. It could also mean that a single licence covers more than one state. Because of the intellectual property rights involved, or the parties involved or the geographical scope, an international element is brought into the licence. That brings private international law and, in particular, choice of law into the picture.

I have argued repeatedly that the parties to such a licence contract have the freedom to choose the applicable law and that they are well advised to make use of that option. Indeed, I have argued that the alternative option (that of determining the applicable law in the absence of a choice made by the parties) is often a recipe for disaster.[1] Legal certainty and predictability are then often lost completely. It is not the aim of this chapter to re-examine that issue completely. I will therefore leave to one side the freedom of the parties to choose the applicable law; nor will I examine the system for choice of law in the absence of a choice made by the parties contained in Article 4 of the Rome Convention 1980.[2] Instead I will focus briefly on the new regime in Article 4 of the Rome I Regulation,[3] and will argue that, whilst this is an improvement,

---

[1] See J.J. Fawcett and P.L.C. Torremans, *Intellectual Property and Private International Law* (Clarendon Press 1998) 556–76.

[2] Rome Convention 1980 on the law applicable to contractual obligations (consolidated version) [1998] OJ C 27/34. See J.J. Fawcett and P.L.C. Torremans, *Intellectual Property and Private International Law* (Oxford University Press 2011) Chapter 14.

[3] Regulation (EC) No. 593/2008 of the European Parliament and of the Council of 17 June 2008 on the law applicable to contractual obligations (Rome I) [2008] OJ L 177/6.

it does not solve the main issue. The escape clauses will still be used in far too many cases and there will still be a lack of legal certainty and predictability. That will lead me to a proposal for an alternative model.

2. ARTICLE 4 ROME I AS AN ATTEMPT TO IMPROVE ON THE ROME CONVENTION APPROACH OF THE 1980S

2.1 The New System

As already indicated, an attempt to address at least some of the issues that arose in relation to Article 4 of the Rome Convention 1980 has been made in Article 4 of the Rome I Regulation, and this system will apply to contracts concluded from 17 December 2009. The presumption-based approach has been replaced by a list of rules that determine the applicable law for certain types of contract. Article 4(1) refers to the law of the habitual residence of the seller for sale of goods contracts, to the law of the habitual residence of the franchisee for franchise contracts, to the law of the habitual residence of the distributor for distribution contracts, and so on. Article 4(2) then deals with all types of contract that are not found in the list and the characteristic performance rule that was established in the Convention is retained for these (although without the presumption aspect).[4] The characteristic performance rule is also applied to those cases where elements of the contract are covered by more than one of the rules of Article 4(1). Articles 4(3) and 4(4) then refer to what was Article 4(5) of the Convention. There may, first of all, be an apparent closer connection with another country. The law of that other country will apply if this manifestly closer connection is clear from all the circumstances of the case. If Articles 4(1) and 4(2) do not allow for the identification of the applicable law, the law of the country with which the contract is most closely connected offers the ultimate fall-back position.

The Regulation therefore works with fixed rules and the characteristic performance rule for all other contracts, with the closest connection as an escape route. In the absence of formal presumptions the latter should be used sparingly, but in practice its criteria are the same as those in the Convention system. Therefore, there may not be an enormous change. The insertion of the word 'manifestly' in Article 4(3) is, of course, an attempt to go in the other

[4] R. Plender and M. Wilderspin, *The European Private International Law of Obligations* (Sweet & Maxwell 2009) 188 et seq.

direction and to use the escape clause sparingly,[5] but the complex nature of intellectual property contracts is likely to undo any such improvement over the old Article 4(5).[6] This is not to say, though, that the former approach of the English courts should be continued, but that a reduction in comparison with the former Dutch approach, which was also later approved by the Court of Appeal, is unlikely to materialize.

2.2 No Standard Rule for Intellectual Property Contracts

The latter is no doubt also helped by the fact that intellectual property contracts do not easily fall within either Article 4(1) or Article 4(2). The original proposal for a Rome I Regulation contained a specific rule for intellectual property contracts in Article 4(1) and this would have led to the application of the law of the licensor or assignor. With the colleagues from the European Max Planck Group for Conflict of Laws in Intellectual Property (CLIP),[7] we argued that this rule was unsound. There was no clear definition of what is an intellectual property contract. Plenty of franchise and distribution contracts contain strong intellectual property components and there would have been a conflict between the various rules in Article 4(1) as a result of the overlap. The rules would then also have clashed, as in an intellectual property context the franchisee, for example, would have been the licensee rather than the licensor. Under the mechanism in Article 4(2) the rules would then have cancelled each other out, which would have defeated the whole idea of having a special rule for intellectual property contracts. It is also by no means clear that the choice for the law of the country of the licensor or assignor could have been justified in all cases in a characteristic performance/closest connection context. Intellectual property contracts can, after all, be very different in nature. Or, as it was put in the CLIP Comments:

> The wide variety of contracts relating to intellectual property rights also calls for a differentiated solution instead of one strict, clear-cut rule. Even though the application of the law of the assignor or transferor of the intellectual property right might be appropriate in simple contracts which resemble an outright sale – such as an assignment or license for consideration in the form of a lump sum payment – this does not hold true as a general rule. More complex intellectual property transactions often include an explicit or implicit duty of the licensee to exploit the intellectual property right, sometimes supplemented by clauses indicating quantities of production

---

5 See J.J. Fawcett, 'A United Kingdom Perspective on the Rome I Regulation', in N. Boschiero (ed.), *La Nuova Disciplina Communitaria della Legge Applicable ai Contratti* (*Roma I*) (G. Giappichelli Editore 2009) 209.

6 Plender and Wilderspin, above note 4, 194 et seq.

7 See http://www.cl-ip.eu.

> or modalities of use, while the licensor does not accept any commitment beyond the toleration of use of his rights. This casts doubt on the proposition that it is the licensor who effects the performance characteristic of the contract (as it is the licensee who accepts the commercial risks linked to the exploitation). It may also be the case that the intellectual property rights licensed or assigned are mainly exercised in the country of the licensee's or transferee's habitual residence or principal place of business. Another example of an intellectual property contract where the performances of both parties are essential and characteristic is a contract to publish and distribute a book.[8]

It is therefore satisfying to see that the specific rule for intellectual property contracts has been dropped altogether. One should add, however, that the fact that intellectual property contracts do not form a homogeneous group (such as, for example, sale of goods contracts) and are instead very diverse in nature does also mean that the determination of the characteristic performance will not be a straightforward affair either. The exercise will have to be conducted on a case-by-case basis, and it is to be expected that for highly complex intellectual property contracts recourse will frequently be had to the closest connection escape route. This is in essence a result of the complex nature of many intellectual property contracts, rather than any deficiency in Article 4.

2.3 Application of Article 4 to Contracts in Relation to Intellectual Property Rights

Most of the following analysis has its value in relation to both the Rome Convention 1980 version of Article 4, as well its Rome I Regulation version. The different use of the concept of characteristic performance in both versions has its importance, though, in relation to international intellectual property contracts. The Convention looks at groups or types of contracts and attempts to identify a single characteristic performance for each group or type.[9] That approach is particularly problematic for international intellectual property contracts. As highlighted above, this is not a clearly defined group: inside the

---

8 CLIP, Comments on the European Commission's Proposal for a Regulation on the Law Applicable to Contractual Obligations (Rome I) of 15 December 2005 and the European Parliament Committee on Legal Affairs' Draft Report on the Proposal of 22 August 2006, 4 January 2007, available at: http://www.cl-ip.eu.

9 This point is made strongly in the Giuliano-Lagarde Report where it is said that '[f]or each *category* of contract it is the characteristic performance that is in principle the relevant factor in applying the presumption for determining the applicable law, even in situations peculiar to certain contracts, as for example in the contract of guarantee where the characteristic performance is always that of the guarantor, whether in relation to the principal debtor or the creditor': Report on the Convention on the law applicable to contractual obligations by Mario Giuliano, Professor, University of Milan, and Paul Lagarde, Professor, University of Paris I [1980] OJ C-282/1.

group there are various types of contract and in general the contracts are very varied and diverse in nature. It is therefore almost impossible to define a characteristic performance, especially if it has to go beyond an individual contract and apply to a group of contracts. In practice, the group approach was almost ignored and contracts were looked at on an individual basis. In that respect the Rome I Regulation version is more promising. Article 4(2) looks at the characteristic performance of 'the contract', without having the same baggage as its equivalent in the Convention since the categories approach is now clearly found in and limited to Article 4(1).

Having discarded Article 4(1) and the groups of contracts (from which international intellectual property contracts are missing), one looks more at individual contracts. That might offer more of a perspective to identify a characteristic performance. One could, in this line of thought, see the characteristic performance as the 'key', 'central' or 'vital' performance of the contract. There may still be more than one of these, but at least the chances of finding a single characteristic performance increase this way. There is, though, another element that has its importance. The performance one is looking for must also characterize the contract. In other words there is more to it than being a 'key' performance. It shapes the contract, also to its nature. One way or another, the concept of a type of contract comes back in, if only to situate the individual contract amongst its peers. Be that as it may, the Rome I Regulation version offers more guidance and chances to arrive at the characteristic performance of an international intellectual property contract, even if it remains far from an obvious exercise.

Part of the complication is not only the fact that a single contract often seems to contain more than one characteristic performance, which renders it impossible to identify 'the' characteristic performance, but also the fact that intellectual property often forms only a part of a larger contract that is wider in scope. The starting point is clearly that the exercise is conducted for 'the contract'– the whole potentially wide and large contract. The Convention tool of *depeçage* could have its use here – for example, in the context of a joint venture contract that contains among other parts an intellectual property licence, a training framework for staff, the construction of production sites involving transfer of know-how, and so on. One could then split the joint venture contract into its components and determine the applicable law to each of them, using the characteristic performance technique. The Rome I Regulation rules out this principle, making it unlikely that a single characteristic performance can be identified, that is unless one wants to be flexible and interpret the term 'the contract' in Article 4(2) as each severable part of the larger contract that could have been concluded as a separate contract. This is clearly imaginative, but it is also a rather radical departure from the wording of Article 4(2). On that basis the practice is not to be encouraged, even if it will effectively lead to the application of Article 4(4) of the Rome I Regulation to even more cases.

2.4 Franchise and Distribution Contracts

The absence in Article 4(1) of the Rome I Regulation of a specific rule for a class of international intellectual property contracts does not, however, make the provision completely useless for such contracts. There will indeed be plenty of franchising or distribution contracts that will contain a strong intellectual property component. As long as these remain clearly franchising or distribution contracts[10] nothing stands in the way of the application of the law of the country where the franchisee or the distributor respectively has its habitual residence under the relevant bit of Article 4(1). That law will then apply to the whole contract, including the intellectual property component. There is even no reason to exclude the contract from the franchise or distribution agreement category and rule in those cases where the intellectual property licence is clearly the *raison d'être* of the whole contract and, as such, is also the dominant factor. As long as there is a trigger – the franchise or distribution element – for paragraph 1 and there is no conflict between the various points in that paragraph, the application of Article 4(2) will not be triggered.[11] The only escape route is Article 4(3) for those cases where the contract is manifestly more closely connected with another country. In practice these connections can, of course, arise from the non-core elements that come on top of the franchise or distribution element, as well as from the specificities of the franchise[12] or distribution element. Under the Rome Convention version this could be another case where *depeçage* might have come in handy to separate out the intellectual property part and apply a separate law to it in case a single law for the whole contract was impossible to be identified, but the structure of the Rome I Regulation clearly does not envisage such a scenario.

---

10 Otherwise Art. 4(2) will apply and require the identification of the closest connection. If that is not possible Art. 4(4) will apply and one will look for the closest connection.

11 Art. 4(1) requires the characterization of the contract as belonging to one of the special types of contract listed in its various points. As Art. 4(1) is the starting point and as Art. 4(2) only proposes a different solution in two narrow sets of circumstances, it is submitted that a somewhat wider characterization is to be preferred instead of a narrow one that denies, for example, a franchisee agreement characterization simply because there is one element present in the contract, such as an intellectual property licence, that goes beyond the strict substantive law franchise concept.

12 This may, for example, refer entirely to a territory other than that where the franchisee has its habitual residence.

It can be added that in a jurisdiction context the suggestion has been made that intellectual property licence contracts are contracts for the provision of services. That could bring these contracts within the scope of Article 4(1)(b) of the Rome I Regulation. The Court of Justice has emphatically rejected that suggestion in a jurisdiction context,[13] and there is therefore no good reason to resurrect the idea in a choice of law context. Article 4(1)(b) can therefore be left to one side.

Despite the positive points in the new version of Article 4 and the number of intellectual property related contracts that can find a home in the categories of franchise and distribution contracts, it is clear that numerous intellectual property related contracts will cause difficulties when Article 4(2) is applied to them in the absence of an Article 4(1) rule that covers them. Often there will be more than one characteristic performance, or alternatively it may not be possible to identify a characteristic performance. And there may in almost any case be close, if not closer, connections to several (other) countries. All this still points to the regular use of the escape clause and that in itself is a problem that deserves further analysis in order to see whether a better solution (specific to intellectual property related contracts) can be proposed.

3. A CRITICAL ANALYSIS OF THE PROBLEM, LEADING TO A PROPOSAL

We remain faced, therefore, with a general rule the application of which to complex intellectual property contracts is not certain and may lead to unpredictable results. On too many occasions the escape clauses that are now Articles 4(3) and 4(4) of the Rome I Regulation will be used. Maybe there is another approach that departs even more from current practice that can address these issues and provide more certainty and predictability. A careful re-examination of the issues is required to explain why the alternative may succeed where all others have failed.

3.1 The Re-examination

This brings us back, one more time, to choice of law for intellectual property related contracts in the absence of an express choice of law by the parties. This was a difficult and problematic issue under Article 4 of the Rome Convention 1980, and whilst Article 4 of the Rome I Regulation has no doubt proved to be

13 Case C-533/07 *Falco Privatstiftung v Gisela Weller-Lindhorst* [2009] ECDR 14.

an improvement, it can by no means be argued that all problems have now been solved. Let us be straightforward about the matter, though; there will probably never be an easy solution for this problem. The existing models work well for what we called simple intellectual property related contracts. There is no problem if there clearly is one characteristic performance in the contract or one closest connection. The problem only arises in relation to complex areas where there are multiple mutual obligations of equal value and importance. Narrowing down the potentially high number of characteristic performances and close connections to a single closest connection or a single characteristic performance then becomes difficult as there are no clear criteria for the exercise that are not arbitrary. This problem does not only arise in relation to intellectual property contracts, but it is fair to say that there are proportionally more complex contracts in relation to intellectual property, so the difficulty is more easily perceivable in relation to these contracts and is seen as a more acute problem in this field. These are, on top of that, made worse by the fact that there is no uniformity inside the category of intellectual property related contracts. The boundaries of the category are ill-defined and within the category one finds subcategories of contracts with very different characteristics. Criteria that seem of use and value in relation to some of these contracts are therefore useless and without value when it comes to other contracts.

3.2 No Intellectual Property Specific Rule at Present, but then …

These problems of definition and diversity lead to the conclusion that it may not be straightforward to reform the current Article 4 of the Rome I Regulation by adding a specific choice of law rule for intellectual property contracts. But it does not stop there. The high proportion of complex contracts in this field also means that the fall-back position – the general characteristic performance rule – does not work well in this area. Paragraphs 3 and 4 are intended to cover the exceptional cases where there is a closer connection than that indicated by the characteristic performance, or where no characteristic performance can be determined. But in relation to intellectual property contracts one often finds oneself in a situation where it is these exceptional rules that apply, rather than the general rule. Even then, determining the closest connection is not a straightforward affair. This hints at the fact that reform may be needed on this point.

3.3 Subtle Changes and the Abuse of the Escape Clause

It should be acknowledged, however, that a subtle reform has already taken place when the Regulation replaced the Convention. Often emphasis is placed on the fact that the characteristic performance rule, whilst still subject to exception in paragraphs 3 and 4, is no longer a presumption rule, but a rule of general application where the category specific rules in paragraph 1 do not apply or contradict each other in a specific case. This ultimately does not change that much for intellectual property contracts as they are largely unaffected by paragraph 1, but paragraph 2 now specifically refers to the characteristic performance of 'a' contract. In origin a characteristic performance was something that all contracts in a certain category of contracts had in common. One was supposed to determine the characteristic performance for contracts for the sale of goods, and so on. The solution then applied to all contracts falling within that category. That never worked for the diverse and ill-defined category of contracts in relation to intellectual property; *de facto* one ignored that element of the rule and looked for the characteristic performance in the contract at hand on a contract-by-contract basis. The version of the characteristic performance rule that is now found in Article 4, paragraph 2 of the Rome I Regulation eliminates this need to bend the rule, as it specifically refers to the characteristic performance of the contract and as it applies at a stage when the categories and their rules have not yielded a result for a specific contract. It is therefore normal to apply the rule on a contract-by-contract basis, rather than to a whole category of contracts.

Reform is therefore focused on the unduly high frequency of use of paragraphs 3 and 4 despite this modest step forward. Part of the solution is formed by the realization that the characteristic performance test has little added value in those cases where it is no longer applied to a category of contracts. Whether one calls it a characteristic performance or not, one is effectively looking for the closest connection between that contract and a country and its legal system. Guidance as to the factors that are to be taken into account in terms of connections and how the balancing act is to be operated by the court are steps in the right direction. Another part of the solution is the recognition that such a solution and such an approach need to be intellectual property specific. It is simply not possible to come up with guidance in terms of a list of connecting factors that will be relevant for every single (type of) contract. In that sense, criticism of Article 4 based on the absence of specific guidance is unfair as it has to cover any type of contract. Even by making the guidance intellectual property specific, one cannot easily achieve a clear-cut answer, as the category of intellectual property related contracts remains diverse and ill-defined in terms of boundaries. Nevertheless, progress can be made on this basis.

The situations to which the rule needs to be applied are simply too diverse for a simple rule that would favour the application of the law of the licensor/assignor (or another simple rule that would systematically favour the law of the licensee/assignee) to be justifiable. However well crafted, such a rule would necessarily retain an arbitrary character in a wide range of situations.

This is clear when one considers the approach proposed in § 315(2) of the ALI Principles:[14]

> In the absence of a choice-of-law agreement, the contract law of the State with the closest connection to the contract governs. The contract is presumed to be most closely connected to the State in which the assignor or the licensor resided at the time of the execution of the contract.

3.4 Factors and the Balancing Act

One is therefore left with a range of relevant factors and connecting factors. Each of these needs to be given its proper value in the specific circumstances of the case and then a full-blown balancing act needs to be carried through. One needs to acknowledge that the factors that are to be taken into account will not necessarily point either to the law of the licensor or to the law of the licensee. The intellectual property right itself is by definition a vital factor in relation to these contracts. Every single contractual obligation imposed on either party is founded on the intellectual property right and its existence and scope. Any licence or assignment necessarily refers to a territory or territories where the intellectual property right is in existence. This must bring into the balancing act a reference to a third law – one related to the intellectual property right. We are referring here to the law of the country for which protection is sought or, if one wishes to look at it that way, the law governing the right as such in the place where the licence is to be carried out or in the territory to which the assignment refers. The presence of this important third connection makes the balancing test easier to operate in a large number of cases. A significant overlap between two of the connections must point the court in a certain direction. Nothing is predetermined and factors must be given their proper weight, but, for example, an overlap between the place of establishment of the licensee and the territory for which the licence has been granted will point in the direction of the closest connection being with that country, and it therefore becomes likely that the law of that country will be the applicable law to the contract in the absence of a choice of applicable law made by the parties. In practical terms this means that the balancing test will yield the law of the licensee in circumstances where this is appropriate as it will present *de facto* more cases of overlap with the law of the country for which protection is sought.

[14] American Law Institute, Principles Governing Jurisdiction, Choice of Law and Judgments in Transnational Disputes, available at: http://www.ali.org/doc/2007_intellectualproperty.pdf.

Such a balancing act remains a daunting task, though, and the burden of proof is significant. In the latest stages of the CLIP project it was therefore felt that a mere balancing test would leave too much uncertainty that might deter both the court and the parties. This is undesirable and any way to increase predictability and certainty must be a positive evolution for the parties involved in these contracts, which are often high-value contracts. A clear-cut rule cannot replace the balancing act, but it may equally be incorrect to see the balancing act and the clear-cut rule as alternatives that necessarily exclude one another. In a second stage, a clear-cut rule can add to the balancing act of all relevant factors. It is therefore proposed that the balancing act should remain the starting point, and if it clearly yields a closest connection or a clearly characteristic performance, nothing else is required. There will be plenty of cases, though, where a clear winner will not emerge. A clear-cut rule that appears at that stage by means of a rebuttable presumption will then add guidance and a form of certainty and predictability for both the court and the parties involved. Which form should such a clear-cut rule take, though? Two scenarios can be distinguished. They have a common element. In the absence of a clear closest connection with either licensee or licensor (otherwise we would not get to this stage) the strong factor that remains must be the intellectual property right that is by definition the key element of the contract. If that right is limited to a single territory (that is, the licence or assignment is granted for a single territory), that element points to the law of that territory as the applicable law. The law of the country for which protection is sought will then be presumed to be the applicable law. The second scenario takes on board the inevitable truth that one cannot apply several laws (of the various countries for which the licence or assignment is granted) to a single contract. But implementation in many countries in the absence of a pronounced strong link with the licensee must mean that the right takes centre stage. The right is then created by the licensor and on that basis the ultimate fall-back position for a presumption for a clear-cut rule brings us in these cases to the application for the law of the licensor.

The clear-cut rules will not only provide a solution for those cases where the balancing of factors does not yield a clear solution. And the fact that the presumption element makes it a flexible solution that allows all elements of the very diverse intellectual property contracts to be taken into account properly at any stage is simply not valid for the final stage of the test. The fact that a presumption exists as the ultimate fall-back position will also indirectly provide guidance for the court when applying the balancing test. It makes it clear what the ultimate alternative is and, at the same time, it also provides an indication of the value that the law of the country for which protection is sought and the intellectual property right as such will normally have in these cases. In that way it also alleviates the balancing task to hand and provides an additional level of certainty and predictability.

4. BY WAY OF CONCLUSION: THE PROPOSAL

The approach that is proposed can therefore be summarized as follows:[15]

1. In the absence of a contractual choice of law, the contract shall be governed by the law of the state with which the contract is most closely connected.
2. In contracts having as their main object the creation of protectable subject matter or the transfer or licence of intellectual property, the court shall take into consideration in determining the state with the closest connection:

   (a) as factors tending to the law of the state in which the transferee or licensee has its habitual residence at the time of the conclusion of the contract:

   - the transfer or licence concerns intellectual property rights granted for the state of the habitual residence or place of business of the transferee or licensee;
   - the transferee or licensee has the explicit or implicit duty to exploit the right(s);
   - the royalties or other form of money consideration is expressed as a percentage of the sale price;
   - the licensee or transferee has a duty to report on its efforts to exploit the right(s);

   (b) as factors tending to the law of the state in which the creator, transferor or licensor has its habitual residence at the time of the conclusion of the contract:

   - the transfer or licence concerns intellectual property rights granted for the state of the habitual residence or place of business of the transferor or licensor;
   - the transferee or licensee has no other explicit or implicit duty but to pay a flat sum as money consideration;
   - the licence is for single use;
   - the creator of the protectable subject matter has the duty to create that matter.

---

15 Based on Art. 3:502 of the CLIP Principles; see the Draft available at http://www.cl-ip.eu.

3. If no clear decision can be made under paragraph 2 and the transfer or licence concerns intellectual property rights for only one state, it shall be presumed that the contract is most closely connected with that state. If the transfer or licence concerns intellectual property rights for multiple states, it shall be presumed that the state with which the contract is most closely connected shall be the state in which the creator, transferor or licensor has its habitual residence at the time of the conclusion of the contract.

3. Emerging escape clauses? Online exhaustion, consent and European copyright law

Guido Westkamp

1. INTRODUCTION

Article 4(2) of the European Union Copyright Directive (EUCD)[1] obliges member states to implement the exhaustion doctrine in national copyright laws. Exhaustion occurs once a copy of a work has been put on the market by, or with consent of, the copyright owner. That rule has long been accepted as a core principle of European IP law. It is derived from the preceding jurisprudence as regards, predominantly, parallel imports under primary EU law – that is, the rules on the prohibition of anticompetitive agreements and the subsequent application of the exhaustion doctrine under the rules on the free movement of goods. It was further expressly established in secondary legislation, including the relevant directives in the remit of trade marks, designs, computer programs and databases. What distinguishes the treatment of exhaustion under the EUCD is the fact that, for the first time, it is expressly explained that exhaustion occurs only and apodictically with respect to the putting into circulation of physical copies.

Recital 44 asserts that the question of exhaustion does not arise in the context of online delivery of (digital) works, which is generally understood to mean that the owner of copyright maintains full control over the digital dissemination of digital works. Above and beyond impacting upon the question of whether exhaustion may occur online, a broader issue is at stake here. Historically, the exhaustion rule developed out of the notion of an implied licence. The latter was an attempt to explain the loss of control rights of IP owners following the first act of exploitation. The implied licence doctrine

1 Directive 2001/29/EC of the European Council and Parliament on the Harmonisation of Certain Aspects of Copyright and Related Rights in the Information Society (European Union Copyright Directive), OJ L167, 22 June 2001, at 10.

was developed by German scholar Josef Kohler,[2] who himself extended that model of explanation towards a broader notion of exhaustion[3] in order to enable an extension to those disputes where there was no contractual agreement.

The express exclusion of exhaustion is now increasingly subjected to rather divergent treatment under national law. Questions have arisen that not only affect the exhaustion rule under Article 4(2) EUCD as such. Courts in Germany, as will be explained later, have indeed applied the exhaustion rule, in the context of used software licences, to situations concerning online delivery.

In addition, German jurisprudence now establishes a broader principle of implied consent as regards copyright enforcement on the internet, a principle that historically paved the way for the discovery of exhaustion as a general clause limiting control rights. These approaches reflect the context between exhaustion as a more general exclusionary principle, applied by way of analogy, and consent as an escape clause in order to preserve a certain degree of competitive freedom. If these approaches are considered to be deviations from Article 4(2) EUCD, problems emerge under European law.

This contribution will portray the respective decisions rendered by the German Federal Court of Justice and will assess their potential impact upon European copyright law in general and the ensuing issue of the division of capacities in the evolution of copyright law between national systems (including existing differences in legal methodology) and European jurisprudence.

From the outset, it is certain that the recent application of the exhaustion and implied consent rules does not effortlessly agree with the more rigid protection standard established under European law. Consequentially, there is potential in the exhaustion rule – understood broadly as a principle limiting control rights – to develop into a broader meta-limitation to copyright. That tension prompts further intricate questions. Hence, how far can a rigid understanding of the exhaustion rule be justified under European law? Is it true to say that the jurisprudence of the Court of Justice establishes a rigid restriction of the exhaustion to physical transfers?[4] Is European law – prior to the transposition

---

2 Josef Kohler, *Deutsches Patentrecht* (J. Bensheimer 1878) 100, § 56: this relied on the construction of an implied licence *adincertaspersonas*.

3 Josef Kohler, *Handbuch des deutschen Patentrechts in rechtsvergleichender Darstellung* (J. Bensheimer 1904) 457 (rejecting his implied licence doctrine as incorrect, unnecessary and insufficient).

4 See, e.g., European Commission Green Paper of 27 July 1995 on Copyright and Related Rights in the Information Society COM(95)382 final, 45 et seq.: 'The question of the exhaustion of rights does not arise in the same way where services rather than goods are to be supplied. If there is an intellectual property right which makes a service subject to authorization, the act of supplying that service will be subject to authorization every time. Unlike what happens where the intellectual property is incorporated into a product, such as a video cassette of a film, therefore the

of the EUCD – coercive in, specifically, excluding exhaustion and related concepts in the context of online delivery and related uses such as by image search engines, and establishing an insurmountable legal principle? If not, how can national law internalize concepts above and beyond that restriction that aims to establish broad meta-restrictions? Can, and will, the Court of Justice, especially within the problematic system of interpretation under the preliminary ruling procedure, accept national deviations from the text and spirit of the EUCD?

The starting point here will be a short assertion of the standard argument that favours a constriction of exhaustion to physical goods as a matter of European law and, in that context, the accepted wisdom prevailing in Europe will be assessed initially. That analysis will be followed by a brief investigation into the scope and recognition of aspects of 'online exhaustion' – a question now pending before the Court of Justice – and will conclude with a portrayal of the problems surrounding the notion of implied consent outside contractual licensing agreements as a – different – metaphor for a general consumption doctrine that safeguards technological development and the public interest in unfettered access. Finally, some observations will be made on the relationship between European copyright law and national law, and therein between the freedom enjoyed by national courts and the Court of Justice.

2. THE EUROPEAN EXHAUSTION DOCTRINE AND COPYRIGHT CATEGORIZATION

Article 4(2) and Recital 29 EUCD are the result of a long-established jurisprudence of the Court of Justice concerning the interface between the principle of the free movement of goods and territorial intellectual property rights, including copyright.[5] As is well known, the principle of exhaustion was first applied in the context of (as is now) Article 101 TFEU on the prohibition of anticompetitive agreements,[6] and later the application of the principles of the free movement of goods[7] in order to resolve the conflict that had arisen because IP

---

broadcasting of a film or the showing of a film in a cinema does not exhaust the holder's right to authorize or prohibit the broadcasting, projection or cable retransmission thereafter.'

[5] See Recital 29 EUCD, above note 1.

[6] Cases 56 & 58/64 *Consten and Grundig v Commission* [1966] ECR 299; Case 40/70 *Sirena v Eda* [1971] ECR 69; Case 58/80 *Dansk Supermarked v Imerco* [1981] 3 CMLR 590; Case 170/83 *Hydrotherm Gerätebau v Andreoli* [1984] ECR 2999.

[7] The territorial restraint resulting from territorial IP rights was considered to be

owners were relying on territorial IP rights in order to recreate national boundaries to prevent parallel or re-imports,[8] often to maintain price differences between different national markets.[9]

It is also well known that the Court of Justice approached that conflict in a manner that was frequently criticized by IP lawyers.[10] It first invented the distinction between exercise and existence, which proved problematic. The Court held that, whereas the existence of rights remained unfettered by community law, it had competence under the Treaty to evaluate the exercise of IP rights.[11] In later decisions, the Court reverted to a principle of the specific subject matter of IP rights to distinguish those remits of primary European law that may affect the exploitation of goods protected by IP rights from those where the territorial effect might continue.[12] Effectively, however, the Court of Justice would usually prohibit any attempt based on territorial IP rights so as to create artificial boundaries at the expense of a free circulation of goods.[13] This went as far as allowing exhaustion even in cases where goods were first marketed in countries that did not provide for IP protection and where, consequently, the IP owner could not reap any reward based on that right. The Court of Justice did not always expressly rely on the concept of exhaustion in all of these cases, though clearly it had found the exhaustion, derived from a comparative evaluation of the law in (some) member states convincing to

---

a measure having equivalent effect: see Joined Cases 55 & 57/80 *Musik Vertrieb Membran v Gesellschaft für musikalische Aufführungsrechte* [1981] ECR 147.

8 The Court first established that Art. 36 (now Art. 30) does not restrict the scope of application of the competition provisions: see *Consten and Grundig v Commission*, above note 6. It later applied Art. 36 by way of analogy to cases concerning Art. 85(1) (see Case 24/67 *Parke Davis v Probel* [1968] ECR 85) until it finally directly applied Arts 28–30 (formerly 30–36) on any exercise of intellectual property rights: see *Sirena v Eda*, above note 6; Case 78/80 *Deutsche Grammophon v Metro-SB-Grossmärkte* [1971] ECR 487; Case 192/73 *van Zuylen Frères v Hag AG* [1974] ECR 731; Case 16/74 *Centrafarm v De Peijper Winthrop* [1974] ECR 1183.

9 Giuliano Marenco and Karen Banks, 'Intellectual Property and Community Rules on Free Movement' [1990] *European Law Review* 224.

10 Friedrich-Karl Beier, 'Industrial Property and the Free Movement of Goods' [1990] IIC 131.

11 See, for instance, *Centrafarm v De Peijper Winthrop*, above note 8.

12 *Deutsche Grammophon v Metro*, above note 8; latter approaches to defining the 'specific subject matter' include, as regards trade marks: Case 102/77 *Hoffmann La Roche & Co AG v Centrafarm Vertriebsgesellschaft Pharmazeutischer Erzeugnisse mbH* [1978] ECR 1139 (the essential function of the trade mark was considered to be the guarantee of origin to the consumer or ultimate user; further *Centrafarm and De Peijper Winthrop*, above note 8 (the guarantee to market the product for the first time).

13 The issue of what amounts to a proper exercise is a matter of community law and for the ECJ to decide: see Case 144/81 *Keurkoop BV v Nancy Kean Gifts BV* [1982] ECR 2853.

support its distinction.[14] However, the Court of Justice – as far as copyright is concerned – similarly stated that exhaustion would not occur with respect to services such as the public performance of films: a licence providing for the right to exploit a movie in one member state consequently did not include the right to show it in another.

It is this grid of argument that was later imposed upon secondary legislation. It is apparent that Article 4(2) EUCD was attached systematically to acts of distribution and that consequently distribution was understood to derive from the principle of free movement of goods. In contrast, the respective rights of communication to the public, in particular the right to make available works interactively, is then attached to the freedom to provide services. Following that logic, exhaustion – as an element of primary European law – cannot occur in the latter case. Effectively, then, the national transposition of the exclusive rights incorporates a European logic into national law that may be based upon entirely divergent rationales, and superimposes an alleged 'principle' ultimately based on the division between goods and services that, in such exclusivity, does not exist. Automatically, the division between goods and services under primary EU law is then superimposed upon national law, thus altering the potentially different approach to exhaustion, especially where national law might have employed that doctrine in relation to different exclusive rights or as a more flexible principle.[15] Hence, if that division, derived from the diverging treatment of limitations upon the respective fundamental freedoms, can be fully justified so as to constrain exhaustion to cases of physical distribution, the current jurisprudence in German courts would initially contradict fundamental European principles. However, it may be suggested that a simple transposition – prematurely equating the exclusive right to control distribution with the principles of free movement of goods and other rights with the freedom to

---

14 *Hoffmann La Rochev Centrafarm*, above note 12. The court did not, however, introduce the exhaustion principle as a novel conceptual approach, but stated that it had already existed under case law on Art. 30 EC. Further case law then consistently and expressly reaffirmed the exhaustion rule: see Case C-19/84 *Pharmon BV v Hoechst AG* [1985] ECR 2281, [1985] WL 311768, [1985] 3 CMLR 775; Case 35/87 *Thetford Corporation and Another v Fiamma SPA and Others* [1990] Ch 339; Case 341/87 *EMI Electrola Gmbh v Patricia Im- und Export* [1989] ECR 79; Case 395/87 *Ministere Public v Tournier* [1989] ECR 2521; Case C-9/93 *IHT Internationale Heiztechnik GmbH v Ideal Standard GmbH* [1994] ECR I-2789; Case C-267/95 *Merck & Co Inc v Primecrown Ltd* [1996] ECR I-6285; Case C-427/93 *Bristol Myers Squibb Co v Paranova A/S* [1996] ECR I-3457; Case C-352/95 *Phytheron International SA v Jean Bourdon SA* [1997] ECR I-1729; Case C-200/96 *Metronome Musik GmbH v Music Point Hohkamp GmbH* [1998] ECR I-1953, [1999] EMLR 93.

15 See, e.g., the decision concerning exhaustion in the case of cable rights: BGH 7 November 1980, I ZR 24/79 – *Kabelfernsehen in Abschattungsgebieten*.

provide services – is misguided; if so, the general exclusion of exhaustion under Article 4(2) EUCD for anything delivered online cannot be conclusive.

A closer inspection of the 'character' of the exhaustion doctrine as applied in the jurisprudence of the Court of Justice indeed reveals that, rather than aiming to establish a categorization of exclusive rights (between material uses and communication rights, thus allocating the exhaustion doctrine to one category only), it was always concerned with creating a formula that would permit a full recognition of the requirements of an emerging internal market.[16] In that sense, exhaustion denotes a flexible formula, or collision clause, that permitted the Court to employ a principle accepted in most member states (at the time) that allowed for the conflict to be resolved by applying a reasonably convincing methodology. As far as a conflict with the principles of free movement of goods is concerned, the Court of Justice had to apply the test set out in the Treaty – that is, whether an attempt to prevent parallel imports was a measure having equivalent effect and, more critically, whether such measure (that is, the exercise of a national norm by which such import may be prevented) was justified. It was certain from the text that the protection of intellectual property rights was deemed to be a legitimate reason to justify such a measure, and it is that element in the test under Article 30 that required a more sophisticated approach.

At this juncture, European law did not provide for a general rule by which the exercise of rights derived from national IP rights could be overcome. This created an imbalance and, as far as the principle of free movements of goods was concerned, an unpersuasive factual extension of exploitation rights. Owners of IP rights who were able to take advantage of the emerging internal market additionally would have benefitted from an all-embracing safeguard of their territorial rights that would have resulted in adversely affecting considerably the functioning of the freedom to trade in goods; this would have led to a deterioration in the principle aim of the Treaty to create a market without borders. The result of that approach – the loss of control rights that then

---

16 Clearly, it is far beyond the scope of this contribution to sketch out fully the history of the exhaustion rule and its manifold intricacies. See, for example, Valentine Korah, *An Introductory Guide to EC Competition Law and Practice* 298 (Hart Publishing, 7th edn 2000); P. Müller-Graff, 'Die Rechtsangleichung zur Verwirklichung des Binnenmarktes' (1989) 24 *Europarecht* 151, 152; H. Mertens de Wilmars, 'The Case Law of the Court of Justice in Relation to the Review of the Legality of Economic Policy in Mixed-Economy Systems' [1982] *Legal Issues of European Integration* 1, 3; H. Matthies, 'Die Verfassung des Gemeinsamen Marktes', in *Das Europa der Zweiten Generation: Gedächtnisschrift für Christoph Sasse* (Nomos 1985) 115, 117; Manfred Koenigs, 'Rechtsfragen der einheitlichen europäischen Akte für den gewerblichen Rechtsschutz', in Manfred Bohlig (ed.), *Lohn der Leistung Und Rechtssicherheit, Festschrift für Albert Preu zum 70. Geburtstag* (C.H. Beck 1988) 277.

extends to the entire territory of the EU – is easily justifiable. Traders cannot legitimately benefit from the freedoms enshrined in the Treaty and the individual advantages these bring about, and concurrently partition that market by non-harmonized national property titles. Reliance on exhaustion thus was a technique to overcome the language of Article 30 EC, and indeed it was the only option. The Court of Justice could, unquestionably, express a preference neither for the protection of IP rights nor for a general rule completely rescinding IP rights without violating the Treaty language and the system of rules and limitations enshrined under Article 30 EC. It required a rule that, methodically, resulted in a balancing exercise. The exhaustion principle thus appeared as an ideal candidate: as a normative principle already enshrined in the laws of member states, and similarly so because – as a principle rather than a norm – it allowed a further differentiation and evolution of the law, if only hypothetical.

The doctrinal strategy employed by the Court of Justice relied, specifically, upon the notion of consent.[17] In construing 'consent' as a broad entry requirement for the occurrence of exhaustion, the Court of Justice furnished itself with a flexible doctrinal concept. It thus became irrelevant whether the agreement contained anticompetitive restrictions because it would be caught under Article 28 (formerly Article 30) EC, which would necessarily supersede any right to prevent parallel imports. The key to this is the emphasis placed on consent, which the Court of Justice then interpreted to refer to the entire territory of the Treaty and which it equated with entering into a licensing agreement, including compulsory licences.[18] This allowed both a step back from the more restrictive requirements under Article 81 EC (Article 101 TFEU), and also invoked a legal rule under which the entering into a licence agreement as such was sufficient. In turn, that interpretation developed into an understanding that every act of putting an article into circulation resulted in exhaus-

[17] See Case 15/74 *Centrafarm BV v Sterling Drug Inc.* (1974) 2 CMLR 480, 486–7, 507 (addressing the right to first put into circulation, either directly or by an authorized party, and the right to sue for infringement); *Keurkoop v Nancy Kean Gifts*, above note 13; Case 187/70 *Merck v Stephar* (1981) CMLR 463 (stating that patent law does not give a right to monopoly profits. A patentee cannot prevent re-importation of goods previously marketed in another member state even though the invention was not patentable there); Cases 267 & 268/95 *Merck v Primecrown Ltd* [1997] FSR 237 (stating that the substance of a patent right was the exclusive right to put the invention on the market for the first time); *Musik Vertrieb Membran v Gesellschaft für Musikalische Aufführungsrechte*, above note 7 (holding there is no right to additional royalties for a copyright collecting society); see also Ulrich Loewenheim, 'Schallplattenimporte und freier Warenverkehr' (1985) 95 UFITA 41, 60; Robert M. Merkin, 'The Interface between Anti-trust and Intellectual Property' [1985] ECLR 377, 391.

[18] *Merck v Stephar*, ibid.

tion, even where the place of first circulation was a country in which no rights existed or where the owner could not be rewarded—a scenario which was held to result in rendering IP rights a *nudumius*.[19] This would denote that territorial restrictions in licensing contracts cannot affect the occurrence of exhaustion as a matter of the proprietary scope of the IP right. Such understanding, however, would presuppose that the Court of Justice's jurisprudence referred to establishing a true limitation on the exercise of national IP rights. Consent, in this respect, was not employed as a predetermining normative rule but constituted the principle aspect for resolving and guiding the proportionality test – mostly, but not necessarily in favour of free circulation.[20] If this is correct, the status of consent and, subsequently, its effects upon exhaustion can be analysed more closely in the light of the function of the IP right and, more specifically, the scope to which a licensor may bind his buyers and licensees.

In other words, the use of the term exhaustion in the jurisprudence concerning the interface between the justifiable scope of territorial IP rights and the principle of free movement of goods, derived from a comparative assessment of existing national laws, reflects the need for the creation of a flexible assessment model. In so doing, the Court of Justice appears to have employed the exhaustion principle indeed, not as a rigid normative rule but as a collision clause that fundamentally paves the way for further differentiation. Clearly, that differentiation – as is apparent in the attempt to formulate a doctrinally convincing formula – remains difficult to imbue with fully convincing rules. The approach taken thus far – that is, to rely upon the notion of the specific subject matter – in itself is of little assistance in clearly determining the scope of control rights. In particular, the jurisprudence remains clear in that attempts to obstruct parallel imports will not be tolerated, and that assertion specifically conveys the impression that exhaustion will remain as a cemented principle. The only ascertainable area of importance where the balancing exercise would

---

19 Karl-Friedrich Beier, 'Beherrschende Marktstellung und Ausübung gewerblicher Schutzrechte', in Harm P. Westermann and Wolfgang Rosener (eds), *Festschrift für Karlheinz Quack* (Walter de Gruyter 1991) 31; Clifford D. Miller, 'Magill: Time to Abandon the "Specific Subject-matter" Concept' [1994] 10 EIPR 415, 419.

20 See, e.g., the arguments raised in relation to self-induced liability of the licensor by putting goods on the market. These are unconvincing because Art. 30 relates to the restrictive practice enabling a patentee under national law and is not concerned with individual behaviour. These views clearly sought to explain the decision in *Merck v Stephar*, above note 17. See Koenigs, above note 16; F.A. Mann, 'Industrial Property and the EEC Treaty' (1975) 24 *International & Comparative Law Quarterly* 31, 34; Friedrich-Karl Beier, 'Industrial Property and the Free Movement of Goods' [1990] 21 IIC 131; Hermann Cohen Jehoram, 'Articles 30–36 EEC and Intellectual Property' [1982] *Social Economisch Wetgeving* 374.

result in favouring the IP owner is trade mark law, where it is fundamentally accepted that exhaustion does not occur where further distribution results in a loss of the origin function of the trade mark.[21] Again, the trade mark example supports the view that the exhaustion rule is but a metaphor rather than a principled concept.

2.1 Categorization and European Exhaustion in Secondary Legislation

However, that general jurisprudence does not detract from the fact that exhaustion remains a collision clause rather than a rule that monolithically allocates the exhaustion principle to one category of exclusive rights under copyright law. In a similar vein, the general flexible character of the exhaustion rule as a collision clause is mirrored when considering the potential to divide markets by way of licences and thus to attempt to circumvent the occurrence of exhaustion in those cases where goods are being put into circulation on (geographical or product) markets not covered by the licensing agreement. Clearly, such licensing clauses would prima facie violate the prohibition to enter into anti-competitive agreements. Increasingly, however, that general prohibition[22] – formulated at a time when the internal market was not fully established – is becoming subject to debate. These aspects of competition law and their impact upon IP licensing agreements obviously cannot be covered here in meticulous detail. However, it should be noted that certain block exemptions under Article 101 (3) TFEU at least appear to permit IP owners to control more generously the exploitation of works by licensees.[23] The trend here is to permit non-

---

21 See Art. 7 European Trade Mark Regulation. In relation to trade marks, the ECJ has developed the concept of the essential function, which subsequently found its way into the Trade Mark Regulation: see Case C-273/00 *Sieckmann v Commission* [2002] ECR I-1737 (stating the essential function is 'to guarantee the identity of the origin of the marked product or service to the consumer or end-user by enabling him to distinguish that product or service from others without confusion'). See further, F. Urlesberger, '"Legitimate Reasons" for the Proprietor of a Trade Mark Registered in the EU to Oppose Further Dealings in the Goods after they have been put on the Market for the First Time' (1999) 36 CMLR 1195.

22 See *Hoffmann La Roche v Centrafarm*, above note 12. The practice in the 1970s and 1980s, in particular, was hostile towards any territorial restraint: European Commission Decision 76/29 in *AOIP v Beyrard* [1976] 1 CMLR D14; *Bronbemaling v Heidemaatschappij* (75/570/EEC) [1975] 2 CMLR D67; in Case 258/78 *Nungesser and Eisele v Commission* [1982] ECR 2015, the ECJ allowed open exclusive licences. The 1985 Patent Licensing Regulation similarly only allowed non-exclusive and open exclusive licences: see Art. 1(1)(1)–1(1)(5) Regulation 2349/85. See Korah, above note 16,283.

23 For example, under Art. 4(b) of the Vertical Restraints Regulation 1999 (below note 24), the seller may restrict the territory 'into which…b) the restriction of

dominant firms to enter into licensing clauses that aim to restrict markets.[24] Whether exhaustion then occurs after the product has been put on the market, however, remains unresolved.[25] In addition, although the relationship between block exemptions and permissible restrictions on trade, on the one hand, and the rules on the free movement of goods, on the other, has not yet received a full analysis by the Court of Justice, some observations may be made that further underline the character of the exhaustion rule as a flexible collision clause.[26] A clause that, following on from what is permitted under the respective block exemptions, is deemed not to be anticompetitive may logically be pro-competitive. Certainly, it is the intention underlying, in particular, the block exemption as regards technology transfers to provide more contractual freedom with a view to give an incentive to innovate; here it is made clear that, provided certain market share thresholds are not reached, the parties are free

---

the territory into which, or of the customers to whom, the buyer may sell the contract goods or services', except '– the restriction of active sales into the exclusive territory or to an exclusive customer group reserved to the supplier or allocated by the supplier to another buyer, where such a restriction does not limit sales by the customers of the buyer'; VRR, Recital 3: 'This category includes vertical agreements for the purchase or sale of goods or services where these agreements are concluded between non-competing undertakings, between certain competitors or by certain associations of retailers of goods; it also includes vertical agreements containing ancillary provisions on the assignment or use of intellectual property rights.'

24 See the approach taken under the Technology Transfer Regulation (TTR), Commission Regulation 772/04, [2004] OJ L 123, 11; and the Vertical Restraints Regulation, Commission Regulation 2790/1999, [1999] OJ L 336, 2. The details concerning the effect of permissible licensing restrictions on the occurrence of exhaustion cannot be discussed here. See, in detail, Guido Westkamp, 'Intellectual Property, Competition Rules and the Emerging Internal Market: Some Thoughts on the European Exhaustion Doctrine' (2007) 11 *Marquette Intellectual Property Law Review* 291, 311 et seq. See further, James S. Venit, 'In the Wake of Windsurfing: Patent Licensing in the Common Market' [1986] *Fordham Corporate Law Institute* 517, 528–9 (B. Hawk (ed.), 1987).

25 Steven D. Anderman, *EC Competition Law and Intellectual Property Rights* (Clarendon Press 1998) 97 et seq. The 2004 TTR apparently allows the territorial reservation for buyers. See further Valentine Korah, *An Introductory Guide to EC Competition Law and Practice* (Hart Publishing, 8th edn 2004) 287 (stating that even though a clause may be caught under Art. 81(1), the licensor may still be able to rely on national patent rights). The correct view, it is submitted, is to treat the agreement in accordance with Art. 81(1), whereas the question of exhaustion in cases of illegitimate restrictions (here an export ban imposed between individual licensees) is to be treated under Arts 28–30 EC.

26 See, e.g., BGH, 4 May 2000, I ZR 256/97 = (2001) GRUR 51; OLG Hamburg (1998) ZUM-RD 2 – *PerfumeBottle* (on the application of the exhaustion doctrine to acts of publicly showing works protected by copyright rather than to the distribution right, which effectively aligned the effects of exhaustion under trade mark and concurrently applicable copyright law).

to agree any clause they wish without the risk of falling foul of Article 101 (1) TFEU. Such a clause continues to bind the licensee; but whether it may have absolute (*in rem*) effect in preventing exhaustion is an open matter.

Two views may be distinguished: either, the principle of free movement applies in such a situation regardless, despite the fact that the competition rules would permit such a restriction, or indeed the current rules on exhaustion are being relaxed so as to permit an *in rem* effect against, for instance, third parties who acquire protected goods at a later stage in the licensing chain. That view may be supported by the observation that an increasingly established internal market may tolerate less prohibitive rules[27] and that therefore the jurisprudence might move away from an assessment of the impact of restriction on the principle of the free movement of goods towards concentrating solely on competition aspects. That view is further, from a comparative perspective, supported by the treatment of such a clause under US antitrust law, where it has been held that a trade mark licence that aimed to divide geographical markets was permissible. In that sense, the approach under the rules on free movement would have to be modified. Where a particular restriction is permitted as a matter of competition law, it can hardly be ascertained that the same restriction must fail – when enforced vis-à-vis third parties – under the specific subject matter test. In such a case, the preferable option is to consider the third limb of the test established under the free movement of goods rules – that is, whether the restriction on free movement caused by such an agreement constitutes an arbitrary restriction.

If, then, the view is correct that the exhaustion rule – in either direction – cannot be considered as a monolithic doctrine, but more so a flexible tool that may be adapted, importantly, to the specific requirements that arise at differ-

---

27 § 261 of the US Patent Act allows territorial restrictions even as applied to a common national market, but it does curtail the patent owner's control after the first sale to the consumer: see 36 USC § 261 (2000). This solution would mean a significant step away from the reward notion. The licensor would be able to control the distribution up to the point when the article is physically in the hands of the consumer: *United States v Arnold, Schwinn & Co.*, 388 U.S. 365 (1967) (finding a territorial distribution illegal under § 1 of the Sherman Act because it harmed competition among distributors. That decision sparked controversy which, in turn, generated a considerable amount of scholarly work focusing on the economic effects of vertical arrangements. Territorial restraints could be used to address the 'free-rider phenomenon'); *Continental TV Inc. v GTE Sylvania, Inc.*, 433 U.S. 36 (1977) (reversing the position and concluding that a *per se* illegal approach to territorial restraints was fallacious). The Court pointed out that vertical restraints should be evaluated under the rule of reason. The lawfulness of a particular vertical restraint will depend upon whether the restraint on balance restricts or promotes competition: *National Society of Professional Engineers v United States*, 435 U.S. 679 (1978) (interpreting 35 USC § 261 so as to allow territorial divisibility of patent distribution licences to the whole or any specified part of the United States).

ent stages of the creation of an internal market, it follows that the rigidity with which the European legislator has excluded exhaustion in any case of 'service' is misguided. At least as far as the free movement of goods is concerned, nothing in the jurisprudence actually indicates, in addition, that the Court of Justice was concerned with establishing a demarcation line between the different exclusive rights under copyright. It was concerned, on the contrary, with establishing a concept allowing, on the basis of the consent expressed, a viable balancing mechanism that in itself does not incorporate any strict rule in favour or against a loss of control rights, and one that additionally functions as a concept that permits the recognition of an increasingly more lenient attitude towards restrictive clauses. Hence, the transgression from the jurisprudence as regards the primary towards a rule informing, as of now, national copyright law is certainly much less persuasive then it appears. The categorization of the exclusive rights under copyright law, therefore, does not follow from the jurisprudence of exhaustion, and the relationship between primary and secondary legislation should not be concocted. Accepting that the restriction enshrined in Recital 29 EUCD is mandatory in constituting a principle of European IP law is an untenable hypothesis.

2.2 The Exclusion of Services

Similarly, then, the fact that the Court of Justice had excluded exhaustion in the case of licences concerning the public performance of works[28] requires a more holistic interpretation. The Court, as is well known, did state that the right to control a public performance was not subject to exhaustion. However, it remains open whether that assertion indeed related to an interpretation of exclusive rights or whether it was merely concerned with the application of primary European law. In the latter case, the exclusion of exhaustion, eventually taken as a monolithic principle cemented in stone and applying to any right of communication under secondary copyright legislation, becomes significantly less convincing. The first aspect to bear in mind here is that the factual details of the case rather unequivocally concerned the freedom to provide services given that it concerned a public performance, and in that regard the decision is not fully transferable to cases where the question of a loss of control rights concerns the delivery of individual works as part of such service. The initial categorization as either a service or a product thus remains a matter that is deduced from primary European law rather than from substantive copyright law. It should, in this respect, also be noted that, according to

---

[28] See Case 262/81 *Coditel v Cine Vog Films* (*Coditel II*) [1982] ECR 3381, 15–20.

the Court of Justice, the rules on the free movement of goods and the freedom to provide services are not mutually exclusive.[29] Hence, the limitations that apply to the principle of the movement of goods may apply concurrently to justify a violation of the free services provision, in that a service may concurrently be categorized as a modality of sales.[30] National laws thus may be subject to an analysis under both the freedom to provide services and the free movement of goods, in which case the assessment ultimately results in a general balancing between national freedom and the requirements of the primary aims of the treaty.[31] Secondly, and more importantly, the structure of the rules on the freedom to provide services differs from a systematic perspective from those on the free movement of goods. Article 48 EC does not contain a limitation that requires, or permits, the Court of Justice to have regard to a list of justifications as is found under Article 30(2) EC. In other words, once a violation of the freedom to provide services is established, it is not feasible to have regard to a collision such as that established under Article 30(2) EC. Clearly, the Court of Justice was limited by the categorization of the licensing agreement as having a service as its object. The route towards creating a general and principled collision clause is necessarily blocked in such a case, given that the limitations imposed upon restriction of the free movement of goods and services respectively are based on divergent structures. Article 49 EC (Article 56 TFEU) simply prohibits any restriction on that freedom. The fact that the Court rejected exhaustion here does not prevent it from establishing a functionally identical principle[32] in future (such as, hypothetically,

---

[29] On the convergence between the principles of the free movement of goods and services (advertising as a modality of sale within the meaning of the jurisprudence in *Keck*), see Joined Cases C-34–36/95 *Konsumentenombudsmannen v Svenska Förlag De Agostini (Svenska) Förlag AB* [1997] ECR I-3843.

[30] *Konsumentenombudsmannen v Svenska Förlag De Agostini*, ibid. The goods to be marketed were collectable parts for a children's reference book on dinosaurs produced by an Italian manufacturer. The advertisements were broadcast from the UK, inter alia into Sweden, where media law prohibits advertisements targeted at children. Here, the Court assessed the impact of the prohibition on both fundamental principles, yet apparently did not treat the justification of the Swedish media law provision in question differently under Arts 28–30 and 49 EC.

[31] For criticism, see Oliver Remien, *Zwingendes Vertragsrecht und Grundfreiheiten* (Mohr Sieback 2003) 193 et seq. On the broader impact of the two categories upon private law, see further, Jürgen Basedow, 'Privatrechtsvereinheitlichung Privatrechtsvereinheitlichung und Marktintegration', in *Festschrift für Ernst-Joachim Mestmäcker zum siebzigsten Geburtstag* (Nomos 1996) 347, 353 et seq.

[32] See BGH, 4 May 2000, I ZR 256/97 (2001) GRUR 51 – *Perfume Bottle;* BGH, BGHZ 79, 350, 356 et seq. – *Exhaustion of Cable Program Copyright.* The latter approach was given up in BGH, 17 February 2000, I ZR 194/97 – *Einzigartige Chanel.*

regards 'online exhaustion' cases with respect to individual works); nor does it rule out, exclusively, the possibility that national courts may apply the exhaustion principle to works disseminated via a service.

Secondly, the fact that the EUCD employs the term 'service' shows only that, as a matter of simple logic, the right to provide a service itself cannot be exhausted; otherwise, indeed, not a lot would be left of any exclusive right.[33] The language itself, therefore, is open to a broader analysis. In particular, it does not follow that the mere fact that a particular work is made accessible through a service must exclude the occurrence of exhaustion or, for that matter, the application of any meta-norm that abrogates control rights after such work had been licensed. The treatment of individual copies and the service under which these are disseminated must initially be distinguished.[34]

In conclusion, it appears that the rigidity with which the EUCD allocated the exhaustion rule to the distribution right is grossly overestimated. There are clear differences in applying the exhaustion rule as a metaphor to enable a balancing test that permits the recognition of the treaty aims, and the exhaustion rule as it was understood and applied within national legal systems as a provision applicable within a discrete system of national intellectual property law. The initial categorization as a product or service thus remains a matter of primary European law and not a matter of establishing substantive rules under national IP law; even then that categorization is neither mutually exclusive, nor does it necessarily follow that European law may not intervene in the case of services in order to constrain control rights, albeit not necessarily on the basis of the exhaustion doctrine as applied in relation to physical products. If this is correct, the exclusion of exhaustion as regards any 'online service' can neither be supported by relying on the jurisprudence concerning the free movement of goods, nor can it prevent its application (by way of analogy) under national law. The construction of the distribution right as pertaining to physical goods only, therefore, cannot be deduced from the fact that it was predominantly in the area of the free movement of goods that exhaustion was accepted. Similarly, it does not follow logically that exhaustion – or, indeed,

[33] That view was accepted in OLG München, 3 August 2006 – 6 U 1818/06, (2008) MMR 601, JurPC Web-Dok 141/2006, available at: http://www.jurpc.de/rechtspr/20060141.htm; OLG Frankfurt, Order made 12 May 2009, 11 W 15/09, available at http://openjur.de/u/30875.html; LG Berlin, 14 July 2009, 6 O 67/08, JurPC Web-Dok 240/2009, available at: http://www.jurpc.de/rechtspr/20090240.htm (last visited 18 January 2012). See also Gerald Spindler, 'Der Handel mit Gebrauchtsoftware – Erschöpfungsgrundsatz quo vadis?' (2008) *Computer und Recht* 69, 70 et seq.

[34] Note also that a similar problem arises under Art. 6(4)(4) EUCD, which excludes the opportunity for member states to allow beneficiaries of limitations to enforce these in relation to services. It is not clear whether that exclusion is to apply in general to all individual works or merely to claims for access to a service.

any general clause aimed at constraining control rights past an act of first publication – must be tied to the distribution right. The division between goods and services under primary EU law and the division between physical and non-physical acts of exploitation remain discrete categories. Whilst it is necessarily true that the first is informed by the fundamental aims of European integration, the latter must remain a matter of ensuring a level-headed evolution of copyright law and the specific requirements of a general balance between the public interest and the scope of control rights.

2.3 Summation

In summary, nothing in the history and application of the European exhaustion doctrine coerces the European legislator to expressly constrain exhaustion to acts of physical sales. This becomes, as mentioned, utterly clear when considering that

(i) the use of the term 'exhaustion' followed from a comparative assessment of national laws in which that term existed, and as such promised the most elegant solution to the conflict between the principle of free movement of goods and continued territorial effects of intellectual property rights;
(ii) the issue of exhaustion and the division of exclusive rights under copyright law are two entirely independent concerns; therefore, the fact that exhaustion was the preferred solution to (mainly) attempts to restrict the impact of the territorial effect in cases that fell within the remit of the rules on the free movement of goods is an aspect that must clearly be distinguished from the categorization of exclusive rights under copyright law;
(iii) the notion of exhaustion – understood as a general principle which is tied to diverging national considerations and rationales – remains distinct depending on whether one addresses it from the perspective of European or national law; and
(iv) the ultimate problem lies in the fact that secondary legislation by way of directives has caused a concoction of these principles and has led to the misguided view that exhaustion remains a narrow limitation applicable to acts of physical sales, which after transposition excessively narrows judicial freedom of movement at the expense of a meaningful evolution of copyright law in the light of highly dynamic commercial realities.

3. NATIONAL DISOBEDIENCE?

If unconditional reliance on primary EU law is an inapposite basis for excluding exhaustion in the context of online services, one may ask why the legislative decision was taken to limit exhaustion so rigidly under the EUCD. Two observations spring to mind. First, it may be conceivable that the Commission, in drafting the Directive, had in mind a particular business model that required monopolistic control rights enjoyed by right holders.[35] That remains an impression and cannot be entirely substantiated, though certainly the Commission was adamant to permit right holders (and here, in particular, the entertainment industry[36]) the opportunity to enter into direct licensing agreements; with such a business model in mind broad consumption clauses and meta-restrictions do not easily agree. Clearly, then, one may presume that the EUCD was silently drafted around that central tenet, built upon the assumption that such unfettered control rights prompt the facilitation of online services controlled by right holders, and that ultimately such 'high degree of protection' was desirable.[37] The second is that, certainly, any extension of the exhaustion rule towards a national meta-limitation to copyright – something akin to the US fair use doctrine – would, of course, have resulted in limiting the harmonizing effect of the Directive and would have shattered the system of permissible limitations under Article 5 EUCD. It should also be added that, necessarily, the EU was bound by the WIPO Treaties and that therefore Article 3 WCT[38] (the making available right) had to be implemented 'as is'.

These considerations already show that European law itself, in heeding the aim of harmonization, must leave little scope for national courts to create general escape clauses under copyright law nationally, and that the impact of international copyright law upon the freedom enjoyed in Brussels similarly limits more holistic approaches. To these aspects I will return later. At this juncture, the sole remaining question is whether the exclusion of exhaustion

---

35 The Directive employs the terms 'authors' and 'right holders' indistinctly. It is uncertain whether, for example, an exclusive licensee – in the absence of own neighbouring rights – should therefore enjoy the same level of protection.

36 The Commission has initially adopted the view that collective licensing structures should be phased out and replaced broadly by direct licensing agreements supported by digital rights management. See, on the ensuing work programme and related initiatives of the Commission, Giuseppe Mazziotti, *EU Digital Copyright and the End User* (Springer 2008) 387 et seq. See also Commission Recommendation of 18 May 2005 on collective cross-border management of copyright and related rights for legitimate online music services [2005] OJ L 276/54, 21 October 2005, 54–7.

37 See Recitals 2, 3 and 6 EUCD, in particular.

38 WIPO Copyright Treaty, adopted in Geneva, 20 December 1996, available at: http://www.wipo.int/treaties/en/ip/wct/trtdocs_wo033.html.

can reasonably be justified by substantive copyright law. Overall, that question certainly is way too broad to be analysed here in detail, specifically so given that the Directive remains rather opaque on the fundamental rationale of copyright. In other words, it appears difficult to place the exclusion of exhaustion into a system that is free from contradiction, since the Directive operates not only within a closed system that leaves rather little freedom of movement, but also because any such rigidity reduces the chances for a reasonable adaptation and evolution of copyright in the light of highly dynamic market and public interest realities. That said, the underlying policy rationale of the EUCD – though not expressly asserted in the text – might indeed explain, though not entirely justify, a complete exclusion of exhaustion and comparable meta-norms.

3.1 National Law: Online Exhaustion and the Used Software Licensing Cases

The first instalment towards a broadening of the exhaustion rule was made, following decisions by the German Federal Supreme Court, in 2011. The Court did not permit 'online exhaustion' but referred several questions to the Court of Justice in the context of the practice to resell used software. Although not directly applicable to the EUCD,[39] the decision may, in future, nevertheless prompt a development towards a broader recognition of the public interest.

The issue before the Court concerned the practice of reselling 'used' software licences – that is, bulk program licences that had previously been purchased or downloaded and eventually resold once no longer required. The central issue concerned the loss of control of the original copyright owner following a purchase of such software and respective licence keys online. The prevailing view as to the legitimacy of such a resale practice had been that the exhaustion rule – enshrined, as far as computer program copyright is concerned, in Article 69d (3) of the German Authors Right Act 1965 – made such practice unlawful. This position was based largely on the two premises that (i) the necessary installation by the acquirer required an act of reproduction not subject to the exhaustion rule, and (ii) the exhaustion rule was applicable only with regard to acts of physically placing into circulation a physical embodiment of the program. Other commentators took a more lenient view and referred to the basic rationale of the exhaustion rule to preserve market transparency and thus permit unconstrained circulation of any works. That

[39] The EUCD does not extend to computer program copyright. Therefore, initially Recital 29 and Art. 4(2) EUCD cannot be applied to software as such.

position was underlined by reference to the commercial realities: clearly, where online delivery increasingly (and in the case of software today, almost entirely) substitutes for a physical transaction of works, the copyright owner deserves less, not more protection. In particular, online delivery saves the owner immense transaction costs.

The two opposite views thus emerged from entirely divergent perspectives: an exclusion of exhaustion may certainly be the preferred view under a strict doctrinal construction of the statutory text, which excludes exhaustion principally on the premise that the copy in question was acquired through a service and was, therefore, previously made available rather than distributed in a physical form. German commentators therefore believe that in such case an application of the exhaustion rule, even by way of analogy, must be barred,[40] and also because that position may be based on the alleged intention of the (European) legislator to limit exhaustion to physical copies, as was enshrined expressly later in the EUCD. Whilst doctrine certainly remains important, such an intrinsic view often blocks a broader perspective under which the rationale of the exhaustion rule may be perceived through the lens of market realities and associated aspects of the degree to which the respective participants, and the public interest in free circulation and limited monopolies, can be recognized fully.

The OLG Hamburg, as of today, appears to be the only court in the European Union to have taken such a more holistic view. It held that the commercial resale of used software licences and licence keys was permissible – a consequence of applying the exhaustion rule by way of analogy. The decisions resonate with the decision in the *OEM* case, in which the court clearly preferred market transparency over an absolute effect of contractual clauses restricting the acquirer of copies from selling into particular product markets.[41] In that decision, the Court preferred market transparency over monopoly and dismissed the claim on the basis of exhaustion. It held that the owner of software copyright was prevented from separating product markets at different levels of trade and that consequently a contractual prohibition imposed on the first licensee did not allow the claimant to circumvent the effects of exhaustion after consent had been given to place the software into circulation.[42]

---

40 See Gerhard Schricker and Ulrich Loewenheim, *Urheberrecht, Kommentar* (C.H. Beck 3rd edn 2007), annotation 33 to § 69c; Thomas Dreier and Gernot Schulze, *Urheberrechtsgesetz, Kommentar* (C.H. Beck 3rd edn 2008) annotation 25 to § 69.

41 BGH, 6 July 2000,I ZR 244/97 – *Microsoft/OEM Software*. See further, Guido Westkamp,'The Limits of Open Source: Consumer Protection, Exhaustion and Co-Existence with Copyright Law' [2008] 1 *Intellectual Property Quarterly* 14–57.

42 A division of product markets is permissible under Art. 31 of the German Authors Right Act 1965; however, there are limits where the goods marketed have been

The particular problems concerning the possible exhaustion in other cases of 'used' software have received divergent treatment. The legal implications are complex. First, as in the *OEM decision*, the first acquirer of a program copy is usually bound by a licensing clause prohibiting any resale or redistribution. Second, even where it is found that the exhaustion rule may apply, at least by way of analogy, to instances of 'online distribution', the fact that any further operation of the programs requires an act of reproduction must still be overcome – an issue then relating to the question of the status of a third party acquirer as a lawful acquirer under Articles 5(1) and 4(2) of the Computer Program Directive.[43] In general, the intricacies under German law – as regards distribution in both a physical form and an initial distribution by way of download – are far too complex to be analysed here in detail. The issues relate not only to the interpretation of the Computer Program Directive, but additionally to questions under the law of obligations that are outside the remit of this contribution.[44]

The business model in question is based upon the 'resale' of used software. Such software copies are acquired from, mainly, entities who had entered into licensing agreements with the owner of copyright, and who later wish to dispose of licences that were no longer needed. When no longer required (in particular, where a new version of the software was available), the licensee would then 'sell' the licences acquired to the defendant, who would make, for example, the respective programs available to third parties for download or would provide the program on disks, of course at a fraction of the original price. Such a business model reduces the opportunity to control the market for different software versions; the defendant, in offering used software, clearly offers copies that to a large extent may substitute for the acquisition of newer versions.

The Federal Court of Justice has, at the time of writing, presented some issues concerning the exhaustion rule under the Computer Program Directive for preliminary ruling,[45] starting from the notion of a physical acquirer in

---

redistributed by non-licensees. This generally depends on the proximity of the markets subdivided and thus upon considerations of market transparency and the need to allow for free circulation of copyright protected goods.

[43] Directive 2009/24/EC on the legal protection of computer programs, 23 April 2009 [2009] OJ L 111/16.

[44] See, for example, BGH, *In Re Half-Life 2,* 11 February 2010 – I ZR 178/08, concerning unfair contractual terms in software licensing agreements with end consumers under Art. 307(2)(1) of the German Civil Code.

[45] Case C-128/11 *Oracle International Corp. v Used Soft GmbH* (Reference No. 2011/C194/11). See further, Matthias Leistner, 'Editorial: "Used" Software before Europe's Top Court – the German Federal Supreme Court Refers the *Oracle v Used Soft* Case to the European Court of Justice' [2011] IIC 503.

cases where there is neither a licensing agreement with the owner of copyright nor an acquisition of property in a physical carrier. These affect both the question of exhaustion'online', as well as the consequential issue of whether an acquirer with no contractualties with the rights owner may be characterized as a lawful acquirer. In short, where exhaustion may occur online, the effect – via the lawful acquirer provision – would practically be to extend to the reproduction right. The first aspect – whether exhaustion may occur following a download of the initial copy from a website – may require some sophisticated analysis by the Court of Justice.The Court here may follow the view that the EUCD, in limiting exhaustion to the transfer of physical copies, establishes a general principle; alternatively (and hopefully) the Court will provide a more insightful guidance that permits a closer inspection of the commercial expectations of the parties. The principal argument in favour of permitting exhaustion in such a case concerns the fact that simply the act of downloading replaces a physical transfer of an individual copy.[46] Therefore, the question is broader than appears at first sight: it depends on the rationale of the exhaustion rule under national law rather than under European law. Again, different positions may be taken.

It may be argued that exhaustion occurs at any time when remuneration was paid for the first act of exploitation, which clearly would speak in favour of the acquirer. It may similarly be argued that exhaustion occurs in order to allow for the free circulation of goods – a rationale that would require a more critical evaluation of the markets and the scope of the monopoly. In any case, these issues can hardly be answered currently by taking recourse to a narrow and literal interpretation of the exhaustion rule under the Computer Program Directive, specifically so where such recourse relies on the EUCD and its express exclusion of 'online exhaustion'. Similarly, it is certain that if online exhaustion is permissible in cases of download, an end consumer who had

---

46 This is by no means a novel position. See Eric Tjong Tjin Tai, 'Exhaustion and Online Delivery of Digital Works' [2003] EIPR 207; B. Knies, 'Erschöpfung Online?' (2002) *GRUR Int* 314; see further, Janusz Piotr Kolczyński, 'Exhaustion of Copyright of Computer Software Online: A European (Polish, German, Austrian) and US Perspective' [2011] EIPR 578; Friedrich Ruffler, 'Is Trading in Used Software an Infringement of Copyright? The Perspective of European Law' [2011] EIPR 375; Andreas Wiebe, 'The Principle of Exhaustion in European Copyright Law and the Distinction between Digital Goods and Digital Services' (2009) *GRUR Int.* 214; Thomas Hoeren, 'Die Online-Erschöpfung im Softwarebereich: Fallgruppen und Beweislast' (2010) MMR 447; for a more restricted view see, for example, Sabine Korthaus and Katharina Garbers-von Boehm, 'Keine Erschöpfung im Online-Bereich: Überprotektionismus oder notwendige Differenzierung?', in H.-P-Götting and A. Lunze (eds), *Überprotektion durch geistiges Eigentum? Festschrift zum 10 jährigen Jubiläum des Studiengangs* (*International Studies in Intellectual Property Law*) (Nomos 2009) 129, 133.

acquired such software must be categorized as a lawful acquirer. The aim of the 'lawful acquirer' provision certainly was to create a balance between the right to control temporary reproductions in the operation of a computer and the fact that the reproduction right is not subject to exhaustion. Thus, a lawful acquisition may be one where a licensing agreement is in place or where the purchaser acquired property in a copy. In the latter case, exhaustion would normally have occurred where the copy was acquired on a physical carrier. In such a situation, the rights owner would hypothetically be able to prevent the normal use of the program based on the reproduction right. The function of the 'lawful acquirer' provision therefore lies solely in furnishing the user with the minimum right to load and run the program and thus to align the usual effect of exhaustion with restricting the continuing right to control reproductions.[47]

Overall, the Court of Justice is well advised to allow national courts a flexible approach in such matters: the business model clearly stands and falls with the ultimate use rights that a user may be granted as a matter of statutory law. But the key aspect remains the scope of the monopoly right vis-à-vis the permission to create business models partly relying on the innovative strength of the copyright owner. Certainly, such a situation requires a balancing test rather than an initially cemented allocation of rights. The dispute therefore reflects many of the intricacies that arise in those cases where third parties rely on existing limitations to act, for commercial purposes, for the beneficiary of limitations as 'agents'.[48] Fundamentally, the Court of Justice will also have the opportunity to consider the scope of judicial freedom of movement left to national courts. This is specifically so as regards the impact of national law upon the way in which provisions ultimately rooted in potentially divergent national concepts (such as the broad notion of 'lawfulness'), or the potential of national law to exceed the literal meaning of secondary law in employing nationally accepted methodologies such as an application by way of analogy. Arguably, it appears that, once the meaning of 'lawfulness' is established in favour of any acquirer, the BGH would tend also to permit exhaustion online.

The fundamental aspect of the jurisprudence portrayed here appears, obviously, to lie in developing recognition of broader perspectives. As such, the decision is – still – limited to computer program copyright. Certainly, the

[47] It should be noted that, therefore, the 'lawful acquirer' provision does not require contractual consent. Therefore, any mode of acquisition under national law is sufficient. This becomes clearer when considering that otherwise a purchase of (physical) software copies that had previously been acquired in good faith without the consent of the rights owners would not be possible.

[48] See, in detail, Guido Westkamp, 'The Three-Step Test and Copyright Limitations in Europe: European Copyright Law between Approximation and National Decision Making' (2008) 55 *Journal of the Copyright Society of the USA* 401.

Court would have encountered significantly more daunting difficulties where the same issues arise with respect to traditional works, since in this case clearly the question of European construction before national courts will arise. At this juncture, the strictures on the exhaustion doctrine that have been imposed by the European legislator will ultimately require guidance from the European Court of Justice; this writer does not share the hope that, following the extremely narrow construction of general freedoms under existing European copyright law, the Court would find in favour of an application of the exhaustion rule. These aspects appear decisive for the more all-embracing problem of how meta-norms can be created under European copyright law, and will be considered later.

3.2 The Consent Doctrine as a General Escape Clause?

A development similar to the doubts that have arisen in relation to online exhaustion concerns the recent decisions by the German Federal Court of Justice concerning the implications of image search engines depicting artistic works as thumbnails. The dispute arose between Google and an artist who was annoyed (or hopeful to receive some compensation) to find that the search engine had indexed images of her paintings, depicted on her own website, and eventually shown on Google's image search results page. Whilst it is immediately clear that allowing the claimant to enforce copyright vis-à-vis the search engine technology would result in a complete breakdown of technology for which there is a huge public demand, the dispute similarly highlights the inelasticity in the normative order of copyright under European law, as implemented.

In short, the Court asserted that the claimant could not enforce her copyright against the act of making available by the defendant, despite the fact that unequivocally Google had violated her right to make the images available (in accordance with Article 3(1) EUCD, as implemented in Article 19a of the German Author's Right Act),[49] and the finding that no statutory limitation was applicable.[50] Instead, the Court asserted that the claimant had consented to that use. This deviated from the position taken by the second instance court, in

[49] The depiction on the results page additionally constituted an act of reproduction, though the Court was not further concerned with that given that such reproduction took place abroad, i.e. on the Google server in the United States.

[50] The Court assessed whether the use of the images on the search engine's results page might fall under the limitations of a free use, a free adaptation and the right to make citations. The Court also rejected the argument that the use on the results page fell within the exemption for transient copies under Art. 5(1) EUCD, as implemented in Art. 44a of the German Authors Right Act.

which the same conclusion was reached on the basis of finding that the claimant's conduct was contradictory.[51] The rationale upon which the decision is founded is highly indicative of the conflict between the need to foster the development of internet technology and the rigidity of the EUCD. The most important aspect is that the decision factually permits the diffusion of the normative hierarchy as embodied in the EUCD. First, the term 'consent' was not understood so as to mean the expression of authorization under the law of copyright contracts. The Court was clear that the fact that the claimant herself had placed the images on her website did not permit the assumption that she had declared an implied offer to license any aspect of copyright. This assertion is important: it denotes that any future application of such'consent doctrine', as applied here, applies irrespective of considerations rooted in the law of obligations in general, and which particularly bars the objection that such consent may be repudiated at a later point in time. Instead, the fact that the objection to such use was indeed expressly noticeable (the claimant had placed a copyright warning on the website) was entirely immaterial, and likewise it was held that the mere placing of the images on the artist's website did not amount to a permission to use. The Court went on to explain that, irrespective of the legal character of any such expression of will, the claimant had to accept the use by Google as a matter of a 'simple consent'. It explained that such 'simple consent'[52] may be assumed in all cases in which works are being placed on the internet[53] without technologically barring access.[54]

---

[51] More specifically, this was based on the principle of *venire contra factum proprium* (the conduct of the claimant – placing the works on her website – was in contradiction to her refusal to allow typical internet uses): see OLG Jena (2008) *Multimedia und Recht* 408.

[52] That is, a form of consent that does not create rights exercisable by a third party but a defence. For a similar approach in the US, see Rachel Clark Hughey, 'Implied License by Legal Estoppel' (2003) 14 *Albany Law Journal of Science & Technology* 53.

[53] The key passage gives the following explanation. The simple consent to a violation of an author's right is to be distinguished from a transfer of use rights with effect *in rem* and an obligatory permission to use. A simple permission renders such an act legitimate, yet the defendant does not acquire any rights based on a licence or a contractual permission to use. Therefore, the 'simple permission' doctrine does not require an express or implied declaration of will, and in that sense silence (and absence of communication) may be taken to be sufficient where it concerns the will to opt-out or not. It follows, therefore, that anything in the previous conduct of a claimant may be taken into account in order to assess the potential legitimacy of a violation of copyright. The result is, essentially, synonymous with a limitation for the benefit of the public interest.

[54] Google provides an option to opt out of searches: see Google Webmaster Help Center, at http://www.google.com/support/webmasters/bin/answer.py?answer=35303 (last visited 23 January 2012).

Thereby, the Court went well beyond a notion of an 'implied licence' as one that requires some form of agreement between the parties.[55] The effect, doctrinally, is that the violation becomes legitimate, thus creating a defence. In that sense, the Court established an additional limitation outside the enumeration of acceptable limitations under Article 5 EUCD. In particular, such permission may be assumed in all cases where technological means have not been applied.[56] This is notable particularly because, in effect, the Court broadly transposed an aspect of the exclusion from liability by third party providers – such as the safe harbour provision for the benefit of host providers – into a dispute that concerns a primary infringement of copyright.[57]

3.3 Towards a General Escape Clause? The Emerging Discrepancy between Harmonization and Evolution

The Court, therefore, was clearly adamant to unearth a doctrinal escape clause by which the insurmountable fact that copyright had been violated could be

---

[55] On the construction of an implied licence under UK law see, most recently, *Newspaper Licensing Agency v Meltwater* [2011] EWCA Civ 890 at 51; *SAS Institute Inc. v World Programming Ltd* [2010] ECDR 15. In the case of statutory limitations and the recognition of the public interest, UK law similarly has adopted a more lenient approach based upon the notion of freedom of information: see Jonathan Griffiths, 'Copyright Law after *Ashdown* – Time to Deal Fairly with the Public' [2002] *Intellectual Property Quarterly* 240. See also the findings of the Gowers Review on the inflexibilities of the current fair dealing provisions: *Gowers Review of Intellectual Property* (HMSO 2006) 41 and 65. Functionally, adopting a US-style fair use test would venture in a similar direction as has German law: see Robert Burrell, 'Reining in Copyright: Is Fair Use the Answer?' [2001] *Intellectual Property Quarterly* 361. However, whether such a general clause may be sufficient, or whether a general implied licence approach is preferable, has been questioned in the US: see John S. Sieman, 'Using the Implied License to Inject Common Sense into Digital Copyright' (2008) 85 *North Carolina Law Review* 885. Practically, the EU Commission might still reject a – rather hypothetical – legislative stipulation of an implied consent or related doctrine on the basis that European private law remains too divergent on that point and that therefore general harmonization in that area should be awaited.

[56] This follows from the decision in BGH, 6 December 2007, I ZR 94/05, (2008) GRUR 245 at 27 – *In Re Printer and Plotter*. The claimant then maintains the right to repudiate that permission, though only from the point in time at which effective technological protection means have effectively been applied.

[57] Indeed, the BGH also referred to Art. 14 of the Directive on Electronic Commerce to (obiter dictum) support its concept. However, the decision reverses the relationship of rule and exception: the safe harbour provisions are based upon knowledge of infringing acts committed by third parties. The decision ventures, arguably, beyond this in relying on the principle that underlies the safe harbour provisions – that is, to facilitate an unfettered freedom to provide internet services and thus to reduce risk in order to incentivize technological development.

overcome. In many respects, the extension of the implied licence doctrine, which requires a declaration of will, towards a doctrine that allows courts simply to rely upon the claimant's conduct, resonates with more expansive balancing approaches, such as the fair use rule under US copyright law that incorporates a public interest test,[58] a general recognition of communication freedom as a directly applicable defence or, indeed, an exhaustion (or, maybe more fittingly, consumption) rule that courts may employ to flexibly react to changing expectations of the public. The connection between a broadening of the notion of exhaustion and a meta-limitation based on the concept of a 'simple permission' is conspicuous.

In reality, the decisions discussed here corroborate that European copyright legislation – which understands itself as a closed system of rules applicable to copyright in general and to digital uses in particular – cannot provide an inherently logical and workable framework to regulate the heteronomous interests affected by it.[59] To use the language of systems theory, then, copyright law itself can no longer be described as autopoietic – that is, a self-producing system that permits the necessary structural coupling[60] between the legal and other relevant social systems, in this regard the system of network economies and network communication that would be adversely affected by a stringent application of the intrinsic normative hierarchy reflected in the EUCD.[61] Clearly, the legal system must detect operational possibilities that permit the internalizing of necessary developments.

These advances, however, become increasingly limited the more that European harmonization is deemed desirable. If the EUCD itself demands supremacy, its threefold aim – (i) to *concurrently harmonize* the law in order to foster market integration[62] (and specifically so in relation to music and film), (ii) to implement international protection standards following from the

---

58 See specifically, James Grimmelmann, 'The Structure of Search Engine Law' (2007) 93 *Iowa Law Review* 1.

59 A notable aspect concerns the underlying explanatory doctrine of German law as rooted in the protection of the author's personality. The decision did not address the – thorny – issue of how the refusal to protect the exclusive right of the author was explicable in the light of the general doctrine that authors maintain, as much as possible, control over their rights. In fact, it was the rejection of principles of copyright contract law that in itself allowed the Court to circumvent that fundamental issue; the German Authors Right Act unequivocally stipulates that the construction of a licence agreement must be interpreted in an 'author-friendly' manner, meaning that the right to control the use of works remains with the author as much as is feasible.

60 See, e.g., Jean-Pierre Dupeuy, 'On the Supposed Closure of Normative Systems', in G. Teubner (ed.), *Autopoietic Law: A New Approach to Law and Society* (Walter de Gruyter 1988) 51.

61 See, e.g, Dan Wielsch, *Zugangsrechte* (Mohr Siebeck 2009) 23 et seq.

62 The EUCD is based upon the capacity clause under Art. 95 EC.

1996 WIPO Treaties and (iii) to conclusively regulate all aspects of digital uses – will be compromised where national courts seek to find solutions outside the text of secondary legislation, and in particular by relying on the use of principles that may be accepted in one national system but may not in others. Such normative refinement, informed by constantly changing interests and realities, is clearly necessary but apparently the limits imposed by both the Directive and the ensuing constricted capacity to adjudicate under Article 234 EC bar such refinement, and in particular the internalization of external normative concepts. European law may then permit the construction of individual norms, if reflected in the text, but it can hardly establish and internalize *principles* derived from national law that are not part of its accepted *acquis*,[63] and that are emerging only as consequences of national decision making. If the possible advances that have been instigated by the decisions discussed here are treated as 'limitations' upon the exclusive rights enshrined in relevant secondary legislation, the doors are opened to the critical questions of (i) whether the reduction in protection in such cases is in compliance with the three-step test, and in particular (ii) whether open clauses such as an implied consent or permission doctrine,[64] extracted and taken out from any relationship with contract law, can indeed be subject to the test at all and, if so, whether such a clause would pass the 'certain special cases' step . To that difficulty, the fact that the test – as enshrined in Article 5(5) EUCD – now forms part of statutory law in some member states, thus limiting potentially the application of national limitations – must be added.[65] Thus, from the perspective of European law, the conflict is one between evolution and harmonization. An

---

63 The reason – in copyright law – perhaps also lies in the fact that the Directive purports to enshrine a specific rationale of copyright (ultimately, as noted, to foster online services and to permit direct licensing agreements), whereas the general rationale of copyright, starting from the division between investment and personality based models of explanation, hinders a general consent as to the aim that copyright law should reflect as a matter of national law.

64 The development in the US is compellingly identical. There, courts have likewise cautiously expanded the initial implied consent doctrine, which is similarly related to the first sale rule, to cases where an escape clause was clearly felt necessary. See, in relation to hyperlinking, *Kelly v Arriba Soft Corp* , 77 F. Supp. 2d 1116, 1118–19 (C.D. Cal. 1999) (hyperlinking was permissible under the fair use test given that it included a transformative use): *ACLU vReno*, 929 F. Supp. 824, 836 (E.D. Pa. 1996), aff'd, 521 U.S. 844 (1997); *Field v Google Inc.*, 412 F. Supp. 2d 1106 (D. Nev. 2006) (implied licence in relation to search engine uses).

65 The fact that it remains debated whether the US fair use clause complies with the three-step test under international law proves the capacity of the test as an additional limiting clause upon any rule that may be applied to restrict copyright protection by applying broad principles.

emerging potential discrepancy between national canons and rules of statutory interpretation – a field not yet fully explored in academic writing with respect to intellectual property harmonization, and copyright in particular – further adds to the difficulties.

That far-reaching predicament can, obviously, not be fully analysed here, though some 'closing remarks' will be made. For example, the advances made under German law relied on German legal methodology, where the application of a rule by way of analogy is a standard method. This is different in the UK where statutory law must generally be interpreted literally, in order to reflect the will of Parliament and thus to constrain the generous freedom enjoyed by courts to set precedents.

4. SUMMATION: THE EUROPEAN CANON

Is it reasonable, then, to imagine the European Court of Justice accepting the approach taken by the German courts? Would the Court of Justice – bearing in mind the potential to reduce the impact upon a harmonizing effect that permitting an evolving meta-restriction on European copyright *acquis* will generate – allow national courts to ultimately and independently conduct broad balancing tests, and to choose themselves the parameters for such assessment on the basis of national considerations?[66] In that respect, the interpretation of copyright norms rooted in secondary European legislation as handed down by the Court of Justice tends to be narrow and literal – understandably so when considering that a protection-friendly interpretation logically serves best the aim to harmonize in tightening the rules of the *acquis*. Perhaps the only way by which a more holistic interpretation of the exhaustion rule may be reached would lie in a close investigation of the origin and history of the European exhaustion doctrine and in setting a precedent that clearly expresses the – in comparison to national laws – limited scope of application as a tool to identify and regulate specific problems under European primary law. As mentioned above, the possible solutions instituted by the German Federal Court of Justice

---

[66] Cf. the comments made in Case C-5/08 *InfopaqInternational A/S v Danske Dagblades Forening* [2009] ECR I-6569: 'The need for uniform application of Community law and the principle of equality require that where provisions of Community law make no express reference to the law of the Member States for the purpose of determining their meaning and scope, as is the case with Article 2 of Directive 2001/29, they must normally be given an autonomous and uniform interpretation throughout the Community.' Consequently, if no limitations under national Danish law are available, the entire problem is reduced to the existence of a temporary copy.

will more effortlessly result in establishing a principle that may provide a workable basis for a more particularized legal evolution, allowing reliance upon a fundamental meta-norm.

However, the prospects for such development at the European level appear bleak, if the generally apodictic and partially hyperbole decisions are anything to go by. As far as copyright law is concerned, the *Infopaq* decision gives a first impression. Here, the Court of Justice stated that:

(a) the transient copying of eleven words[67] in a scanner amounted to an act of reproduction to which the exception under Article 5(1) EUCD would not apply given that these copies would have their own economic significance; and
(b) the scope of limitations was drastically reduced in asserting that limitations had to be construed narrowly.[68]

Importantly, the latter assertion was based upon an alleged principle of European law, rather than on a principle of copyright law. That apodictic jurisprudence creates an imbalance and causes a division between European law and more lenient, and insightful, national approaches.[69] The limpid tendency towards a preference for stringent protection, and thus a harmonizing effect, cannot be questioned, and the need for an autonomous interpretation of community law so frequently emphasized, adds to a continuously freezing conceptualization of protection standards.[70]

---

67 UK jurisprudence claims, despite the position taken by the Court of Justice that the skill and labour threshold still applies: *Newspaper Licensing Agency v Meltwater*, above note 55.

68 For a full discussion of the implications of the *Infopaq* decision, see Guido Westkamp, 'Code, Copyright, Competition: The Subversive Force of Para-Copyright and the Need for an Unfair Competition-based Re-Assessment of DRM Laws after *Infopaq*' (2011) 58(2) *Journal of the Copyright Society of the USA* 601, 623. The alleged principle of narrow interpretation is notably derived from the general case law rather than deduced from copyright principles.

69 Although the Court of Justice indeed applies a certain 'general' principle, it does so without further exploration of the merits of such a principle of narrow interpretation, but simply reverts to entirely distinct legal areas to construe an allegedly applicable principle, deduced from the initial connotation of the term 'limitation or exceptions', as used in Article 5 EUCD.

70 The Court of Justice refers to: Case C-245/00*Stichting ter Exploitatie van Naburige Rechten (SENA) v Nederlandse Omroep Stichting (NOS)* [2003] ECR I-1251 at [23], and Case C-306/05 *Sociedad General de Autores y Editores de Espana (SGAE) v Rafael Hoteles SL* ECR I-11519 at [31]) (in relation to the meaning of the 'public' under Art. 3 EUCD, stating that the term must be interpreted autonomously and that national preconceptions are to be disregarded).

Multifarious questions then arise. Should national courts have the sole capacity to determine the meaning of indeterminate legal language, such as the term 'lawfulness', as a term much tied to fundamental national concepts? To what extent can European law, based on the highly abstract modus of an interpretation of secondary legislation by preliminary rulings, actually venture beyond a literal interpretation of norms so as to achieve the level of clarity, immersion and view for matters beyond the literal text that national supreme courts have exhibited?[71] How far, if at all, may comparative law assist in creating a more flexible system?

As a general conclusion, it appears that the division between the capacities of national courts and the European Court of Justice under Article 234 EC requires a more robust investigation. It is notable that, in contrast to the broader area of European private law itself and the highly advanced research that has been undertaken in the past years there, the implications of elements of national legal principles and rules on construction, and their interaction with statutory copyright law have not, as far as is discernible, been explored in academic literature. These aspects will become increasingly important where national courts seek to construe escape clauses that reflect changing expectations by taking recourse to their own arsenal of methods and principles external to copyright law, rather than aim to solidify legal harmony for its own sake. Certainly, the interpretation of European copyright norms should be directed towards a broader aim than merely to create an autonomous body of rules.

71 See also Jan Brinkhof, 'Some Thoughts on the Proposal for a European and European Union Patent Court', in Götting/Schlüter, *Nourriture de l'Èsprit, Festschrift für Dieter Stauder* (2010) 30 et seq.

4. An American tale: the unclear territorial application of the first sale rule in United States copyright law (and its impact on international trade)

Irene Calboli*

1. INTRODUCTION

The relationship between copyright protection, the 'first sale' rule and international trade has traditionally been a complex matter in the United States.[1] Section 106 of the Copyright Act grants copyright owners the right to prevent third parties from, inter alia, copying and distributing unauthorized copies of their copyrighted works.[2] These exclusive rights, however, are limited by the copyright first sale rule, which is also known as the principle of 'copyright

* This chapter was originally presented at the 30th Annual ATRIP Congress, 'Intellectual Property at the Crossroads of Trade', Faculty of Law, National University of Singapore, 24–27 July 2011. I would like to thank the Congress participants for useful conversation, comments and suggestions following the presentation of this chapter. I also thank Kristin Hagen for research assistance and the students on my International Intellectual Property course for interesting discussion.

[1] The literature on this topic is extensive. In general, on the relationship between intellectual property protection and international trade, see Christopher Heath, 'Parallel Imports and International Trade' [1997] IIC 623; John C. Hilke, 'Free Trading or Free-Riding: An Examination of the Theories and Available Empirical Evidence on Gray Market Imports' (1988) 31 *World Competition Law & Economics Review* 75; Herman Cohen Jehoram, 'Prohibition of Parallel Imports through Intellectual Property Rights' [1999] IIC 495; Herman Cohen Jehoram, 'International Exhaustion versus Importation Right: A Murky Area of Intellectual Property Law' (1966) 4 *GRUR International* 280; Charles Worth, 'Free Trade Agreements and the Exhaustion of Rights Principle' [1994] 1 EIPR 40. In previous works, I have analyzed the tensions between the first sale rule in trademark law and international trade: see Irene Calboli, 'Market Integration and (the Limits of) the First Sale Rule in North American and European Trademark Law' (2011) 51 *Santa Clara Law Review* 1241; Irene Calboli, 'Trademark Exhaustion in the European Union: Community-Wide or International? The Saga Continues' (2002) 6 *Marquette Intellectual Property Law Review* 47.

[2] 17 USC § 106(a) (1994).

exhaustion'.[3] Under this principle, a third party who has lawfully acquired a copyrighted work can further sell or otherwise dispose of the work without the consent of the copyright owner whose exclusive rights are exhausted after the first lawful sale of the work.[4] As this chapter elaborates, this principle was originally adopted by the Supreme Court in the early twentieth century in the leading case *Bobbs-Merrill v Straus*[5] to balance the exclusive rights of copyright owners with the rights of retailers, second-hand dealers and consumers to freely resell or otherwise dispose of the possession of the copyrighted products that they had legitimately purchased. Congress codified this principle in the Copyright Act of 1909 and later in section 109(a) of the Copyright Act of 1976, which states that the owners of copyrighted works 'lawfully made under this title' are entitled 'to sell or otherwise dispose of the possession of that [work]' without the 'authority of the copyright owner'.[6]

While enacting section 109(a), however, Congress did not clarify the territorial application of the first sale rule as part of the statutory language – notably whether the exclusive rights of copyright owners are exhausted only when products are first sold in the United States or whether these rights are also exhausted after a first sale in a foreign jurisdiction.[7] Not surprisingly, this lack of guidance has created much uncertainty and controversy, particularly with respect to the application of the first sale rule in the context of international trade. Generally, copyright owners (particularly corporations trading in copyrighted products) are interested in distributing their products in multiple foreign markets, yet they usually oppose the parallel importation of 'gray market products' – genuine (non-piratical) products, which are imported into one country from unauthorized importers after copyright owners have sold the products in another country.[8] Copyright owners particularly oppose gray

---

3 17 USC § 109(a) (1994).

4 See e.g., 2–8 Melville B. Nimmer and David Nimmer, *Nimmer on Copyright* (Matthew Bender/Lexis Nexis 2011) §8.12; John A. Rothchild, 'Exhausting Extraterritoriality' (2011) 51 *Santa Clara Law Review* 1187, 1187–8; Lisa A. Zakolski, 'Copyright and Literary Property' (2011) 18 *American Jurisprudence* 2d.

5 *Bobbs-Merrill Co. v Straus*, 210 U.S. 339 (1908).

6 17 USC § 109(a).

7 See discussion below at Part 2.

8 The literature on this topic is also extensive. Among the most recent scholarship on the topic, see in general Ryan L. Vinelli, 'Bringing Down the Walls: How Technology is Being Used to Thwart Parallel Importers Amid the International Confusion Concerning Exhaustion of Rights' (2009) 17 *Cardozo J. International & Comparative Law* 135; William Richelieu, 'Gray Days Ahead?: The Impact of Quality King Distributors, Inc. v L'anza Research International, Inc.' (2000) 27 *Pepperdine Law Review* 827; John C. Roa, 'Gray Market Goods and the First Sale Doctrine: The Last Nail in the Coffin?: Quality King v L'anza Research International, Inc. 523 U.S. 135 (1998)' (1999) 20 *Mississippi College Law Review* 211.

market products because they want to control the international distribution (and price) of their products and fear the competition (and the resulting loss of profits) that the importation of gray market products could create in the markets where they already distribute the same products (usually at a higher price).[9] As a result, copyright owners have traditionally argued that gray market products should not be considered to be lawful imports into the United States under the language of section 109(a) of the Copyright Act.[10] To support their claims, they have invoked section 602(a)(1) of the Copyright Act, which explicitly states that the 'importation into the United States' of a copyrighted work acquired outside the United States 'without the authority of the [copyright] owner' should be considered 'an infringement of the exclusive right [of] distribut[ion],' and should thus be forbidden.[11]

This corporate opposition to gray market products is not unanimously shared, however, among the judiciary and in academic circles. Notably, some courts and scholars have argued that, because the provision in section 602(a)(1) is an extension of the rights granted to copyright owners by section 106, the exclusive rights granted by section 602(a)(1) are also limited by the language of section 109(a).[12] According to these courts and scholars, the first sale rule would thus extend to all products 'lawfully made under this title' regardless of the actual place where these products are first offered for sale, and section 602(a)(1) would not apply in the context of gray market copyrighted products. Against this position favoring gray market products, other courts and scholars have nevertheless stressed that copyright protection is based on a strict principle of territoriality and that, as a result, section 109(a) could not be applied extraterritorially.[13] Specifically, supporters of the latter approach have argued that the limitation provided by section 109(a) to the exclusive rights of copyright owners can apply only to domestic sales of copyrighted products and does not extend to foreign sales.

Because of these conflicting interpretations on such an important issue, in the late 1990s the Supreme Court entered the debate on the territorial application of the first sale rule in copyright law and granted certiorari in a case

---

9 See, e.g., Donna K. Hintz, 'Battling Gray Market Goods with Copyright Law' (1994) 57 *Albany Law Review* 1187.

10 Ibid.

11 17 USC §602(a)(1) (2008). In 2008, the US Congress amended the Copyright Act and redesigned what previously was s. 602(a) of the statute as 602(a)(1): Act of 13 October 2008, Pub. L. 110–403, Title I, § 105(b)–(c)(1), 122 Stat. 4259. This chapter refers to ss 602(a) and 602(a)(1) of the Copyright Act interchangeably.

12 See, e.g., *Sebastian International Inc. v Consumer Contacts (PTY) Ltd.*, 847 F.2d 1093 (3d Cir. 1988); Richelieu, above note 8, 843.

13 See e.g., *Subafilms Ltd v MGM-Pathe Comm. Co.*, 24 F.3d 1088, 1095–98 (9th Cir. 1994); Rothchild, above note 4, 1217; Hintz, above note 9, 1197.

involving gray market copyrighted products: *Quality King v L'anza.*[14] Unfortunately, the Supreme Court's decision in *Quality King* did not resolve the contrasting interpretations of sections 109(a) and 602(a)(1) of the Copyright Act. Moreover, a concurring opinion by Justice Ginsburg injected even more ambiguity in the interpretation of the statutory language 'lawfully made under this title' in section 109(a).[15] Absent a clear nationwide precedent, courts in the United States remained divided on the issue in the years following the decision in *Quality King*. Eventually, in 2010, the Supreme Court again granted certiorari in a case involving gray market copyrighted products, *Costco v Omega*,[16] hoping finally to clarify this important aspect of copyright law and international trade. Once again, however, the Court could not reach a satisfactory decision in the case – this time it could not even reach *a* decision, and the justices divided equally, affirming the decision of the Court of Appeals (and the nationwide split on the issue) without addressing the merits of the dispute.[17] Because of the pressing need for clarification regarding the issue, in April 2012 the Supreme Court finally once again granted certiorari in another case involving gray market copyrighted products, *Kirtsaeng v Wiley & Sons, Inc.*, on appeal from Courts of Appeals for the Second Circuit ('Second Circuit').[18] To date, the oral arguments for this case are scheduled to take place in the fall of 2012 and a decision is anticipated by the end of 2012.

This chapter addresses this hotly debated topic in copyright law in the United States, and explores the intricate relationship among sections 106, 109(a) and 602(a)(1) of the Copyright Act and the impact of the Supreme Court's decisions on the application of the first sale rule with respect to gray market products and international trade.[19] The chapter proceeds as follows. Section 2 describes the scope of copyright protection and the copyright first

---

[14] *Quality King Distributors, Inc. v L'anza Research International, Inc.*, 523 U.S. 135 (1998).

[15] Ibid., at 154 (Ginsburg J concurring).

[16] *Costco Wholesale Corp. v Omega, SA*, 131 S. Ct. 565 (2010).

[17] Ibid. (stating only '[t]he judgment is affirmed by an equally divided Court').

[18] *Kirtsaeng v John Wiley & Sons, Inc.*, 132 S. Ct. 1905 (U.S. 2012).

[19] Because of the complexity of this topic and the limited scope of this chapter, the focus is on the analysis of the territorial application of the first sale rule in copyright law in the United States. The chapter does not address other issues relating to the relationship between copyright enforcement and the international trade in general; nor does it elaborate on the economic aspects, positive and negative, of the importation of gray market products for corporations and national economies. Similarly, this chapter does not address the antitrust issues that can arise as a result of the exercise of copyright protection with respect to gray market products nor other means to control product distribution, such as licensing clauses, contracts or torts. Finally, this chapter does not explore the effect of the internet and e-commerce on the traditional application and interpretation of the first sale rule in copyright law.

sale rule in the United States; in particular, it outlines the provisions of sections 106, 109(a) and 602(a)(1) of the Copyright Act, and addresses the controversy surrounding the interpretation of, and the interplay among these provisions. Section 3 recounts the Supreme Court's attempts to resolve the conflicting judicial interpretations in this area, first in *Quality King v L'anza in* 1998 and later in *Costco v Omega* in 2010. Notably, it highlights the Supreme Court's failure to clarify, to date, the territorial application of section 109(a) of the Copyright Act and the continuing uncertainty that surrounds the first sale rule in copyright law in the United States. Section 4 concludes the chapter and examines the decision that has been issued by the Second Circuit in the case that is currently pending before the Supreme Court. Ultimately, Section 4 underscores the urgent need for the Supreme Court to resolve the ambiguity that continues to dominate this area in *Kirtsaeng*. Should the Supreme Court not be willing, or able, to do so, this chapter calls upon Congress to act and clarify, once and for all, the geographical extent of the application of the first sale rule in copyright law in the United States.

2. NATIONAL OR INTERNATIONAL? SECTION 109(A) OF THE COPYRIGHT ACT AND THE UNCLEAR TERRITORIAL APPLICATION OF THE COPYRIGHT FIRST SALE RULE IN THE UNITED STATES

Based upon the Intellectual Property Clause in the Constitution,[20] section 106 of the Copyright Act grants authors the exclusive right to control the reproduction, adaptation, distribution, display and public performance of their original works of authorship.[21] These exclusive rights are expressly limited, however, by the provisions of sections 107 to 122.[22] Included among these

---

[20] The Constitution grants Congress 'the power' to 'promote the progress of science and the useful arts, by securing for limited times to authors and inventors the exclusive right to their respective writings and discoveries': US Constitution, Art. 1, § 8, Cl. 8. See,e.g., 1-1 Melville B. Nimmer and David Nimmer, *Nimmer on Copyright* (Matthew Bender/Lexis Nexis 2011) §103(a); *New York Times Co. v Tasini*, 533 U.S. 483, 519 (2001); *Twentieth Century Music Corp. v Aiken*, 422 U.S. 141, 156 (1975); *Mazer v Stein*, 347 U.S. 201, 219 (1954) (stating '[t]he economic philosophy behind the clause empowering Congress to grant … copyrights is the conviction that encouragement of individual effort by personal gain is the best way to advance public welfare through the talents of authors … in 'science and useful arts').

[21] 17 USC § 106(a).

[22] Section 106 of the Copyright Act begins with the language 'Subject to sections 107 through 122': 17 USC § 106(a).

limitations to the exclusive rights of copyright owners is the 'first sale rule', as codified in section 109(a); according to this rule 'the owner of a particular copy or phonorecord lawfully made under this title … is entitled without authority of the copyright owner, to sell or otherwise dispose of the possession of that copy or phonorecord'.[23] Originally adopted by the Supreme Court in *Bobbs-Merrill v Straus* in 1908,[24] the first sale rule was created to balance the exclusive rights of copyright owners to control their copyrighted works with the rights of those who had lawfully purchased those works, such as consumers, retailers and second-hand dealers. In particular, the first sale rule has traditionally been justified based on the assumption that copyright owners should not revert to copyright law to control the distribution of a copyrighted work after that work has been offered for sale in the marketplace, either directly by the copyright owners or with their consent.[25] On the contrary, '[t]o add the right of exclusive sale the authority to control all future retail sales … would give a right not included in the terms of the statute, and [in the Supreme Court's view] extend its operation … beyond its meaning'.[26] As scholars have repeatedly noted, in addition to preventing monopolies in the distribution of copyrighted products, the first sale rule has also been justified by the rule against the restraint of the alienation of private property,[27] which translated in granting to the lawful purchasers of copyrighted works the right to fully enjoy the possession of these works, and thus the right to resell or otherwise dispose of the works.[28]

After the Supreme Court's decision in *Bobbs-Merrill*, courts in the United States continued to apply the first sale rule.[29] Congress codified this doctrine

---

23 17 USC § 109(a). See also Zakolski, above note 4; 2–8 Nimmer & Nimmer, above note 4, §8.12; Rothchild, above note 4, 1187–8.

24 *Bobbs-Merrill Co. v Straus*, above note 5.

25 Ibid., 351.

26 Ibid., 350 (stating that '[the] purchaser of a book, once sold by the authority of the owner of the copyright, may sell it again, although he could not publish a new edition of it').

27 See, e.g., *Columbia Pictures Industries, Inc. v Redd Horne, Inc.*, 749 F.2d 154, 160 (3d Cir. 1984); HR 987, 98th Cong., 2d Session (1984) (highlighting that the first-sale doctrine is rooted in the rule against restraint on alienation of property).

28 See 2–8 Nimmer & Nimmer, above note 4, §8.12[A] (stating that '[the] continued control over the distribution of copies is not so much a supplement to the intangible copyright, but is rather primarily a device for controlling the disposition of the tangible personal property that embodies the copyrighted work' and that 'the policy favoring a copyright monopoly for authors gives way to the policy opposing restraints of trade and restraints on alienation').

29 See, e.g., *Buck v Jewell-La Salle Realty Co.*, 283 U.S. 191 (1931); *Motion Picture Patents Co. v Universal Film Mfg. Co.*; *Victor Talking Mach. Co. v Kemeny*, 271 F. 810 (NJ 1921); *Free Sewing Machine Co. v Bry-Block Mercantile Co.*, 204 F. 632 (D.C. Tenn. 1913).

into the Copyright Act of 1909 and later into the statutory language of section 109(a) of the 1976 revision of the Copyright Act.[30] While enacting section 109(a), however, Congress did not specify the territorial application of the first sale rule. In particular, Congress did not specify whether the rule applies to sales taking place only in the national territory or also to foreign sales of copyrighted products. Generally, national practices have traditionally distinguished between countries adopting a 'national' first sale rule – where the exclusive rights of copyright owners are exhausted only if the first sale of a copyrighted work has taken place within the national territory – and countries adopting an 'international' first sale rule – where the exclusive rights of the copyright owners are exhausted after the first sale of a copyrighted work anywhere in the world.[31] Hence, while drafting the language of section 109(a), Congress merely specified that the first sale rule applies to all copyrighted works 'lawfully made under this title,' and it did not indicate whether this language included works sold in a foreign jurisdiction.[32] Not surprisingly, as a result of the growing corporate interests in controlling the distribution (and prices) of copyrighted products in separate national markets, the interpretation of the language of section 109(a) and the territorial application of the first sale rule has caused heated debate, particularly with respect to the importation of unauthorized 'gray market' copyrighted works.[33] Copyright owners can, in fact, legitimately oppose the importation of gray market copyrighted products as copyright infringement only if the country to which the products are imported – the United States in this case – has adopted a domestic regime of national first sale rule.[34] As a result, copyright owners have vigorously asserted that the United States has adopted a regime of national first sale to prevent the importation of gray market products.

Absent a clear indication in section 109(a) of the Copyright Act, those supporting the position that the United States follows a regime of national copyright first sale law have thus pointed to the language of section 602(a)(1)

---

30 17 USC § 109(a).

31 Frederick M. Abbott, 'Parallel Importation: Economic and Social Welfare Dimensions', International Institute for Sustainable Development, June 2007, 5, available at: http://www.iisd.org/pdf/2007/parallel_importation.pdf. See also Vincent Chiappetta, 'The Desirability of Agreeing to Disagree: The WTO, TRIPS, International IPR Exhaustion, and a Few Other Things' (2000) 21 *Michigan Journal of International Law* 333.

32 17 U SC §109(a). Note that the statutory language does not clarify whether 'lawfully made under this title' should be interpreted as 'made in the United States'; nor does it clarify whether it applies to items copyrighted in the United States but manufactured abroad. See discussion below at Sections 3 and 4.

33 See, e.g., Vinelli, above note 8, 151; Richelieu, above note 8, 827.

34 Vinelli, ibid., 151.

of the Copyright Act, which directly provides that the 'importation into the United States, without the authority of the owner of copyright under this title, of copies or phonorecords of a work that have been acquired outside the United States is an infringement of the exclusive right [of] distribut[ion]'.[35] As repeatedly noted by scholars, since gray market products are imported into the United States without the consent, and thus 'the authority,' of copyright owners, 'manufacturers holding copyrights to their products, or to some aspect of their products' packaging, would seem to derive a solid measure of legal protection [against gray market products] from section 602(a)'.[36] On the other side, those who support the position that the Unites States follows an regime of international copyright first sale have argued that the right to control the 'importation' of copyrighted products per section 602(a)(1) of the Copyright Act is also subject to limitation provided by section 109(a), and thus to the first sale rule.[37] Notably, supporters of the interpretation that the first sale rule applies also to foreign sales have argued that the right provided to copyright owners by section 602(a)(1) of the Copyright Act is an extension of the rights granted to copyright owners by section 106, which in itself is subject to the first sale rule per section 109(a). Thus, they argued, the limitation of section 109(a) should apply also to section 602(a)(1), and in turn to imported copyrighted products.[38]

Because of the complexity of the issue and the interests at stake for all involved parties – copyright owners, retailers, second-hand dealers, libraries, consumers, and so on – much debate has characterized this area of copyright law. Not surprisingly, not only have scholars and practitioners disagreed over the territorial application of the copyright first sale rule in the United States, but courts have also adopted diverging positions on the interpretation of section 109(a) and its interplay with section 602(a)(1).[39] One of the most notorious conflicts in this respect, which continues essentially unresolved today, was the judicial split between the Court of Appeals for the Third Circuit ('the Third Circuit') and the Court of Appeals for the Ninth Circuit ('the Ninth Circuit'). In particular, in its 1988 decision in *Sebastian International v*

---

[35] 17 USC § 602(a)(1). See also Kristine Boylan, 'Life after Quality King: A Proposal for Evaluating Gray Market Activities' (1999) 27 *AIPLA Quarterly Journal* 109.

[36] Richelieu, above note 8, 829.

[37] See Willie Skinner, 'Preventing Gray Markets: Is Copyright Law the Answer? (1999) 26 *Syracuse Journal of International Law & Commerce* 315, 328; Hintz, above note 9, 1212.

[38] Hintz, ibid.,1212.

[39] Ibid., noting that there have traditionally been two groups of cases where courts have addressed the applicability of the Copyright Act to parallel imports: cases that permit importation, and cases that do not allow importation.

Consumer Contacts, the Third Circuit adopted the position that the first sale rule in copyright law was international[40] and stated that the 'first sale by the copyright owner extinguishes any right later to control importation of those copies' regardless of the place of sale.[41] In reaching its decision, the Third Circuit argued that the first sale rule finds its rationale in the fact that copyright owners are rewarded for their work upon the first sale of their copyrighted articles and thus copyright owners should not control the distribution of those copyrighted articles after they have enjoyed such reward(ing sales),[42] regardless of whether these (rewarding) sales have taken place domestically or abroad.[43] The Third Circuit finally noted that the Copyright Act does not suggest that one who sells copies abroad should be rewarded more (by not having to be subject to the first sale rule) than one who sells domestically.[44]

Contrary to the Third Circuit, the Ninth Circuit repeatedly supported the position that the first sale rule in copyright law applied only to domestic sales of copyrighted products.[45] Specifically, in 1991, in *BMG Music v Perez*, the Ninth Circuit held that section 109(a) exhausts the distribution right of copyright owners only if the first sale occurred in the United States and construed the 'lawfully made under this title' language of section 109(a) to exclude copyrighted copies sold in foreign countries.[46] In 1994, in Parfums *Givenchy*, the Ninth Circuit confirmed this position and underscored that

> the logical outcome of a ruling that [a] US copyright owner is precluded from interfering with US distribution of copies manufactured and lawfully sold abroad would be to deprive the US copyright holder of the power to authorize or prevent imports of the copies once the copies are sold abroad.[47]

---

40 *Sebastian International, Inc. v Consumer Contacts (PTY) Ltd.*, above note 12.

41 Ibid., 1099.

42 Ibid., 1096–7 (quoting *Burke & Van Heusen v Arrow Drug*, 233 F. Supp. 881, 884 (E.D. Pa. 1964)).

43 Ibid., 1099.

44 Ibid., stressing that if s. 109(a) applied only to copies sold in the US, copyright owners selling copies abroad would receive a purchase price and a right to limit importation, whereas copyright owners selling copies domestically would only receive the purchase price.

45 *BMG Music v Perez*, 952 F.2d 318 (9th Cir. 1991); *Parfums Givenchy, Inc., v Drug Emporium*, 38 F.3d 477 (9th Cir. 1994). Prior to *BMG Music* and *Givenchy*, another court, the District Court for the Eastern District of Pennsylvania, interpreted the 'lawfully made under this title' language of s. 109(a) of the Copyright Act to mean 'lawfully made in the United States'. The decision was affirmed, without opinion, by the Third Circuit: *Columbia Broadcasting Systems., Inc. v Scorpio Music Distributors., Inc.* 569 F. Supp. 47, 50 (E.D. Pa. 1983) aff'd without opinion, 738 F.2d 424 (3d Cir. 1984). See also discussion below at 3.1.

46 *BMG Music*, ibid., 319.

47 *Parfums Givenchy*, above note 45, 481.

In the same decision, the Ninth Circuit added that copyright owners could prevent unauthorized imports until there has been a 'first authorized sale' in the United States, regardless of the place of manufacture of the products.[48] As described in the following paragraphs, the Ninth Circuit reconfirmed its position in favor of an exclusively national application of the first sale rule in copyright law in the cases *L'anza v Quality King* in 1996,[49] and *Omega v Costco* in 2008.[50] In both cases, the Supreme Court granted the petition for certiorari in order to resolve the conflicting interpretations between the Third Circuit and the Ninth Circuit.[51] Still, as elaborated below, even after the Supreme Court's decisions, the territorial application of the first sale rule and the interpretation of the language 'lawfully made under this title' in section 109(a) of the Copyright Act continue to remain far from clear.

3. THE SUPREME COURT ON THE TERRITORIAL APPLICATION OF THE COPYRIGHT FIRST SALE RULE IN THE UNITED STATES: MUCH ADO ABOUT NOTHING (YET)?

3.1 Copyright First Sale Act One: *Quality King v L'anza* (or the 'Round-Trip Story')

The Supreme Court first attempted to clarify the conflict of interpretation between the Third Circuit and the Ninth Circuit – the territorial application of the first sale rule and the interplay between the interpretation of sections 109(a) and 602(a)(1) of the Copyright Act – in *Quality King Distributors, Inc. v L'anza Research International, Inc.* in 1998.[52] This dispute concerned high-end hair care products, which were originally manufactured in the United States, but had been exported and sold in a foreign jurisdiction and reimported into the United States without the authorization of the product manufacturer (and copyright owner), L'anza.[53] The case was relevant under copyright law

---

48 Ibid., 482–3.

49 *L'anza Research International., Inc. v Quality King Distributors, Inc.*, 98 F.3d 1109 (9th Cir. 1996).

50 *Omega SA v Costco Wholesale Corp.*, 541 F.3d 982, 984 (9th Cir. 2008).

51 *Quality King Distributors, Inc v L'anza Research International., Inc.*, above note 14 (stating 'because [the Ninth Circuit's] decision created a conflict with the Third Circuit … we granted the petition for certiorari).

52 Ibid.

53 Ibid., 139 (stating that the record is unclear as to 'whether the initial purchaser was the [authorized] distributor in the United Kingdom or the [unauthorized] distribu-

because L'anza registered the labels and the instructions that were affixed to the hair care products' packaging with the US Copyright Office.[54] Like most corporations that sell products in separate national markets (at different prices), L'anza adopted an international distribution policy that prohibited foreign distributors from selling L'anza products outside their domestic jurisdictions and did not authorize the reimportation of L'anza products into the United States.[55] In 1993, several quantities of L'anza products were nevertheless reimported into the United States without L'anza's consent.[56] Quality King Distributors acquired these products after they had been reimported into the US, and distributed them to unauthorized retailers at discounted prices.[57] L'anza sued Quality King, alleging that the unauthorized distribution of L'anza hair care products constituted copyright infringement under sections 106, 501, and 602(a)(1) of the Copyright Act.[58]

Quality King, however, raised the first sale defense under section 109(a) of the Copyright Act and argued that L'anza's exclusive rights with respect to the copyrighted material affixed to the hair care products were exhausted after the first lawful sale of the products in the foreign markets.[59] Quality King thus argued that it could lawfully dispose of and sell L'anza hair care products in the United States regardless of L'anza's consent, without being liable for copyright infringement.[60] Despite Quality King's claim, the District Court granted summary judgment in favor of L'anza, holding that the first sale doctrine did not apply because the first sale of the products occurred outside the territory of the United States.[61] Quality King appealed but the Ninth Circuit affirmed the decision of the District Court.[62] Following its previous decisions, the Ninth Circuit repeated that the first sale rule in copyright law is applicable only to those sales that have taken place within the national territory. Notably, the Ninth Circuit affirmed the District Court's holding, which stated that 'Congress enacted [section] 602(a) to provide a copyright owner protection

---

tor in Malta … but it is undisputed that the goods were manufactured by L'anza and sold … to a foreign distributor').

54 Ibid., 138.

55 Ibid., 139.

56 Ibid., 139.

57 Ibid.

58 Ibid.

59 Ibid.

60 Ibid.

61 *L'anza Research International., Inc. v Quality King Distributors, Inc.*, 1995 WL 908331, 1 (C.D. Cal. 1995). The District Court reasoned that since the goods were intended to be sold to a foreign distributor for foreign distribution, the first sale occurred outside of the US, and fell within the 'acquired abroad' language of s. 602(a) Copyright Act, ibid.

62 *L'anza Research*, above note 49.

'where the copies … were lawfully made but their distribution in the United States would infringe the US copyright owner's exclusive rights'.[63] The Ninth Circuit also confirmed the reasoning of the District Court that, since '[t]he legislative history makes no reference to the place of manufacture of the goods … the emphasis is on 'the mere act of importation' of copies whose distribution would infringe the copyright owner's exclusive rights'.[64] As a result, the Ninth Circuit agreed with the District Court that, regardless of where the copies were originally manufactured, 'if the copies are sold outside the United States, the first sale defense does not extinguish the right later to prohibit unauthorized importation of those copies'.[65] 'To hold otherwise … would undermine the stated purpose of section 602.'[66]

Quality King, however, petitioned the Supreme Court. The Supreme Court granted certiorari and considered 'whether the first sale doctrine endorsed in section 109(a) is applicable to imported copies'[67] in addition to copies first sold in the United States. Before addressing the question, the Supreme Court noted that this was an 'unusual' copyright case because L'anza was not seeking to prevent unauthorized copying of its copyrighted material but rather to protect 'the integrity of its method of marketing'[68] – its price differentiation strategy in separate national markets. Despite this observation, the Supreme Court proceeded to address the interplay among the relevant sections of the Copyright Act. Ultimately, the Supreme Court reversed the Ninth Circuit and concluded that section 602(a)(1)of the Act does not 'categorically prohibit … unauthorized importation of copyrighted materials',[69] but rather unauthorized importation infringes upon the rights granted under section 106(a), which is expressly limited by section 109(a). In particular, the Supreme Court rejected L'anza's argument that section 602(a)(1) would be superfluous if it could not be used against 'non-piratical ("lawfully made") copies' and noted that section 602(a)(1) is broader than section 109(a) of the Copyright Act. The Supreme Court said specifically that, while both provisions may apply in the same situation, they retain independent significance.[70] The Supreme Court also rejected

63 *L'anza Research*, above note 61, 1.
64 Ibid., 3.
65 Ibid.
66 Ibid.
67 *Quality King*, above note 14, 138.
68 Ibid., 140.
69 Ibid., 144.
70 Ibid., 152. The Supreme Court pointed out that s. 602(a) Copyright Act permits bringing a private action against unauthorized importers, whereas the enforcement of s. 602(b) is vested in the Customs Service: ibid., 146. The Court also noted that s. 109(a) provides a defense against s. 602(a) only with respect to the 'owners' of lawfully made copies, while such defense is not available to 'non-owners' such as

the Solicitor General's argument that 'importation' is 'neither a sale nor a disposal of a copy under section 109(a)'.[71] Instead, the Supreme Court underscored that the right to 'sell or otherwise dispose of' an item clearly includes the right to ship an item abroad, and therefore importation naturally constitutes a first sale that is included under the meaning of the language of section 109(a) of the Copyright Act.[72]

Still, the Supreme Court's decision fell short of addressing the territorial extent of the first sale rule in copyright law directly. Notably, the Supreme Court did not specify whether the language of section 109(a) of the Copyright Act could be applied to all products copyrighted (but not necessarily made) in the United States, which had been lawfully offered for sale in a foreign jurisdiction and then imported into the United States without the authorization of the copyright owners.

To complicate matters further, in a short concurring opinion, Justice Ginsburg wrote that the hair care products at issue could be lawfully imported into the United States only because the case at issue involved a 'round trip' importation: the 'travel of copies … from the United States to places abroad, then back again'.[73] Justice Ginsburg additionally underscored that she was only joining the majority in recognizing that the decision in *Quality King was* not resolving 'cases in which the allegedly infringing imports were manufactured abroad';[74] she cited sources stating that copyright protection is 'territorial' and that the language 'lawfully made under this title' in section 109(a) must mean 'lawfully made in the United States'.[75] Not surprisingly, Justice Ginsburg's opinion added to the existing uncertainty over the territorial application of the provision of section 109(a). In addition, Justice Ginsburg's interpretation of the language 'lawfully made under this title' as meaning 'lawfully made in the United States' injected a new layer of complication into the debate

---

bailees, licensees, or those in unlawful possession of the copies: ibid., 147. Finally, the Court pointed out that s. 602(a) applies to a category of copies that were 'lawfully made' but 'not under the law of the United States Copyright Act, but instead, under the law of some other country': ibid., 147.

71 Ibid., 152.

72 Ibid., 152.

73 Ibid., 153 (Ginsburg J concurring).

74 Ibid. (Ginsburg J concurring).

75 Ibid. (Ginsburg J concurring) (citing William F. Patry, *Copyright Law and Practice* (1997 Supp.) 166–70 and 10 Paul Goldstein, *Copyright* (2nd edn 1998) § 16.0, 16:1–16:2). Justice Ginsburg adopted the position that had previously been adopted in *Scorpio*, which stated that the defendant's arguments 'would be more persuasive were it not for the phrase – lawfully made under this title – in §109(a). I conclude that the section grants first sale protection to the third party buyer of copies which have been legally manufactured and sold within the United States and not to purchasers of imports': *Columbia Broadcasting Systems*, above note 45, 49.

by suggesting that products manufactured 'outside the United States' and copyrighted in the United States could altogether be excluded from the application of section 109(a) because these products would 'not [be] lawfully made under this title'.[76]

As criticized by scholars and members of the judiciary after the decision in *Quality King,* this interpretation of section 109(a) would severely restrict the application of the first sale rule even within the territory of the United States (national first sale rule) as a result of the growing number of products manufactured outside the United States (frequently by US companies) and later imported to and sold in the United States.[77] Still, as highlighted below, this seems to be precisely the position adopted by the Second Circuit in August 2011 in *John Wiley & Sons v Kirtsaeng*, the latest case on the issue that is currently pending before the Supreme Court and that should be decided by the end of 2012.[78]

3.2 Copyright First Sale Act Two: *Costco v Omega* (or the 'Untold Nine-Word Story')

A little over a decade after its decision in *Quality King,* the Supreme Court again granted certiorari in a case involving the territorial application of the first sale rule and the interpretation of section 109(a) of the Copyright Act: *Costco v Omega.*[79] This time, the dispute did not concern a 'round trip' of copyrighted products manufactured in the United States. On the contrary, this case involved copyrighted products (luxury watches) which had been manufactured and first sold outside the United States by Omega and its authorized foreign distributors, and had then been imported into the United States without Omega's consent.[80] Notably, several quantities of the Omega 'Seamaster' watch were bought by unauthorized third parties from authorized Omega distributors outside the United States and brought into the US without Omega's authorization.[81] Eventually, Costco Wholesale Corporation bought the watches and sold them to the public in California at considerably lower prices than the authorized Omega dealers in the United States.[82] The 'Seamaster' watches, however, carried a small engraved design on their reverse side, the 'Omega Globe Design', which Omega had registered with the

76 Richelieu, above note 8, 850–5; Roa, above note 8, 234.
77 See discussion below in Part 4.
78 *Kirtsaeng v John Wiley & Sons, Inc.*, above note 18.
79 *Costco Wholesale Corp. v Omega SA*, above note 16.
80 *Omega SA v Costco Wholesale Corp.*, above note 50.
81 Ibid.
82 Ibid.

US Copyright Office.[83] Omega thus challenged the unauthorized importation of the watches as copyright infringement under the Copyright Act.[84]

Against Omega's claim, Costco argued that the initial foreign sale of the watches had exhausted Omega's rights to those specific batches of watches under the first sale rule provided by section 109(a) of the Copyright Act.[85] To this end, Costco argued that the Supreme Court ruled in *Quality King* that the first sale rule as per section 109(a) applied to copyrighted products even when they had first been sold outside the United States, and then imported into the US without the authorization of the copyright owner in the United States. This time the District Court ruled, without explanation, in favor of Costco. Omega nevertheless appealed to the Ninth Circuit[86] which reversed the decision of the District Court and ruled in favor of Omega. While deciding the case, the Ninth Circuit first addressed whether the Supreme Court's decision in *Quality King* required the Ninth Circuit to overrule its precedents, which allowed the first sale defense to be applied only where the copies at issue were manufactured or first sold in the United States under the authority of the copyright owner.[87] The Ninth Circuit concluded, however, that its precedents were not 'clearly irreconcilable' with the Supreme Court's decision in *Quality King* and, as a result, its precedents were not overruled. The Ninth Circuit then ruled that, since Omega's watches were not manufactured in the United States, the first sale defense under section 109(a) of the Copyright Act did not apply in this case because Omega's watches were not 'lawfully made under this title'.[88]

Once again, the Ninth Circuit analysed the interplay among the relevant sections of the Copyright Act – sections 106, 109(a)and 602(a)(1) – and focused its decision, again, on the interpretation of the language 'lawfully made under this title' under section 109(a).[89] Ultimately, the Ninth Circuit agreed with the position expressed by Omega, which was based upon Justice Ginsburg's concurring opinion in *Quality King*, that the language must be construed to mean 'lawfully made in the United States'.[90] Therefore, the Ninth Circuit ruled that the first sale defense under section 109(a) does not apply to

83 Ibid., 984.
84 Ibid.
85 *Omega*, above note 50, 984.
86 Ibid.
87 Ibid., 983. The court framed the issue differently from the issue the parties brought on appeal, which was whether the copyright first sale doctrine applies to the sale in the United States of a US copyrighted work that was manufactured and first sold abroad.
88 Ibid., 984.
89 Ibid.
90 Ibid., 984.

products manufactured abroad and imported into the United States.[91] To hold otherwise would impermissibly extend the reach of the Copyright Act extraterritorially[92] or, as the Ninth Circuit put it, '[t]o characterize the making of copies overseas as 'lawful … under [Title 17]' would be to ascribe legality under the Copyright Act to conduct that occurs entirely outside the United States, notwithstanding the absence of a clear expression of congressional intent in favor of extraterritoriality'.[93] Ultimately, the Ninth Circuit confirmed its previous interpretation of section 109(a) in *BMG Music*[94] and *Parfums Givenchy*,[95] and reversed the District Court, holding that the first sale rule did not apply in the case at issue because the products had been manufactured in Switzerland.[96]

Costco, nonetheless, petitioned the Supreme Court, which once again granted certiorari. This time, the question presented to the Supreme Court was whether section 602(a)(1) of the Copyright Act applies to copies manufactured abroad by copyright owners.[97] To answer this question, the Supreme Court needed to assess, again, the interplay among sections 106, 109(a), and 602(a)(1) of the Copyright Act, and to provide guidance on the interpretation of the language 'lawfully made under this title' in section 109(a) of the Copyright Act. Notably, the Court needed to explain specifically whether the wording 'lawfully made under this title' meant, in fact, 'made in the United States'. Because of the importance of the Supreme Court's decision – which would finally clarify the territorial application of section 109(a), as well as whether the provision applies to all products sold in the United States 'under the authority' of the copyright owners and not only to those that are 'made' in the national territory – it was anxiously awaited in many circles. Yet, the final

---

91 Ibid., 987.

92 Ibid., 987–8 (citing Restatement (Second) of Foreign Relations Law of the United States § 38 (1965) and *EEOC v Arabian American Oil Co.*, 499 U.S. 244, 248 (1991)).

93 Ibid., 988 (citing 17 USC §109(a); *Subafilms Ltd v MGM Pathe Communications Co.*, above note 13, 1096. See also Curtis A. Bradley, 'Extraterritorial Application of US Intellectual Property Law: Principal Paper: Territorial Intellectual Property Rights in an Age of Globalism' (1997) 37 *Virginia Journal of International Law* 505; John K. Kelsh, 'Subafilms Ltd v MGM-Pathe Communications Co., the Berne Convention, and the Extraterritorial Application of the Copyright Act' (1996) 90 *Northwestern University Law Review* 1839.

94 *BMG Music v Perez*, above note 45.

95 *Parfums Givenchy v Drug Emporium*, above note 45.

96 *Omega v Costco*, above note 50, 990. On the Ninth Circuit's decision, see Samuel Brooks, 'Battling Gray Markets through Copyright Law: Omega SA v Costco Wholesale Corporation' (2010) *Brigham Young University Law Review* 19.

97 See, e.g., Lindsay R. Aldridge, 'Costco v Omega and the First Sale Doctrine' (2011) 12 *North Carolina Journal of Law & Technology* 325, 239.

outcome of the decision was not the one that many expected. After Justice Kagan recused herself, as a result of her previous role in the same case as the US Solicitor General (arguing in favor of Costco and the importation of the Omega watches),[98] the other eight justices could not find a majority for or against the claim brought forward by Costco. Ultimately, the justices divided equally on the issue and issued a nine-word, per curiam decision, affirming the Ninth Circuit's holding – '[t]he judgment is affirmed by an equally divided Court'– thus leaving the interpretation of section 109(a) of the Copyright Act on the territorial application of the copyright first sale rule in the United States in murky waters.[99]

The Supreme Court's (non)decision in *Costco v Omega*, however, did not signal the end of this dispute. Interestingly, after the ruling, Costco brought charges against Omega for copyright misuse in the US District Court for the Eastern District of California.[100] Notably, Costco argued that Omega affixed the 'Omega Globe Design' to the watches to use copyright law to oppose the unauthorized importation of Omega watches[101] and bypass the first sale rule in trademark law, which permits the importation of unauthorized gray market products carrying a mark protected in the United States when the products are controlled by the same commercial source inside and outside the national territory.[102] In November 2011, the District Court granted summary judgment in favor of Costco and ruled that Omega was liable for copyright misuse. Most notably, the court dismissed Omega's argument that the 'Omega Globe Design' served the purpose of 'promot[ing] the creativity and aesthetics of the Omega Globe Design itself, and to increase the value that the design gives to the watch', and stated that, even though those aspects of the design were in

---

98 Ibid.

99 See, e.g., Eric Bensen, 'What Does a 4-4 Tie Say About the Future of the First Sale Doctrine?' (2011) *Emerging Issues* 5538; Aldridge, above note 97, 239.

100 *Omega SA v Costco Wholesale Corp.*, CV 04-05443 (E.D. Cal. 2011). This case is currently under appeal in front of the Ninth Circuit and a decision on the case is awaited by the end of 2012 or the beginning of 2013. See also Michael A. Rosenhouse, 'Sufficiency of Copyright Misuse Defense to Allegations of Copyright Infringement Pursuant to Federal Copyright Law' (2010) 185 ALR Fed. 123; Brett Frischmann and Dan Moylan, 'The Evolving Common Law Doctrine of Copyright Misuse: A Unified Theory and its Application to Software' (2000) 15 *Berkeley Technology Law Journal* 865; Aaron Xavier Fellmeth, 'Copyright Misuse and the Limits of the Intellectual Property Monopoly' (1998) 6 *Journal of Intellectual Property Law* 1.

101 *Omega v Costco*, ibid, 2.

102 Although Costco did not directly raise this question (the difference between trademark and copyright first sale rules), Omega's use of copyright protection was evidently driven by the stronger protection that, in particular under the precedents of the Ninth Circuit, copyright law grants against gray market products. Generally, on the first sale rule in trademark law, see Calboli, 'Market Integration and (the Limits of) the First Sale Rule', above note 1, 1262–3.

fact protected by copyright law, this protection could not be used as a defense against Costco's rightful claim of copyright misuse with respect to the facts in issue.[103] Although it was a much needed ruling in an increasingly controversial area of intellectual property rights – the use of copyright protection for 'methods of marketing' and the 'cumulation' of copyright and trademark protection for the same article in order to exploit the strengths of both protections – this decision did not, however, add any new element to the interpretation of the language of section 109(a) of the Copyright Act and the territorial application of the first sale rule.

4. THE SAGA CONTINUES: THE STILL UNCLEAR TERRITORIAL APPLICATION OF THE COPYRIGHT FIRST SALE RULE IN THE UNITED STATES (AND ITS IMPACT ON INTERNATIONAL TRADE)

After the Supreme Court's non-precedential decision in *Costco*, much uncertainty continued to characterize the interpretation of section 109(a) of the Copyright Act and the relationship between sections 109(a) and 602(a)(1), particularly with respect to the application of the first sale rule to copyrighted goods manufactured abroad and imported into the United States.[104] Based upon the existing judicial precedents, there is no doubt that section 109(a) applies to copyrighted products made in and first sold in the United States, for which the exclusive rights of copyright owners are exhausted upon the first sale of the products in the market.[105] Following the Supreme Court's decision in *Quality King*, section 109(a) seems to apply also to copyrighted products that are made in the United States, exported abroad, and reimported into the national territory with or without the consent of the copyright owner – the so-called 'round-trip' gray market products.[106] To date, however, and at least until the Supreme Court's decision in *Kirstsaeng*, the application of the first sale rule to foreign manufactured gray market products that are imported into the United States remains a matter for the individual courts to decide based upon the (diverging) precedents governing each federal circuit.[107] In other words, different courts in different circuits can rule that the importation of foreign manufactured gray market products into the United States is either a lawful importation or a copyright infringement.

---

103 *Omega*, above note 100, 2.
104 See discussion above at Part 3.
105 Ibid.
106 *Quality King*, above note 14, 153.
107 Aldridge, above note 97, 325.

The Second Circuit decision in *John Wiley & Sons v Kirtsaeng,*[108] the only decision that has been issued in this area by a Court of Appeal since *Costco*, and that is currently pending in front of the Supreme Court directly exemplifies the possible conflict of judicial interpretations. Generally, the Second Circuit confirmed the position that the interplay of sections 109(a) and 602(a)(1) of the Copyright Act should be interpreted as dictating a rule of national copyright first sale based on territoriality[109] and ruled that the defendant, Kirtsaeng, was not entitled to a first sale defense under section 109(a) against the claim of copyright infringement brought by the plaintiff, Wiley & Sons.[110] Kirtsaeng, a Thai student living in the United States, asked friends and family to ship to him foreign editions of textbooks printed abroad by a Wiley subsidiary; Kirtsaeng subsequently sold the books online in the United States, earning profits of over one million dollars. Wiley sued, claiming copyright infringement.[111] The jury found Kirtsaeng liable for willful infringement and he appealed. As in *Costco v Omega*, the issue on appeal was whether section 109(a) applied as the textbooks were not manufactured in the United States.[112]

In addressing the appeal, the Second Circuit once again analysed the interplay between sections 106, 109(a) and 602(a)(1) of the Copyright Act and the meaning of the language 'lawfully made under this title'; as a result, the court found that that this language could not refer to goods manufactured outside the United States.[113] Like previous courts, the Second Circuit repeated that this interpretation was the only possible interpretation of section 109(a) compatible with section 602(a)(1).[114] Otherwise, the Second Circuit stated, section 602(a)(1) would have 'no force… in the vast majority of cases'.[115] Still, the Second Circuit directly relied on the language of Justice Ginsburg's concurrence in *Quality King* to determine the outcome of the case, concluding that 'the Supreme Court's unambiguous language, though dicta, [was] sufficient to resolve' the case at issue.[116] By relying on Justice Ginsburg's concurrence,

108 *John Wiley & Sons, Inc. v Kirtsaeng*, 652 F.3d 210 (2d. Cir. 2011) cert. granted, 132 S. Ct. 1905 (U.S. 2012); See also *Pearson Education, Inc. v Liu*, 656 F. Supp. 2d 407 (S.D. NY 2009) (holding *dubitante* in a case also dealing with imported textbooks, that the first sale rule does not apply to foreign manufactured goods).

109 The Second Circuit directly relied on Justice Ginsburg's concurrence in *Quality King*, above note 14, 153 (Ginsburg J concurring).

110 Ibid., 225 (holding that 'the first sale doctrine does not apply to copies manufactured outside of the United States').

111 Ibid., 213 (claiming copyright infringement under s. 501(a) of the Copyright Act).

112 Ibid.

113 Ibid., 221.

114 Ibid., 221.

115 Ibid.

116 Ibid. See also Aldridge, above note 97, 330.

however, the Second Circuit departed from the position previously adopted in similar cases by the Ninth Circuit, which had repeatedly affirmed that, while section 109(a) does not apply to foreign manufactured goods that are imported into the United States without the consent of the copyright owners, section 109(a) does apply to foreign manufactured products after their first authorized sale in the US. Instead, the Second Circuit stated: 'While perhaps a close call … in light of its necessary interplay with section 602(a)(1), section 109(a) is best interpreted as applying only to works manufactured domestically'.[117] Based upon the Second Circuit's decision, only domestically manufactured products would thus be subject to the first sale rule – regardless of whether they are sold nationally or reimported into the United States under the rule in *Quality King* – while section 109(a) would not apply to foreign made products, even after their authorized sale in the United States.[118]

Not surprisingly, the Second Circuit's decision has been criticized for its extensive implications for the viability of secondary markets in an economy increasingly dominated by foreign manufactured products.[119] Most notably, the Second Circuit decision was not unanimous. One of the sitting judges, Judge Murtha, wrote an important dissenting opinion, noting precisely the fact that the majority's opinion would incentivize negative economic policies and discriminate between domestic and foreign manufactured products and, paradoxically, favor the latter over the first category of goods.[120] In particular, Judge Murtha stated that to interpret the language 'lawfully made under this title' as 'made in the United States' was incorrect since section 109(a) of the Copyright Act does not make reference to the place of manufacture of the products, but instead focuses on whether the products are made 'lawfully'.[121] As a result, Judge Murtha argued that copyrighted products offered for sale in the United States are 'lawful' under the Copyright Act and thus should be subject to the first sale doctrine, regardless of the place of their first sale.[122] If

---

[117] *John Wiley & Sons*, above note 108, 221 (noting that the Ninth Circuit holds that s. 109 applies also to foreign manufactured works sold in the US, but that holding has not been adopted by other Courts of Appeal).

[118] See discussion above at 3.1.

[119] See, e.g., Abigail Phillips, 'Poking More Holes in the First Sale Doctrine', *Electronic Frontier Foundation*, 19 August 2011, available at: https://www.eff.org/deeplinks/2011/08/poking-more-holes-first-sale-doctrine (last visited 30 November 2011); Michael Kelley, 'Court Rules First Sale Doctrine Only Applies to Works Manufactured in US', *Library Journal*, 17 August 2011, available at: http://www.libraryjournal.com/lj/home/891663-264/court_rules_first_sale_doctrine.html.csp (last visited 30 November 2011).

[120] *John Wiley & Sons*, above note 108, 224–9 (Murtha J dissenting).

[121] Ibid., 226 (Murtha J dissenting).

[122] Ibid.

Congress wanted to limit the application of the first sale rule to works manufactured in the United States, Judge Murtha noted, Congress would have done so expressly, as it did in other parts of the Copyright Act.[123] Judge Murtha also argued that it was not Congress' intent to provide more copyright protection for foreign goods than for domestic ones, and thus provide an incentive for copyright owners in the United States to manufacture their goods abroad to bypass the application of section 109(a). Probably even more relevant, Judge Murtha disagreed with the Ninth Circuit's 'imperfect solution' – 'that the first sale doctrine can apply to copies made outside the United States but only after there has been one authorized sale [in the United States]'.[124] Ultimately, Judge Murtha agreed with the majority that this was a 'close call', yet he concluded that 'the first sale doctrine applies to foreign manufactured [products]', regardless of the place of manufacture and whether the products have been imported into the United States with or without the authorization of the copyright owners.[125]

Following the Second Circuit's decision, Kirtsaeng petitioned the Supreme Court to grant certiorari and again to clarify the application of section 109(a) of the Copyright Act to foreign manufactured products.The Court granted certiorari and should decide the case before the end of 2012. This time, the intervention of the Supreme Court on the issue was even more pressing than it was in the past. By finding that section109(a) of the Copyright Act does not apply to foreign manufactured products, the Second Circuit's opinion clearly did not seem to consider the risks of this position for the conduct of international trade, as well as its impact on secondary markets, and even libraries and consumers.[126]

Ultimately, the first sale rule is what enables the public to exert control over the products consumers buy, to borrow books from libraries, to donate or gift new books, DVDs and even toys, or to resell used articles that are still protected under copyright law such as books, paintings and any other artistic work. Against this interest of the public, however, recent judicial precedents have granted copyright owners a growing control over their products and have restrained the ability of retailers and consumers to alienate property, compete in the market, or simply dispose of their own possessions.[127] After Justice Ginsburg's concurrence in *Quality King*, reselling anything made abroad had already become highly controversial. Now it directly seems to constitute copyright infringement under the jurisdiction of the Second Circuit.[128]

---

123 Ibid., 226–27 (Murtha J dissenting).

124 Ibid., 228 (Murtha J dissenting).

125 Ibid., 229 (Murtha J dissenting).

126 Aldridge, above note 97; Justin Yedor, 'Lacking Swiss Protection: The First-Sale Doctrine in Costco v Omega' (2011) 6 *Duke Journal of Constitutional Law & Public Policy Sidebar* 126; Bensen, above note 99.

127 Ibid.

128 Tun-Jen Chiang, 'Unanswered Questions after Costco v Omega', Prawfs

This situation, as Judge Murtha pointed out, however, is not, and cannot be, what Congress intended when it enacted section 109(a) of the Copyright Act. Accordingly, it is imperative that the Supreme Court finally clarifies the meaning of the language 'lawfully made under this title' in section 109(a) in its decision in *Kirtsaeng* later this year. Should the Court, once again, not reach a majority or not clearly address (and resolve) the issue, the time has come for Congress to directly enter this debate and to address this fundamental aspect of copyright law with an appropriate legislative amendment that would, again finally, clarify the territorial application of the copyright first sale rule in the United States with respect to *all* copyrighted products offered for sale in the national territory regardless of their place of manufacture.[129]

5. CONCLUSION

The relationship between the exclusive rights of copyright owners per section 106 and the limits set by the first sale rule per section 109(a) of the Copyright Act is undoubtedly complex as a result of the conflicting interests of those affected: copyright owners, consumers, retailers, second-hand dealers, libraries, and so on. This relationship becomes even more complex when the application of the first sale rule in copyright law intersects with the international trade of copyrighted products across separate national markets – namely with products first sold in a foreign jurisdiction and reimported into the United States without the authorization of the copyright owners. As this chapter has highlighted, copyright owners have traditionally opposed the arbitrage of copyrighted products from low-cost countries to the United States because these products create additional competition in the national market, which in turn jeopardizes copyright owners' profits as well as their ability to control distribution (and price discriminate) in separate domestic jurisdictions. As a result, copyright owners have repeatedly invoked section 602(a)(1) of the Copyright Act, which prohibits the unauthorized importation of copyrighted products and defines such importation as copyright infringement. Still, jurisprudential precedents on the interpretation and interplay of sections 109(a) and 602(a)(1) have historically proved to be conflicting and, even after

---

Blawg, 14 December 2010, available at: http://Prawfs Blawg.blogs.com/Prawfs Blawg/2010/12/unanswered-questions-after-costco-v-omega.html (last visited 30 November 2011) (noting that the confusion in this area is creating deterrents for businesses such as eBay, Netflix, and others with similar business models).

129 Richelieu, above note 8, 858; Doris R. Perl, 'The Use of Copyright Law to Block the Importation of Gray-Market Goods: The Black and White of it All' (1990) 23 *Loyola of LA Law Review* 645, 680.

two Supreme Court decisions on the topic, the interpretation of the territorial application of first sale rule per section 109(a) remains unclear.

Despite this uncertainty, recent judicial decisions by the Ninth and Second Circuits seem nonetheless to increasingly favor the interpretation that section 109(a) applies only to products offered for sale in the national territory. More problematically, the Second Circuit recently followed Justice Ginsburg's concurring opinion in *Quality King* and suggested that the language of section 109(a) 'lawfully made under this title' should be interpreted as 'lawfully manufactured in the United States'. This interpretation, however, excludes from the application of the first sale rule foreign manufactured products that are copyrighted in the United States, even after their authorized importation and first sale in the country. As objected to by several scholars and members of the judiciary, if confirmed nationwide, this position would provide greater copyright protection for foreign manufactured than for domestically manufactured products, which would in turn incentivize copyright owners to manufacture products abroad rather than domestically – per se a 'bad' policy, it has been argued, and unlikely to have been Congress' intent.

Because of the important interests at stake, the time has come for the Supreme Court to resolve this unsustainable and confusing status quo and clarify, once and for all, the meaning of the language 'lawfully made under this title' per section 109(a) of the Copyright Act in its awaited decision in *Kirtsaeng*. Should the Supreme Court not be willing to do so, Congress should step into the debate and address the interpretation of section 109(a) directly with an appropriate legislative amendment and clarify, again once and for all, the actual meaning of the provision and the territorial application of the copyright first sale rule with respect to *all* copyrighted products offered for sale in the United States, without discriminating between domestically and foreign manufactured products.

5. The need to harmonize intellectual property licensing law: a European perspective

Jacques de Werra

1. INTELLECTUAL PROPERTY LICENSING AS A KEY ELEMENT OF INNOVATION POLICY

The key role of intellectual property in the shaping of a successful innovation policy has been duly identified in Europe as well as in many other parts of the world: intellectual property constitutes an important component of the regulatory architecture supporting a competitive knowledge-based economy. This role has been confirmed in numerous official European Union (EU) documents and statements, particularly in the Communication of the EU Commission of 24 May 2011, which states that 'European IPR legislation must provide the appropriate "enabling framework" that incentivises investment by rewarding creation, stimulates innovation in an environment of undistorted competition and facilitates the distribution of knowledge'.[1] The European Commission even expressed the view that 'IP is the capital that feeds the new economy'. This focus on intellectual property should, however, not hide the fact that intellectual property rights (IPRs), as well as the intellectual property regulations which protect them, cannot perform miracles by themselves and cannot fully achieve the declared goal of feeding the new economy if IPRs, as commercial assets, cannot be put to efficient use by third parties with the authorization of the IP owner. This was duly confirmed by the European Commission, which stated that a 'better use of IP portfolios by means of licensing and commercial exploitation is central to successful business models'.[2]

1 Single Market for Intellectual Property Rights boosting creativity and innovation to provide economic growth, high quality jobs and first class products and services in Europe, COM(2011) 287 final.

2 Ibid.

This consequently requires the stakeholders (intellectual property owners and users) to be in a position to rely on and have trust in a clear and predictable regulatory framework, which not only defines and protects intellectual property rights as such but also enables and facilitates intellectual property transactions and, most particularly, intellectual property licence transactions.

In other words, an efficient intellectual property policy, which generates equitable benefits for all stakeholders, must not be limited to the definition of exclusive intellectual property rights and of their limits (which are the classical issues governed by intellectual property regulations), but should also include policies on the commercialization of such rights by way of contracts: such a policy must also regulate intellectual property commercial law.[3]

Even if the central role of intellectual property transactions as well as the need to facilitate and promote them have been duly identified (particularly by the European Commission), there are at present no global, or even European, policies governing intellectual property commercial law, and specifically intellectual property licensing law. There is indeed, as of today, no uniform body of law governing intellectual property licensing transactions within Europe, even if complex intellectual property licensing issues have recently been litigated up to the European Court of Justice (ECJ).

On that basis, the goal of this chapter is to discuss certain aspects of European intellectual property licensing law in the light of recent case law and regulations in order to show that there is a need to develop a more unified framework to govern IP licensing law in Europe.

[3] Reference can be made here to the remarkable project (proposed at the UNCITRAL Third International Colloquium on Secured Transactions, 1–3 March 2010, Vienna: see http://www.uncitral.org/uncitral/en/commission/colloquia/3rdint.html) for a 'Concept Proposal for a Model Intellectual Property Contracting Law' (drafted by L. Brennan and J. Dodd) who rightly state that '[i]ntellectual property (IP) assets have become important in everyday global commerce. [...] The world economy has experienced profound changes, with information products and services now driving increased productivity and growth. Contracts support both the creation and distribution of such information. As a result, there is a growing need to develop common legal rules to guide and support commercial contracting practices involving IP'. One specific area which will not be addressed in this chapter is the issue of the treatment of licence agreements in bankruptcy proceedings, and particularly in the bankruptcy of the licensor; in this scenario local bankruptcy rules significantly diverge, and this can lead to significant difficulties; for a recent illustration, see *In re Qimonda AG*, 2011 WL 5149831 (Bankr. E.D.Va. 2011) (protecting the US-based licensees of a German bankrupt licensor under the protective US bankruptcy rules, which are favourable to licensees).

2. THE PRESENT STATUS OF EUROPEAN INTELLECTUAL PROPERTY LICENSING LAW

While intellectual property licensing agreements are not regulated at the European level, even if they are succinctly mentioned in certain European regulatory instruments,[4] licensing contract law issues have been at the heart of several recent decisions given by various courts (particularly the ECJ). As these decisions tend to show the difficulties that result from the current non-harmonized status, the aim of the following paragraphs is to present them in some detail. This case law illustrates the difficulties faced by the courts when confronted with (i) the application of the principle of exhaustion anchored in European intellectual property law in a licensing context (see 2.1 below), (ii) the characterization of licensing agreements from the perspective of private international law (see 2.2 below) and (iii) the issue of whether a licensee has standing to sue for infringement (see 2.3 below).

2.1 Under What Circumstances Can the Exhaustion Principle Apply in the Case of Products Commercialized as a Result of a Breach of a Licensing Agreement by the Licensee? The ECJ *Dior–Copad* and *Greenstar–Kanzi* Cases

Two recent decisions of the ECJ show the complex interaction between the European and well established concept of exhaustion of rights, the nationally based scope and reach of licence agreements and the consequences of their breach.[5] These cases discuss the thorny issue of whether the owner of intellectual property rights can exercise its exclusive rights and sue for infringement when a (former) licensee and/or a third party commercialize products

---

4 For a review of the relevant regulations (which will not be enumerated here in view of the focus made on the relevant provisions at stake in the recent case law), see Peter Stiel, *Leistungstörungen bei Lizenzverträgen aus Sicht des europäischen Rechts* (Herbert Hutz 2009) 5 et seq. It is worth noting that beyond intellectual property regulations as such, intellectual property licensing is also regulated under competition law, particularly under a technology transfer perspective, as resulting from Commission Regulation (EC) No. 772/2004 of 7 April 2004 on the application of Article 81(3) of the Treaty to categories of technology transfer agreements (with the accompanying Guidelines on the application of Article 81 of the EC Treaty to technology transfer agreements), and also from the Commission Regulation (EU) No. 330/2010 of 20 April 2010 on the application of Article 101(3) of the Treaty on the Functioning of the European Union to categories of vertical agreements and concerted practices; this aspect will not be further analysed in this chapter.

5 The recent decision of the ECJ of 3 July 2012 in Case C128/11 *Used Soft GmbH v Oracle International Corp is* not analysed here.

which were initially manufactured and distributed under the framework of the relevant licence agreement.

In the *Dior–Copad* case,[6] the ECJ had to decide for the first time on the question of the effect of a trade mark licence agreement on the exhaustion of the right of the owner of the licensed trade mark.[7] The dispute arose out of a trade mark licence agreement entered into between Christian Dior couture SA ('Dior') and Société industrielle de Lingerie ('SIL') for the manufacture and distribution of luxury corsetry goods under the Dior trade mark. Clause 8.2(5) of the licence agreement provided that 'in order to maintain the repute and prestige of the trade mark the licensee agrees not to sell to wholesalers, buyers' collectives, discount stores, mail order companies, door-to-door sales companies or companies selling within private houses without prior written agreement from the licensor, and must make all necessary provision to ensure that that rule is complied with by its distributors or retailers'.

After bankruptcy proceedings were initiated against SIL, it sold goods bearing the Dior trade marks to Copad International, which operates a discount store business. Dior subsequently initiated legal proceedings for trade mark infringement against SIL and Copad before the French courts. The French Cour de Cassation ultimately referred the following questions to the ECJ for a preliminary ruling:

1. Must Article 8(2) of [the then in force 89/104 Directive now consolidated in Directive 2008/95/EC] be interpreted as meaning that the proprietor of a trade mark can invoke the rights conferred by that trade mark against a licensee who contravenes a provision in the licence agreement prohibiting, on grounds of the trade mark's prestige, sale to discount stores?
2. Must Article 7(1) of that directive be interpreted as meaning that a licensee who puts goods bearing a trade mark on the market in the [EEA] in disregard of a provision of the licence agreement prohibiting, on grounds of the trade mark's prestige, sale to discount stores, does so without the consent of the trade mark proprietor?
3. If not, can the proprietor invoke such a provision to oppose further commercialisation of the goods, on the basis of Article 7(2) of [the Directive]?

The ECJ answered these questions as follows:

1. Article 8(2) … is to be interpreted as meaning that the proprietor of a trade mark can invoke the rights conferred by that trade mark against a licensee

[6] Case C-59/08 *Copad SA v Christian Dior Couture SA, Vincent Gladel, as liquidator of Société Industrielle Lingerie (SIL) and Société Industrielle Lingerie (SIL)* [2009] ECRI-03421, OJ C141/16, 23 April 2009.

[7] See the Opinion of Advocate General Kokott of 3 December 2008 in Case C-59/08, ibid.

> who contravenes a provision in a licence agreement prohibiting, on grounds of the trade mark's prestige, sales to discount stores of goods such as the ones at issue in the main proceedings, provided it has been established that that contravention, by reason of the situation prevailing in the case in the main proceedings, damages the allure and prestigious image which bestows on those goods an aura of luxury.
>
> 2. Article 7(1) ... is to be interpreted as meaning that a licensee who puts goods bearing a trade mark on the market in disregard of a provision in a licence agreement does so without the consent of the proprietor of the trade mark where it is established that the provision in question is included in those listed in Article 8(2) of that Directive.
> 3. Where a licensee puts luxury goods on the market in contravention of a provision in a licence agreement but must nevertheless be considered to have done so with the consent of the proprietor of the trade mark, the proprietor of the trade mark can rely on such a provision to oppose a resale of those goods on the basis of Article 7(2) of Directive 89/104 ... only if it can be established that, taking into account the particular circumstances of the case, such resale damages the reputation of the trade mark.

Even if this decision raises many interesting issues which would call for a closer analysis, the goal here is to focus on certain findings made by the ECJ that relate to the limits of the power of control of a trade mark owner on goods which have been initially manufactured and commercialized under a trade mark licence in the light of the exhaustion principle.

The ECJ found in this respect that where a licensee puts goods bearing the licensed trade mark on the market, this is to be viewed, as a rule, as an act done with the consent of the trade mark owner so that it triggers the application of the exhaustion principle, pursuant to Article 7(1) of Directive 2008/95.[8]

However, the ECJ also held that a licence agreement does not offer unrestricted protection to third parties who have acquired the relevant goods from a licensee under the shield of the exhaustion principle while a 'licence agreement does not constitute the absolute and unconditional consent of the proprietor of the trade mark to the licensee putting the goods bearing the trade mark on the market'.[9] In this respect, as stated by the ECJ, Article 8(2) of Directive 2008/95 expressly enables the trade mark owner to invoke its trade mark rights against a licensee in the event of breach of certain contractual conditions listed in this provision.[10] Article 8(2) indeed provides that

> [t]he proprietor of a trade mark may invoke the rights conferred by that trade mark against a licensee who contravenes any provision in his licensing contract with regard to:

---

8 *Copad v Dior*, above note 6, para. 46.
9 Ibid., para. 47.
10 Ibid., para. 48.

(a) its duration;
(b) the form covered by the registration in which the trade mark may be used;
(c) the scope of the goods or services for which the licence is granted;
(d) the territory in which the trade mark may be affixed;
(e) the quality of the goods manufactured or of the services provided by the licensee.

An important finding made by the ECJ in this case is to confirm that the list of contractual provisions of Article 8(2) (as listed above) is exhaustive.[11] This consequently means that trade mark infringement remedies are not available to a trade mark owner against its licensee except in the specific circumstances listed in Article 8(2).

The ECJ held in this case that Article 8(2)(e) could be applicable subject to the decision to be made by the national (French) courts in the light of the circumstances of the case.[12]

The second, and more recent, decision of the ECJ, *Greenstar–Kanzi Europe NV v Hustin and Goossens*,[13] concerned Community plant variety rights under Regulation 2100/94, as amended by Regulation 873/2004 on Community plant variety rights. The issue at stake was whether the owner of the exclusive right could bring an infringement action against a third party which had obtained material from a former licensee who had breached certain conditions in the licence agreement entered into with the owner. As in the *Dior–Copad* case, this required an assessment of whether, and if so to what extent, the principle of exhaustion (as anchored in Article 16 of Regulation 2100/94) could protect the third party who had legitimately acquired the relevant goods from an ex-licensee against infringement claims raised by the owner of the right, in spite of the breach of the licence agreement committed by the former licensee.

The former licensee in this case (Nicolaï) had obtained the exclusive right to grow and market apple trees of a given protected new variety (Nicoter) provided that (as per the condition contained in the licence agreement) Nicolaï

> will not dispose of or sell any product covered by the licence unless the other party signs in advance the grower's licence referred to in Annex 6 (where the other party is a grower) or the marketing licence referred to in Annex 7 (where the other party is a trader).[14]

---

11 Ibid., para. 49.

12 See the decision of the French Cour de Cassation on 2 February 2010, Ref. 06-16202 (following the decision of the ECJ), Bulletin 2010, IV, No. 25.

13 Case C-140/10 *Greenstar-Kanzi Europe NV v Jean Hustin and Jo Goossens*, 20 October 2011, [2011] OJ C362/10, 20 October 2011. For a comment, see Gert Würtenberger, 'Plant Variety Rights and Breach of Licence' (2012) 7(3) *Journal of Intellectual Property Law & Practice* 161.

14 *Greenstar–Kanzi*, ibid., para. 12.

Article 27 of Regulation 2100/94 provides in this respect (under the title 'Contractual exploitation rights') that:

> 1. Community plant variety rights may form in full or in part the subject of contractually granted exploitation rights. Exploitation rights may be exclusive or non-exclusive.
> 2. The holder may invoke the rights conferred by the Community plant variety right against a person enjoying the right of exploitation who contravenes any of the conditions or limitations attached to his exploitation right pursuant to paragraph 1.

In spite of the very broad wording of Article 27(2) of Regulation 2100/94 (referring to 'any of the conditions or limitations attached to his exploitation right'), the ECJ adopted a more restrictive approach in order to limit the right of control of the right holder.

By invoking the principle that the 'protection enjoyed by the holder is not to be excessive',[15] the ECJ decided that the right holder could not invoke its right against a licensee (or a third party having acquired the relevant goods from the licensee) for the types of breach of the licence agreement which would not affect and vitiate the consent of the holder to the placing of the goods on the market, and thus would have no effect on the exhaustion of the holder's right.[16] As expressed by the Advocate General, 'an infringement of the conditions attached to prior authorization cannot be treated in the same way, in law, as an absence of authorization enforceable on others'.[17] In other words, the ECJ essentially held that the exhaustion principle can apply in the case of a breach of the licence agreement by the licensee because, in such a case, the holder had basically authorized the marketing of the relevant products by the licensee and has also been remunerated for the commercialization of the goods. In contrast, in the situation in which the holder has not authorized at all the marketing of the relevant products, no exhaustion can take place.

In the light of this reasoning, the ECJ held that the holder is entitled to bring an action for infringement against a third party (having obtained materials from a licensee who has breached certain obligations of the licence agreement entered into with the holder) only if the contractual obligations violated by the licensee would 'relate directly to the essential features of the Community plant

---

[15] Ibid., para. 41 (referring to Recital 14 of the Directive which provides that 'the introduction of the principle of exhaustion of rights must ensure that the protection is not excessive').

[16] Ibid., para. 41.

[17] Opinion of the Advocate General Jääskinen of 7 July 2011 in Case C-140/10, para. 57.

variety right'[18] in issue. Given that the relevant contracts and clauses in issue in this case were not submitted to the ECJ, the Court stated that it could not characterize the provisions of the licence agreement in order to decide whether the relevant provisions would meet this condition and that it was for the referring court to make such an assessment.

The result of this decision is that the exhaustion principle can apply unless the breach committed by the licensee relates to the 'essential features' of the plant variety right, whereby the definition of what would constitute an essential feature of such right remains quite uncertain.

What is the impact of these two decisions on the European intellectual property licensing landscape?

An initial comment, which is striking in the light of these decisions, is that the relevant rules – which define the conditions under which an owner of an IPR (and licensor) can sue for infringement against a licensee or against a third party who has acquired goods from the licensee – are not identical and can even significantly diverge; this results from a comparison between Article 8(2) of the 2008/95 Directive and Article 22(2) of Regulation 207/2009 (for national and Community trade marks, respectively), Article 22 of Regulation 6/2000[19] (for Community designs),[20] and Article 17 of Regulation 2100/94 (for Community plant varieties).[21]

This divergence of regimes is quite problematic in that it seems hardly conceivable that an owner of various intellectual property rights – which can,

---

[18] *Greenstar–Kanzi*, above note 13, para. 44.

[19] Art. 32(2) Regulation 6/2002 provides: 'Without prejudice to any legal proceedings based on the law of contract, the holder may invoke the rights conferred by the Community design against a licensee who contravenes any provision in his licensing contract with regard to its duration, the form in which the design may be used, the range of products for which the licence is granted and the quality of products manufactured by the licensee.'

[20] Directive 98/71/EC of the European Parliament and of the Council of 13 October 1998 on the legal protection of designs does not contain any rules on this issue.

[21] Even though the European patent regulatory environment is still moving and uncertain (and also from a jurisdictional perspective in view of the Opinion of the ECJ 1/09 of 8 March 2011 on the compatibility with EU law of the draft agreement on the creation of a European and Community Patent Court, available at: http://curia.europa.eu/juris/document/document.jsf?text=&docid=80233&pageIndex=0&doclang=EN&mode=lst&dir=&occ=first&part=1&cid=402571), it can be noted that certain draft documents also regulate this issue (in a different manner/wording); see Art. 19(2) of the Proposal for a Council Regulation on the European Union patent (approved at the European Union's Competitiveness Council of 4 December 2009): 'The rights conferred by the EU patent may be invoked against a licensee who breaches any restriction in the licensing contract'.

of course, as frequently occurs in practice,[22] be licensed together in the same licence agreement – has different remedies depending on the type of right in issue and on the type of contractual condition which has been breached. It seem sequally inappropriate that regulations define standards only for industrial property rights without doing so for unregistered rights, and particularly for copyrights, as experience shows that the interaction between copyright infringement remedies and contractual remedies can also be quite delicate.[23]

More fundamentally, these regulations tend to hide the basic principle that the owner of an intellectual property right should have the right to invoke infringement of its IPR committed by its licensee if, and only if, the licensee commits an act which falls within the scope of the exclusive right granted to the owner under the relevant intellectual property regulations but which is not covered by the licence.[24]

Viewed in this light, the existing regulations, and particularly those adopted with respect to trade marks, are inappropriate to the extent that they do not (fully) comply with this basic principle in that intellectual property infringement remedies are available only in the case of infringement of the relevant rights. A quick review of the individual conditions set out in Article 8(2) of Directive 2008/95 confirms this analysis.

This provides first that the owner of a trade mark can invoke its trade mark right against a licensee who contravenes any provision in his licensing contract with regard to its duration (Article 8(2)(a)). This wording does not constitute a proper standard to the extent that it is possible (at least theoretically) for a licence agreement to be entered into for the term of the trade mark

---

[22] It being noted that the *Greenstar–Kanzi* case, which essentially deals with Community plant variety rights, also has a trade mark aspect in that the apples are marketed under the 'Kanzi' trade mark.

[23] For a recent example (an open source software licence), see *Jacobson v Katzer*, 535 F.3d 1373 (Fed. Cir. 2008); for a discussion of this case and of the subtle distinction between contractual covenants and licence conditions, see Robert B. Gomulkievicz, 'Clarifications and Complications in Enforcing Open Source Software Licenses', in Jacques de Werra (ed.), *Research Handbook on Intellectual Property Licensing* (Edward Elgar Publishing, forthcoming), see http://www.ip-licensing.info.

[24] See the crystal clear reasoning made by the Honourable Madam Justice Heneghan (Federal Court of Canada) in *Harmony Consulting Ltd v G.A. Foss Transport Ltd*, 2011 FC 540 (2011) (available at: http://decisions.fct-cf.gc.ca/en/2011/2011fc340/2011fc340.html) at para. 261: 'In simple terms, the Plaintiff argued that any violation of the licensing agreements constituted a violation of copyright. This argument is inherently flawed and cannot succeed as "...copyright infringement does not arise out of a breach of contract"; see *Corel Corp. v Guardian Insurance Co. of Canada* (2001) 26 CCLI (3d) 39 (OSCJ) at para. 22. As I have explained, copyright is violated only if the defendant has performed, or authorized, an act that only the owner can do within the confines of the Copyright Act'.

(assuming that the trade mark owner does not wish to extend the protection of the trade mark after the term of the licence agreement), and that the licensor will contractually impose on the licensee the prohibition to use the trade mark after the termination of the licence agreement. In such a case, it is obvious that at the end of the term of the licence agreement (which would then coincide with the term of protection of the trade mark), the trade mark owner would not be in a position to invoke an alleged infringement of its trade mark right as it would no longer exist (even if it may potentially invoke a contractual breach of the licensee's obligations). For this reason, this first condition, as presently drafted, seems inappropriate. The same argument applies – even more blatantly – to Article 22(2) of Regulation 6/2002 (for Community designs) for which this scenario appears to be more likely than it is for trade marks, in view of the limited duration of design protection.

In addition, the wording of Article 8(2)(a) does not clearly address the complex issue of whether infringement remedies are available in the event of early termination of the licence: indeed, this provision refers only to a contractual provision relating to the 'duration' of the licence. It appears most doubtful that a licensor would benefit from infringement remedies in the event of early termination of the licence agreement if such termination is not justified; in such a case this would be assessed under the national contract law governing the licence agreement in issue.[25] Therefore, it is only if the early termination of the licence is legitimate that the licensor would be in a position to invoke the infringement of its intellectual property rights against the licensee.

Article 8(2)(b) then provides that the owner of the trade mark can invoke its trade mark right against a licensee who contravenes any provision of the licence agreement with regard to the 'form covered by the registration in which the trade mark may be used'. Even if it is conceivable that disputes will arise frequently between licensors and licensees regarding the way in which the licensed trade mark can be used,[26] it is doubtful that the absolute wording of Article 8(2)(b) is adequate. It could (at least in theory) be that the form or graphical appearance of the trade mark is so different from the trade mark as initially licensed that the new form would not be infringing the trade mark right by applying the standard test of trade mark infringement – similarity of the signs. Again, it appears questionable whether this provision will change the standard test resulting from the application of substantive trade mark law principles.

---

25 See James J.D. Wagner, 'Licence Enforcement' (2012) 7 *Journal of Intellectual Property Law & Practice* 176.

26 For a recent illustration, see *Sunstar, Inc. v. Alberto-Culver Co.*, 586 F.3d 487 (7th Cir. 2009) (addressing the question whether a Japanese licensee, Sunstar, is authorized to use *variants* of the licensed trade mark under a 'Senyoshiyoken licence').

Similar reasoning can also be made about Article 8(2)(c), which makes it possible to invoke trade mark infringement remedies in the case of breach of contractual provisions relating to 'the scope of the goods or services for which the licence is granted'. It is indeed conceivable that a licensee may use the trade mark unduly in connection with products or services which hypothetically are totally unrelated to those claimed for the licensed trade mark. In those circumstances, the application of standard trade mark law principles would not allow the trade mark owner to prevent the use of the licensed trade mark by the licensee in connection with products or services not similar to those claimed for the trade mark (subject to the protection of well-known trade marks).[27]

Along the same line, the condition set out in Article 8(2)(d) – under which the trade mark owner is in a position to sue for trade mark infringement a licensee who contravenes any provision in his licensing contract with regard to the 'the territory in which the trade mark may be affixed' – can be problematic. This can be illustrated by the scenario in which a multiterritorial trade mark licence covers different EU countries (in each of which valid national trade marks have been registered and licensed); the licensee breaches the licence agreement by using the licensed trade mark in another EU country (Z) in which no trade mark has been registered by the owner/licensor. Based on the wording of Article 8(2)(d), this could be a situation in which the trade mark owner could invoke its trade mark right against the licensee, while in reality this would, of course, not be possible because of the absence of trade mark protection in the relevant country (Z).

The final condition, Article 8(2)(e), relating to'the quality of the goods manufactured or of the services provided by the licensee', is problematic in view of the difficulty of perceiving its scope of application, as is revealed by the *Dior–Copad* case. It is quite obvious that courts will have a difficult time in assessing to what extent the relevant breach of the licence agreement 'damages the allure and prestigious image which bestows on those goods an aura of luxury'.[28]

In addition to these specific issues relating to each of the conditions in Article 8(2), the wording of the provision is problematic for additional, and perhaps more fundamental, reasons.

---

27 Art. 5(1)(b) Directive 2008/95 provides that '[t]he proprietor shall be entitled to prevent all third parties not having his consent from using in the course of trade: [...] any sign where, because of its identity with, or similarity to, the trade mark and the identity or similarity of the goods or services covered by the trade mark and the sign, there exists a likelihood of confusion on the part of the public'.

28 First finding of the ECJ.

First, the fact of enumerating in a limitative manner the types of contractual provision that can trigger infringement remedies if breached is dangerous for the interests of the licensor. The reason is that many different types of breach of a trade mark licence agreement can lead to the early termination of the agreement as a result of the breach. By focusing on the identified provisions, Article 8(2) seems to exclude the availability of infringement remedies for any other types of breach.

Take, for example, the case of a trade mark licensee who is late in payment of the contractual royalties and who still has not paid them in the additional period the licensor may have granted to the licensee (30 days, for example). In such a scenario, it is conceivable that the licensor is entitled to terminate the licence agreement upon what would be considered a material breach of the agreement committed by the licensee. This termination would remove all permission for the use of the trade mark by the licensee, given that such use would no longer be permitted by the licence agreement.[29] In such circumstances, it would appear logical that the licensor should be in a position to invoke trade mark infringement remedies against the ex-licensee. However, this does not appear to be possible in the light of the exclusive causes of infringement action listed in Article 8(2), breach of the financial obligations by the licensee not being among them. It appears legitimate to hold that a licensee cannot be threatened by infringement actions in the case of minor breaches of the licence agreement. The question arises, though, whether the parties are free to decide that any breach of the agreement will trigger the availability of infringement remedies for the benefit of the licensor. This could be implemented by making the grant and maintenance of the licence to use the relevant IPRs subject to compliance by the licensee with the terms of the agreement so that the licence (the right of use) is conditional on compliance with the terms of the licence.

Even if this could be justified by the principle of freedom of contract, it still appears that a good argument could be made to protect the licensee against such a risk and consequently to limit infringement remedies to cases of material breaches of the licence agreement. This may be the underlying rationale of Article 8(2) of Directive 2008/95 and of the ECJ decision in the *Greenstar–Kanzi case* (discussed above), which held that the holder was entitled to bring an action for infringement against a third party (having obtained materials from a licensee who had breached certain obligations of the licence agreement entered into with the holder) *only* if the contractual obligations

---

[29] It is, of course, again up to the substantive contract law to define what shall constitute a material breach of the licence agreement.

violated by the licensee 'relate directly to the essential features of the Community plant variety right'.[30]

Secondly, Article 8(2) of Directive 2008/95 limits the availability of trade mark infringement remedies against a licensee to cases in which the licensee 'contravenes any provision in his licensing contract'. This wording (at least on the basis of other languages: 'clause' or 'Bestimmung'[31]) seems to imply that such conditions should be expressly regulated in the licence agreement. The question then arises of what happens if there is no *contractual* clause defining the relevant condition and the scope of the licensed right of use. To take one example (in the light of Article 8(2)(b)), should the trade mark owner be in a position to invoke its trade mark right for a violation by the licensee 'of the form covered by the registration in which the trade mark may be used' even if the licence agreement contains no provision whatsoever on this specific issue? In the affirmative – and potentially against the wording of Article 8(2) – this would require an exploration of this issue under the relevant contract law governing the trade mark licence agreement at issue; this can prove to be complex (in the absence of an EU-wide harmonized solution). In the negative, it would seem somehow surprising (to say the least) that the regulation could create unequal treatment between trade mark owners who have included the relevant clauses in their licence agreements and those who have failed to do so: it appears awkward indeed that the availability of non-contractual remedies (trade mark infringement remedies) depends on the presence or absence of certain contractual clauses in the relevant trade mark licence

A third area of concern over Article 8(2) arises from the reference made in the provision to the rights of the 'proprietor of a trade mark' to invoke its trade mark rights against a licensee. In view of this wording, the question is whether this provision can also apply in a sublicensing scheme so that a licensee and sublicensor can benefit from the rights granted under Article 8(2). In view of the wording of this provision, which clearly and exclusively refers to the trade mark owner ('proprietor of a trade mark'), it appears quite uncertain that a trade mark licensee (even an exclusive licensee) could be in a position to invoke such protection, even if this appears to be legitimate.

---

30 *Greenstar-Kanzi*, above note 13, para. 44.

31 In German : '[…] gegen einen Lizenznehmer geltend machen, der in Bezug auf Folgendes gegen eine Bestimmung des Lizenzvertrags verstößt'; in French : '[…] à l'encontre d'un licencié qui enfreint l'une des clauses du contrat de licence […]'; the case law of the ECJ confirms that an EU regulatory provision must not be interpreted in a single language but must rather be interpreted and applied in a uniform manner in the light of all its versions in all the languages of the Union, as the ECJ reminded in its decision in the trade mark/internet domain name dispute in Case C-569/08 *Internetportal und Marketing GmbH v Richard Schlicht*, 3 June 2010, [2010] ECR I-04871, OJ C209, 7.

The result of these developments is that the present regulation raises intricate questions of delineation and interaction between contract remedies and intellectual property remedies, which are not optimally solved as of today. It is therefore important to ensure a sufficient degree of consistency and harmony between the regulations applicable to the different types of intellectual property right in respect of the conditions and the consequences of any breach of IP licence agreements within Europe.

2.2 Is a Licence Agreement a Contract for the Provision of Services? The ECJ *Falco* Case

In the lack of a standard official definition or even understanding of the nature and concept of intellectual property licensing at the level of the EU, the relevant bodies, and particularly the courts, are forced to develop their own understanding of what constitutes the true nature of an intellectual property licence, which can happen in somewhat unexpected circumstances. This is precisely what occurred in the most interesting *Falco* case, which was decided by the ECJ in April 2009.[32]

The ECJ had to decide whether a licence agreement – defined as a contract under which the owner of an IPR grants its contractual partner the right to use that right in return for remuneration – constitutes a contract for the provision of services within the meaning of Article 5(1)(b) of Council Regulation 44/2001 of 22 December 2000 on jurisdiction and the recognition and enforcement of judgments in civil and commercial matters.

The Court answered negatively to this question by stating that 'the concept of services implies, at the least, that the party who provides the services carries out a particular activity in return for remuneration'.[33] In the light of this requirement, the Court decided that it cannot be inferred from a licence agreement that the licensor provides such a service,[34] because 'the owner of an intellectual property right does not perform any service in granting a right to use that property and undertakes merely to permit the licensee to exploit that right freely',[35] whereby the ECJ expressly made reference to the opinion of the Advocate General in connection with this finding.[36]

---

32 Case C-533/07 *Falco Privatstiftung und Thomas Rabitsch v Gisela Weller-Lindhorst* [2009] ECR I-03327, 23 April 2009; for a detailed analysis of this case from a private international law perspective, see Benedetta Ubertazzi, 'Licence Agreements Relating to IP Rights and the EC Regulation on Jurisdiction' [2009] IIC 912. (See also Benedetta Ubertazzi, 'Lizenzverträge und die EG-Zuständigkeitsverordnung' (2010) *GRUR International* 103.)

33 *Falco*, ibid., para. 29.

34 Ibid., para. 30.

35 Ibid., para. 31.

36 Ibid., para. 31 referring to para. 58 of the Opinion of Advocate General

A detailed analysis of the opinion of the Advocate General given in this case is of utmost interest as it reveals and confirms the difficulties of defining what constitutes an intellectual property licence agreement from a European perspective.

In order to decide whether a licence agreement constitutes a contract for the provision of service (under Regulation 44/2001), the Advocate General first had to face the difficulty that licence agreements are creatures of local contract law. She thus stated that the 'starting point [for a definition of a licence agreement] must be the definition of a licence agreement offered by the referring court [in this case, the Austrian Oberster Gerichtshof]'.[37] In this respect, it is interesting to note that the Advocate General expressly relied on the terminology of the referring court, which used the terms 'licence agreement',[38] while noting that 'the concept of a licence agreement is defined more narrowly in some Member States'.[39] However, the Advocate General confirmed that it was necessary to conduct an analysis beyond the local contract law of the referring court given that the judgments of the ECJ are binding on all national courts so that the 'definition of a licence agreement offered by the law of other Member States and by the provisions of Community law, if any, must also be taken into account'.[40]

The Advocate General thus had to face the most difficult task of finding common denominators and common features of licence agreements between the diverse regulatory or judicial solutions adopted by the Member States.

Not surprisingly, the Advocate General had to state at the very beginning of her analysis that licence agreements are 'regulated differently in the various Member States'[41] and that Community law only refers to licence agreements in a sporadic manner without effectively regulating them – that is, without laying down provisions – 'on the conclusion of a licence agreement and [on] its characteristics'.[42]

Trsetenjak of 27 January2009 in Case C-533/07, available at: http://eurlex.europa.eu/LexUriServ/LexUriServ.do?uri=CELEX:62007CC0533:EN:HTML.

37 Ibid., para. 48.

38 It can be noted (and regretted) that the Opinion of the Advocate General does not identify the law which governed the licence agreement which was in dispute and was entered into between Austrian-based licensors (Falco Stiftung and Thomas Rabitsch) and a German-based licensee (Gisela Weller-Lindhorst), whereby the licence covered Austria, Germany and Switzerland.

39 See note 4 of the Opinion, in which the Advocate General notes that, in certain countries, the term 'licence agreement' is used only with respect to the licensing of industrial property rights and not with copyright.

40 *Falco*, Opinion of Advocate General Trsetenjak in Case C-533/07, above note 36, para. 48.

41 Ibid., para. 49.

42 Ibid., para. 50 (stating that 'Community law on the protection of intellectual

While the Opinion of the Advocate General provides a quite impressive and remarkable account of the status of licence agreements under the legal orders of the Member States,[43] it cannot hide the wide diversity of ways in which such contracts are treated under the respective national legal orders. This absence of a harmonized approach to licensing was confirmed by the review made by the Advocate General of the limited European intellectual property legal texts which only refer to licence agreements without defining them in any manner.

The Advocate General thus noted (among other references) that Recital 30 of Directive 2001/29/EC of the European Parliament and of the Council of 22 May 2001 on the harmonization of certain aspects of copyright and related rights in the information society provides that the exclusive rights of the authors may be transferred, assigned or subject to the granting of contractual licences, without prejudice to the relevant national legislation on copyright and related rights, thereby leaving it to the relevant national law to address the issue of contractual licences.

Similarly, Article 22(1) of Council Regulation (EC) No. 207/2009 of 26 February 2009 on the Community trade mark provides that a Community trade mark may be licensed for some or all of the goods or services for which it is registered and for the whole or part of the Community, and such a licence may be exclusive or non-exclusive.

Coming to the issue of whether a licence agreement can constitute a contract for the provision of services, which requires some 'active conduct',[44] the Advocate General held that this was not the case because the licensor does not 'perform any action that consists in active conduct'.[45]

In this respect the Advocate General held that the licensor 'authorises the licensee to exploit the intellectual property right that is the subject of the licence' and that 'the active conduct required of the licensor consists in signing the licence agreement and in making the object to which the licence relates physically available so that it can be used', whereby those 'actions cannot, in [her] opinion, be defined as a "service"'. As a consequence, the Advocate General concluded that the granting of a licence cannot be regarded as a 'service' within the meaning of Article 5(1)(b) of Regulation No. 44/2001.[46]

---

property does govern the possibility of granting licences, but it does not lay down provisions on the conclusion of a licence agreement and its characteristic features').

[43] The Opinion enumerates and discusses in detail numerous regulatory, doctrinal and case law sources that expose the legal treatment of licence agreements in the Member States: ibid., paras 48–52, and corresponding footnotes 32–49.

[44] Ibid., para. 57.

[45] Ibid., para. 58.

[46] Ibid., para. 58.

While this conclusion can be approved, the reasoning adopted for supporting this view raises difficulties (if not concern) as it reveals the problems resulting from the absence of a common understanding of the nature of licence agreements in Europe. Even if one can share the opinion that the 'active conduct' of the licensor cannot be assimilated to the provision of a service by the licensor within the meaning of Article 5(1)(b) of Regulation No. 44/2001, the description of the 'active conduct' of the licensor which was made by the Advocate General remains quite problematic.

As quoted above, the Advocate General described the active conduct of the licensor in terms of two actions: 'signing the licence agreement' and 'making the object to which the licence relates physically available so that it can be used'. However, the mention of each of these two actions raises serious doubts as to the understanding of the nature of intellectual property licences.

By referring first to the signing of the licence agreement, the Advocate General's Opinion could be understood as implying that all licence agreements are in writing. This is not the case in all Member states, or even under European law (as interpreted by national courts).[47] Secondly, and more fundamentally, the Advocate General's statement that a licensor adopts active conduct by 'making the object to which the licence relates *physically* available so that it can be used' (emphasis added) is problematic because it may infer that there is an obligation on the licensor to deliver *a physical item* to the licensee under any intellectual property licence agreement. This is not the case in view of the intangible nature of intellectual property goods which are the object of licence agreements: for instance, a trade mark licence does not require the licensor to deliver any physical item to the licensee since the licensee can simply refer to and use the licensed trade mark as taken from the relevant publicly accessible trade mark registry for this purpose.[48] This statement by the Advocate General can thus be perceived as a revelation of a frequently encountered misunderstanding in intellectual property transactions: the need to clearly distinguish the issue of the transfer of physical objects which may potentially incorporate the intangible goods protected by the relevant intellectual property rights, on the one hand, and the assignment or licensing of the intellectual property rights as such, on the other.

In short, even if the outcome of the *Falco* case can be approved, it (and particularly the opinion of the Advocate General) still reveals the absence of any harmonized European concept of IP licence agreements, as well as the risk

---

47 This issue is discussed at 2.3 below.

48 This may still be the case in certain circumstances, such as for copyright/neighbouring right licences in the course of which the licensor makes available to the licensee a master version (of a recording) of the licensed intellectual goods: see Ubertazzi, 'Licence Agreements Relating to IP Rights', above note 32, 933–4.

of misconceptions about the real nature of such agreements and the difficulties that can result from this situation.

2.3 Does a Licensee Have Standing to Sue Third Party Infringers?

The absence of a harmonized solution at the European level is also felt over the issue of whether, and under what conditions, a licensee has standing to sue third party infringers; this is quite frequently litigated around the world in the absence of a regulatory solution.[49] It should be noted from the outset that European IP law offers some elements of a solution,[50] but these do not fully resolve the issues which arise in practice, as is illustrated by recent case law.

This can be evidenced by the very interesting decision of the UK High Court of Justice in May 2011 in *Jean Christian Perfumes Ltd/Jigsaw European Sales Ltd v Sanjay Tharkar*.[51] The question in this case was as follows. Does an oral licensee of a Community Trade Mark have locus to sue for infringement? Article 22(3) of Regulation 207/2009 provides that, unless precluded by contract, a licensee may bring proceedings for infringement if he has the consent of the trade mark owner.

Regulation 207/2009 does not require any formalities for a Community trade mark licence, in contrast to the assignment of Community trade marks which must be made in writing under Article 17(2).

In contrast, section 28(2) of the UK Trade Marks Act 1994 provides that a licence for a UK registered trade mark is not effective unless it is in writing and signed by or on behalf of the grantor; it thus subjects the effective licensing of a UK trade mark to the written form.

Based on the interpretation of these regulations, the High Court, Chancery Division (John Baldwin QC) held that 'an oral licensee of a Community trade mark may bring proceedings for infringement if he has the consent of the proprietor of the mark'.

In doing so, the Court granted privileged treatment to the oral licensee of a Community trade mark compared with that of a licensee of a UK trade mark,

---

49 For a recent US example, see *HyperQuest, Inc. v N'Site Solutions, Inc.*, 632 F.3d 377, 97 U.S.P.Q.2d (BNA) 1492 (7th Cir. 2011).

50 See, e.g., Art. 32(3) of Regulation (EC) No. 6/2002 of 12 December 2001 on Community designs (OJ EC No. L3 of 5 January 2002) which provides: 'Without prejudice to the provisions of the licensing contract, the licensee may bring proceedings for infringement of a Community design only if the right holder consents thereto. However, the holder of an exclusive licence may bring such proceedings if the right holder in the Community design, having been given notice to do so, does not himself bring infringement proceedings within an appropriate period'.

51 [2011] EWHC 1383 (Ch) (High Court of Justice, Chancery Division, 27 May 2011).

which would not have the same power given that under UK trade mark law a licence must be made in writing. Such privileged treatment could also apply to an international trade mark licence agreement. As a result of the *favor validitatis principle*,[52] such a licence could still be held to be valid even if not made in writing.

This case shows that it would appear to be appropriate to adopt a European-wide solution which would apply equally to all types of intellectual property right, and which would specify the conditions under which a licensee would have standing to sue third party infringers. The proposed regulation should also define whether such standing should be reserved to exclusive licensees and whether it should be conceived as a default rule from which the parties could contractually derogate.

In this respect reference can be made to Directive 2004/48/EC of the European Parliament and of the Council of 29 April 2004 on the enforcement of intellectual property rights; unfortunately this leaves the issue open by offering Member States the flexibility to decide whether licensees are to have power to initiate legal action to protect the relevant IPRs by providing that

> Member States shall recognise as persons entitled to seek application of the measures, procedures and remedies referred to in this chapter: […] b) all other persons authorised to use those rights, in particular licensees, in so far as permitted by and in accordance with the provisions of the applicable law.

This absence of a European-wide solution to address the conditions and consequences of standing to sue is not adequate: it means that a licensee with the benefit of a multiterritorial intellectual property licence covering various EU states would not necessarily have the right to sue third party infringers in a uniform manner in the relevant territories in the absence of a harmonized solution regulating this issue at the regional level. The issue of standing to sue also evidences the lack of a European-wide definition of basic intellectual property licensing concepts, specifically the respective notions of exclusive and non-exclusive licences,[53] whereby certain regulations grant standing to sue only to exclusive licensees.

---

[52] As anchored in Art. 11(2) of the Rome I Regulation (Regulation (EC) No. 593/2008 of the European Parliament and of the Council of 17 June 2008 on the law applicable to contractual obligations.

[53] On this issue, see Stiel, above note 4, 8; see also Gunda Plaß, 'Die Rechtsstellung des Markenlizenznehmers nach', § 30 III and IV MarkenG, (2002) GRUR 1029, 1031 (describing the various national regimes in the Member States relating to the standing of a trade mark licensee).

3. CONCLUSION

By focusing on certain aspects relating to European intellectual property law, this chapter has evidenced the difficulties that result from the present non-harmonized status of intellectual property licensing within the European Union. This focus does not hide the fact that other areas also call for harmonization – such as[54] (and starting with) the very issue of the definition of a licence agreement and, in particular, whether covenants not to sue would qualify as a licence,[55] and the issue of the conditions under which intellectual property rights jointly owned by several co-owners can be licensed to third parties. In this respect, it must be remembered that, even if the ECJ can valuably contribute to the debate (as shown by the cases discussed in this chapter), its role is not that of a regulator. A court is not necessarily equipped to define the key elements of a given contractual *typus*, such as the licence agreement.[56]

This lack of harmonization is regrettable at a time when there appears to be momentum for building a European contract law (as reflected in the recent proposal for a regulation on a Common European Sales Law).[57] It is therefore necessary to ensure that aspects of intellectual property licensing law are reflected in the European contract framework which is presently being envisioned,[58] given that its declared goal is – noticeably – also to regulate transactions on 'digital content'[59] (which must generally be viewed as licensing

---

54 Of course, without claim to any exhaustivity.

55 See the decision of the State Court of Mannheim (Landgericht Mannheim, 23 April 2010, Docket No. 7 O145/09,GRUR-RR 2011, 49) which contrasts with the diverging US decision in *ICOS Vision Systems Corporation NV v Scanner Technologies Corporation,* Case No. 10 Civ. 0604 (PAC) (S.D.N.Y. 15 February 2012).

56 On the process of the creation of a so-called 'small European contract law' ('petit droit européen des contrats') as coming from the ECJ case law in matters outside contract law (such as intellectual property law), see the interesting comment of Jean-Sylvestre Bergé, 'A propos du "petit droit européen des contrats": de quelques exemples récents en droit de la propriété intellectuelle', *Revue des contrats*, April 2010 N. 2, 725 (commenting on the ECJ *Dior–Copad* decision (as presented in this chapter) and the C-32/08 *FEIA* cases (dealing with the conditions of assignment of design rights). On the process of the definition of contractual types by the ECJ, see Saskia Kümmerle, 'Güter und Dienstleistungen, Vertragstypenbildung durch den EuGH', in *Vertragstypen in Europa, Historische Entwicklung und europäische Perspektiven* (Sellier 2011) 295 et seq. (commenting on the *Falco* case at 317 et seq.).

57 Proposal for a Regulation of the European Parliament and of the Council on a Common European Sales Law, 11 October 2011, COM(2011) 635 final, 2011/0284 (COD).

58 The issue of whether the basic conditions of action at the EU level are met in this context have been voluntarily left aside in this chapter: see the Proposal, ibid., 8 et seq.

59 Defined as 'data which are produced and supplied in digital form, whether or

agreements and not as contracts of sale). This is also appropriate in view of the upcoming creation of the pan-European online music licensing framework which is contemplated by the recent proposal for a Directive of the European Parliament and of the Council on collective management of copyright and related rights and multi-territorial licensing of rights in musical works for online uses in the internal market, released on 11 July 2012.[60] It can, however, be noted that this draft regulation does not contain any provision relating to the regulation of licensing contracts as such.

As a final note, if intellectual property law 'facilitates the distribution of knowledge'[61] and feeds the knowledge-based economy, intellectual property rights must be able to circulate in an efficient manner in order to maximize their use and benefits. This requires an efficient *vehicle* for this purpose and an enabling contractual law framework governing intellectual property transactions constitutes such a vehicle. It is therefore time to conceptualize and develop the contractual vehicle that will enable the efficient commercialization and licensing of intellectual property rights within Europe.[62]

---

not according to the buyer's specifications, including video, audio, picture or written digital content, digital games, software and digital content which makes it possible to personalise existing hardware or software': Art. 2(j) of the Proposal, above note56.

[60] COM(2012) 372/2); available at: http://ec.europa.eu/internal_market/copyright/docs/management/com-2012-3722_en.pdf.

[61] Single Market for Intellectual Property Rights, above note 1.

[62] See Nicolas Binctin, 'Pour un Code communautaire de la propriété intellectuelle', in *Droits de propriété intellectuelle, Liber amicorum Georges Bonet* (Litec 2010) 51, 60 (pleading for the introduction of a European intellectual property code that will include provisions on certain intellectual property contracts); Stiel, above note 4, 257 (concluding his thesis by calling for the adoption of a European intellectual property contract law – 'Immaterial gütervertragsrecht'– which would define the key features of intellectual property licence agreements); see more generally Ansgar Ohly, 'Europäisches Grundsätze des Geistigen Eigentums', in Matthias Leistner (ed.), *Europäische Perspektiven des Geistigen Eigentums* (Mohr Siebeck 2010) 190, 208 (calling for a scientific contribution to the creation of common European intellectual property principles); it must be noted in this respect that efforts have been recently made in order to create a European framework for copyright law in the remarkable Willem Project for a European Copyright Code: see http://www.jipitec.eu/issues/jipitec-1-2-2010/2622/wittem-group-european-copyright-code.pdf. On the harmonization of European copyright contract law, see Marina P. Markellou, 'Est-il nécessaire de consacrer un droit d'auteur contractuel au niveau européen?', in *The Work of George Koumantos and the Current Issues in Copyright, Symposium in Memoriam of George Koumantos* (Sakkoulas 2011) 299 et seq. Moving beyond Europe, a global harmonization would also be of the utmost value; for such an effort, see the *Research Handbook on Intellectual Property Licensing* (Edward Elgar Publishing, forthcoming), see http://www.ip-licensing.info.

6. Commercialization of genetic resources: leveraging *ex situ* genetic resources to shape downstream IP protection

Dana Beldiman

1. INTRODUCTION

Plant and microbial genetic resources exist in natural habitats and culture collections worldwide. Their scientific and economic value is rapidly gaining in importance, even though the laws governing them do not support ease of use. Genetic resources are subject to the overlapping jurisdiction of the Convention on Biological Diversity (CBD) and the Agreement on Trade Related Aspects of Intellectual Property (TRIPS). Neither of these regimes operates in a particularly access-friendly manner with respect to biological resources with imminent commercial potential. The CBD entitles countries to share benefits arising out of the use of resources originating in their territories. The scope, nature and duration of CBD obligations, and consequently of potential claims, are, however, often vague. Patent laws enacted under TRIPS, in a context of a strong growth market, fragmented patents and expensive product development, tend to function sub-optimally and allow formation of blocking patents and patent thickets. In combination, these regimes encourage a race to extract value by the beneficiaries of the entitlements created, which tends to diminish the ability to exploit high-value biological resources.

A change in the current system is unlikely, despite a growing need for facilitated accessibility and transferability of biological resources. However, intervention through contractual means is possible. The *ex situ* collections that hold genetic materials operate as contractual points of articulation between countries of origin and recipients and/or prospective developers. In that capacity collections are in a position both to negotiate clarification of CBD obligations and, by virtue of their control over the biological materials, to impose IP-related conditions on recipients.

Against this conceptual background, the World Health Organization (WHO) Framework for Pandemic Influenza Preparedness (PIP) provides the opportunity for empiric analysis. The Framework's goal is to facilitate the availability of influenza-related medicines in the event of pandemics. Its IP treatment defaults to national patent laws. In the context of the influenza-related medicines industry – characterized by a strong growth market, narrow patents and high-cost product development – national patent laws are unlikely to achieve the Framework's goal of widespread availability of influenza-related drugs at affordable prices. On the contrary, it is more probable that one player would seek to monopolize all relevant technologies and emerge as single source, or, in the alternative, that a patent thicket would discourage development.

Would alternate IP treatment help to mitigate this result and better achieve the PIP Framework's objective? If so, what treatment would be appropriate for biological resources with imminent commercial prospects? This chapter proposes the concept of a 'rebundling' of IP rights: the prospective patentee would relinquish its entitlement to full exclusivity under patent law, in exchange for freedom to operate from a patent perspective plus access to other material recipients' technology. The 'rebundling' could take the form of a patent pooling arrangement and would give multiple players a chance to participate in the market.

From a practical perspective, the patent pool would be mandated by the *ex situ* collection's Material Transfer Agreement, under which genetic materials are transferred to prospective developers. It would leverage release of the biological materials against the agreement to 'rebundle' patent rights: the greater the value of the biological materials, the greater the incentive to join. And finally, coming full circle, in the optimal scenario contractual certainty regarding CBD obligations could be obtained and would provide an added incentive to participate in a patent pool.

2. *EX SITU* GENETIC RESOURCES AND THEIR ECONOMIC VALUE

Genetic resources are materials 'of plant, animal, microbial or other origin containing functional units of heredity'.[1] They reside in natural ecosystems or habitats worldwide (*in situ* genetic resources), or, once they have been

1 UN Convention on Biological Diversity (CBD), Art. 2. The definition of 'biological resources' differs slightly in that it includes genetic resources, organisms or parts thereof, populations, or any other biotic component of ecosystems with actual or potential use or value for humanity: CBD Art. 2. On the assumption that viruses contain functional units of heredity and have actual or potential value for humanity, they would qualify as genetic or biological resources: Frederick Abbott, 'Unweaving our Tangled Patent Web: Negotiating a Framework for the Sharing of Influenza Viruses with

collected, in collections (*ex situ* genetic resources),[2] where they are validated, characterized and stored for purposes of scientific research and commercial use. Most *ex situ* collections contain plant genetic resources (biological materials derived from plants), or microbial genetic resources (microscopic biological material such as bacteria, fungi, yeasts, algae and viruses).[3] An estimated 1,300 plant genetic resource collections exist worldwide and more than 500 collections of microbial genetic resources are of record.[4]

Microbial and plant resources form the building blocks of biological research that underlies important industries such as human health and pharmaceutics,[5] agricultural productivity and food security,[6] adaptation to climate change and sustainable agriculture,[7] energy,[8] and so on. The understanding of possible uses of such resources is still evolving.[9] For instance, only 1 per cent of the world's microbial resources have been characterized.[10] Further scientific development of microbial and plant resources is likely to have a profound impact on all fields of human endeavor.

Human Pandemic Potential', Presentation at Swiss Federal Institute of Intellectual Property, 26 March 2009, available at: http://ebookbrowse.com/abbott-untangling-web-pdf-d72377873. The terms 'genetic resources' and 'genetic materials' will be used interchangeably.

2 '*Ex-situ* conservation' means the conservation of components of biological diversity outside their natural habitats: CBD, above note 1, Art. 2.

3 Tom Dedeurwaerdere, 'Self-governance and International Regulation of the Global Microbial Commons: Introduction to the Special Issue on the Microbial Commons' (2010) 4(1) *International Journal of the Commons* 390–403, 393, available at: http://www.thecommonsjournal.org/index.php/ijc/article/view/215/144.

4 More than 500 collections are registered with the World Federation of Culture Collections (WFCC). Since many collections are not registered, this number does not reflect the total number of collections worldwide. Michael Halewood, 'Governing the Management and Use of Pooled Microbial Genetic Resources: Lessons from the Global Crop Commons' (2010) 4(1) *International Journal of the Commons* 404–36, 412.

5 Approximately one half of the world's medicines are estimated to contain compounds of plant origin: Halewood, ibid., 428.

6 Ibid., 422.

7 Ibid., 423.

8 Charles McManis and Eul Soo Seo, 'The Interface of Open Source and Proprietary Agricultural Innovation: Facilitated Access and Benefit-Sharing under the New FAO Treaty' (2009) 30 *Washington University Journal of Law & Policy* 405, 406, citing Judy Keen, 'Midwest Farms Reap Benefits of Ethanol Boom', *USA Today*, 2 October 2006, 10A ('US plants can produce more than 5 billion gallons of ethanol per year, and that number will rise sharply as new facilities come on line').

9 Jerome H. Reichman, 'A Compensatory Liability Regime to Promote the Exchange of Microbial Genetic Resources for Research and Benefit Sharing', in Paul F. Uhlir (ed.), *Proceedings of the Symposium on Designing the Microbial Research Commons* (National Academies Press, forthcoming 2012).

10 Ibid.

The increase in interest in microbial and plant resources dates back only a few decades. The introduction, towards the end of the twentieth century, of new biotechnological research technologies, methods for the isolation and cultivation of microbial strains,[11] technologies relating to the freezing and shipping of samples,[12] and other technologies have resulted in intensified research. Along with it came the global realization of the considerable economic importance and commercial potential of microbiological resources,[13] followed in turn by increased worldwide collection and exploitation.[14]

3. THE APPLICABILITY OF DIFFERENT LEGAL REGIMES

In the course of their lifecycle, genetic resources are successively transferred downstream[15] from their original natural habitat, to *ex situ* collections and on to recipients in research and industry, ultimately to form the basis for innovation in a variety of industries. As a result of these transfers, genetic resources become subject to different legal regimes – specifically, benefit sharing laws enacted under the Convention on Biological Diversity and national patent laws enacted under TRIPS. Under the CBD laws, countries of origin treat genetic resources as subject to the sovereign authority of the country and exact benefit sharing in exchange for their release, whereas under national IP laws genetic resources and their derivatives are appropriated by commercial users.[16]

This legal treatment operates, separately and combined, to obstruct the free transferability of genetic resources and to diminish their ultimate usefulness

---

11 Dedeurwaerdere, 'Self-governance', above note 3, 390.

12 The increase in global exchanges of microbial and genetic resources is in part as a result of improved technologies for the handling and long-term maintenance of living microbiological samples, such as freezing and freeze-drying, easier and safer shipping of samples, etc: Tom Dedeurwaerdere, 'Global Microbial Commons: Institutional Challenges for the Global Exchange and Distribution of Microorganisms in the Life Sciences' (2010) 161(6) *Research in Microbiology* 414–21, 414, available at: http://biogov.uclouvain.be/staff/dedeurwaerdere/global_microbial_commons.PDF.

13 See generally, Dedeurwaerdere, ibid.

14 See generally, ibid.

15 The terms 'upstream' and 'downstream' describe the position of players with reference to the research and development continuum, starting with research and continuing on to final commercialization.

16 See below text accompanying notes 22 et seq.

for research, in particular for commercial applications.[17] CBD obligations, which apply in the early stages of the genetic resources' lifecycle, give rise to legal uncertainty as a result of their unspecified nature and unclear duration. Patent laws, which apply in the later stages of the lifecycle, may cause patent thickets and blocking positions, particularly where the genetic resources have imminent commercial utility. In combination, these 'encumbrances' risk preventing the widespread, affordably priced commercialization of products deriving from *ex situ* genetic resources.

3.1 The Early Stage Legal Regime

The increased collection and exploitation for commercial purposes of biologic resources led to concerns about the conservation of genetic resources and the loss of global biological diversity.[18] In response to instances of appropriation by private firms of other countries' genetic resources for their own benefit, resource-rich countries began to demand the right to share in benefits that result from commercial use of such resources.[19] This movement resulted in the adoption of the CBD in 1993 along with new ownership rules for genetic resources. The 'common heritage' doctrine that had previously governed genetic resources[20] was abandoned in favor of a rule that grants member countries sovereign rights over the genetic resources located in their territories and the right to share in benefits arising out of their use.[21]

---

17 Non-commercial use of genetic resources tends to be less impacted for a number of reasons, including high enforcement costs combined with limited recovery possibilities: see generally, Rebecca Eisenberg, 'Noncompliance, Nonenforcement, Nonproblem? Rethinking the Anticommons in Biomedical Research' (2008) 45 *Houston Law Review* 1959.

18 'Probably the most immediate threat to human welfare posed by the loss of biological diversity arises from the shrinkage of the plant gene pools available to agricultural scientists and farmers': McManis, above note 8, 412.

19 Sabrina Safrin, 'Hyperownership in a Time of Biotechnological Promise: The International Conflict to Control the Building Blocks of Life' (2004) 98 *American Journal of International Law* 641, 668; McManis, above note 8, 418, noting that the movement towards creating international rules relating to protection of genetic resources is a relatively recent one.

20 Safrin, ibid., 654.

21 'Recognizing the sovereign rights of States over their natural resources, the authority to determine access to genetic resources rests with the national governments and is subject to national legislation': CBD, above note 21, Art. 15.1. 'Each Contracting Party shall take … measures, … with the aim of sharing in a fair and equitable way the results of research and development and the benefits arising from the commercial and other utilization of genetic resources with the Contracting Party providing such resources': CBD, Art. 15.7.

3.1.1 The Convention on Biological Diversity (CBD)

The CBD's objectives include conservation of biological diversity and 'fair and equitable sharing of the benefits arising out of the utilization of genetic resources'.[22]

Its terms reflect the concern among biodiversity-rich developing countries that resources removed and appropriated by firms from developed countries would be depleted, without providing benefit to the countries of origin.[23] To counteract such practices,[24] the CBD grants its members sovereign rights and national control over the raw genetic materials (including plants, animals and micro-organisms) located within their national boundaries.[25] Countries are thus entitled to control access to genetic resources and demand fair and equitable sharing of any benefit derived from their use. As a quid pro quo for access to the genetic resources of developing countries,[26] the CBD aims to encourage support for developing countries of origin through monetary benefit sharing, technology transfers, capacity building, sharing of and collaboration in research, training, providing human resources, and so on.[27]

To date, the CBD has more than 190 member countries.[28] With a growing number of countries implementing the CBD and a generally heightened sense of the value of genetic resources,[29] countries rich in such resources are placing increased emphasis on compensation for access to those resources.[30]

---

22 CBD, ibid., Art. 15.

23 Safrin, above note 19, 654. The concern over 'biopiracy' has been voiced by many developing countries: see James O. Odek, 'Bio-Piracy: Creating Proprietary Rights in Plant Genetic Resources' (1994) 2 *Journal of Intellectual Property Law* 141, 141.

24 Ibid.

25 CBD, above note 1, Arts. 15.1 and 15.7.

26 CBD, ibid.; the Bonn Guidelines on Access to Genetic Resources and Fair and Equitable Sharing of the Benefits Arising out of their Utilization (available at: http://www.cbd.int/doc/publications/cbd-bonn-gdls-en.pdf) and the Nagoya Protocol on Access and Benefit-sharing (available at: http://www.cbd.int/abs) specify the type of benefit sharing that might be required, and provide for a national central authority to deal with issues that arise from it.

27 CBD, ibid., the Annex to the Nagoya Protocol, ibid., provides an extensive list of Monetary and Non-Monetary Benefits.

28 CBD, ibid., List of Parties, available at: http://www.cbd.int/convention/parties/list.

29 Safrin, above note 19, 204.

30 Lawrence Helfer, *Human Rights and Intellectual Property: Mapping the Global Interface* (Cambridge University Press 2011) 393. '[T]he frictionless exchange of biological materials within a global commons, which prevailed during the early days of modern life sciences, now seems to be reversed … as more and more biological materials are enclosed behind national and privatized fences, or only accessible under very restrictive license conditions': Dedeurwaerdere, 'Self-governance', above note 3, 391.

3.1.2 The uncertainty of CBD obligations

There seems little doubt that the CBD access and benefit sharing provisions apply to *in situ* genetic resources located in their natural habitat in countries of origin.[31] To what extent, absent express contractual provisions,[32] CBD obligations also cover *ex situ* genetic resources, or whether such obligations are exhausted by the transaction between depositor and collection, remains unclear.[33] Assuming such obligations apply, their scope under national legislation may vary considerably and lack specificity.[34] Certainty regarding the CBD's coverage of the genetic layer – the most useful and potentially lucrative aspect of biological resources – is critical, and includes coverage of DNA isolates and genetic information extracted from genetic resources, the relevance of the persistence of the original materials' molecules in isolated or purified DNA, coverage of derivatives and byproducts of the original genetic resources, and so on. Finally, assuming such aspects are covered, the nature of the shared benefit owed also remains to be clarified.[35]

Because these uncertainties cannot be factored into decisions to develop commercial products, claims under national laws enacted pursuant to the CBD may become obstacles to investment and commercialization.[36]

---

31 CBD, above note 1, Arts. 8 and 15.

32 Survey data show that most new materials are deposited without conditions: Dedeurwaerdere, 'Self-governance', above note 3, 395. Nine major culture collections use formal deposit forms but this fact does not preclude future assertion of benefit sharing claims, against either the collection or downstream users.

33 Frederick Abbott, 'An International Legal Framework for the Sharing of Pathogens', ICTSD, *Intellectual Property and Sustainable Development Series*, Issue Paper 30, October 2010, 24 et seq., available at: http://ictsd.org/i/publications/89485/?view=MoreDetails.

34 Certain national laws define the scope of ownership in some detail, including whether they include byproducts or derivatives at a genetic level. For instance, under the Andean Pact's Common System, sovereign ownership covers raw genetic material and derivatives of such genetic resources, such as molecules: Safrin, above note 219, 650. On the other hand, coverage may be subject to limitations, e.g. 'products which may contain portions or extracts of plants and animals in unrecognizable and physically inseparable form' which are not subject to its national sovereignty under India's Biological Diversity Act 2002: Safrin, ibid., 651, note 71, See also Keith Aoki, 'Free Seeds, Not Free Beer: Participatory Plant Breeding, Open Source Seeds, and Acknowledging User Innovation in Agriculture' (2009) 77 *Fordham Law Review* 2275, 2296.

35 The Nagoya Protocol, above note 26, lists both 'monetary' and 'non-monetary' benefit sharing. A manufacturer may prefer to provide monetary or in-kind benefit over transfer of technology. Yet, unless negotiated in advance, it is conceivable that a claim may be based on any type of benefit listed in the Nagoya Protocol.

36 Halewood, above note 4, 423.

3.2 The Later Stage Legal Regime

At the later stage of the innovation cycle, when the commercial endpoint of their development is sufficiently clear, genetic resources become subject to national patent laws enacted under TRIPS.

3.2.1 WTO Trade Related Aspects of Intellectual Property (TRIPS)[37]

The TRIPS Agreement was negotiated at about the same time as the CBD. Designed to 'promote effective and adequate protection of intellectual property rights',[38] the TRIPS Agreement requires member states to enact national patent laws that have the effect of protecting both plant and microbial genetic resources.[39] Its mandatory minimum standards provide for national patent protection of inventions in 'all fields of technology'.[40] Technology includes biotechnology and covers micro-organisms and microbiological processes.[41] Patent protection of plants is optional, but member states who opt against such protection must protect plant varieties by 'an effective *sui generis* system or by any combination thereof'.[42] In short, microbial genetic resources fall under national patent laws as micro-organisms, while plant genetic resources may be protected by either patent or plant variety protection laws,[43] such as the *sui generis* system that protects breeders' rights in plant varieties.[44]

Patent laws grant the patentee the right 'to prevent third parties not having the owner's consent from the acts of: making, using, offering for sale, selling, or importing' the patented product or process.[45] Commercial firms are likely

---

[37] Trade Related Aspects of Intellectual Property Agreement (TRIPS), available at: http://www.wto.org/english/docs_e/legal_e/27-trips.pdf.

[38] TRIPS was concluded in 1993, as part of the Uruguay Round of Multilateral Trade Negotiations which created the World Trade Organization.

[39] TRIPS, Preamble, para. 1.

[40] TRIPS grants protection to inventions in any field of technology that are new, display an inventive step and are capable of industrial application: TRIPS, Art. 27.

[41] TRIPS, Art. 27.3(b) creates an optional exemption for 'plants and animals other than micro organisms, and essentially biological processes for the production of plants or animals other than non-biological and microbiological processes'.

[42] TRIPS, Art. 27.3(b).

[43] International Convention for the Protection of New Varieties of Plants (Union Internationale pour la Protection des Obtentions Vegetales) (UPOV), adopted in 1961, and last amended in 1991, available at: http://www.wipo.int/wipolex/en/other_treaties/details.jsp?treaty_id=27.

[44] The UPOV grants plant breeders protection to plant varieties that are new (novel), clearly distinguishable by one or more important characteristics (distinct), homogeneous in their sexual reproduction or vegetative propagation (uniform), and stable in their essential characteristics (stable): UPOV, Art. 6.

[45] TRIPS, above note 38, Art. 28.1(a).

to make maximum use of TRIPS-enabled provisions in all jurisdictions in which the Convention has been implemented.[46]

3.2.2 The impact of patent laws

Certain conditions – which include a strong growth market, narrow and fragmented patents, a congested patent scene and expensive development – will cause the patent system to function sub-optimally with respect to genetic resource-based products with clear commercial prospects.[47] Specifically, the prospect of successful commercialization based on a scarce resource, such as genetic resources, may cause parties to seek to monopolize the market by use of patent law. Alternatively, companies might be daunted by patent thickets: that is, impediments such as a large number of licenses to be obtained for freedom to operate, high associated transaction costs, stacked royalty obligations, uncertainty regarding the grant of patents, uncertainty regarding the ability to secure all necessary licenses, and so on.[48] Without intervention, these conditions risk interference with optimal commercialization and the social usefulness of genetic resources-based products.

4. THE ROLE OF *EX SITU* COLLECTIONS AND MATERIAL TRANSFER AGREEMENTS

Beneficiaries of entitlements under CBD and TRIPS laws, discussed above, are likely to race to extract value from potentially successful genetic resources-based products. This race risks interfering with, or even preventing the transfer, research and development of these resources.[49] The following will explore use of the contractual structure surrounding transfers of genetic resources between depositors, *ex situ* collection and recipient to mitigate these effects.

Ex situ culture collections contain genetic material deposits received from donors worldwide.[50] The role of the collections is to maintain the materials and make them available to third parties for research or commercial

---

46 The deadline for full implementation by least developed countries of the TRIPS provisions is 2016: see http://www.wto.org/english/thewto_e/whatis_e/tif_e/org7_e.htm.

47 See below text accompanying notes 103 et seq.

48 See below text accompanying notes 126 et seq.

49 See below text accompanying notes 126 et seq.

50 There is a push for harmonized models of distributing materials to the relevant community: Halewood, above note 4, 423.

purposes.[51] Collections are self-governing and have quasi-legislative powers over most aspects relating to the genetic resources they maintain.[52]

Collections contract with both depositors and recipients and thus act as an interface between the two sides.[53] On the recipient side, most collections use a material transfer agreement (MTA), a contractual instrument the main objective of which is to establish conditions relating to the transfer of physical genetic material. However, a collection may also use the MTA to regulate aspects beyond the mere material transfer.[54] Using its ability to withhold or release genetic resources materials as leverage, a collection is free to impose conditions in exchange for release of genetic resources.[55] In this way, an MTA can effectively serve to address two important aspects that risk giving rise to obstacles to downstream exploitation: (i) the uncertainty regarding CBD benefit sharing obligations, and (ii) the allocation of IP rights in a way that avoids downstream patent thickets or monopolization of genetic resources-related technologies by a single party.[56]

---

51 Some collections treat genetic resources as public goods: Dedeurwaerdere, above note 12, 397. Maintenance of collections requires a number of complex tasks, including validation of samples, characterization, implementing tracking mechanisms, and so on.

52 Aoki, above note 34, 2289.

53 Recipients of *ex situ* genetic resources from collections are typically university laboratories, pharmaceutical companies and small R&D companies.

54 The concept of leveraging access to *ex situ* genetic resources for creating funds that promote benefit sharing is not new. 'In exchange for access to this communal seed treasury held in governmental and international seed banks, private parties that incorporate materials from the multilateral system into commercial products must pay a percentage of their profits into a trust account … to promote benefit-sharing and conservation of genetic resources, particularly with regard to farmers in developing countries': Laurence R. Helfer, 'Using Intellectual Property Rights to Preserve the Global Genetic Commons: The International Treaty on Plant Genetic Resources for Food and Agriculture', in Keith E. Maskus and Jerome H. Reichman (eds), *International Public Goods and Transfer of Technology under a Globalized Intellectual Property Regime* (Cambridge University Press 2005) 217, 219–20.

55 'Culture collections clearly have rights in the material they manage and preserve. Having these rights they also can specify the conditions under which they distribute the material': Dedeurwaerdere, above note 12, 372 et seq.; Aoki, above note 34, 2302. However, the terms and conditions under which distribution occurs must be in conformity with international law: Halewood, above note 4, 423.

56 It is recognized that most genetic resources do not realize their value until toward the end of their use: Dedeurwaerdere, above note 3, 394. Most likely, those genetic resources with more immediate commercial potential provide greater leverage.

4.1 Benefit Sharing Obligations under the CBD

Because the collection is in the best position to negotiate dovetailed conditions governing materials intake on the one side, and conditions governing release of materials on the other,[57] an MTA can, in principle, help to overcome uncertainty regarding the applicability, scope and duration of potential benefit sharing obligations.[58]

How to approach the question from a strategy standpoint, however, is far from clear. Addressing the issue may create a previously non-existent obligation, the beneficiary of which might never have asserted its rights. Silence on the topic would maintain the uncertainty and leave open the possibility of inflated claims downstream. From the perspective of a recipient and prospective developer of materials, clarity would be welcome, as would the resulting increase in value of the materials received.[59] In the optimal case, a collection could thus attempt to obtain a waiver of benefit sharing. Alternatively, specifics regarding the nature and scope of benefit sharing should be negotiated.[60] Obtaining clarity would benefit not only subsequent transferees, but also the collection,[61] in that imposing obligations on recipients could help to build credibility with depositors.

4.2 Allocation of Intellectual Property Rights

In addition to seeking clarity on the benefit sharing aspect, a collection is in a position to favor certain policy outcomes by affirmatively influencing downstream behavior[62] regarding IP ownership.[63] For instance, conditioning the release of collection materials on an agreement not so seek patent protection, combined with a reach-through provision, could be effective throughout the lifecycle of the materials and their derivatives. This type of provision is

---

57 Dedeurwaerdere, above note 12, 372 et seq.

58 See above text accompanying note 31.

59 It is assumed that clarity regarding rights and obligations under CBD laws would increase the value of the materials.

60 Such specifics would include whether monetary or non-monetary compensation is at issue, royalty rates, whether and to what extent the obligations extend to derivatives, genetic information, and so on.

61 Specificity on whether the donor is entitled to assert future benefit sharing claims against the collection or any downstream user or whether such rights have been exhausted by any already existing benefit sharing provisions will enhance the strength of subsequent transfers.

62 See Halewood, above note 4, 423 note 17.

63 Commercial transactions would be facilitated to a greater extent as currently the conditions for commercial use in the microbial field differ considerably: Dedeurwaerdere, above note 12, 366.

conceptually akin to an open source license in the software field and its policy outcome would favor broad access.[64] On the other hand, if the policy goal were to ensure widespread and affordably priced commercialization, an MTA might address the following aspects.

As a first consideration, IP rights in the materials themselves (microbial or plant genetic resources) must be allocated. Most national patent laws prohibit patenting of both the physical and the information layer of the materials as discoveries or phenomena which occur in nature.[65] Less clear is the status of isolated or purified genes,[66] the patentability of which depends on the extent of the changes made to the underlying material.[67] Consistent with the view that *ex situ* genetic resources, as released by the collection, are products of nature, an MTA would most likely provide that neither the collection nor any recipient is entitled to obtain patent protection for the materials themselves, in the form released by the collection.[68] Silence on this issue involves the risk that recipients might obtain patents on genetic inventions in jurisdictions with more liberal patenting laws[69] and possibly preclude others from using the technology in the respective jurisdiction.

The second and possibly most important consideration is the allocation of IP rights relating to derivatives of the materials released from the collection. Derivatives are the result of follow-on research or incremental improvements that, by way of an inventive effort, effect changes in the underlying materials.[70]

---

[64] Robin Feldman, 'The Open Source Biotechnology Movement: Is It Patent Misuse?' (2004) 6 *Minnesota Journal of Law Science & Technology* 117, 118.

[65] The materials would be excluded as discoveries: see *Diamond v Chakrabarty*, 447 U.S. 303 (1980); EPC 52.2(a).

[66] The treatment to be given to isolated or purified genetic sequences remains unclear under patent laws: *Association for Molecular Pathology v Myriad* Genetics, US Court of Appeals, Federal Circuit, No. 2010–1406, 29 July 2011, and some treaty texts; see Helfer, above note 30, 399.

[67] See *Association for Molecular Pathology v Myriad Genetics*, ibid., holding that an isolated gene has a markedly different chemical structure than that found in nature, which makes it a distinct chemical entity that is patentable, while some questions remain as to purified genes.

[68] How the term 'as released by the collection' is to be interpreted is unclear, as commented upon in connection with Art. 12.3(d) International Treaty on Plant Genetic Resources for Food and Agriculture, available at: http://www.planttreaty.org; Helfer, above note 30, 399; McManis, above note 8, 455.

[69] For example, the US: *Diamond v Chakrabarty*, above note 65, and *Association for Molecular Pathology v Myriad Genetics*, above note 66, or the EU: EU Biotechnology Directive 98/44/EC.

[70] Often multiple sequential improvements are required to assemble a product: A. Krattiger and S.P. Kowalski, 'Facilitating Assembly of and Access to Intellectual Property: Focus on Patent Pools and a Review of Other Mechanisms in Intellectual Property Management', in A. Krattiger, R.T. Mahoney, L. Nelsen et al. (eds), *Health*

Most innovation occurs in small incremental steps.[71] To the extent they meet the patentability requirements, improvements are generally patentable under the national laws of TRIPS member countries.[72] IP rights to improvements can be allocated in different ways.

At one end of the spectrum, improvements may be freely appropriated by the improver and, as appropriate, patented. Patent protection generally tends to promote commercialization. An MTA's silence on downstream IP treatment would therefore, in principle, also favor commercialization as, by default, national patent laws would apply. In some instances, however – particularly in the biotech field where designing around is often not a viable solution – issuance of one or more patents may block the entire field, making it inaccessible to new inventors.[73] This scenario would limit the number of patent holders and reduce competition. Unrestricted patenting is thus not always conducive to widespread, affordably priced commercialization. At the other end of the spectrum, patenting of improvements would be prohibited in much the same way as in an open source software license.[74] This scenario may be an even more serious deterrent to investment into commercialization, as investors into product development would be concerned about the absence of exclusive rights.

In the ultimate analysis, neither of these models is satisfactory. As will be shown below, a hybrid model which allows patenting but rebundles patent rights to allocate them among multiple parties may be the most effective in favoring commercialization, with the added benefit of not foreclosing on third parties from accessing the technology.[75]

---

and Agenetic Resources in Cultural Innovation: A Handbook of Best Practices (MIHR and PIPRA 2007) Chapter 2.8, available at: http://www.ipHandbook.org. For the view that the issue of sequential improvement is not well solved by the patent system, see J. Reichman, 'Intellectual Property in the Twenty-First Century: Will the Developing Countries Lead or Follow?' (2009) 46 *Houston Law Review* 1115–85.

[71] Matthew Conigliaro et al., 'Foreseeability in Patent Law' (2001) 16 *Berkeley Technology Law Journal* 1045, 1053 ('Generally, pioneering advances provide great leaps in society's collective progress, while technological improvements provide the multitudes of incremental steps necessary to realize the full potential of major, as well as minor, discoveries').

[72] To be entitled to patent protection, inventions must display novelty, an inventive step (non-obviousness) and are capable of industrial application (usefulness): TRIPS, above note 37, Art. 27.

[73] Linda J. Demaine and Aaron Xavier Fellmeth, 'Reinventing the Double Helix: A Novel and Nonobvious Reconceptualization of the Biotechnology Patent' (2002) 55 *Stanford Law Review* 303, 418; see also below text accompanying notes 116 et. seq.

[74] Feldman, above note 64, 118.

[75] While most innovation occurs by way of sequential incremental improvement, the issue of allocation of rights to such improvements is not well solved by the patent system: see Reichman, above note 70.

A final important consideration is whether the MTA's terms and conditions are binding on the recipient alone, or whether downstream transferees are also bound by the provisions (with reach-through effect).[76] If the contractual obligations bind only the parties to the agreement, the contracting party's transferee may handle IP unrestrictedly. For a more extensive reach, the obligations created must attach to ('run with') the genetic resources and their derivatives.

Having set the conceptual framework regarding the legal status of *ex situ* genetic resources under the CBD and TRIPS and the role that collections can play in terms of smoothing the path of genetic resources towards ultimate use, we now turn to a discussion of how these concepts can work in practice, using as an example the WHO agreement for sharing influenza virus samples.[77]

5. THE WHO PANDEMIC INFLUENZA PREPAREDNESS FRAMEWORK FOR THE SHARING OF INFLUENZA VIRUSES AND ACCESS TO VACCINES AND OTHER BENEFITS (PIP)

The PIP is the product of long-drawn negotiations conducted by the WHO relating to access to and dissemination of influenza virus samples. The framework agreement was concluded in May 2011 and approved by the World Health Assembly (WHA) in June 2011.[78] Negotiation of the PIP was largely triggered by Indonesia's refusal to share H5N1 influenza samples with the international research and pharmaceutical community during the H5N1 influenza pandemic of 2007.[79] The PIP consists of a framework agreement (the Framework) and two proposed standard MTAs.[80] It covers the 'H5N1 virus and other influenza viruses with human pandemic potential'.[81]

---

[76] Michael Heller and Rebecca Eisenberg consider that reach-through provisions in principle can be advantageous to both patent holders and researchers: Michael Heller and Rebecca Eisenberg, 'Can Patents Deter Innovation? The Anticommons in Biomedical Research' (1998) 280 *Science* 698, 699.

[77] Pandemic Influenza Preparedness Framework for the Sharing of Influenza Viruses and Access to Vaccines and other Benefits (PIP), available at: http://www.who.int/influenza/pip/en/.

[78] Its funding scheme has been described as innovative and sustainable: participating manufacturers who use WHO Global Influenza Surveillance and Response System (GISRS) will contribute collectively 50% of running costs of use. In exchange, they have no further payment obligations for receipt of the materials or follow-on obligations in case of commercialization: PIP Framework, ibid., Art. 78, Art. 6.14.

[79] Reuters, 'Indonesia, Baxter sign pact on bird flu vaccine', available at: http://www.reuters.com/article/2007/02/07/idUSJAK76679._CH_.2400.

[80] PIP Framework, above note 77, Art. 78, SMTA, Art. 1 and 2. Two different

The PIP attempts to strike a balance between public health needs and the ability to successfully commercialize proprietary medicines in small and uncertain markets.[82] From an IP perspective, the guiding principles of the PIP Framework recited in the Introductory Principles recognize both that 'intellectual property rights do not and should not prevent Member States from taking measures to protect public health' and 'that intellectual property rights are an important incentive in the development of new health care products, but insufficient to meet the need for the development of new products to fight diseases where 'the potential paying market is small or uncertain'.[83]

The tension inherent in these guiding principles is reflected in the negotiations and the ultimately agreed upon version of the Framework. Some proposals have sought to prohibit the patenting of influenza biological materials outside the WHO system altogether.[84] Others have required parties who made 'patent or other intellectual property rights' claims based on the virus samples received, to 'disclose in the patent application, the country from where [the samples] were collected'.[85] If commercialization were to result in financial gain, contributions should be made to the WHO's Coordinated International

---

standard MTA forms are provided, depending on whether the recipient party is 'participating' or 'non-participating' in funding the WHO GISRS Centers (hereafter SMTA1 and SMTA2).

81 PIP Framework, ibid., Art. 78, Art. 2.1(i).

82 PIP Framework, Preamble: 'intellectual property rights do not and should not prevent Member States from taking measures to protect public health' and 'that intellectual property rights are an important incentive in the development of new health care products. However, this incentive alone does not meet the need for the development of new products to fight diseases where the potential paying market is small or uncertain': PIP Framework, ibid., Art 78, Preamble, PP13.

83 PIP Framework, ibid., Preamble, PP13.

84 This proposal was made by Bolivia, whose position was that the 'patenting of influenza biological materials in particular in a pandemic preparedness context', is against public health interests and thus contradicts the primary objective of the WHO's activities: Report by the Open-Ended Working Group of Member States on Pandemic Influenza Preparedness: Sharing of Influenza Viruses and Access to Vaccines and Other Benefits, CORRIGENDUM, A64/8 Corr1, 12 May 2011, available at: http://apps.who.int/gb/ebwha/pdf_files/WHA64/A64_8Corr1-en.pdf. In the spirit of cooperation Bolivia eventually withdrew this proposal, but indicated that it would reserve 'its rights to seek a prohibition of patenting of influenza biological materials outside WHO': Catherine Saez, 'WHO Members on Verge of New Framework for Pandemic Flu Response', 23 May 2011, available at: http://www.ip-watch.org/weblog/2011/05/23/who-members-on-verge-of-new-framework-for-pandemic-flu-response.

85 Charles Lawson, 'Who Shall Live When Not All Can Live? Intellectual Property in Accessing and Benefit-sharing Influenza Viruses through the World Health Organization' (2011) 18(3) *Journal of Law and Medicine* 554–76, note 123, citing A/PIP/IGM/4, note 119 Annex, Appendix 3 at [31]–[32].

Sharing of Influenza Viruses & Benefits Agreement.[86] A further proposal made was that for

> IPR … obtained on inventions derived from the use of the Materials, the holder [provider] of such rights should grant to WHO a non-exclusive, royalty free license, which WHO will sub-license to interested developing countries for the purpose of maximizing availability of critical benefits on a non-profit basis, such as vaccines and antivirals for pandemic influenza preparedness purposes.[87]

None of these proposals were included in the final version. The final agreed version merely provides that the owner of deposited materials agrees to their 'onward transfer and use',[88] without further restrictions.

The Framework does, however, contain several voluntary provisions. SMTA2, the MTA applicable to recipients outside the GISRS system,[89] allows for certain options for voluntary benefit sharing measures. A recipient may select from two out of six different choices, four of which relate to payment and pricing benefits. The remaining two relate to the licensing and transfer of IP.[90] To the extent that technology is licensed to WHO, it may be sublicensed to manufacturers in developing countries.[91]

In short, from an IP rights perspective, no mandatory provision is included, except the one prohibiting parties from seeking intellectual property rights in the materials.[92] Both the Framework and the MTAs are silent regarding down-

---

86 Ibid. However, the question of whether the influenza virus can properly be considered a 'genetic resource' covered by the benefit sharing provisions of the CBD has apparently been resolved in favor of including the influenza virus among genetic resources: Abbott, above note 1.

87 Lawson, ibid., 569, citing A63/48, note 162, Annex (Appendix 2, White Paper 1 and at [4.1.3], [4.1.5] and [4.3].

88 PIP Framework, above note 77, Art. 78, Art. 5.1.2. and SMTA, Arts. 1 and 2.

89 Materials may be distributed to recipients, any manufacturer or laboratory that is qualified, i.e. which meets appropriate biosafety guidelines and best practices: PIP Framework, Art, 6.3 bis. Recipients may be 'outside the WHO GISRS', in which case SMTA1 governs, or 'within the WHO GISRS' and governed by SMTA2.

90 Recipients may (a) grant to manufacturers in developing countries licences on mutually agreed terms that should be fair and reasonable including, in respect of affordable royalties, taking into account development levels in the country of end use of the products, on technology, know-how, products and processes for which it holds IPR for the production of (i) influenza vaccines, (ii) adjuvants, (iii) antivirals and/or (iv) diagnostics or (b) grant royalty free licences to manufacturers in developing countries or grant to WHO royalty-free, non-exclusive licenses on IPR, which can be sublicensed, for the production of pandemic influenza vaccines, adjuvants, antivirals products and diagnostics needed in a pandemic: PIP Framework, above note 77, Art. 78; SMTA2, Art. 4.1.1 A5.

91 PIP Framework, ibid., Art. 78, SMTA2. Art. 4.1.1 A6.

92 PIP Framework, ibid., Art. 78, SMTA1 and SMTA2, Art. 6.1.

stream IP issues. This leaves recipients free to treat as fully proprietary all derivatives from samples received from WHO Centres, while recipients may, on a voluntary basis, grant licenses to manufacturers in developing countries or to the WHO, with a right to sublicense.[93] The structure of the options is such that recipients can meet their obligations by providing product (vaccines or treatment courses) or monetary compensation instead. Given commercial realities, it is likely that owners of critical patents will select these options over the licensing options.[94]

The next section will consider how development of influenza-related drugs would unfold under the terms of the PIP Framework described above and how the failure to address IP rights can impact upon the PIP Framework's broader objectives of ensuring widespread supply of influenza-related medicines.

6. THE MTA AT WORK

The broader goal of the PIP Framework is to ensure the reliable and adequate supply of medicines in the event of a pandemic, in quantities and at an overall cost level that is affordable to both developed and developing countries. How effectively this goal can be achieved is contingent on the interrelation of a number of factors, including market conditions, the characteristics of the industry and governing IP provisions.

The following section will discuss how these three factors interrelate in terms of achieving the PIP Framework's goal as described above. The discussion will show that, given the influenza medicine industry and market conditions, the PIP Framework's current IP treatment is not optimally designed to promote its stated goals. Instead, this chapter proposes an alternative approach to IP issues, in the form of a patent pooling arrangement for all patents derived from virus samples obtained from the WHO Centres. This chapter suggests that this approach is overall more likely to achieve broad availability of influenza medicines, along with greater flexibility with respect to non-commercial uses and satisfying obligations that may arise under the CBD.

We will start with a discussion of the influenza industry and market.

---

93 PIP Framework, ibid., Art. 78, SMTA2. Art. 4.1.1. A5 and A6.

94 The nature of benefit sharing can impact upon different stakeholders differently: technology transfers (sharing of knowledge) compared to royalties favors access and increases the flow of information. Benefit sharing in kind (providing benefit in the form of product) favors the manufacturer, as product is available to the manufacturer at marginal cost, whereas the benefit to the recipient can be up to market price.

6.1 The Influenza Medicine Market

Influenza-related medicines[95] include products intended for prevention, diagnostic and treatment of influenza, both in pandemic situations and for preventive purposes.

Since the pandemics of the H1N1 and H5N1 influenza strains in 2005 and 2009 respectively, governments, national health care organizations and international organizations have provided increased support and funding for antiviral research and development programmes, product development and pandemic prevention.[96] Furthermore, governments, healthcare organizations and other players have begun to stockpile antivirals as a method of preparedness and disease containment in case of a pandemic. As a result, sales in the influenza-related drug industry have grown at a much faster rate than has the overall pharmaceutical market.[97] Statistics show that sales have more than tripled from $2.2 billion in 2004 to $7 billion in 2009, and the total market is expected to reach $10 billion by 2015.[98]

The high market growth rate and the availability of funding are attractive to players in the industry. Many diverse organizations, both commercial and non-commercial – including government, academia, small R&D companies and vaccine manufacturers – are now active in the upstream influenza drug space.[99]

This heightened activity is correlated with intensified patenting. One study notes that a sharp rise in patent applications based on the H5N1 virus occurred just shortly after the outbreak of the H5N1 2005 pandemic.[100] Specifically, the study identified 63 applications under the Patent Cooperation Treaty (PCT) for influenza vaccines in 2010, compared to 19 applications in 2001.[101] The appli-

---

[95] Influenza-related medicines are part of the 'biologics' subset of the pharmaceutical industry in which products are created from living organisms (such as vaccines, antibiotics, rDNA products): Hillary Greene, 'Patent Pooling Behind the Veil of Uncertainty: Antitrust, Competition Policy' (2010) 90 *Boston University Law Review* 1397, 1407.

[96] See http://www.healthcarepackaging.com/archives/2009/09/global_influenza_market_to_be.php.

[97] 'Global Pandemic Influenza Preparedness Market Forecast 2010–2015', Market Research Media, available at: http://www.marketresearchmedia.com/2009/04/24/pandemic-influenza-market/.

[98] Ibid.

[99] Greene, above note 95, 1410.

[100] Edward Hammond, 'An Update on Intellectual Property Claims Related To Global Pandemic Influenza Preparedness', Third World Network, 8 April 2011, available at: http://www.twnside.org.sg/title2/IPR/pdf/ipr15.pdf.

[101] The applications considered in this study include only the patents narrowly derived from this particular strain.

cants include pharmaceutical manufacturers, biotech companies and research centres, coming mainly from the United States, Belgium, Switzerland, the Netherlands and France. A further study, performed under the auspices of WIPO at about the same time, indicates a similar rise in patent applications for the H5N1 and the H1N1 viruses.[102] Both studies refer strictly to patents based on the H5N1 and H1N1 virus strains. They do not include any of the other technologies that may be necessary for the development of influenza diagnostics, prophylactics and therapeutics products.

These statistics generally indicate that the influenza drug industry is characterized by a concentration of numerous players and intensive patent activity in a relatively small space.

6.2 Patenting in the Influenza Drug Field

Besides the concentration of patent activity in the influenza space, the narrowness and fragmentation of biotechnology patents in general also contributes to the difficulties of drug development in this field.

Claims on different aspects of drug development – such as adjuvants or other formulation technologies, sequences, production technologies or combinations thereof – are generally contained in separate patents.[103] The manufacture of influenza drug products consequently requires assembly of multiple patented technologies mostly owned by different patentees.[104] The need for several patents to be aggregated to produce a viable product[105] means that they have to be licensed from other patentees in order to achieve freedom to operate in the space.[106] To accomplish this, a drug developer would have to

---

102 While providing valuable analysis on the types of patent filed, the WIPO study, in its own terms, does not evaluate the situation from a 'freedom-to-operate' perspective: WIPO Patent Search Report on Pandemic Influenza Preparedness (PIP) Related Patents and Patent Applications, 1 April 2011 (the WIPO Report) 31, available at: http://www.wipo.int/patentscope/en/programs/patent_landscapes/documents/patent_landscapes/influenza_full_report_01_04_2011.pdf.

103 Greene, above note 95, note 15, citing Edward Hammond, 'Some Intellectual Property Issues Related to H5N1 Influenza Viruses, Research and Vaccines, The Sunshine Project, Third World Network, July 2007, available at: http://www.sunshine-project.org/flu/patent_report.pdf.

104 Krattiger and Kowalski, above note 70, 132: 'An invention must be assembled by putting together the patents and other forms of intellectual property from third parties.'

105 See Dan L. Burk and Mark A. Lemley, 'Biotechnology's Uncertainty Principle' (2004) 54 *Case Western Reserve Law Review* 691, 738.

106 Aoki describes a similar situation in the field of genetic resources which result in an anticommons in the field of biology. 'These 'transformation technologies' combine information 'from many areas of biology, including crop genetics, breeding,

traverse a 'patent thicket' in order to assemble the necessary technologies.[107] This process is associated with high transaction costs, complex negotiations, delays and uncertainty.[108]

The regulatory environment under which the pharmaceutical industry operates adds further uncertainty and cost. In major drug-producing countries, the pharmaceutical industry is heavily burdened by regulatory requirements. The path from patented invention to a marketable drug is expensive and uncertain. Many patented or patentable inventions remain on the shelves at research centres because bringing the invention to the market stage is too costly and uncertain.[109] A drug developer must contend with the uncertainty and cost of regulatory approval and clinical trials. Additionally, production in the biologics industries is subject to particularly rigorous manufacturing standards. Combined, these conditions result in a cost of bringing a drug to the market that ranges close to $1 billion.[110]

Given these circumstances, companies might be daunted by the combination of high development costs and the uncertainty of being able to secure freedom to operate from a patent perspective[111] (the number of licenses to be

---

agronomy, pest control and agro-ecology' that make 'innovation ... cumulative, in the sense that each invention builds on previous inventions, and complementary, in the sense that each invention contains elements derived from more than one source. ...What these various proprietary claims on plant phenotype, genotype, and gene sequences within the plant begin to create is an 'anticommons'. Here, an 'anticommons' entails a situation in which a particular resource is underutilized because of too many bottlenecks where several permissions must be obtained due to overlapping property/ownership claims': Aoki, above note 34, 2297.

107 Greene, above note 95, note 18. Parties wishing to commercialize must find their way through the 'tangled, twisted mass of IPRs, which criss-cross the established walkways of commerce, rather, it requires numerous contracts with multiple, independent right holders': Robert Merges, 'Contracting into Liability Rules: Intellectual Property Rights and Collective Rights' (1996) 84 *California Law Review* 1293, 1296. An anticommons, a related concept, is an accumulation of 'too many IP rights in "upstream" research results that could ... restrict "downstream" research and product development by making it costly and burdensome to collect all the necessary licenses': Michael Heller and Rebecca Eisenberg, 'Can Patents Deter Innovation? The Anticommons in Biomedical Research (1998) 280 *Science* 698; Eisenberg, above note 17, 1060. A player would be faced with an anticommons if the burden of negotiating the licences necessary is disproportionate to the expected value of the product or the expected gain.

108 See generally, Greene, above note 95.

109 A. Rai, J. Reichman, P. Uhlir and C. Crossman, 'Pathways Across the Valley of Death: Novel Intellectual Property Strategies for Accelerated Drug Discovery' (2008) 8 *Yale Journal of Health Policy, Law and Ethics* 53, 61.

110 Greene, above note 95, 1411.

111 Empirical evidence indicates that in the field of genetic inventions, commercialization of the final product is jeopardized when more than one to three licences are necessary to develop the product: Eisenberg, above note 17, 1064 note 27.

obtained for freedom to operate,[112] associated transaction costs, stacked royalty obligations, uncertainty regarding the grant of patents,[113] uncertainty regarding the ability to secure all necessary licenses,[114] and so on) and their incentive to invest diminished.[115]

Finally, certain biotechnology inventions, particularly biologics at a sub-cellular level, will operate as blocking patents. Biotechnology patents in general are difficult, if not impossible, to invent around. A patent granted on a natural biologic, such as a gene, protein or cell line, embodies the process of understanding and experimenting with foundational material over an extended period of time.[116] A party which isolates the respective gene holds considerable advantage over other researchers and its patenting of the invention may result in its control over uses of the gene, including diagnostics, prophylactics and treatment based on the respective sequence.[117] A blocking patent developed or acquired by a single player would prevent others from entering the field.[118]

These extreme scenarios – monopolization by a single party or congestion as a result of too many players – point to a sub-optimal functioning of the patent system under the specific conditions of the influenza drug market described above (a strong growth market, narrow and fragmented patents, a congested patent scene and expensive development). Drug development under the PIP Framework is likely to follow largely the same pattern, resulting in a patent thicket or single player scenario. If so, the PIP's goal of reliable and widespread availability of affordably priced influenza related drugs will not be achieved.

It is posited that the extreme scenarios described above arise from the absence of specific IP ownership allocation. A directed reallocation of patent

---

112 'The greater the number of essential licensors, the greater the total risk of bargaining breakdown': Eisenberg, ibid., 1073.

113 In reality the validity of a patent is only determined once an appellate level court has ruled on it.

114 See generally, Greene, above note 95.

115 See Krattiger and Kowalski, above note 70, 56.

116 Demaine and Fellmeth, above note 73, 303.

117 Greene, above note 95, 1404.

118 TRIPS, above note 37, Art. 31(l) permits use without the authorization of the rightholder of a first patent for exploitation of a second patent provided 'the invention claimed in the second patent shall involve an important technical advance of considerable economic significance in relation to the invention claimed in the first patent'. Depending on the degree of 'significance' the dependent patent is required to have – e.g. the UK Patents Act 1977, s. 48A(1)(b)(i)(4) requires an 'important technical advance of considerable economic significance'; the German Patent Law of 2001, Art. 15 requires 'indispensable in the public interest' – anti-blocking statutes may not provide a significant amount of relief.

rights requiring all patents based on the virus samples received to be joined in a patent pool, would largely avoid similar scenarios.

6.3 A Patent Pool as an Alternative Solution

Patent pools are conceptually premised on a contractual variance of the contours of legislatively allocated intellectual property rights. Full patent rights are 'rebundled' to grant rights sufficient to ensure freedom to operate and function in the market.[119] In a congested space, 'rebundling' allows a more flexible and efficient allocation of rights. Pooling may help players assemble the necessary technologies and reduce transaction costs, thereby stimulating overall product development. It may also support non-commercial uses and create allowances for CBD obligations. A patent pool is likely to enjoy broader acceptance because it seeks to reconcile the interests of all stakeholders.

Patent pools are informally defined as agreements 'between two or more patent owners to license one or more of their patents to one another or third persons'.[120] The members of the pool assign their rights in patents and patent applications to a separate administering entity,[121] which then licenses these rights in rebundled form to pool members and third parties, upon terms and in accordance with rules agreed upon by the members.[122] By providing participants with freedom to operate from a patent perspective, product development is stimulated.[123]

---

119 The concept of contractually rebundling IP rights with the intent to direct the innovation process has been given relatively little attention. But see Michael Carroll, 'One Size Does Not Fit All: A Framework for Tailoring Intellectual Property Rights' (2009) 70 *Ohio State Law Journal* 1361, who proposes a tailoring framework for IP rights.

120 Jeanne Clark, Joe Piccolo, Brian Stanton and Karin Tyson, 'Patent Pools: A Solution to the Problem of Access in Biotechnology Patent', US Patent and Trademark Office, 5 December 2000, available at: http://www.uspto.gov/web/offices/pac/dapp/opla/patentpool.pdf. 'Just as there is no formal legal definition of the term "patent pool", there are no national or international laws or regulations guiding the formation of patent pools': Ed Levy, Emily Marden, Ben Warren, David Hartell and Isaac Filaté, 'Patent Pools and Genomics: Navigating a Course to Open Science?' (2010) 16 *Boston University Journal of Science and Technology Law* 75, 82.

121 Merges, above note 107, 1299.

122 Merges, ibid., 1340. Josh Lerner and Jean Tirole, 'Public Policy toward Patent Pools', in Adam B. Jaffe, Josh Lerner and Scott Stern (eds), *Innovation Policy and the Economy*, Vol. 8 (University of Chicago Press 2008) 157–86, 159.

123 Lerner and Tirole, ibid., 159; Krattiger and Kowalski, above note 70, 56; Merges, above note 107, 1299.

With the growth of the biotechnology industry, bioinformatics and related industries, patent pools have increasingly come under consideration in the life science field.[124] Industry resistance to patent pools is decreasing and governments tend to encourage at least those pools perceived to provide a social benefit.[125]

6.3.1 Considerations in establishing a patent pool

Depending on their specific licensing terms, patent pools present the risk of being anticompetitive. The underlying agreements are subject to review by antitrust authorities on whether their competitive benefits outweigh the potential harm to competition.[126]

In general, competition authorities view patent pools as pro-competitive. The US Department of Justice Guidelines (IP Guidelines) point to the fact that pools provide benefits such as 'integrating complementary technologies, reducing transaction costs, clearing blocking positions, and avoiding costly infringement litigation'.[127] The US Patent and Trademark Office (USPTO) has

---

124 'The value of patent pooling within the biotechnology and related fields has received considerable attention, primarily by commentators, owing to the perceived promise of improved social welfare (including decreased transaction costs, increased pricing efficiency, and faster innovation) and despite the acknowledged potential for antitrust issues': Greene, above note 95, note 69.

125 Sarah Boseley, 'Big Pharma Shows Willingness to Pool HIV and Aids Drug Patents', *The Guardian*, 10 February 2011, available at: http://www.guardian.co.uk/society/sarah-boseley-global-health/2011/feb/10/drugs-pharmaceuticals-industry; 'G8 Encourages Drug Companies to Work with Medicines Patent Pool', available at: http://g8live.org/access-for-all-medicines-patent-pool-gains-recognition-in-communique/.

126 The Department of Justice (DOJ) inquiry is focused on the issues of (1) whether the proposed licensing program is likely to integrate complementary patent rights and, if so, (2) whether the resulting competitive benefits are likely to be outweighed by competitive harm posed by other aspects of the program: DOJ US Antitrust Guidelines for the Licensing of Intellectual Property, 1995 (IP Guidelines), available at: http://www.justice.gov/atr/public/guidelines/0558.pdf. The DOJ's assessment of whether patent pools would be deemed pro- or anticompetitive are set out in the IP Guidelines. In essence the IP Guidelines provide that pooling arrangements are pro-competitive when they (a) integrate complementary technologies, (b) reduce transaction costs, (c) clear blocking positions, (d) avoid costly infringement litigation, and (e) promote the dissemination of technology. On the other hand, indicia of anticompetitiveness would be that (a) the excluded firms cannot effectively compete in the relevant market for the good incorporating the licensed technologies, (b) the pool participants collectively possess market power in the relevant market, and (c) the limitations on participation are not reasonably related to the efficient development and exploitation of the pooled technologies. See also Krattiger and Kowalski, above note 70, 142.

127 IP Guidelines, ibid.

also opined favorably on the formation of patent pools, because 'the social and economic benefits of the pooling of biotechnological products outweigh their costs'.[128]

In evaluating the acceptability of an individual patent pool in the biotechnology area, it must be kept in mind that the IP Guidelines contemplate primarily patent pools in the electronics industry, which are largely organized around industry standards and may respond to different needs. Much of antitrust law in the biotech area is still limited to 'merely importing existing norms developed within the standard-setting context' without addressing specific issues raised by the biotechnology industry,[129] despite the existence of a good number of scholarly writings on the topic.[130]

Electronics industry precedents limit pool membership to 'essential' patents[131] and concomitantly exclude 'substitute' patents.[132] A more liberal interpretation of the 'essentiality' requirement has been suggested for biotechnology pools.[133] Because the development of biotechnology or pharmaceuti-

---

128 Clark et al., above note 120, 2–3.

129 Greene, above note 95, note 171, citing Josh Lerner and Jean Tirole, 'Efficient Patent Pools' (2004) 94 *American Economic Review* 691, 691 ('questioning whether, though not addressing specifically the biotechnology industry, "the reluctance to form pools may be due to the ambiguities surrounding the manner in which proposed pools will be evaluated")'.

130 For example, Krattiger and Kowalski, above note 70; Courtney G. Scala, 'Making the Jump from Gene Pools to Patent Pools: How Patent Pools Can Facilitate the Development of Pharmocogenomics' (2009) 41 *Connecticut Law Review* 1631; Rebecca Goulding, Emily Marden, Rachael Manion and Ed Levy, 'Alternative Intellectual Property for Genomics and the Activity of Technology Transfer Offices: Emerging Directions in Research' (2010) 16 *Boston University Journal of Science & Technology Law* 194; Patrick Gaulé, 'Towards Patent Pools in Biotechnology?', Ecole Polytechnique Fédérale de Lausanne, College of Management of Technology, *CDM Working Papers Series*, CEMI-Report-2006-010, April 2006, available at: http://infoscience.epfl.ch/record/85505/files/WP%20Gaul%C3%A9%20-%20Pool_22_04_06.pdf.

131 Because the IP Guidelines require the pool to contain only 'essential patents' (i.e. those which are necessary to implement the technology), the implication is that substitutes, either within or outside the pool should be accepted: Lerner and Tirole, above note 122, 160.

132 The DOJ business review letters exclude 'substitute' technologies: Greene, above note 95, 1439. Whether government pronouncements in this regard hold true with respect to the biotech, and in particular the antiviral industry, remains to be seen. In general, an individual pool is likely to pass muster under competition rules if it (1) serves no ancillary purpose, (2) allows independent licensing by participants, (3) includes only essential patents, and (4) avoids grant-backs.

133 Some scholars believe that there is no harm to competition as long as at least one valid essential patent is included in the pool and independent licensing by all patentees is permitted: see generally, Richard Gilbert, 'Antitrust for Patent Pools: A Century of Policy Evolution' [2004] *Stanford Technology Law Review* 3.

cal products requires assembly of a large number of patents, the technological relation between them is often unclear, particularly at a time before the product has been developed.[134] At the time of the pool's formation it is therefore difficult, if not impossible, to determine whether any given patent pool is 'essential', rather than 'substitutable'. Applying the 'essential' patent limitation in the context of an influenza virus patent pool, for instance, would be based on a mere assumption of their technological relation. An erroneous decision in this regard could render the pool useless. This speaks for relying on the 'safe harbor' model suggested by Lerner and Tirole, according to which antitrust compliance could be achieved by meeting only two criteria: that the pool should (1) serve no ancillary purpose, and (2) allow for independent licensing of the individual patents by their owners.[135] Based on this approach, determination of essentiality would become secondary.

6.3.2 The SARS patent pool

Relatively few precedents of biotechnology patent pools exist.[136] The only pool in the influenza field is the genomic patents pool involving the SARS virus (severe acute respiratory syndrome 'coronavirus').

Following the SARS outbreak in 2003,[137] a number of institutions, including major research centres such as the Berhardt Nocht Institute, the British Columbia Cancer Agency (BCCA), the US Center for Disease Control (CDC), and Hong Kong University began simultaneously to sequence the SARS virus. Each of these institutions had filed patent applications with the USPTO on the

---

134 Greene, above note 95, 1437. Whether government pronouncements in this regard hold true with respect to the biotech, and in particular the antiviral industry remains to be seen.

135 Lerner and Tirole suggest, based on a study of 63 different patent pools, that uncertainties with respect to antitrust scrutiny can be reduced by adhering to a 'safe harbor' model, which (1) serves no ancillary purpose and (2) allows for independent licensing of the individual patents by their owners: Lerner and Tirole, above note 122, 172.

136 Examples include the Medicines Patent Pool UNITAID pool for antiretroviral medicines: see http://www.medicinespatentpool.org and http://www.wipo.int/wipo_magazine/en/2011/03/article_0005.html; and the AvGFP Green Fluorescent Protein: see E. van Zimmeren, 'From One-Stop to One-Stop-Shop: Patent Pools and Clearinghouse Mechanisms as Pragmatic Solutions for Patent Thickets and Non-cooperative Patent Holders in Genetic Diagnostics?', IPSC 2006, Berkeley, 10–11 August 2006.

137 WHO, 'Global Alert and Response: Summary of Probable SARS Cases with Onset of Illness from 1 November 2002 to 31 July 2003', 26 September 2003, available at: www.who.int/csr/sars/country/table2003_09_23/en; see also Matthew Rimmer, 'The TRIPS Agreement and Access to Essential Medicines' (2004) 5(2) *Melbourne Journal of International Law* 335, 336.

genomic sequence of the coronavirus, along with a general description of how the knowledge contained therein would be converted into diagnostics and treatments.[138]

The number of prospective patent holders gave rise to the concern that patent rights to the SARS genomic sequence would be fragmented. Interference proceedings were anticipated as a result of the quasi-simultaneous filing by multiple entities and the uncertainty over patent rights was feared to result in manufacturers delaying making investment decisions.[139] To overcome these concerns, all patent holders agreed to a 'cooperative pooling', combining their technologies by licensing them to a separate entity that would make them available to licensors and third parties by way of non-exclusive licenses.[140] Because it took an extended period of time to agree which patents to include, to craft the pool structure agreement and its licensing terms and to ensure that antitrust and other regulations were met,[141] the SARS outbreak was contained before completion of the pool. While the pool's activity continues, it does so with less intensity. A business review was not requested, and therefore the proposed structure has not been ruled upon by the DOJ,[142] and remains inconclusive as to its ultimate success.[143]

Nonetheless, the SARS pool suggests a few practical steps. Overall, advance development of a legal blueprint for the formation of similar patent pools would be useful, as circumstances will inevitably demand urgency. The blueprint should consider, inter alia, that influenza virus pools are likely to consist in part or entirely of patent applications.[144] The risk of non-issuance would therefore have to be neutralized.[145] Further, because of the lengthy R&D process, the commercial endpoint is often not clear until the end of the development process.[146] Determinations of essentiality and substitutability at

---

138 Levy et al., above note 120, 90.

139 James H.M. Simon, Eric Claassen, Carmen E. Correa and Albert D.M.E. Osterhaus, 'Managing Severe Acute Respiratory Syndrome (SARS) Intellectual Property Rights: The Possible Role of Patent Pooling' (2005) 83(9) *Bulletin of the World Health Organization*, available at: http://www.scielosp.org/ scielo.php?pid=S0042-96862005000900017&script=sci_arttext&tlng=e.

140 Simon et al., ibid., 708; Levy et al., above note 120, at 91.

141 Levy et al., ibid., 91.

142 Ibid.

143 Finally, a number of other pooling arrangements exist, such as the pool for neglected tropical diseases formed by drug manufacturer GlaxoSmithKline, and one for diagnostic genetics, which creates patent pools for technical standards and other technology platforms: see http://www.wipo.int/wipo_magazine/en/2011/03/article_0005.html.

144 Levy et al., above note 120, 91.

145 Ibid.

146 In the SARS context, the relationship between the patents and specific

the stage of formation are therefore virtually impossible. Arguments regarding the pool's legality under antitrust laws should be part of the blueprint.[147]

Assuming that an influenza-based patent pool can successfully overcome these hurdles and address the requisite antitrust problems,[148] it would provide considerable benefits over individual licensing, including promoting participation of multiple players in the market,[149] stimulating innovation by granting access for research purposes, allowing more efficient pricing,[150] and so on. Pooling of patents derived from the influenza virus would thus mitigate the problems associated with obstacles to commercialization posed by a multi-player, fragmented IP industry. If so, the PIP Framework would have benefited from a provision of this nature in its SMTA. In addition, as will be discussed below, the MTA's terms and conditions could be designed so as to accommodate social concerns as well.

7. THE FINAL BALANCE

Assuming that a patent pool is both overall beneficial and legal under the circumstances at hand, the critical question of practical feasibility remains: would prospective recipients of an influenza virus agree to an MTA that requires joining a patent pool? After all, the prospect of market exclusivity as a result of a patent grant is likely to be an, if not the most, important factor in deciding to develop a pharmaceutical product. By joining a patent pool the individual patentee agrees to relinquish its exclusivity and to potentially share the market with others. Absent an adequate quid pro quo a company is unlikely to enter into such an agreement.

Two considerations weigh in favor of joining a patent pool. First, joining a patent pool is a condition to accessing the genetic resources.[151] If the potential

---

commercial products that might incorporate the patents' teachings differed from the historical precedents. In the SARS case, as for genomics in general, commercial therapeutic and prophylactic products can be placed on the market only after a lengthy research and development process, and the range of possible commercial endpoints remains only partially defined until well into the development process: Levy et al., ibid., 92.

147 See above text accompanying notes 132 et seq.

148 Some commentators suggest that patent pools are mostly appropriate in mature industries, in particular surrounding industry standards: Krattiger and Kowalski, above note 70, 141; Rimmer, above note 137, 358.

149 The usefulness of a patent pool increases with the number of patents required for assembling a product, and the number of individual transactions required to do so: Merges, above note 107, 1341.

150 Greene, above note 95, 117.

151 See above text accompanying notes 62 et seq.

market for the product to be developed is strong, as in the influenza-related medicines market, access constitutes a powerful inducement. Second, by joining a patent pool a player would obtain freedom to operate from a patent perspective and avoid the risk of blocking patents and patent thickets. The larger the number of recipients and the larger the number of patents required to produce the drug, the more attractive and safe a patent pool will appear.[152] The benefit of joining the pool would then balance out any detriment resulting from relinquishment of the patent exclusivity.

8. REMAINING CONSIDERATIONS

Two additional considerations might disturb the balance: (i) allowing free non-commercial use of patented inventions, and (ii) possible benefit sharing obligations under the CBD.

8.1 Non-commercial Use[153]

Notwithstanding its desirability from a social and scientific perspective,[154] free non-commercial use has the potential to reduce a drug developer's revenue and might at first sight appear to be a deterrent. This concern may be outweighed by two considerations. First, non-commercial use is accepted by many as a matter of course, as patent laws in many jurisdictions already exempt non-commercial, research or experimental use to various degrees.[155] Second, a non-commercial use provision might well weigh in favor of a pool's pro-competitiveness in the event of antitrust scrutiny, and may even serve to fulfil potential CBD obligations, if the benefits of the non-commercial use

---

[152] The usefulness of a patent pool increases with the number of patents required for assembling a product, and the number of individual transactions required to do so: Merges, above note 107, 1341.

[153] Even though this distinction is not always easy to make and could open up new areas of uncertainty: see Mark Harvey and Andrew McMeekin, 'Public or Private Economies of Knowledge: The Economics of Diffusion and Appropriation of Bioinformatics Tools' (2010) 4(1) *International Journal of the Commons*, 481–506, 484.

[154] By removing downstream restrictions on the rights of others to experiment, innovate, share or exchange the genetic resources: Aoki, above note 34, 2302.

[155] Many countries have enacted experimental use exceptions. Their scope varies, e.g., 35 USC, § 271(e)(1) (limited to use for regulatory approval); Germany, 'Klinische Versuche I' (BGH GRUR 1996, 109) and 'Klinische Versuche II' (BGH, Mitteilung 1997, 253) (allowing use for clinical trials); UK Patents Act 1977, s. 60; Patent Law of Japan, s. 69(1).

provisions were to specifically target developing countries or the country of origin. In short, an MTA provision granting free non-commercial use to the patents licensed to the pool may well be a neutral consideration and not detract from the general balance of the agreement. Consequently, nothing would opt against inclusion of a provision to this effect in the MTA requirement directing formation of a pool.[156]

8.2 Benefit Sharing

Finally, unless the *ex situ* collection has successfully negotiated clarity regarding CBD obligations (existence, scope and nature of such obligations),[157] no legal obstacle would prevent a country of origin from claiming benefit sharing under the CBD against a successful drug developer. The greater the commercial success of a particular influenza-related drug, the greater the chance that such claims might be made. While this aspect could operate as a deal breaker to the MTA because of its irremediable legal uncertainty, given the current state of the law the possibility may be ignored as being too unlikely.

8.3 Enforceability of a Pooling Agreement

This leads to the final vulnerability of the proposed structure. A party who reluctantly agrees to an MTA that requires patent pooling may too easily prevent the pool's formation by stalling negotiations, disagreeing on terms and conditions, and so on, without being in actual breach of the MTA. The entire structure would then become illusory. To provide the MTA with 'teeth', failure to form a pool could trigger a default to an arrangement akin to a compensatory liability-type regime.[158] Under such a rule a recipient entitled to use deposited material would be required to pay a pre-established royalty on any revenue obtained from commercial use of the materials. This compensatory liability obligation is incurred contractually, *ex ante*.[159] In the present

---

156 While the PIP Framework's multiple benefit sharing provisions might, under certain circumstances, have a similar effect, they do not systematically provide an assured flow of information as would a non-commercial use exception.

157 See above text accompanying notes 31 et seq.

158 The compensatory liability regime proposed by Professor Jerome Reichman for the microbial commons is characterized by the fact that 'the depositor would not forfeit all rights to benefit from downstream commercial applications, and instead share in them, should such applications emerge': Reichman, above note 9; see also Jerome H. Reichman, 'Of Green Tulips and Legal Kudzu: Repackaging Rights in Subpatentable Innovation' (2000) 53 *Vanderbilt Law Review* 1743.

159 The approach can also be viewed, on the one hand, as giving the depositor an *ex ante* conditional entitlement to collect royalties in the event of successful

scenario, a royalty obligation would be imposed on revenue based on products derived from virus samples, in the event a patent pool is not established.[160] The key to the success of this arrangement is a high royalty rate. Because the default scenario is primarily intended to be a deterrent, the royalty rate would have to be unattractive compared with the potential gains under the patent pool option.[161]

In conclusion, the proposed structure includes a number of conditions that would burden prospective recipients of biologic materials. Whether some or all of these conditions will be acceptable is a function of the strength of the market. At one end of the spectrum, a particularly strong market, such as that for influenza-related drugs, may well support the conditions discussed, while, at the other end, for a purely research oriented application, the combined requirements of relinquishing patent exclusivity, non-commercial use, potential CBD obligations and default option, may prove too heavy a burden.

9. CONCLUSION

The commercial usefulness of valuable genetic resources, such as influenza virus samples, may be diminished by uncertain benefit sharing obligations under the CBD and the suboptimal performance of the patent system, given certain market and industry conditions.

This chapter proposes mitigating these results by using the contractual structure that surrounds the transfers of genetic resources between *ex situ* collections and recipients to clarify benefit sharing obligations and to require that all patents based on the genetic resources received be assigned to a patent pool. The proposed structure is intended to stimulate innovation and incentivize investment, so as to support broader-based availability of products derived from biological resources.

---

commercialization and, on the other, giving the recipient a conditional licence to use: Reichman, above note 9.

[160] For genetic resources with imminent commercialization potential, a compensatory liability regime as proposed by Professor Reichman is, however, likely to be less effective, as it does not address the suboptimal functioning of the patent system which is likely to occur in e.g. the influenza-related medicine industry, as a result of blocking patents and patent thickets.

[161] The patent pool, as envisioned here, is a tool to control the 'race' to patent and the ensuing suboptimal functioning of the patent system, with respect to genetic resources with imminent commercial prospects. Setting a low royalty rate would encourage parties to default into a compensatory liability mode, 'buy' their exclusivity in the market by way of a low royalty and avoid sharing technologies with potential competitors. Accordingly, the royalty rate set must be sufficiently high to operate as a deterrent.

Evaluation of the legal feasibility of the proposed patent pool model indicates that from the antitrust perspective it is likely to be legally supportable. Furthermore, from a practical perspective, under the specific circumstances of the influenza virus industry (a strong growth market, narrow and fragmented patents, a congested patent scene and expensive development) the option of a patent pool constitutes a sufficient inducement for parties to relinquish their full patent rights in exchange for freedom to operate from a patent perspective.

Overall, the success of the proposed contractual arrangement is conditioned on the existence of a strong market, as the prospect of successful commercialization enhances the value of the genetic resources and increases their leveraging power. This model is likely to be inapplicable for research activities given the absence of an immediately apparent commercial applicability.[162]

---

162 Furthermore, non-commercial use generally follows a different model. It is not impacted upon by the concerns that arise in circumstances of imminent monetary gains. A general sharing ethos 'social norms of communalism' among academic researches create conditions that differ from commercial pursuits. See Dedeurwaerdere, above note 12, 240. Furthermore, enforcement is more limited against non-commercial entities: see generally, Eisenberg, above note 17.

7. Managing online music rights in the European Digital Single Market: current scenarios and future prospects

Giuseppe Mazziotti

1. INTRODUCTION

Boosting the music business in the internet age has proven to be a tough proposition. Online copyright infringement still has the edge over legitimate music. Moreover, the music industry has faced dramatic losses in the offline markets that have not been offset by the increase in revenues from the online music sector. In Europe the situation is more complex than that in the US since the European Union (EU) does not have a single copyright system and the enforcement and management of exclusive rights in musical compositions, music performances and sound recordings still takes place mostly on a country-by-country basis, despite the international reach of the internet.

The launch and full development of innovative services and an EU-wide online music business that could create a credible alternative to digital piracy is being hindered, at a time when there is a shift of content from end-user devices to the 'Cloud'. Newly emerged and successful music platforms such as iTunes, Pandora's randomized music streams, and Spotify's on-demand music deliveries are very good examples of commercial services that can compete effectively and prevail over unauthorized filesharing.

In recent years the EU Commission – the government and policy maker of the EU – took the music business into great consideration while continuing to develop the copyright harmonization process undertaken as of 1991 through the adoption of several directives. Recently, the EU Commission focused on ensuring a higher legal protection and on granting stronger economic incentives to copyright holders wishing to make their content available online on an EU-wide basis. In the absence of a unified copyright system, such as that created in the US by its federal laws, the ultimate goal of European lawmakers has been that of creating a licensing system for a 'Digital Single Market' which would clear all music rights online in all the countries of the EU.

2. ONLINE RIGHTS

When speaking about online music, one should always bear in mind that the legitimate supply of online services presupposes the clearance of the rights in both musical compositions – that is, as they appear on a pentagram and in music sheets made available by a music publisher – and the rights in the sound recordings. The latter have to do with the performances of musical compositions – the so-called 'neighbouring' rights. In the EU legal framework, performing artists and recording producers enjoy the same set of rights for their performances and sound recordings that authors and, indirectly, music publishers enjoy for their compositions. This means that three layers of full property rights' protection coexist on the same digital goods exploited by online music services.[1]

Until recently, the most significant distinction between rights in musical compositions and in sound recordings in EU copyright laws was given by their respective terms of duration. For musical compositions this was 70 years after the author's death, and for sound recordings it was 50 years from the date of publication or communication of the sound recording to the public. An EU Directive of September 2011 extended the term of protection for sound recordings and performances incorporated into sound recordings from 50 to 70 years.[2] As clearly stated in the Commission's impact assessment that accompanied the directive proposal of 2008, the extension of the term of protection was aimed at helping record producers and music performers financially at a time when piracy increasingly reduced the economic incentives to invest in artist and repertoire research and, inevitably, reduced the earnings of music performers.[3] The original intent of the EU Commission was that of extending

---

1 The enforcement of rights in sound recordings logically (and legally) depends on the previous enforcement of author rights in musical compositions, in such a way that each act of performance, recording, broadcasting (or webcasting) of a musical work protected by copyright must be authorized by the copyright owner in order to be lawful.

2 See Art. 1(2) Directive 2011/77 of the European Parliament and of the Council of 27 September 2011 amending Directive 2006/116/EC on the term of protection of copyright and certain related rights, [2011] OJ L265/1 (EU). This Directive ended up establishing a distinction between, on one hand, the term of protection of sound recordings and fixations of performances incorporated into sound recordings, whose term was extended from 50 to 70 years and, on the other hand, the term of protection of broadcasts and fixations of performances other than in sound recordings, which remains subject to the previous 50-year term (cf. Art. 1(2)(a)).

3 See Commission of the European Communities, 'Impact Assessment on the Legal and Economic Situation of Performers and Record Producers in the European Union', Commission Staff Working Document accompanying the Proposal for a Council Directive amending Directive 2006/116 on the term of protection of copyright

rights in sound recordings until 95 years from the date of publication, which would have ensured in Europe the same duration of protection granted to sound recordings – as 'works made for hire' – under US copyright law.[4]

3. LICENSING

The EU Commission has been very active in recent years in order to make the licensing of online music rights smoother and effectively pan-European. As things stand, an online service provider or a digital music retailer wishing to use musical compositions for its online or mobile exploitations needs to clear two categories of rights conferred to authors under copyright laws: mechanical or reproduction rights and public performance rights. The advent of digital technologies has increasingly blurred the distinction between these two categories, which are otherwise clearly separated in the offline world.

Even if *online* rights already exist on the market and in the day-to-day practice of European collecting societies, the 2001 'Information Society' Directive – the most comprehensive attempt at harmonizing national copyright laws – failed to clarify whether the exclusive right to make content available online in an interactive way encompassed acts of reproduction necessary for digital delivery.[5] If online rights constitute a specific combination of mechanical and performance rights for online applications, such as downloading or streaming services, then legitimate music services should simultaneously clear both classes of rights.

---

and certain related rights, Brussels, 16 July 2008, available at: http://ec.europa.eu/internal_market/copyright/docs/term/ia_term_en.pdf (EC Commission, 'Impact Assessment').

[4] See EC Commission, 'Impact Assessment', ibid., 61. The Commission's proposal was eventually amended by the EU Parliament in the course of the co-decision procedure, which led to the adoption of the final text of the Directive. Interestingly, in fixing a 70-year term of protection for sound recordings, Directive 2011/77 obliges EU Member States to confer certain rights to music performers for the 20-year period of extended protection: (a) a right to termination of the contracts through which performers have assigned or transferred the rights in their performances to record producers if the producer does not offer copies of the phonogram for sale in sufficient quantity or does not make it available to the public, by wire or wireless means, within a year from the notification by the performer of his or her intention to terminate the contract (see Art. 1(2)(a) of Directive 2006/116, as amended by Directive 2011/77), and (b) a right to supplementary remuneration for each full year of extended protection (see the new version of Art. 1(2)(b) to (e)Directive 2006/116). These new provisions state expressly that music performers cannot validly waive the above-mentioned rights.

[5] See Art. 3(2) Council Directive 2001/29, 2001 OJ L167/10 (EC).

4. NEW RULES

From 2005 onwards, the EU Commission took action to facilitate the acquisition of all online music rights by online music distributors on an EU-wide basis.[6] This has proved to be a very difficult undertaking since the national collecting societies of authors and music publishers in EU countries have traditionally operated on a strictly national basis and are *de facto* or legal monopolies. They have concluded agreements of mutual representation for the management of their respective music repertoires in their sole country of business. At the same time, collecting societies have developed different rules and contractual practices for the transfer and management of the mechanical and public performance rights, and this has led to the creation of parallel ownership regimes for each of these rights.

The most important distinction in this regard is probably that which concerns the assignment of mechanical rights in the UK and continental European repertoires. There is a philosophical and cultural difference underlying the notion of *copyright* and *author*'s rights in both territories. In the UK, music publishers have historically been the sole proprietors of mechanical rights through their own collective rights management organization, after having acquired them from the authors. Instead, in continental Europe, authors and music publishers usually co-own the same rights under the shield of their respective collecting societies (these societies have sought to protect authors from the bargaining power of the publishers and have ultimately become authors' unions).

The EU Commission sought to break up this well-established system in order to enable a smooth management of online music rights on a pan-European basis. The main idea was that of dismantling national barriers that restricted rightholders from issuing EU-wide licences for digital uses of their musical compositions and that forced commercial users of such compositions to seek authorizations in every EU country through the local collecting societies. At the same time, according to this reform plan, individual rightholders should have been allowed to opt for a collective rights manager of their choice, irrespective of the country of domicile of the rightholder or of the copyright manager.

To pursue these ends, the Commission opted first for a non-binding recommendation in 2005, which was addressed to EU Member States and collecting societies. This recommendation urged them to reconsider the existing structure

6 See EC Commission,'Study on a Community Initiative on the Cross-border Collective Management of Copyright', 7 July 2005, available at http://ec.europa.eu/internal_market/copyright/docs/management/study-collectivem gmt_en.pdf.

of online rights management.[7] At a later stage, the Commission decided to tackle directly the mutual representation agreements that European collecting societies concluded with each other under the aegis of the International Confederation of Societies of Authors and Composers (CISAC). This happened through an antitrust decision (known as 'the CISAC decision') of 2008 that found the clauses of territorial exclusivity and the membership requirement of economic residence embodied in these agreements illegal since they were deemed to constitute cartels restricting competition on the EU market for services of copyright management.[8] As a result, this antitrust decision ordered the 24 collecting societies of the European Economic Area to withdraw these clauses from their mutual representation agreements and to bring to an end cartels on territorial segmentation of collective licensing for online, satellite and cable transmissions.[9]

5. ONE-STOP LICENSING PROBLEMS

This change of licensing rules for online music rights paved the way not only for effective competition between different collecting societies at the European level, but also, and most importantly, for a completely new form of competition among distinct music repertoires, which are now offered to commercial users by new and separate licensing bodies under their own contractual conditions and at their own prices.

These new licensing bodies take the form of either joint ventures that major international music groups have established with the biggest collecting societies in Europe (in order to centralize the licensing of their Anglo-American and Latin-American music repertoires)[10] or strategic alliances of national

---

7 See Commission Recommendation of 18 October 2005 on Collective Cross-Border Management of Copyright and Related Rights for Legitimate Online Music Services, [2005] OJ L276/54.

8 See Commission Decision relating to a Proceeding under Article 81 of the EC Treaty and Article 53 of the EEA Agreement, COM(2008) 3435 final, 16 July 2008, 1, 5, available at: http://ec.europa.eu/competition/antitrust/cases/dec_docs/38698/38698_4567_1.pdf.

9 Ibid., 73–75, Arts 1 and 4 (membership clauses) and 3 (territorial exclusivity). The addressees of the decision were: AEPI (Greece), AKKA/LAA (Latvia), AKM (Austria), ARTISJUS (Hungary), BUMA (the Netherlands), EAU (Estonia), GEMA (Germany), IMRO (Ireland), KODA (Denmark), LATGA-A (Lithuania), OSA (Czech Republic), PRS (UK), SABAM (Belgium), SACEM (France), SAZAS (Slovenia), SGAE (Spain), SIAE (Italy), SOZA (Slovakia), SPA (Portugal), STEF (Iceland), STIM (Sweden), TEOSTO (Finland), TONO (Norway) and ZAIKS (Poland).

10 Major international music publishers such as EMI Music Publishing and

societies in southern and northern Europe that seek to consolidate and license jointly their local music repertoires for digital uses.[11]

Unfortunately, the new licensing scenario for online music is far from settled, at least for the new licensing bodies of the international major music groups, which together account for more than two-thirds of the global music market. These economic entities, which own vertically integrated publishing and recording businesses, would certainly take advantage of the opportunity to license complete packages of rights in their digital music, including rights in musical compositions, performances and sound recordings either by themselves or through a specialized agent.

However, the sole rights that music publishers have been able to successfully withdraw from the repertoire of works administered by national collecting societies and confer to their own specialized licensing agents are the mechanical rights in the Anglo-American music repertoires. As recalled above, that is owing to the fact that UK music publishers, as their counterparts in the US, have traditionally acquired and owned such rights on an exclusive basis and they have managed them through their own collecting societies. For foreign uses, UK music publishers have traditionally appointed sub-publishers, which are members of national collecting societies, and have conferred on them a mandate for the management of mechanical rights on a local basis in every country of exploitation. This means that UK music publishers own and administer mechanical rights and can dispose of them without the author's approval, and can easily withdraw the foreign collecting societies' rights to represent their music repertoire by merely letting the agreements with sub-publishers expire.

Sony/ATV Music Publishing appointed as agents for their repertoires at the European level new licensing bodies: EMI appointed CELAS Gmbh, co-owned jointly by GEMA (Germany) and PRS for Music (UK); Sony appointed PAECOL Gmbh, which is a 100% subsidiary of GEMA. Other major publishers such as Universal Music Publishing and Warner Chappell opted for a slightly different version of the same model, which did not imply the creation of new organizations but merely appointed one or more national collecting societies as exclusive or non-exclusive agents of the publishers' repertoires. For instance, music publishers like Sony and Peer Music and the collecting societies of Central and South America conferred a mandate to SGAE (Spain) within the Pan-European Licensing (PEL) initiative for the management of their music repertoires for EU-wide online exploitations.

[11] See initiatives such as ARMONIA, launched by SIAE (Italy), SACEM (France) and SGAE (Spain), and that of the pre-existing licensing body established by the Baltic and Nordic collecting societies (Nordisk Copyright Bureau), which has become a licensing hub for mechanical and online rights management and for the collection and distribution of royalties beyond the territories within which the cross-border system previously operated (i.e., Sweden, Norway, Denmark, Finland, Iceland, Lithuania, Latvia and Estonia).

On the other hand, music publishers cannot withdraw or easily transfer *public performance rights*, since these rights – even under UK contractual practice – are normally owned or co-owned by authors and have traditionally been managed by collecting societies, whose approval or consent is therefore indispensable for any kind of withdrawal or rights transfer. So far, national collecting societies (and the music authors they represent) have proved to be reluctant to change the way in which they manage their public performance rights for online uses. As acknowledged by the same EU Commission in a position paper of October 2009, in spite of the bilateral renegotiation of mutual representation agreements imposed by the 2008 CISAC decision, EU collecting societies still license their public performance rights for online music services on a national basis.[12]

6. CURRENT SCENARIOS

The current situation in the online music business clearly shows that some sort of simplification is needed in order to make the EU-wide licensing of online music rights smooth and economically convenient for rightholders, commercial users and, ultimately, consumers. If the creation of a unified copyright system at the EU level is not yet a concrete option, lawmakers might consider amending the existing legal framework through measures aimed at drastically reducing legal uncertainty and transaction costs.

6.1 Major Music Publishers

The creation of strong business partnerships with the new licensing arms of the major collecting societies in Europe (that is, PRS, GEMA, SACEM and SGAE) placed major music publishers in a position to negotiate directly all the conditions of management of their online rights, obtaining a preferential regime which contradicts the traditional principle of non-discrimination between rights holders and their repertoires. However, it would be misleading to present this strong alliance between major publishers and major collecting societies as a sudden or unexpected breakthrough. A preferential regime for the repertoires of the major music publishers was already granted, to a certain extent, through the fixing of lower commission fees for the management

12 See DG INFSO and DG MARKT, 'Creative Content in a European Digital Single Market: Challenges for the Future', 22 October 2009, 6, available at http://ec.europa.eu/avpolicy/docs/other_actions/col_2009/reflection_paper.pdf.

services provided by collecting societies for the clearance of major music publishers' mechanical rights under the so-called Cannes Agreements.[13]

This preferential treatment was linked to a centralized rights clearance system for mechanical rights developed in the EU during the 1970s.[14] At that time, the larger Western European collecting societies started clearing mechanical rights for the whole volume of records produced by the four or five major international record producers for all EU countries by themselves (by excluding other European collecting societies from this business).[15] Because, in the case of vertically integrated music groups, the entity that owns the major record producer is also (directly or indirectly) the owner of the publishing rights, the licence fees paid by record producers to the collecting society are allocated to the publishing branch of the same major entity after deduction of management fees.[16] As a result of the Cannes agreements, these management fees are lower in the case of a major music publisher.[17]

More generally, major publishers have been able to influence the decision-making process of music rights management through the participation of their representatives in the activities and in the resolutions of the governing bodies of national collecting societies. As provided under the Common Declaration on Governance in Collective Management Societies and on Management of

---

13 See Maria M. Frabboni, 'Collective Management of Copyright and Related Rights: Achievements and Problems of Institutional Efforts towards Harmonisation', in Estelle Derclaye (ed.), *Research Handbook on the Future of EU Copyright* (Edward Elgar 2009) 373, 385–8. Originally negotiated in 1997 with all collecting societies in Europe, and renewed in 2000, the Cannes Agreement between major music publishers and mechanical copyright collecting societies was renegotiated and renewed in 2002. This was an extension of the previous agreements and concerned in particular the maximum administration fees that collecting societies could charge their members for services of rights clearance concerning reproduction of sound recordings on physical carriers.

14 Ibid., 386. See also Peter Gyertyanfy, 'Collective Management of Music Rights in Europe after the CISAC Decision', 41 *International Review of Intellectual Property and Competition Law* 59, 60.

15 See Frabboni, above note 13, 386 (explaining that the practice of centralized agreements for the clearance of mechanical rights is based on an extensive interpretation of the reciprocal representation agreements concluded by collecting societies and on the grounds of the well established concerted negotiation taking place between BIEM (umbrella association of mechanical copyright collecting societies) and IFPI (International Federation of the Phonographic Industry), which contract on behalf of their members).

16 See Gyertyanfy, above note 14, 60.

17 See Hellenic Foundation for European and Foreign Policy, 'Collecting Societies and Cultural Diversity in the Music Sector 95–96', June 2009 (hereinafter 'ELIAMEP Study'), available at: http://www.europarl.europa.eu/committees/en/studiesdownload.html?languageDocument=EN&file=28328.

Online Rights in Music Works, issued by the International Confederation of Music Publishers (ICMP) and the European Grouping of Societies of Authors and Composers (GESAC) in 2006, now one-third of the seats on the board of directors of collecting societies is reserved for music publishers.[18]

The new mono-repertoire licensing models in the online music sector indisputably increase the bargaining power of major music publishers, especially in their relationships with the specific collecting societies (or subsidiaries of them) they appoint as their exclusive or non-exclusive licensing agents. Major music publishers can easily impose the adoption of licensing and management conditions for their repertoires (for both online or offline uses) by threatening the withdrawal of their online rights and repertoires, which would lead to significant losses in the turnover of the licensing entities involved.[19]

The enhanced subjection of collecting societies to the leverage of major publishers inevitably challenges the well-known principle of equal treatment (or non-discrimination) between repertoires and distinct categories of rights holder. The circumstance that the 2005 recommendation of the EU Commission restated this principle with no practical effects on the operation of the new rights management organizations raises doubts about the adequacy of a mere soft law instrument for safeguarding of the interests of individual authors and small music publisher's interests.

6.2 National Collecting Societies

National collecting societies excluded from the small circle of EU-wide licensors of major publishers' repertoires for digital uses are definitely the most affected stakeholders in the new scenario. Many European collecting societies openly contested the major international music publishers' direct involvement in the organization of new licensing bodies and argued that the loss of mandates for the administration of online rights is likely to reduce their turnover significantly.[20] Moreover, because of the reduction in the number of

---

18 See Violaine Dehin, 'The Future of Legal Online Music Services in the European Union: A Review of the EU Commission's Recent Initiatives in Cross-Border Copyright Management' (2010) 32 *European Intellectual Property Review* 220, 229. See also ELIAMEP Study, ibid., 96.

19 ELIAMEP Study, above note 17, 96.

20 Ibid., 22–23 note 24 (making reference to the Joint Position of collecting societies AEPI (Greece), AKKA-LAA (Latria), AKM (Austria), Artisjus (Hungary), Austro Mechana (Austria), BUMA/STEMRA (the Netherlands), EAU (Estonia), HDS (Croatia), IMRO (Ireland), KODA (Denmark), LATGA-A (Lithuania), Musicautor (Bulgaria), OSA (Czech Republic), SABAM (Belgium), SAZAS (Slovenia), SOZA (Slovakia), SPA (Portugal), STEG (Iceland), TONO (Norway), UCMR-ADA (Romania) and ZAIKS (Poland) on the Recommendation of 18 October 2005).

works managed, these societies claimed that their administration costs would have increased, causing a subsequent reduction in revenues for local authors and music publishers and an inevitable contraction of the culture-supporting tasks that all of them have an obligation to perform under their national laws, reciprocal representation agreements or by-laws.[21]

A recent study on collecting societies and cultural diversity (the ELIAMEP Study) found that the entrustment of major publishers' rights to specialized online rights managers will affect mainly the functioning of small and medium-sized collecting societies.[22] The study argued that – deprived of the Anglo-American repertoire for online exploitations – the economic sustainability of such societies is likely to be seriously endangered with the predictable growth and expansion of the (still immature) EU online market.[23] In the absence of major music repertoires to manage, the profitability of local collecting societies will depend largely on the volume of their remaining repertoire and their commercial appeal.

The ELIAMEP Study evidenced that the music repertoires of the smaller Western European countries and of all Eastern European member states have mostly a local diffusion and do not easily penetrate European markets, for both cultural and economic reasons.[24] To reach this conclusion, the study measured and compared the economic values of the domestic repertoire of a selected number of European countries (the United Kingdom, Germany, Italy and Belgium) by deducting the shares of foreign repertoires from the total revenues of each national collecting society (respectively PRS for Music, GEMA, SIAE and SABAM) and taking account of what each society received for uses of its repertoire abroad (in the EU as well as in the rest of the world). This comparison clearly revealed that the presence of a wide range of foreign repertoires in the EU territory was very limited and music repertoires are exploited mostly at the local level, with the big exception of the international (that is, the Anglo-American and Latin American) repertoire.[25]

---

21 See Dehin, above note 18, 224 (noting that collecting societies within which there is a high degree of solidarity among members apply social and cultural deductions on rights holders' revenues); Gyertyanfy, above note 14, 66 (recalling that collecting societies have agreed so far to limit deductions to a maximum of 10% of all collected revenues).

22 See ELIAMEP Study, above note 17, 97–8.

23 Ibid., 97.

24 Ibid., 98–106.

25 While measuring intra-European trade flows for each of the above-mentioned societies, the ELIAMEP Study found that PRS for Music's revenues coming from other EU collecting societies were 6.71 times higher than the amount distributed by PRS to EU societies. As for the repertoire revenues that PRS for Music received from foreign societies, in 2008, 60.9% came from other EU member states, whereas 15% came from the United States:ibid., 89–91.

The withdrawal of the online rights of the Anglo-American repertoire from the mandates conferred on local collecting societies constitutes a potential threat for local collecting societies and for their music. The economic consequences of the major publishers' withdrawals are still limited today since the licences and revenues relating to online music services remain quantitatively modest.[26] However, this situation has been changing quickly as a result of the predictable expansion of digital music markets following the growth of broadband internet services in Europe.[27]

The fragmentation of repertoires stemming from the centralization of online rights management for single publishers' music titles gives pan-European commercial exploiters a high incentive to seek authorization for the exploitation of only the most commercially appealing repertoires. This entails concrete risks of marginalization for local repertoires that are certainly higher for smaller domestic repertoires, such as those of Eastern European countries and of Western European countries such as Greece, Portugal, the Netherlands, Belgium and the Scandinavian countries.[28]

The only means that small societies have at their disposal, in order to face competition by the biggest repertoires and of the wealthiest rights managers, is to improve the quality of their services (even from a technology-related perspective) and to create regional hubs for the smooth licensing of joint music repertoires.

6.3 Commercial Users of Online Music

The biggest commercial users of digital music (that is, those who are able to devise and launch online music services within the whole territory of the European Union) should have been the main beneficiaries of the restructuring of online rights management. However, very few among these users seem to

---

[26] Ibid., 39, 52, 63, 82 (observing that the value of 2007 digital music sales on the total value of recorded music sales was 6% in Belgium, 5.5% in Germany, 7.2% in Italy and 8.3% in the United Kingdom).

[27] Email interview with Gabriela Lopes, International Federation of the Phonographic Industry (IFPI), Director of Market Research & Analysis, 22 March 2011 (providing updated information on online music revenues in Europe between 2007 and 2010). According to IFPI figures, in 2010 the volume of digital music sales on the total value of recorded music sales in the countries examined in the ELIAMEP Study was, respectively, 9.2% in Belgium, 12.6% in Germany, 15.3% in Italy and 25.2% in the UK: ibid.

[28] See Frabboni, above note 13, 395 (emphasizing that the EU Commission was fully aware of the problems of economic sustainability that the adoption of a pan-European mono-repertoire licensing model would have created for all those collecting societies deriving a large portion of their income from licensing foreign repertoire). See also EC Commission,'Study on a Community Initiative', above note 6, 44.

be satisfied with the fragmentation of music repertoires stemming from the withdrawal of major publishers' rights from the system of reciprocal representation.[29] Major retailers of online music complained that fragmentation of repertoires obliges them to negotiate and enter into multiple licensing agreements with different entities in order to clear all those rights that, under the old-fashioned system, they could easily obtain through a mono-territorial blanket licence from each national collecting society. For instance, one of the most popular providers of music downloads through its iTunes Music Store (Apple), and a large German retailer of music downloads, music videos and ringtones (Deutsche Telekom) expressed their frustration in the context of public consultations held by the EU Commission.[30] Both online music retailers emphasized that their licensing businesses were much smoother before the advent of the new regime and showed a strong preference for the previous mono-territorial global repertoire licences.[31]

---

[29] Nokia, one of the world's largest mobile phone manufacturers, was definitely one of the very few commercial users to publicly disclose its satisfaction with the pan-European mono-repertoire approach to music licensing. In its intervention at the EU Commission Public Hearing on the Governance of Collective Rights Management in the European Union held in Brussels on 23 April 2010, Nokia reported it had experienced 'good progress in reforming the earlier national monopoly-based copyright licensing regime' and it found the 2008 CISAC decision helpful. On that occasion, Nokia mentioned the successful example of its 'Nokia Comes with Music' service, which gives its mobile phone users unlimited access to music downloads for a certain period (typically one year) at the end of which the consumer can keep everything he/she has downloaded. For this service, Nokia entered into pan-European licensing agreements with PRS for Music, Chrysalis Music, Peer Music, Sony/ATV and Warner Chappell. See Public Hearing on the Governance of Collective Rights Management in the EU, Brussels, European Commission, available at: http //ec.europa.eu/internal_market/copyright/management/management_en.htm#hearing (last visited 27 March 2011).

See also Press Release,'PRS for Music, Chrysalis Music, peer music, Sony/ATV and Warner/Chappell Music support Nokia's European Roll Out', PRS for Music, 14 May 2009, available at: http://www.prsformusic.com/aboutus/press/latestpressreleases/Pages/InnovativeComesWithMusicserviceextendingtootherEU.aspx.

[30] See, e.g., Deutsche Telekom Reply to the Commission's Consultation Regarding the Online Distribution of Music, 30 June 2009 (Deutsche Telekom Reply), available at: http://ec.europa.eu/competition/consultations/2009_online_commerce/deutsche_telecom_ag.pdf. See generally 'Online Commerce Roundtable Report on Opportunities and Barriers to Online Retailing', 26 May 2009, available at: http://ec.europa.eu/competition/sectors/media/online_commerce.html (reporting the opinions expressed by Apple in the debate on online retailing of music).

[31] See, e.g., Deutsche Telekom Reply, ibid. Deutsche Telekom writes: 'Although Deutsche Telekom is generally interested in multi-territory licences, there is no advantage for Deutsche Telekom if such multi-territory licences must be acquired from a multitude of right-owners with regard to certain works and/or music repertoires. The

As the new licensing scenario stands, a pan-European service provider wishing to offer the repertoire of the major international music publishers needs to negotiate with its different specialized agents and resort to the traditional management services of national collecting societies (or to one of their regional hubs) if it intends to enrich its service or platform with local music repertoires. This mono-repertoire licensing system evidently requires any lawful commercial user like Apple to identify beforehand which music titles it wants to use and which entity manages those titles; this seems an almost unbearable task.

Commercial users still have to face general legal uncertainty as to the identity of the collective rights managers entitled to grant licences, and the exact scope of such licences (especially in case of split copyright ownership, in which the presence of multiple rights holders makes it difficult to understand who controls the necessary rights). In replying to the 2009 consultation of the EU Commission regarding online distribution of music, YouTube (Google) and Apple raised the issue that, as a result of repertoire fragmentation, commercial users do not know exactly which rights they are clearing or purchasing.[32] This is because of the unfortunate circumstance that many collective rights organizations (still accustomed to the practice of granting blanket licences giving access to global music repertoires) are largely unable to provide commercial users with sufficient repertoire data identifying the relevant rights owners in a certain song. This is particularly unfortunate, YouTube stressed, for devisers of user-generated platforms, who need to know the repertoire data in advance in order to monetize content.[33]

---

effort to find out the numerous rights owners (co-lyricists, co-composers, co-publishers) for each music work contained in broad music repertoire offers is higher than the effort for the acquisition of global repertoire licences from a limited number of collecting societies': ibid.

[32] See 'Apple/iTunes Response to the Commission's Consultation Regarding Opportunities in Online Goods and Services', available at: http://ec.europa.eu/competition/sectors/media/apple_itunes_contribution.pdf; 'Google/YouTube Reply to the Commission's Consultation Regarding the Online Distribution of Music', 15 July 2009 (Google/YouTube Reply), available at: http://ec.europa.eu/competition/consultations/2009_online_commerce/google_youtube.pdf.

[33] See Google/YouTube Reply, ibid., 2. Not surprisingly, in its attempt to legalize the uploads of YouTube's users in Europe, Google is still negotiating and obtaining the old-fashioned mono-territorial licences for the clearance of the online rights of public performance for global music repertoires with national collecting societies such as SACEM (France) and SIAE (Italy). As pointed out in the main text, these societies still manage such rights, on the grounds of their reciprocal representation agreements, even for the Anglo-American repertoires of major international music groups. See also Aymaric Pichevin, 'YouTube Signs with France's SACEM', Billboard.biz, 30 September 2010, available at: http://www.billboard.biz/bbbiz/others/youtube-signs-with-france-s-sacem-1004117894.story; Claudio Tamburino, 'YouTube e SIAE,

For now, the only specialized rights manager who can license full packages of rights for digital uses in Europe, because of its structure, is SGAE (Spain), acting as *de facto* exclusive manager of Sony and Peer Music's Latin American repertoire within the Pan-European Licensing (PEL) initiative. The other specialized agents can *directly* license the sole mechanical shares of their Anglo-American repertoire. However, for the clearance of public performance shares of the same repertoire, online music providers still need to enter into agreements with the national collecting societies.[34]

7. FUTURE PROSPECTS

Politically speaking, EU law has a long way to go before it can establish a single copyright system for online copyrighted content. In the absence of a unified legal framework, reform plans like that undertaken by the EU Commission in the online music sector are likely to fail if EU lawmakers do not create a common playing field for collecting societies and do not harmonize and/or clarify the rules governing the assignment, transfer and online enforcement of copyright through proper legislative tools.

7.1 Fair Competition between EU Collecting Societies

If European collecting societies and other licensing bodies are expected to compete with one another on reasonably fair grounds, they should preferably enjoy a uniform legal treatment and be subject to similar administrative duties and burdens (for example, the pursuit of solidarity or cultural goals), which can greatly influence their profitability.[35] That is why I believe that the establishment of a common playing field for copyright collective management though a proper legislative harmonization initiative is indispensable (long as this initiative may take).[36]

Licenza di Monetizzare', Punto Informatico, 29 July 2010, available at: http://Ωpunto-informatico.it/2958158/PI/News/youtube-siae-licenza-monetizzare.aspx.

[34] Obviously, commercial users are placed in a much easier position in the rights clearance process whenever one of these agents (e.g., CELAS or IMPEL) sublicences the performing rights pre-acquired by national collecting societies and bundles them with the mechanical rights.

[35] See Rita Matulionytė, 'Cross Border Collective Management and Principle of Territoriality: Problems and Possible Solutions in the EU', (2009) 11 *Journal of World Intellectual Property* 467, 479–80 (suggesting the adoption of a directive on collective rights management and discussing, in particular, issues that would be worth harmonizing at the EU level, e.g. the so-called establishment requirement, deductions for cultural and social purposes).

[36] Surprisingly, this is the same view that was expressed by GEMA at the EU

What is also indispensable, in my view, is a conscious and democratic decision about what the advocated competitive relationship between collecting societies should be about. In other words, should such competition be based on the grounds of management services or – as the EU Commission seemed to claim at the time of its 2005 recommendation – on the appeal of music repertoires, regardless of how big or commercially valuable they are at the moment? This seems to me a politically and culturally strategic choice, which should be made carefully and democratically. As things stand in the offline world, music repertoires have very different commercial values and the disproportion between the market power and the territorial penetration of the Anglo-American repertoire and of national repertoires is impressive in Europe.

One wonders why EU law and policy makers should not give all repertoires the chance to be heard and known online, taking the European cultural diversity as an advantage and investing on the potential of new technologies for the promotion and wide diffusion of a vast array of music works. A prospective problem of preservation and promotion of cultural diversity undoubtedly exists and EU lawmakers should take it into consideration in their next moves, as is constitutionally prescribed by a cross-sectional clause of the Treaty on the Functioning of the European Union under Article 167.[37] In this regard,

---

Commission's Public Hearing on the Governance of Collective Rights Management in the EU, held in Brussels on 23 April 2010. On that occasion, GEMA advocated an urgent legislative initiative of the Commission aimed at enacting a directive on collective rights management. The speech delivered in Brussels by the managing director of GEMA's Department of Broadcasting and Online was very critical of the mono-repertoire model that the EU Commission has endorsed so far (and from which GEMA, through its CELAS and PAECOL subsidiaries, seemed to benefit). The GEMA representative said: 'Who still proposes to introduce competition between collecting societies about licensing deals (and secretly hopes to cut his costs) merely repeats the arguments of yesterday. Whereas the discussion of today is about win-win solutions for all involved stakeholders. … During the last ten years we have learned that competition law alone does not provide for solutions. … We need a horizontal framework directive that covers all of the activities of collecting societies': Urban Pappi, 'Relationship between Collective Rights Managers and Commercial Users Intervention at the Public Hearing on the Governance of Collective Rights Management in the EU', 23 April 2010, available at: http://ec.europa.eu/internal_market/copyright/docs/management/hearing20100423/panel_3_gema_en.pdf.

[37] See Consolidated Version of the Treaty on the Functioning of the European Union (TFEU), Art. 167(4), 5 September 2008, [2008] OJ C115, 47: 'The Union shall take cultural aspects into account in its action under other provisions of the Treaties, in particular in order to respect and to promote the diversity of its cultures.' See also Gyertyanfy, above note 14, 71 (criticizing the fact that the word 'culture' does not appear in the 19 paragraphs and in the Preamble of the Recommendation of 18 October 2005).

lawmakers should preferably opt for a licensing model that proves to work smoothly on a pan-European scale and does not end up discriminating and fragmenting the legitimate access to music repertoires by commercial users and consumers.

In this alternative scenario, in my view, collecting societies should compete with each other on the sole ground of their management services without discriminating between different categories of rights holder.

7.2 A Solution for Multi-territorial Rights Clearance

The European Union has already adopted multi-territorial or 'central' licensing solutions that presuppose a single act of rights clearance by commercial users and have an immediate pan-European reach. The legislative adoption of one of these models for the creation of one-stop shops in the management of online music rights is the least disruptive and most practical alternative to the currently unrealistic goal of unification of the national copyright systems and to the consequent creation of single EU entitlements, which would automatically supersede national rights.

This licensing solution for pan-European licensing of copyrighted works already exists under EU law and was implemented under the 1993 Satellite and Cable Directive and, more recently, under the 2010 Audiovisual Media Services Directive.[38] Both directives apply, respectively, a principle of private international law known as 'country of origin' to broadcast transmission signals and to online transmissions of audiovisual content (mainly digital TV services).[39] In both cases, the logic is that of avoiding the cumulative application of several national laws to a single EU-wide act of commercial exploitation of a copyrighted work, by adopting a criterion that identifies a single applicable law.[40] Even though their logic is the same, these two directives

---

38 Council Directive 93/83/ECC, Art. 1.2, [1993] OJ L248 15, 19 (EC) (hereinafter Directive 93/83); Directive 2010/13, Art. 2, [2010] CJ L95, 1 (EU) (codified version) (hereinafter Directive 2010/13), replacing (with no substantive changes) Directive 2007/65, Art. 2, [2007] OJ L332, 27 (EC) (hereinafter Directive 2007/65).

39 See DG INFSO and DG MARKT, 'Creative Content in a European Digital Single Market', above note 12, 17 (discussing the possible legislative extension of the principle of the country of origin of the transmission principle to the realm of online film deliveries). See also Hannah Wardale, 'The New Frontier – The Audiovisual Media Services Directive' (2009) 31 *European Intellectual Property Review* 336, 338 (providing an overview of Directive 2007/65).

40 See Matulionytė, above note 35, 475–8 (discussing the above-mentioned 'single law approach' with regard to the applicability of Directive 2000/31, [2000] OJ L178, 1 (EC) (E-Commerce Directive), and Directive 2006/123, [2006] OJ L376, 36 (EC) (Services Directive) to services of collective rights management). As this author

implement the principle of the law of the country of origin of the transmission in different ways.

Directive 93/83 adopts a country of emission rule, under which satellite broadcasters must clear copyrights just once, in the EU member state from which the programme-carrying signal is uplinked to the satellite under the control and responsibility of the broadcaster (rather than in the various member states where the broadcast is received because of the satellite footprint). In contrast, Directive 2010/13 (which codified the 2007 'modernization' amendment to the 1989 Television without Frontiers Directive) extends a 'country of establishment' rule from traditional television services to both interactive and non-interactive online television services. As a result of the country of establishment principle, providers of audiovisual media services must comply only with the laws (including copyright law) of the EU member state in which the service provider is established, rather than with those of the member states in which the service can be received.[41]

While adopting a 'single law approach', both these directives took steps to prevent opportunistic location of the television service's business establishment or of the point of departure of the transmission in a country with particularly lax copyright norms. First, the single law approach applied only to business establishments or transmission points located within the European Union. Second, these directives embodied measures ensuring a sufficient level of substantive harmonization of member state laws in their respective fields of application. This means that, despite the application of a single national law with EU-wide effects on satellite and online TV services, identical or similar conditions for market players in all EU member states preclude a 'race to the bottom'.

If EU law elaborated and then extended the country of origin principle to all kinds of online music services operated within the European Union, then a multi-repertoire licence acquired in the territory of the country of origin of the communication would automatically cover the whole EU territory. As a matter of consistency, this principle should be extended also to the licensing of rights in sound recordings, in such a way that a licence obtained from rights holders in sound recordings (or from their collecting societies) would automatically have a pan-European reach.

---

concludes, both these directives, which enable service providers to adhere to the single law of their country of establishment, explicitly exclude copyrights and neighbouring rights from their field of application and can hardly be applied to the establishment and functioning of collecting societies.

[41] Directive 2010/13, above note 38, Art. 2 (establishing the criteria according to which a media service provider should be deemed to be established in a given member state: e.g., location of the provider's head office or location of a significant part of its workforce).

It goes without saying that EU lawmakers would need to determine how to concretely adapt the country of origin principle to the realm of online music services. The criterion identifying the single applicable law could be either the country of upload of the copyrighted content to the server connected to the internet or the country of establishment of the service provider. These variations on the country of origin principle would entail the emergence of distinct scenarios, the thorough analysis of which goes beyond the purposes of this chapter.[42]

What matters here, in my view, is that the above-mentioned risk of a 'race to the bottom' in the protection of rights holders – as a consequence of the application of one single national law – would be widely mitigated by the circumstance that member state copyright rules have already been harmonized to a sufficient extent. As has been suggested in this chapter, an even stronger level of harmonization would stem from the creation of a common playing field for collecting societies through the adoption of a directive on collective rights management law.

The pan-European reach of the multi-repertoire licence in the country of origin would derive automatically from the law of that country since, legally speaking, that country would be the only place of use of copyrighted works in the online environment.[43] Under this approach, collecting societies should continue to be bound by the principle of non-discrimination between different categories of rights holder and repertoire and should continue to rely on reciprocal representation agreements in order to give commercial users access to the global music repertoire.

---

42 For instance, EU law would need to establish a secondary criterion identifying the single law of an EU member state if the service provider establishment or the transmission points were not located within the European Union (e.g., opting for the law of the member state with which the online music service or the non-EU provider are most closely connected, in light of, say, the presence of offices or workforce of the same provider).

43 It goes beyond the scope and the purposes of this chapter to discuss the implications of the proposed reform for the determination of the law applicable to copyright infringements affecting works made available online under the above-mentioned 'single law' principle. This aspect is currently disciplined under Regulation 864/2007, Art. 8, [2007] OJ L199 40 (EC), available at: http://eur-lex.europa.eu/ LexUriServ/ LexUriServ.do?uri=OJ:L:2007:199:0040:0049:EN:PDF.Regulation 864/2007, under Art. 8, provides that the law applicable to a non-contractual obligation arising from the infringement of an intellectual property right should be the law of the country for which protection is claimed (*lex loci protectionis*). Ideally, to avoid the application of distinct laws to the management of online music rights and the infringement of the same rights, EU lawmakers could create an exception to the *lex loci protectionis* rule by embracing the principle of the country of origin of the transmission even for the determination of the law applicable to online copyright infringements.

In this prospective framework, all stakeholders would effectively end up treating the European Union as a 'Digital Single Market'. The opportunity for online music providers to offer their services by merely having to clear the necessary online rights in the country in which their content is materially uploaded (or where the provider is established), while paying the same price for all music titles, would greatly reduce today's discrimination between big and small music repertoires, mainstream and local (or niche) repertoires, major recording businesses and small or independent record labels, traditional business models and innovative businesses combining commercial and non-commercial licences. On the rights holders' front, their freedom to select and join a collecting society of their choice for the management of online music rights in the European Union then would ensure that societies would effectively compete and seek to implement the best management conditions for their members (both authors and publishers). As for the economic conditions of licensing, fair competition among collecting societies on licence prices would be ensured through the inclusion in the above-mentioned regulatory framework on collective rights management law of a principle obliging societies and commercial users to take account of the actual and potential audience of the online content transmission on a pan-European basis in determining the amounts of the payments to be made for the rights acquired.[44]

Therefore, with regard to the territorial dimension of the licensing system at issue, the law would mandate the EU-wide character of online music licences in order to avoid artificial restrictions in an intrinsically borderless environment. To a certain extent, the mandatory pan-European dimension of online music licences in the intangible world of copyright would play for diffusion of online music service (and, possibly, for the diffusion of other kinds of online content) the same market-integrating function that the exhaustion principle plays at the EU level in the real (tangible) world for the free circulation of physical items embodying copyrighted works in the EU territory. To this end, the proposed licensing system would sacrifice the freedom of music rights holders to license their rights on a strictly mono-territorial basis and to geo-localize the legitimate online transmission of their works, recordings or performances, in the same way as EU copyright law restricts the national subject matter of the right of distribution when the copyrighted tangible item is placed on the market with the copyright owner's consent.[45]

---

44 Directive 93/83, above note 38, recital 17 (containing a similar principle requiring satellite broadcasters and collective rights organizations to take account of all aspects of the broadcast, such as the actual and the potential audience and the language version, in the determination of the licence price).

45 See Council Directive 2001/29, above note 5, Art. 4.2.

From an economic and cultural perspective, the advocated reform would greatly emphasize the function of reciprocal representation agreements, through which each collecting society builds up its multi-repertoire of 'musical offering' while giving national collective rights managers (even the small and medium size ones) a large incentive to compete with one another on the grounds of the quality, speed and innovative character of their services.

It seems evident to me that such an easier and clearer structure of online music rights licensing would ultimately promote European cultural diversity. A wide and legitimate exploitation of highly diversified stocks of music repertoires would be strongly encouraged; small and independent entrepreneurs, who are completely forgotten and discriminated against in today's licensing system, would be given a much greater incentive to invest in online content services and an effective enjoyment of music 'without frontiers' (that is, on a truly European basis) would become feasible through reasonably inexpensive and equal forms of access to cultural content by the widest portion of EU citizens.

7.3 Types of Rights Covering Online Exploitations

Finally, with regard to the definition of the rights covering online exploitations, it seems clear that today's archaic distinction between *mechanical* and *public performance* rights is no longer justified, neither legally nor economically. It does make sense to keep, for instance, the licensing of streaming music services distinct from that of music downloads, but this should only be an economically relevant distinction, allowing rights holders to price discriminate between licensing solutions corresponding to differentiated forms of exploitation (for example, randomized web radio streams like the service Pandora; music downloads from sources such as iTunes and Beatport; ringtones and Nokia's mobile phone downloads).

Legally speaking, however, keeping the distinction in force in the online environment has proved to be highly detrimental for the development of a mature market for online creative content. In my view, online rights management should no longer be based on old-fashioned categories of rights which were exercised distinctly and transferred to today's rights holders when composers, lyricists and music publishers (John Lennon, Paul McCartney and EMI in the 1960s, for example) could not imagine what the online world and the related forms of commercial exploitation would have been about. As we have seen, the simultaneous implementation of both these old-fashioned categories in online rights clearance processes has entailed in Europe the risks described by the 'tragedy of the anti-commons'.[46]

---

46 In the copyright field, multiple layers of exclusive rights over the same music

I agree with those authors who have called for a radical change in online licensing practices and have proposed the worldwide recognition of a new exclusive right of authorization that functions as a single digital transmission right covering all kinds of online and mobile exploitation.[47] I believe that the existence of a very wide statutory right of making copyrighted content available to the public under Article 3.2 of Council Directive 2001/29 should place the European Union in a position to enforce such a right in conformity with the objective that the directive intended to pursue.

The making available right was the first EU right formulated while having online services in mind, and this right was specifically tailored to cover not just streaming services but also permanent downloads.[48] This new prerogative was not conceived as a new type or category of right, but rather as an extension of the pre-existing right of public performance. Unfortunately, the wording of the 2001 Directive did not make it clear whether or not the sole clearance of the right of making content available would have sufficed in order to make online on-demand transmissions legitimate. As we have seen, the simultaneous application of the rights of digital reproduction has been deemed to be necessary for a legitimate offer of online music services, with an inevitable increase in transaction costs.

In my view, the EU Commission should take action urgently in order to remove this uncertainty and to impose an economically viable and modern interpretation of the exclusive right of making content available to the public. Ideally, this right should be the only one covering online on-demand transmissions and, as a result, the only type of right to be cleared by service providers for online music deliveries, irrespective of the techniques (for example, streaming, downloading, and so on) through which the content is transmitted and placed at the consumer's disposal.

Beyond efficiency and transparency, there are strong legal arguments under Council Directive 2001/29 that might suggest the non-enforceability of

works and over the same sound recording entail the risk of such a situation: see Michael A. Heller, 'The Tragedy of the Anticommons: Property in the Transition from Marx to Markets' (1998) 111 *Harvard Law Review* 621, 623 (coining this expression to describe a coordination breakdown caused by the existence of too many owners over the same resource).

47 See Gyertyanfy, above note 14, 88; see also Bennett Lincoff, 'Common Sense, Accommodation and Sound Policy for the Digital Music Marketplace' (2008) 2 *Journal International Media & Entertainment Law* 1, 9.

48 Recital 23 of Council Directive 2001/29 makes it clear that 'this right should be understood in a broad sense covering all communication to the public not present at the place where the communication originates. This right should cover any such transmission or retransmission of a work to the public by wire or wireless means, including broadcasting'.

mechanical (that is, reproduction) rights and the mere application of the public performance (or making available) rights in the realm of online music services. It should be considered that all acts of digital reproduction which are technically inherent in, and economically inseparable from, acts of making content available to the public can be legally intended to be 'absorbed' by the function of transmitting copyrighted works interactively, which is logically and economically predominant. This rationale is clearly embodied in the wording of the only copyright exception that Council Directive 2001/29 made mandatory for EU member states.[49] This means that acts of reproduction that constitute a technical necessity for, and are inherent in, acts of online content transmissions could easily be deemed to fall outside the scope of the right of digital reproduction since they have, as such, no independent economic significance.

It remains to be seen how the objective of enforcing a single exclusive right of online transmission for online music services can be concretely achieved. The interpretation of EU law is an exclusive competence of the European Court of Justice (ECJ), which might be asked, sooner or later, to shed light on this specific aspect of Council Directive 2001/29. If this happened and the ECJ endorsed the interpretation that has been advocated, there would be no need for a legislative amendment of the current legal framework, since the ECJ's interpretation would constitute a mandatory precedent. Still, the EU could achieve the same objective more realistically through a directive proposal of the EU Commission aimed at recognizing explicitly the autonomous character of the right of making content available for the clearance of online transmissions.

---

49 See Council Directive 2001/29, above note 5, Art 5, which provides: 'Temporary acts of reproduction … which are transient or incidental [and] an integral and essential part of a technological process and whose sole purpose is to enable … a lawful use … of a work or other subject-matter to be made, and which have *no independent economic significance*, shall be exempted from the reproduction right provided for in Article 2' (emphasis added).

PART II

Aspects of the Anti-Counterfeiting Trade Agreement

8. The Anti-Counterfeiting Trade Agreement and criminal enforcement of intellectual property: what consequences for the European Union?

Christophe Geiger

1. INTRODUCTION

The Anti-Counterfeiting Trade Agreement (ACTA) has caused considerable concern,[1] in the European Union (EU) and elsewhere. This was initially generated by the fact that the negotiations for the Agreement, pursued for three years outside any official multilateral framework by the European Commission and ten other countries, were for a long time kept secret, giving rise to all sorts of speculation and fears on the part of the public.[2] At some

[1] In relation to the Agreement, see C. Geiger, 'Weakening Multilateralism in Intellectual Property Lawmaking: A European Perspective on ACTA', (2012) 3(2) *WIPOJ* 166, enhanced version of a Study made at the request of the Committee on International Trade (INTA), Directorate-General for External Policies of the European Parliament, 'The Anti-Counterfeiting Trade Agreement (ACTA): A Comprehensive Assessment from a European Perspective', March 2012, and the Focus Issue on 'Intellectual Property Law Enforcement and the Anti-Counterfeiting Trade Agreement' (2011) 26(3) *American University International Law Review*; K. Weatherall, 'Politics, Compromise, Text and the Failures of the Anti-Counterfeiting Trade Agreement' (2011) 33 *Sidney Law Review* 229; P. Arhel, 'L'accord commercial anticontrefaçon: version finale', Propr. industr. March 2011, 13; J.-C. Galloux, RTDcom. January/ March 2011, 81; M. Stieper, 'Das Anti-Counterfeiting Trade Agreement (ACTA)' (2011) *GRUR International* 124. See also the presentations made by M. Senftleben, M. Barczewski, K. Weatherall, I. Stamatoudi and C.R. McManis at the 2011 ATRIP Congress during the session chaired by Graeme Dinwoodie on the topic 'Trade in Counterfeit Goods – Is ACTA the Right Answer?', Singapore, 26 July 2011 (some of which form part of this volume); M. Blakeney, *Intellectual Property Enforcement: A Commentary on the Anti-Counterfeiting Trade Agreement (ACTA)* (Edward Elgar Publishing 2012).

[2] From a European perspective, see A. Metzger, 'A Primer on ACTA, What Europeans Should Fear about the Anti-Counterfeiting Trade Agreement' (2010) *Journal of Intellectual Property, Information Technology and E-Commerce Law* [JIPITEC] 109. From a more global perspective, see P.K. Yu, 'Six Secret (and Now

point, the European Parliament protested loudly and adopted a resolution by a huge majority,[3] demanding full information from the European Commission on the progress of the negotiations. Under pressure from this resolution, the Commission publicized a first version of the proposed agreement on 21 April 2010[4] and, following the last cycle of negotiations in Tokyo, a consolidated version on 2 October 2010.[5] The final version of the Agreement was released on 3 December 2010 after the legal verification meeting held in Sydney, although this had little impact on the final text.[6]

It should be noted that the final version of the Agreement was far less spectacular than expected, since most of the controversial measures had been abandoned or had had their scope narrowed.[7] However, some problematic aspects

---

Open) Fears of ACTA' (2011) 64(3) *SMU Law Review* 975; C.R. McManis, 'The Proposed Anti-Counterfeiting Trade Agreement (ACTA): Two Tales of a Treaty' (2009) 46(4) *Houston Law Review* 1235; M. Kaminski, 'The Origins and Potential Impact of the Anti-Counterfeiting Trade Agreement (ACTA)' (2009) 24 *Yale Journal of International Law* 247; M. Geist, 'ACTA's State of the Play: Looking Beyond Transparency' (2011) 26(3) *American University International Law Review* 543.

[3] See the Resolution of the European Parliament dated 10 March 2010 on the transparency and state of play of the ACTA (Anti-Counterfeiting Trade Agreement) negotiations: P7_TA-PROV(2010)0058).

[4] ACTA, consolidated text prepared for public release, April 2010, available at: http://trade.ec.europa.eu/doclib/docs/2010/april/tradoc_146029.pdf (last accessed 20 July 2012).

[5] Anti-Counterfeiting Trade Agreement, Consolidated text, reflects changes made during the Tokyo Round in September 2010, Informal Predecisional/Deliberative Draft, 2 October 2010.

[6] The definitive text is available at the website of the Trade DG of the European Commission, which negotiated the Agreement: see http://trade.ec.europa.eu/doclib/docs/2010/december/tradoc_147079.pdf (last accessed 20 July 2012). The Agreement was signed on 1 October 2011 in Tokyo by the representatives of eight of the negotiating parties (Australia, Canada, Japan, Republic of Korea, Morocco, New Zealand, Singapore and the US) and on 26 January 2012 by the European Union and 22 of its Member States (Austria, Belgium, Bulgaria, Czech Republic, Denmark, Finland, France, Greece, Hungary, Ireland, Italy, Latvia, Lithuania, Luxemburg, Malta, Poland, Portugal, Romania, Slovenia, Spain, Sweden and the United Kingdom). On 26 June 2012, the Dutch government decided not to sign ACTA. Other negotiating parties adopted different positions: while Mexico signed ACTA on 11 July 2012 (see the press release available in English at: http://www.impi.gob.mx/work/sites/IMPI/resources/LocalContent/3388/4/IMPI_010_2012_en.pdf (last accessed 20 July 2012)), the Swiss Confederation postponed signature of the Agreement (see the press release available in French, German and Italian at: http://www.news.admin.ch/dokumentation/00002/00015/index.html?lang=fr&msg-id=44484 (last accessed 20 July 2012)).

[7] This was, for example, the case of the controversial 'three strike rules' against internet file sharers, which was present in the earlier version of the Agreement, but had later been dropped, making the 'Digital Chapter' of ACTA less problematic, even if some concerns are remaining as a result of uncertainties in the interpretation of some

remained. This chapter will concentrate on what can be considered to be one of the most problematic of these aspects: the provision on criminal enforcement contained in Article 23. We will show first why criminal enforcement is generally a problematic issue, especially in the EU, and then briefly try to demonstrate why ACTA *is not* the right answer in this regard and that criminal enforcement rules clearly need a differentiated approach – one that is not reflected in the Agreement.[8]

2. CRIMINAL ENFORCEMENT OF INTELLECTUAL PROPERTY, A PROBLEMATIC ISSUE IN THE EUROPEAN UNION

Criminal enforcement of intellectual property rights has always been a controversial issue in the EU.[9] This is mainly as a result of two factors: (i) harmonization in the field of criminal law, and (ii) the extent to which enforcement of intellectual property rights should be subject to criminal law – both of which have always been debated topics.

2.1 Harmonization of Criminal Law

Harmonization at both the European and international levels is a highly sensitive issue, since criminal law is closely linked to moral and cultural conceptions within a society. Criminal law has always been a tool to protect the public interest, the harm to society being the justification for the existence of a criminal penalty. Of course, these conceptions diverge sharply in different parts of the world: the reasons for sending someone to prison are different in the US, France, China, Russia or Singapore. Moreover, traditions regarding criminal procedure vary significantly in the different legal traditions for cultural reasons: while a certain procedure might seem totally normal in a given state, the same procedure might seem rather 'exotic' in another. Sovereignty issues are very strong in criminal law.[10] It is therefore not surprising that, during the negotiation of the TRIPS

---

provisions: see R. Matulionyte, 'ACTA's Digital Chapter: Remaining Concerns and What Can be Done' (2011) 1(3) *Queen Mary Journal of Intellectual Property* 248.

8 See on this issue C. Geiger, 'Of ACTA, "Pirates" and Organized Criminality: How "Criminal" Should the Enforcement of Intellectual Property Be?' [2010] IIC 629.

9 On this question, see C. Geiger (ed.), *Criminal Enforcement of Intellectual Property: A Handbook of Contemporary Research* (Edward Elgar Publishing 2012).

10 See, in this sense, T. Mylly, 'Criminal Enforcement and European Union Law', in Geiger (ed.), above note 9, 215: 'Criminal law – together with the disposition of the police monopoly on the use of force – has traditionally been thought of as an area belonging to the core of national sovereignty and competence'.

Agreement, there were major disagreements concerning the form of IP infringement that should be subject to criminal enforcement.[11] This resulted in a compromise, reducing the mandatory provision of criminal procedures and penalties to cases of wilful trademark counterfeiting or copyright piracy on a commercial scale.[12] It is clear from the negotiations history that Member States were intended, consistent with Article 1.1 of the Agreement,[13] to be allowed considerable flexibility in deciding the manner in which to implement these criminal penalties in their national law.

Moreover, the concept of 'commercial scale' was sufficiently vague to leave enough room for flexible interpretations.[14] Given this internationally sensitive issue, it is also not surprising that the WTO Panel,[15] when asked to provide a more precise definition of the notion of 'commercial scale', remained very cautious and proposed a flexible approach, holding that its interpretation depended on the situation – namely the product and the market in question, and also the extent of the infringement.[16] This flexibility was the

---

11 On the history of the Uruguay round of negotiations and the preparatory work for the TRIPS Agreement regarding criminal enforcement, see A. Adam, 'What is 'Commercial Scale'? A Critical Analysis of the WTO Decision', in WT/DS362/R, [2011] EIPR 342, 346 et seq.

12 Article 61, TRIPS Agreement lays down that 'Members shall provide for criminal procedures and penalties to be applied at least in cases of wilful trademark counterfeiting or copyright piracy on a commercial scale'.

13 Article 1.1 TRIPS Agreement leaves Member States the freedom to choose the manner of implementation of the Agreement's obligations.

14 See H. Grosse Ruse-Khan, 'Criminal Enforcement and International IP Law', in Geiger (ed.), above note 9, 174: 'It is important to highlight the limited scope of Article 61 TRIPS and its inherent flexibilities as well as those external ones which allow WTO Member States to implement criminal procedures tailored to domestic circumstances'.

15 WTO Panel Report, 26 January 2009, *China – Measures affecting the protection and enforcement of Intellectual Property*, WT/DS362/R. For a comment, see R. Creemers, 'The Effects of World Trade Organization Case DS362 on Audiovisual Media in China' [2009] EIPR 568; H. Xue, 'Enforcement for Development: Why not an Agenda for the Developing World?', in H. Li and C.M. Correa (eds.), *Intellectual Property Enforcement, International Perspectives* (Edward Elgar Publishing 2009) 133, and from the same author: 'An Anatomical Study of the United States versus China at the World Trade Organisation on Intellectual Property Enforcement' [2009] EIPR 292; D. Gervais, 'China – Measures Affecting the Protection and Enforcement of Intellectual Property Rights' (2009) 103 *American Journal of International Law* 549; Grosse Ruse-Khan, above note 14, 171; P.K. Yu, 'Shaping Chinese Criminal Enforcement Norms through the TRIPS Agreement', in Geiger (ed.), above note 9, 286; P.K. Yu, 'The US–China Dispute over TRIPS Enforcement', preprinted in (2010) 5 *Drake University Law School Occasional Papers in Intellectual Property Law*, and from the same author 'The TRIPS Enforcement Dispute' (2011) 89(4) *Nebraska Law Review* 1046; Adam, above note 11.

16 According to Adam, ibid., 348, the term 'commercial scale' is a flexible

price to pay in order to reach agreement on criminal enforcement provisions at the international level. However, the consequence was that the enforcement rules in the TRIPS Agreement were considered to be relatively weak, as has been rightly pointed out by scholars such as Jerome Reichman, David Lange and Peter Yu, even referring to the enforcement provisions as the 'Achilles' heel' of the Agreement.[17] This is exactly the reason why stronger provisions on criminal enforcement were included in ACTA. In fact, Article 23 ACTA defines acts carried out on a 'commercial scale' as 'commercial activities for direct or indirect economic or commercial advantage', which broadens the notion and might be less flexible than the market- or product-based interpretation of the WTO Panel.[18]

The same delicate issue of sovereignty can be found in the European Union. The question whether the EU has competence to act in the field of criminal law has always been a debated and unclear issue.[19] It was mainly for this reason that the provisions on criminal enforcement were taken out of the first enforcement directive adopted in 2004.[20] In a subsequent decision of 2005 (a case concerning environmental law), the Court of Justice of the European Union (CJEU) partially clarified that the EU had limited competence in the field of criminal law if the application of effective, proportionate and dissuasive criminal penalties is *necessary to ensure the efficiency of important Community policies*.[21] This very limited competence of the EU regarding criminal law has been reiterated since by the Lisbon Treaty. Article

concept, but the notion remains vague following the decision. According to this author, 'for the time being, it is not possible to establish a clear and precise standard of criminal enforcement measures based on Article 61 of the TRIPS Agreement. Consequently, Article 61 remains an uncertain bare minimum, which may or may not be satisfactory to some parties'.

17 J.H. Reichman and D. Lange, 'Bargaining Around the TRIPS Agreement: The Case for Ongoing Public–Private Initiatives to Facilitate Worldwide Intellectual Property Transactions' (1998) 9 *Duke Journal of Comparative & International Law* 11, 34 et seq.; P.K. Yu, 'TRIPS and Its Achilles' Heel' (2011) 18(2) *Journal of Intellectual Property Law* 479.

18 See, in this sense, Grosse Ruse-Khan, above note 14, 171 et seq. The WTO Panel (above note 15, 7.577) referred to 'counterfeiting or piracy carried on at the magnitude or extent of typical or usual commercial activity with respect to a given product in a given market'.

19 See, on the question of competence, the interesting article by A. Ramalho, 'The European Union and ACTA – Or Making Omelettes without Eggs (Again)' [2011] IIC 97.

20 See Directive 2004/48/EC of the European Parliament and of the Council of 29 April 2004 on the enforcement of intellectual property rights, OJEU L157 of 30 April 2004 corrected in OJEU L195 of 2 June 2004, 16. See in this sense the comment of Mylly, above note 10, 213 et seq.

21 Case C-176/03 *Commission of the European Communities v Council of the European Union* [2005] ECR 7879.

83(2) of the Treaty on the Functioning of the European Union (TFEU) provides only for the possibility of adopting minimum rules concerning the definition of criminal offences and penalties when harmonization of the legislative provisions proves to be *essential* to ensure the effective implementation of a Union policy.[22] The 'essential' nature of criminal penalties is actually debated, since there is already a harmonized framework for civil penalties in the EU, which might be considered to be sufficient and better suited in many cases.[23] As proof, some scholars have also pointed out that criminal law provisions are rarely used in EU countries and play a very subordinate role in practice, especially in the field of patent law.[24] The competence of the EU in the field of criminal enforcement of intellectual property rights, therefore, remains doubtful.[25]

But that is not all. If the EU has exclusive competence regarding common commercial policy, including 'commercial aspects of intellectual property' (Article 207 TFEU), it remains unclear whether criminal enforcement provi-

---

[22] Article 83 (2) TFEU: 'If the approximation of criminal laws and regulations of the Member States proves essential to ensure the effective implementation of a Union policy in an area which has been subject to harmonisation measures, directives may establish minimum rules with regard to the definition of criminal offences and sanctions in the area concerned'. On this provision see S. Peers, 'EU criminal law and the Treaty of Lisbon' [2008] *European Law Review* 517. See also the 'Lisbon' decision of the German Constitutional Court, 30 June 2009, 2 BvE 2/08, stating that: 'only if it is demonstrably established that a serious deficit as regards enforcement actually exists and that it can only be remedied by the threat of a sanction, this exceptional constituent element exists and the annex competence for legislation in criminal law may be deemed conferred' (para. 358 et seq.).

[23] See R.M. Hilty, A. Kur and A. Peukert, 'Statement of the Max Planck Institute for Intellectual Property, Competition and Tax Law on the Proposal for a Directive of the European Parliament and the Council on Criminal Measures Aimed at Ensuring the Enforcement of Intellectual Property Rights' [2006] IIC 970; Ramalho, above note 19, 98. According to Mylly, above note 10, 226, 'the *ultima ratio* nature of EU criminal law measures could well be tested under the principle of proportionality'.

[24] J. Gibson, 'The Directive Proposal on Criminal Sanctions', in Geiger (ed.), above note 9, 245; J. Schmidt, 'The French Case: Comparison Past/Present/Future of Criminal Law', in Geiger (ed.), above note 9, 343: 'Statistics show that in 2001 judicial decisions ordering criminal sanctions of infringement accounted to 0.1% of the total number of the French criminal courts' decisions'; Hilty, Kur and Peukert, above note 23, 972.

[25] Moreover, in its ruling No. 1/94, the ECJ stated that the power to ratify the TRIPS Agreement was divided, i.e. the Agreement required ratification by the Union *and* the Member States: Opinion of the Court of 15 November 1994 on the Competence of the Community to conclude international agreements concerning services and the protection of intellectual property – Article 228 (6) of the EC Treaty [1994] ECR I-05267, paras. 59–60. This would mean that the Members States also need to ratify the ACTA treaty.

sions are necessarily 'commercial aspects of IP'. As it has been argued, 'aspects of IP that relate to commerce and trade might be those which concern, enable, or are the object of commercial transactions – licensing of IP or its securitization are pragmatic examples'.[26] The issue of competence became more and more pressing.[27] Some EU parliamentarians, at the end of May 2011, addressed a letter to the President of the European Parliament asking him to request an opinion of the Court of Justice on this issue.[28] The European Commission finally revealed that the section of the Agreement on criminal enforcement was negotiated on behalf of the Member States and that ACTA needs to be considered as a mixed agreement, for which the European Union's competence is shared with that of the Member States.[29] Anyway, because of the growing opposition to the Treaty in many of the Members States, the European Commission finally announced on 22 February 2012 that it would ask the Court to review the compatibility of the text with primary EU law.[30]

---

26 Ramalho, above note 19, 99.

27 According to Mylly, above note 10, 213, ACTA is likely to become a test case of the EU's competence to criminalize IP infringements internally and externally.

28 Letter of Rebecca Harms to the President of the European Parliament on behalf of the Greens/EFA group, 31 May 2011, available at: http://en.act-on-acta.eu/Letter_to_President_of_the_European_Parliament_regarding_when_the_Parliament_can_ask_the_Court_for_an_opinion (last accessed 20 July 2012). This possibility is granted to the European Parliament by TFEU, Article 218(11) which provides that 'a Member State, the European Parliament, the Council or the Commission may obtain the opinion of the Court of Justice as to whether an agreement envisaged is compatible with the Treaties. Where the opinion of the Court is adverse, the agreement envisaged may not enter into force unless it is amended or the Treaties are revised'.

29 The Commission also concedes that 'a very limited number of Member States may need to adapt their own legislation related to criminal enforcement to comply with the commitments they undertook (ACTA is a mixed EU/Member States competence Agreement). This has been confirmed in very clear terms by the two Opinions of the Legal Service of the European Parliament of 5 October 2011 and of 8 December 2011, answering respectively to questions by the INTA and JURI Committees': '10 Myths about ACTA', text published on the DG Trade website, available at: http://trade.ec.europa.eu/doclib/docs/2012/february/tradoc_149112.pdf (last accessed 20 July 2012)).

30 Statement by Commissioner Karel De Gucht on ACTA (Anti-Counterfeiting Trade Agreement), Press release, Brussels, 22 February 2012. The following question was agreed upon to be asked to the CJEU on 4 April 2012: 'Is the envisaged Anti-Counterfeiting Trade Agreement (ACTA) compatible with the European Treaties and in particular with the Charter of Fundamental Rights of the European Union?' (Update on ACTA's referral the Court of Justice, Press release, IP/12/354, Brussels, 4 April 2012). The referral took place on 10 May 2012 (the European Commission officially referred ACTA to the European Court of Justice Statement by John Clancy, EU Trade Spokesman, Notice, Brussels, 11 May 2012).

The life of ACTA in the EU could, therefore, end prematurely if the Court of Justice were to find it incompatible with the EU treaties.[31]

We have seen that harmonization of criminal law is problematic. This is accentuated by the fact that criminal enforcement of IP is, in itself, a controversial issue in the EU.

2.2 The Extent to which Enforcement of Intellectual Property Rights Should Be Subject to Criminal Law

Even if several EU Member States have criminal enforcement provisions in their IP legislation, the introduction of a harmonized standard for criminal enforcement remains very controversial.[32] A good example is the heated debate caused by the directive proposal on this subject, which ultimately led to its failure[33] and final withdrawal by the Commission in September 2010.[34] One of the most controversial provisions defined the criminal offence as 'any deliberate infringement of an intellectual property right committed on a *commercial scale*, and the attempt at such an infringement, complicity and incitement to commit such an infringement' (Article 3, emphasis added). The

---

[31] It has to be mentioned that the European Parliament declined to consent to the conclusion of ACTA on 4 July 2012. Before the final vote of the Plenary, a postponement was requested until the Court of Justice delivers its Opinion. The Parliament rejected the postponement with 420 against the request, 255 in favour and 9 abstentions, followed by the rejection of the Agreement as such with an overwhelming majority: 478 votes against, 39 in favour and 165 abstentions: European Parliament legislative resolution of 4 July 2012 on the draft Council decision on the conclusion of the Anti-Counterfeiting Trade Agreement between the European Union and its Member States, Australia, Canada, Japan, the Republic of Korea, the United Mexican States, the Kingdom of Morocco, New Zealand, the Republic of Singapore, the Swiss Confederation and the United States of America (12195/2011 – C7-0027/2012 – 2011/0167(NLE)), P7_TA-PROV(2012)0287), available at: http://www.europarl.europa.eu/sides/getDoc.do?type=TA&reference=P7-TA-2012-0287&language=EN&ring=A7-2012-0204 (last accessed 20 July 2012).

[32] See Gibson, above note 24, 245, stating that 'the harmonisation of criminal law and procedure is still in its infancy within the European Union law and so the relationship between the commercial framework of intellectual property and the criminal enforcement of its standards remains an unsettled and unsettling adolescence. The Proposal for a Directive on criminal measures aimed at ensuring the enforcement of intellectual property rights is at the vanguard of the extension of EU competence, some going as far as describing it a competency Trojan Horse'.

[33] Modified Proposal for a Directive of the European Parliament and the Council on Criminal Measures aimed at Ensuring the Enforcement of Intellectual Property Rights, 26 April 2006, COM(2006) 168 final. For a criticism of this text, see Hilty, Kur and Peukert, above note 23, 974, 970; Gibson, above note 24, 245 et seq.

[34] [2010] OJ C252/9, 18 September 2010.

conditions set by this provision were considered by the European Parliament to be too broad and vague, and it requested that acts 'carried out by private users for personal and not-for-profit purposes'[35] should be expressly excluded in order to avoid any ambiguity. There were other areas of disagreement: for example, whether the proposal should apply to all IP rights (as originally proposed) or only to certain IP rights (to exclude patents, for example).[36]

The proposal ultimately failed, which is not surprising since the issue of criminal enforcement is dealt with very differently in the national legislative frameworks of Member States. To start with, not all of them have criminal enforcement provisions.[37] And even when criminal enforcement is provided for, there is no uniformity as to the type of infringement that should be criminalized: All IP rights? Only trademarks and copyrights, and not patents? And what should be the threshold, in that criminal law is in general meant, in most legal systems, to be a measure of last resort?[38]

In addition, in the EU, some fundamental rights issues remain unclear. Are criminal enforcement provisions mandatory on the basis of Article 17.2 of the European Charter of Fundamental Rights[39] ('intellectual property shall be protected'), as the recitals of the failed directive seemed to indicate, or is this provision to be interpreted differently in a more balanced way, which would induce a duty not to strengthen excessively the enforcement ties?[40] And what

35 Position of the European Parliament adopted at first reading on 25 April 2007 with a view to the adoption of Directive 2007/.../EC of the European Parliament and of the Council on criminal measures aimed at ensuring the enforcement of intellectual property rights (EP-PE_TC1-COD(2005)0127). The European Parliament also clarified that 'the fair use of a protected work, including such use by reproduction in copies or audio or by any other means, for purposes such as criticism, comments, news reporting, teaching (including multiple copies for classroom use), scholarship or research, does not constitute a criminal offence'.

36 See Gibson, above note 24, 245.

37 At least not for all IP rights. Patent law is sometimes excluded from criminal liability (this is, for example, the case in the UK). According to Hilty, patent law is a particularly problematic area regarding criminal sanctions: R.M. Hilty, 'Economic, Legal and Social Impacts of Counterfeiting', in: Geiger (ed.), above note 9, 18. For a comparative approach of criminal enforcement provisions in France, UK, Canada, US and China, see the chapters by J. Schmidt, G. Westkamp, D. Gervais and P.K. Yu, in Geiger (ed.), ibid.

38 See Hilty, Kur and Peukert, above note 23, 973; Mylly, above note 10, 246, stating that 'the nature of criminal law as *ultima ratio,* a means of last resort, has been overlooked'.

39 Charter of Fundamental Rights of the European Union, [2010] OJ C83/02, 30 March 2010.

40 On this provision, see C. Geiger, 'Intellectual Property shall be Protected!? Article 17(2) of the Charter of Fundamental Rights of the European Union: A Mysterious Provision with an Unclear Scope' [2009] EIPR 113; J. Griffiths and L.

about issues of competing fundamental rights such as privacy, freedom of expression and due process? [41]

The principle of proportionality of EU legislation is another argument that has been brought forward to demonstrate the need for some harmonization of criminal enforcement provisions of IP rights: there already exist operational civil enforcement mechanisms, which have been harmonized in the EU since the implementation in all Member States of the 2004 Enforcement Directive. These provisions might be considered to be sufficient, especially with regard to the potential for misuse that can result from the threat of criminal penalties and which can have a detrimental effect on competition.[42] The issue of misuse was also raised by the European Parliament in the debate on the directive proposal[43] and in the comment of the Max Planck Institute for Intellectual Property and Competition Law,[44] but it was not addressed in the ACTA draft.

In summary, there are several factors that make the provisions on criminal enforcement problematic in the EU.

It is therefore very surprising and hard to understand why, on 24 November 2010, the European Parliament adopted a resolution[45] in which it considers ACTA to be fully compatible with the *acquis communautaire*. This motivated a group of European academics to draft an Opinion aimed at pointing to the differences between ACTA and European and international intellectual property law, and to the modifications to European law that the ratification of this agreement would involve.[46] This Opinion was sent in

---

McDonagh, 'Fundamental Rights and European IP Law – The Case of Article 17(2) of the EU Charter', in C. Geiger (ed.), *Constructing European Intellectual Property: Achievements and New Perspectives* (Edward Elgar Publishing 2012), at 75.

[41] For more details on this issue, J. Griffiths, 'Criminal Liability for Intellectual Property Infringement in Europe: The Role of Fundamental Rights', in Geiger (ed.), above note 9, 191 et seq.

[42] See in this sense Hilty, above note 37, 18, stating that 'enforcement tools should be moderate enough to allow free competition to increase the supply of available product and services. We should be even more moderate and careful when dealing with criminal law. In its essence, criminal law constitutes a "dangerous weapon" that makes the harm of any enforcement measure even worse'.

[43] Article 7 of the European Parliament's Position of 25 April 2007 (above note 35) required the prohibition of the misuse of criminal procedures and sanctions, especially when they are employed for the enforcement of the requirements of civil law.

[44] Hilty, Kur and Peukert, above note 23, 975. Stressing the need for countermeasures against the misuse of criminal sanctions, see also Hilty, above note 37, 9 and Gibson, above note 24, 245 et seq.

[45] Resolution of the European Parliament dated 24 November 2010 on the Anti-Counterfeiting Trade Agreement (ACTA), P7_TA-PROV (2010)0432.

[46] See the 'Opinion of European Academics on Anti-Counterfeiting Trade Agreement' (2011) 2 JIPITEC 65 (for a French translation of the Opinion, see (2011)

February 2011 to the European Commission and Parliament, and was then widely commented upon.

Surprisingly, the European Commission, in April 2011, issued an official reply in the form of a working document. This deserves to be noticed since it is very rare that the Commission responds to arguments from the academic community and shows that the Opinion was taken very seriously.[47] The Commission, less surprisingly, concludes by stating that

> after close examination of the Opinion, we believe that the Opinion fails to demonstrate, in a convincing manner, that ACTA is not in line with the relevant Community acquis or that it raises legitimate concerns as regards certain fundamental rights.

Nevertheless, interestingly, the Commission replied explicitly to all the arguments that were raised in the Opinion. Some of the clarifications were convincing, some less so. This is the case in particular regarding the concern raised in the Opinion that ACTA would require additional EU legislation, since there is no *acquis* on criminal enforcement. The Commission simply stated that the TRIPS Agreement also contains binding provisions for EU Member States on criminal enforcement and that no EU legislation was necessary to implement those aspects. This seems to be forgetting rather quickly that the Commission, over many years, strongly pushed for a directive on criminal enforcement, and for some commentators 'it is clear that the Commission intends to introduce a new proposal' which is likely to 'include the relevant provision recently agreed in ACTA',[48] especially since enforcement is among the top priorities for its IP strategy. In the meantime, a study drafted by the Institute for Globalisation and International Regulation of Maastricht University, at the request of the European Parliament's Committee on International Trade, came to a similar conclusion as the Opinion, recommending that 'unconditional consent would be an inappropriate response from the European Parliament given the issues identified with ACTA as its stands'.[49]

---

6 *Auteurs et Media*). For a presentation of this opinion, see R. D'Erme, C. Geiger, H. Grosse Ruse-Khan, C. Heinze, T. Jaeger, R. Matulionyte and A. Metzger, 'The Impact of the Anti-Counterfeiting Trade Agreement on the Legal Framework for IP Enforcement in the European Union', in Geiger (ed.), above note 40, at 394.

[47] Commission Services Working Paper, Comments on the 'Opinion of European Academics on Anti-Counterfeiting Trade Agreement', 27 April 2011, reproduced in (2011) 2 JIPITEC 171.

[48] Gibson, above note 24, 265.

[49] European Parliament, Director-General for External Policies, Policy Department, 'The Anti-Counterfeiting Trade Agreement (ACTA): An Assessment', June 2011, EXPO/ B/INTA/FWC/2009-01/Lot7/12, PE 433.859, Recommendation 8.1, 65.

As we have seen, in the field of criminal enforcement, the Anti-Counterfeiting Trade Agreement seems, therefore, not to be the right answer, since it risks undermining the flexibility of the TRIPS Agreement. So what then would be the right answer? This, of course, cannot be presented in detail here; what is sure, however, is that any EU or international framework on criminal enforcement needs a differentiated approach.

3. CRIMINAL ENFORCEMENT IN THE EUROPEAN UNION – THE NEED FOR A DIFFERENTIATED APPROACH

As has been shown, the approach adopted by the WTO Panel for the notion of 'commercial scale' is rather a flexible one, since it is only the counterfeiting activities 'carried on at the magnitude or extent of typical or usual commercial activity with respect to a given product in a given market' that deserve punishment.[50] One can therefore hope that this definition will allow for a case-by-case approach, taking into account also normative considerations. Nevertheless, since public interest objectives lie at the very heart of criminal law, one can wonder if the notion of 'commercial scale' – namely a mainly economic notion based on a market approach – is really the right criterion to decide what should be criminalized or not.[51] In fact, the economic impact is already addressed by means of civil enforcement. Should it not be *something else*, like the aggravated social harm of the infringement (which certainly cannot be measured solely in economic terms) that should lead to a more severe criminal sanction such as imprisonment? Is it really appropriate to treat equally, for example, an internet user who illegally downloads music files from the internet and the activities of (often) mafia-like organizations that mass-produce counterfeit medicines, involving major risks to public health?[52]

---

[50] WTO Panel decision, above note 15, para. 7.577.

[51] See, in this sense, A. Wechsler, 'Criminal Enforcement of Intellectual Property Law: An Economic Approach', in Geiger (ed.), above note 9, 150: 'The solution of policy questions in the realm of the criminal enforcement of IP law requires not only regard to economic evidence but appropriate consideration for moral, philosophical, sociological, and historical dimensions as Beccaria's statement of 1764 still holds true today: "The true measure of crimes is the harm done to society"'.

[52] However, it has been argued that from a public health perspective, it is necessary to differentiate concerns about counterfeit goods that infringe trademarks and medicine suspected of infringing patents: see D. Matthews, 'Counterfeiting and Public Health', in Geiger (ed.), above note 9, 42. According to this scholar, 'the most immediate concern for public health lies with falsified medicines which contain the wrong

Very interestingly, the Max Planck Institute, in its comment on the failed directive proposal on criminal enforcement, suggested making the priority under criminal law 'acts that are particularly dangerous from the viewpoint of public interest' and 'to regulate specific forms of IP infringement falling into that category separately', imposing qualified penalties for those infringements that carry health or safety risks, or that are carried out in the form of organized crime.[53] This approach is convincing: if it might be appropriate to decriminalize certain activities, there are others that deserve far more serious penalties in light of their dramatic consequences in terms of innovation and, above all, because of the danger to consumers[54] that might result from the counterfeiting of certain products (in particular, in the field of medicine).[55]

Another convincing argument towards a new approach for criminal enforcement in the EU is also based on the negative impact that undifferentiated repression can have on the perception of IP in the mind of citizens.[56] The issue of the never-ending battle against file sharing is a good example. One remembers the particularly strict decision by the first instance court in Stockholm on 17 April 2009 on the Swedish file sharing website, The Pirate Bay, which sentenced four of the website's representatives each to one year of

---

or insufficient active ingredients that may be a risk to human health', not necessarily from trademark violations: ibid., 58.

53 Hilty, Kur and Peukert, above note 23, 975. On the issue of criminal enforcement and organized crime, see M.R. Roudaut, 'From Sweatshops to Organized Crime: The New Face of Counterfeiting', in Geiger (ed.), above note 9, 75.

54 Although even there scholars express scepticism regarding the appropriateness of criminal provisions: see, for example, A. Ohly, 'Counterfeiting and Consumer Protection', in Geiger (ed.), above note 9, 40, stating that 'the question remains whether consumer interests strengthen the case for strict enforcement of patents and copyright, in particular by criminal law'. He concludes that 'concerns about product safety and quality should not be put to the cause of strengthening the law of patent or copyright enforcement since the infringement provisions of both legal areas do not distinguish between counterfeiting and imitation'. See also Hilty, above note 37, 23, according to whom 'discussing safety, health and the like in the isolated context of IP laws turns out to be mere window dressing, since stronger IPRs protection by no means *per se* serves the public interest – particularly consumer interests – but primarily helps those who benefit from such a system'.

55 However, the fight against falsified medicines by means of criminal enforcement is also sometimes questioned. According to, for example, C. Correa, 'Anti-Counterfeiting: A Trojan Horse for Expanding Intellectual Property Protection in Developing Countries?', in Geiger (ed.), above note 9, 74, in 'the case of medicines, the fight against sub-standard products should not be addressed through enhanced measures to enforce IPRs, but by strengthening the capacity of drug regulatory authorities with the necessary finance, human resources and equipment'.

56 C. Geiger, 'Introduction', in Geiger (ed.), above note 9, 1; Hilty, above note 37, 9 et seq.

imprisonment and to €2.7 million of damages on the ground of assisting in making copyrighted material available, having therefore provided the means for the main offence (illegal downloading).[57] This decision was welcomed by right holders, favouring the use of the rhetoric of 'punishment' and 'theft' when communicating on file sharing.[58] The results are obvious: the criminalization of a major part of the internet community led to no reduction in illegal downloading.[59] Moreover, the Pirate Bay site and others like it are still online and 'pirate parties' have mushroomed in many parts of Europe – the Swedish Pirate Party even managed to win two seats in the European Parliament after the decision was handed down.

By way of conclusion, a differentiation in terms of criminal enforcement appears to be both inevitable and desirable to guarantee that the IP system will not be rejected, in the long run, by the vast majority and will be able in the future to apply more severe sanctions to those infringements that are causing serious threats to society.[60] Unfortunately, such a differentiated approach to criminal enforcement, taking into account not only economical, but also

---

57 Stockholm District Court, 17 April 2009, Case No. B 13301-06. For comment, see J. Edström and H. Nilsson, 'The Pirate Bay Verdict – Predictable, and Yet …' [2009] EIPR 483. In a decision issued on 26 November 2010 (Case No. B 4041-09), the Swedish Court of Appeal confirmed the criminal liability of the defendants, reduced the original prison terms (with prison sentences now ranging from 4 to 10 months) but increased the damages to €5 million each. See also the decision of the Supreme Court of Finland, 30 June 2010, KKO:2010:47, which upheld the earlier judgment of the Turku Court of Appeal and confirmed the criminal liability of the file sharing service, Finreactor, for copyright infringement through collaboration with the file sharers (it was held that the operator participated with the user in the illegal reproduction and distribution of the work to the public and therefore intentionally infringed copyright). For comment, see P. Honsakasalo, 'Criminal Proceedings against the Administrators of a BitTorrent Tracker: Finreactor KKO:2010:47' [2010] EIPR 591.

58 One still remembers the advertising campaigns pursued by the record industry suggesting that young internet users should be put behind bars for having visited a peer-to-peer site. See more generally about the rhetoric of theft, P.L. Loughlan, 'You Wouldn't Steal a Car … Intellectual Property and the Language of Theft' [2007] EIPR 401.

59 The opposite might even have occurred. For more detail on this issue, see C. Geiger, 'Counterfeiting and the Music Industry: Towards a Criminalization of End Users? The French "HADOPI" example', in Geiger (ed.), above note 9, 386, and A. Peukert, 'Why do "Good" People Disregard Copyright on the Internet?' in Geiger (ed.), ibid., 151 et seq.

60 In this sense, during the TRIPS Agreement negotiations, India and Hong Kong suggested that it is only infringements that have harmed the interests of society or that pose a threat to society , and not merely those of a private party, that should be criminalized: see Adam, above note 11, 346.

ethical, historical and psychological aspects,[61] was not addressed by ACTA. It is therefore doubtful if an implementation of this treaty in the EU would result in progress for the European intellectual property system.[62]

61 For a historical, economical and psychological perspective on criminal enforcement, see the chapters by D. Lefranc, A. Wechsler and A. Peukert, in Geiger (ed.), above note 9.

62 See also C. Geiger, 'The Construction of Intellectual Property in the European Union: Searching for Coherence', in Geiger (ed.), above note 40, at 5.

9. Two tales of a treaty revisited: the proposed Anti-Counterfeiting Trade Agreement (ACTA)*

Charles R. McManis and John S. Pelletier

1. INTRODUCTION

Over the past four years, through a coordinated series of public announcements[1] that seemed to have been stimulated in part by previously leaked documents,[2] details gradually came to light concerning negotiations over a

* This chapter is a reworking and update of a previously published article: Charles R. McManis, 'The Proposed Anti-Counterfeiting Trade Agreement: Two Tales of a Treaty' (2009) 46 *Houston Law Review* 1235. See below notes 11–20 and accompanying text.

[1] See, e.g., Press Release, Office of the US Trade Representative, 'The Office of US Trade Representative Releases Summary of Anti-Counterfeiting Trade Agreement (ACTA) Negotiations', 6 April 2009, available at: http://www.ustr.gov/about-us/press-office/press-releases/2009/april/-office-us-trade-representative-releases-summary-an-0; Press Release, US Trade Representative, 'U.S., Participants Finalize Anti Counterfeiting Trade Agreement Text', 15 November 2010, available at: http://www.ustr.gov/about-us/press-office/press-releases/2010/november/us-participants-finalize-anti-counterfeiting-trad [hereinafter 'USTR, November 2010 Press Release']. The actual summary is available on the US Trade Representative's (USTR) website. Office of the US Trade Representative, 'ACTA: Summary of Key Elements under Discussion', November 2009, available at: http://www.ustr.gov/about-us/press-office/fact-sheets/2009/november/acta-summary-key-elements-under-discussion [hereinafter 'Summary of Key Elements' or 'Summary']. For a discussion of the coordinated nature of the release of this Summary, see below note 95 and accompanying text. For the proposed final text of the ACTA, which was released in December 2010 by the USTR, see the Anti-Counterfeiting Trade Agreement, 3 December 2010, available at: http://www.mofa.go.jp/policy/economy/i_property/pdfs/acta1105_en.pdf [hereinafter ACTA]. All references to chapters, sections and articles discussed in this chapter are with reference to the above-cited draft.

[2] See Discussion Paper on a Possible Anti-Counterfeiting Trade Agreement, available at: http://wikileaks.org/leak/acta-proposal-2007.pdf (last visited 21 November 2009) [hereinafter Discussion Paper]; 'Proposed US ACTA Multi-Lateral Intellectual Property Trade Agreement (2007)', WikiLeaks, 22 May 2008, available at:

proposed new Anti-Counterfeiting Trade Agreement (ACTA). According to the governments involved in these closed-door 'plurilateral' trade negotiations, the purpose of ACTA was simply to help fight the proliferation of counterfeit and pirated goods in international trade.[3] From the outset, however, the

---

http://www.wikileaks.org/wiki/Proposed_US_ACTA_plurilateral_intellectual_property_trade_agreement_(2007); 'Classified US, Japan and EU ACTA Trade Agreement Drafts', WikiLeaks, 11 April 2009, available at: http://wikileaks.org/wiki/Classified_ US%2C_Japan_and_EU_ACTA_trade_agreement_drafts%2C_2009.

[3] See Summary of Key Elements, above note 1. The USTR's characterization of ACTA as a proposed 'plurilateral' agreement seems primarily designed to make it clear that ACTA is neither a 'multilateral' nor a 'bilateral' nor a 'regional' trade agreement, and is thus to be distinguished from: (1) existing multilateral trade agreements administered by the World Trade Organization (WTO), including the Agreement on Trade-Related Aspects of Intellectual Property Rights (TRIPS Agreement); (2) a raft of bilateral free trade agreements that have been negotiated between various trading partners subsequent to the establishment of the WTO; and (3) various regional free trade agreements such as the North American Free Trade Agreement (NAFTA) and those governing trade within the European Union.

Commentators in the US have noted that the USTR and the Executive Branch of the United States government prefer to view ACTA as an executive agreement rather than a treaty: see David M. Quinn, 'A Critical Look at the Anti-Counterfeiting Trade Agreement' (2011) 17 *Richmond Journal of Law& Technology* 16, 5, 12–20, available at: http://jolt.richmond.edu/v17i4/article16.pdf; Eddan Katz and Gwen Heinz, 'The Impact of the Anti-Counterfeiting Trade Agreement on the Knowledge Economy: The Accountability of the Office of the U.S. Trade Representative for the Creation of IP Enforcement Norms Through Executive Trade Agreements' (2009) 35 *Yale Journal of International Law Online* 24, 27–30. These commentators note that, by negotiating ACTA as an executive agreement, the President may enter into ACTA without the approval of Congress. See Katz and Heinz, ibid., 27. However, should ACTA require changes to current US law, it would be 'precluded from sole executive agreement status and would have to come before Congress for approval': see Quinn, ibid., 12–13. See also below notes 232–6 and accompanying text. For an in-depth discussion of the categorization of ACTA under US law and the constitutional ramifications related thereto, see Sean Flynn, 'ACTA's Constitutional Problem: The Treaty is Not a Treaty' (2011) 26 *American University International Law Review* 903, 913–22 (arguing that ACTA is not an Article II treaty, a congressional-executive agreement, or a 'sole' executive agreement – i.e. an agreement with no formal *ex ante* or *ex post* authorization by Congress – under US law and criticizing the USTR's arguments that ACTA is an executive agreement).

By 'counterfeit' the Summary of Key Elements apparently meant mislabeled or otherwise 'fake' goods, while 'pirated' goods apparently meant illicitly copied goods. Nowhere in the USTR's Summary of Key Elements were the terms 'counterfeit' and 'pirated' goods actually defined. However, the final proposed draft does indeed provide definitions of the terms 'counterfeit trademark goods' and 'pirated copyright goods'. See below note 101 and accompanying text, pointing out that the ACTA definitions are similar but not identical to the definitions of the same terms in Art. 51 TRIPS Agreement. See Agreement on Trade-Related Aspects of Intellectual Property Rights, Art. 51 n.14, 15 April 1994, Marrakesh Agreement Establishing the World Trade

negotiations were embroiled in controversy, for at least four reasons. First, while the negotiations initially were carried out behind closed doors, industry representatives were apparently being supplied with information that was not being disseminated to the public.[4] Second, the 'plurilateral' nature of the negotiations aroused suspicions that the ACTA negotiations were but the latest example of 'forum-shifting' – a well-documented tactic that is apparently being deployed by owners of intellectual property (IP) in an effort to ratchet up international standards for the protection of private intellectual property rights (IPRs).[5] These procedural concerns about the conduct of the negotia-

---

Organization, Annex 1C, 1869 UNTS 299, (1994) 33 ILM 1197 [hereinafter TRIPS Agreement]. As the terms themselves suggest, counterfeit goods generally involve misuse of another's trademark, while pirated goods generally involve infringement of another's copyright: see Amarjit Singh, 'Guarding against Spurious and Counterfeit Products Through Effective Enforcement', 5–6 June 2007, 3, available at: http://www.wipo.int/meetings/fr/doc_details.jsp?doc_id=81476; See also below Part 3 (discussing the differences between the definitions of 'counterfeit' and 'pirated' goods).

4 The leaked discussion paper, see above note 2, was reportedly provided to select lobbyists in the intellectual property industry, but not to public interest organizations concerned with the subject matter of the proposed treaty. See 'The Anti-Counterfeiting Trade Agreement (ACTA)', *IP Justice*, available at: http://ipjustice.org/wp/campaigns/acta (last visited 6 March 2012); James Love, 'Who Are the Cleared Advisors That Have Access to Secret ACTA Documents?', *Knowledge Ecology International*, 13 March 2009, available at: http://www.keionline.org/blogs/2009/03/13/who-are-cleared-advisors.

5 Forum shifting is apparently part of a nodally coordinated effort to shift negotiations away from the two international organizations that currently administer multilateral intellectual property agreements – namely the World Trade Organization (WTO), which administers the TRIPS Agreement, see above note 3, and the World Intellectual Property Organization (WIPO), which administers the Paris Convention for the Protection of Industrial Property and the Berne Convention for the Protection of Literary and Artistic Works. See Paris Convention for the Protection of Industrial Property, 20 March 1883, 13 UST 2, 828 UNTS 107, as last revised at the Stockholm Revision Conference, 14 July 1967, 21 UST 1538, 828 UNTS 303, available at: http://www.wipo.int/treaties/en/ip/paris/trtdocs_wo020.html; Berne Convention for the Protection of Literary and Artistic Works, 9 September 1886, as last revised at Paris, 24 July 1971, 25 UST 1341, 1161 UNTS 30, available at: http://www.wipo.int/ treaties/en/ip/berne/trtdocs_wo001.html. For a discussion of forum shifting and nodally coordinated enforcement efforts, see Laurence R. Helfer, 'Regime Shifting: The TRIPS Agreement and New Dynamics of International Intellectual Property Lawmaking' (2004) 29 *Yale Journal of International Law* 1, 14 (describing forum-shifting as a way to 'alter the prevailing legal landscape'); Peter Drahos, 'Securing the Future of Intellectual Property: Intellectual Property Owners and Their Nodally Coordinated Enforcement Pyramid' (2004) 36 *Case Western Reserve Journal of International Law* 53, 62–74 ('[I]ntellectual property owners have sought to achieve the goal of compliance through the creation of an international enforcement pyramid that is nodally coordinated'). For a discussion of the related practice of 'policy laundering' – i.e. disguising the origin of policy decisions, laws or international decisions, including negotiating for

tions, in turn, contributed to two further suspicions about the substantive purpose and scope of ACTA. The first suspicion was that ACTA was simply an effort on the part of intellectual property owners to socialize the enforcement costs of their private IPRs by enhanced civil, criminal, and border enforcement proceedings and remedies.[6] The second suspicion – generated in part by a leaked negotiating document – was that the focus of these civil, criminal and border enforcement provisions would not be limited to targeting commercial trade in counterfeit and pirated physical goods, but would also extend to 'significant willful infringements without motivation for financial gain to such an extent as to prejudicially affect the copyright owner (for example, Internet piracy)'.[7] To the suspicious eye, this verbatim quote from the leaked document clearly seemed to be referring to digital file-sharing – a controversial consumer phenomenon, to be sure, but quite distinct from the issue of commercial trade in counterfeit and pirated physical goods.[8]

A particularly jolting development in the effort by critics to secure more specifics concerning the ACTA negotiations occurred in March 2009 when, notwithstanding President Obama's campaign promises of greater transparency in US government policymaking, the Office of the US Trade Representative (USTR) denied a Freedom of Information Act (FOIA) request for a copy of the ACTA discussion draft and related materials on the ground that they were 'classified in the interest of national security'.[9] While the invocation of national

---

terms in international treaties that might prove too politically unpopular to pass in national assemblies – see 'Policy Laundering', Wikipedia, at: http://en.wikipedia.org/wiki/Policy_laundering, and David Kravets, 'Copyright Treaty is Policy Laundering at its Finest', 4 November 2009, available at: http://www.wired. com/threatlevel/2009/11/policy-laundering/. For examples of the use of bilateral free trade agreements (FTAs) to ratchet up IP standards beyond those mandated by TRIPS, See below notes 91–92, 118–119, 216, 224. For evidence that the ACTA negotiations constituted forum-shifting, See below notes 114, 116–118 and accompanying text.

6 See 'FOIA: Anti-Counterfeiting Trade Agreement (ACTA)', Electronic Frontier Foundation, 17 June 2009, available at: http://www.eff.org/issues/acta [hereinafter FOIA]; Robin Gross, 'IP Justice White Paper on the Proposed Anti-Counterfeiting Trade Agreement (ACTA)', IP Justice, 25 March 2008, available at: http://ipjustice.org/wp/wp-content/uploads/IPJustice_ACTA-white-paper-mar 2008.pdf. For an account of Electronic Frontier Foundation's (EFF) ultimately futile attempt to obtain information about the ACTA negotiations through a lawsuit filed under the US Freedom of Information Act, 5 USC §552 (2006), see FOIA ibid. See also below note 9 and accompanying text.

7 See Discussion Paper, above note 2, 3.

8 See below Part 3 (noting that file-sharing provisions are indeed included in the final text of ACTA).

9 Grant Gross, 'Obama Administration Says Treaty Text Is State Secret', PCWorld, 13 March 2009, available at: http://www.pcworld.com/article/161234/obama_administration_says_treaty_text_is_state_secret.html.

security may have been simply a ruse to camouflage and avoid exacerbating growing divisions among the negotiating parties,[10] it proved useful to take this national security claim at face value, as it offered a starting point for this chapter's predecessor – which sought 'to provide two alternative tales of the treaty with a view to identifying and clarifying the various controversies currently surrounding the negotiations'.[11]

The conclusion of the negotiations has now clarified the extent to which these two speculative tales accurately reflect the final product of the negotiations. On 15 November 2010, the United States, along with its negotiating partners Australia, Canada, the European Union, Japan, Korea, Mexico, Morocco, New Zealand, Singapore and Switzerland, announced that the parties had finalized the text of ACTA.[12] The release of this final draft[13] has provided a number of answers to lurking questions regarding the scope and purpose of ACTA.[14] As indicated above, from the outset of the negotiations,

---

10 For the specific divisions, see below notes 111, 121–122, 131–132 and accompanying text.

11 Charles R. McManis, 'The Proposed Anti-Counterfeiting Trade Agreement (ACTA): Two Tales of a Treaty' (2009) 46 *Houston Law Review* 1235.

12 U.S., Participants Finalize Anti-Counterfeiting Trade Agreement, above note 1; see also John R. Cook, 'U.S. Trade Representative Releases Text of Anti-Counterfeiting Trade Agreement: Critics and Supporters Debate Agreement' (2010) 105 *American Journal of International Law*137.

13 ACTA, above note 1.

14 For comprehensive critiques of the final ACTA draft, see Peter K. Yu, 'Six Secret (and Now Open) Fears of ACTA' (2011) 64 *SMU Law Review* 975; Focus Issue, 'Intellectual Property Law Enforcement and the Anti-Counterfeiting Trade Agreement (ACTA)' (2011) 26 *American University International Law Review* 543–926 [hereinafter Focus Issue]. The six fears Professor Yu discusses in depth track those identified in the predecessor of this chapter: see McManis,above note 11 – namely fears of (1) lack of transparency and accountability; (2) the upward ratchet of the scope of IP protection at home; (3) an analogous upward ratchet in the scope of IP protection abroad; (4) the adverse ('boomerang') effect on US consumers and businesses, particularly small businesses; (5) a new infrastructure for ratcheting up IP protection; and (6) the creation of an ineffective and superfluous treaty. The introduction to the Focus Issue identifies six universal substantive concerns about ACTA – namely that: (1) the scope of ACTA is unclear; (2) uncertainty remains about the relation of IP enforcement within ACTA and privacy rights more generally; (3) there is an absence of balance stemming from the inclusion of enforcement rules but not the limitations, exceptions, and balancing provisions typically found in copyright law; (4) there is continuing uncertainty over in-transit seizures of goods, particularly generic drugs; (5) the injunctive powers specified in ACTA are troublingly broad; and 6) the proposed ACTA institutional structure could usurp the role that WIPO has played in development and technical cooperation. See Michael Geist, 'ACTA's State of Play: Looking Beyond Transparency' (2011) 26 *American University International Law Review* 543. The more modest goal of this chapter is to revisit and identify the denouement of the two tales told in McManis, above note 11.

and following the leaking of an early draft of ACTA, it appeared that ACTA was not only aimed at combating piracy of copyrighted goods and counterfeiting of trademarked goods in international commercial trade, but was also intended to establish more robust intellectual property (IP) enforcement standards for international trade in goods more generally, and also to combat the distinctive problem of digital file-sharing.[15] The final draft clearly confirms these suspicions – for while a majority of the provisions in the final draft target illegal counterfeit and pirated goods in international trade, these same provisions also address IP enforcement efforts in other, more controversial, contexts (albeit still involving trade in physical goods), while Article 27 of ACTA explicitly requires parties to take certain measures to address the enforcement of intellectual property rights in the digital domain.[16]

The conflation of these three distinct concerns not only slowed the ACTA negotiation process but also has created a host of continuing concerns about ACTA that may ultimately undermine its entry into force – or its overall effectiveness as a practical matter.[17] Since the release of the final proposed text, eight countries – the United States, Australia, Canada, Korea, Japan, New Zealand, Morocco and Singapore – have signed ACTA.[18] However, support for ratification among the parties negotiating the final draft is divided and mired in controversy. Within six months of the release of the final proposed text, the Mexican Senate adopted a resolution advising the Federal Executive not to ratify the agreement.[19] On the other hand, one week later the EC recommended ratification of ACTA by the European Parliament without further

---

15 Yu, ibid.,1237.

16 ACTA,above note 1, Art. 27.

17 For comprehensive critiques of the final draft of ACTA, see above note 14. For controversies surrounding ratification, acceptance or approval of ACTA, see below notes 18–24 and accompanying text. For issues surrounding ACTA's effectiveness, See below notes 199–203, 257–258 and accompanying text.

18 Press Release, United States Trade Representative, 'Joint Press Statement of the Anti-Counterfeiting Trade Agreement Negotiating Parties', 1 October 2011, available at: http://www.ustr.gov/about-us/press-office/press-releases/2011/october/joint-press-statement-anti-counterfeiting-trade-ag. However, six of these parities must submit ratification documents in order for ACTA to go into force: ibid. The agreement was opened for signature to participants in the negotiations, along with any members of the World Trade Organization (WTO) on 31 March 2011 and will remain open until 31 March 2013. ACTA, above note 1, Art. 39.

19 Geraldine Jaurez,'Did Mexico Really Pull Out of ACTA? Yes, For Now', Infojustice.org, 28 June 2011, available at: http://infojustice.org/archives/4038. Among the reasons for the advised rejection by the Mexican Senate were that, at least according to Senator Francisco Castellon, the draft is 'not well done' and is unconstitutional: ibid.

review,[20] while the US Trade Representative has taken the view that ratification of ACTA by the US Senate is not necessary.[21] On 25 February 2012, however, the European Parliament (EP) received a petition signed by 2.5 million people from all over the world[22] asking them to 'stand for a free and open Internet and reject the ratification of the Anti-Counterfeiting Trade Agreement (ACTA)'.[23] In response, the EP has begun its own in-depth investigation into the ramifications of signing ACTA, notwithstanding the previous recommendation of the EC.[24] After revisiting the two tales told prior to the approval of the final draft of ACTA, this chapter will offer two additional cautionary tales about ACTA's ultimate impact on the development of intellectual property enforcement standards.

2. TALE # 1: IP PIRACY, ORGANIZED CRIME AND TERRORISM

ACTA proponents have two powerful rebuttal arguments to the criticism that ACTA is merely the latest chapter in an industry-instigated industrialized world effort to impose ever higher standards of IP protection on a reluctant developing world. First, although ACTA is admittedly an industrialized world

---

20 Mike Palmedo, 'EC Recommends that the European Parliament Pass ACTA Without Further Review', Infojustice.org, 5 July 2011, available at: http://infojustice.org/archives/4115.

21 For the USTR's view that ratification by the US Senate is not required, see above note 3 and below notes 230–233 and accompanying text. For a critique of that view, see Yu, above note 11, and sources cited therein.

22 See 'Parliament Receives Petition against ACTA', European Parliament, 28 February 2012 at 1:03 PM, available at: http://www.europarl.europa.eu/news/en/ press-room/content/20120227IPR39337/html/Parliament-receives-petition-against-ACTA.

23 See 'ACTA: The New Threat to the Net', AVAAZ.org, available at: https://secure.avaaz.org/en/eu_save_the_internet/?fp (last visited 6 March 2012).

24 For example, Members of the EP, 'who will be crucial to deciding the treaty's fate in the EU, staged a special workshop on 1 March to grill experts about their insights into ACTA': 'ACTA: Experts Reveal How It Could Affect Civil Liberties and Access to Generic Medicine', European Parliament, available at: http://www.europarl.europa.eu/news/en/headlines/content/20120223STO39243/html/ACTA-how-it-could-affect-civil-liberties-and-access-to-generic-medicine (last visited 6 March 2012). A report presented to the EP in June 2011 recommended that 'unconditional consent [to ACTA] would be an inappropriate response from the European Parliament given the issues that have been identified with ACTA as it stands': Directorate-General for External Polices, Policy Department, 'The Anti-Counterfeiting Trade Agreement (ACTA): An Assessment', 2011, available at:http://www.europarl.europa.eu/committees/en/INTA/studies down load.html?languageDocument=EN&file=43731.

initiative, a fluid, but generally increasing number of developing countries subsequently joined in the negotiations, and Brazil apparently contacted one of the participants about joining the negotiations as well.[25] Second, while the participation of these developing countries may have been window-dressing, as discrete tangible benefits may have been proffered by ACTA's original proponents to encourage such participation,[26] there are nevertheless ample reasons for developing countries, particularly those that became involved in the ACTA negotiations, to be concerned with international trade in counterfeit and pirated goods, as a mounting body of empirical evidence has linked trade in counterfeit and pirated goods with threats to public health and the involvement of organized crime and terrorist organizations.

The starting point for this tale can be traced back at least to October 2000, when the General Assembly of INTERPOL, the world's largest international police organization, approved the addition of IP crime to the organization's official mandate.[27] Shortly thereafter, INTERPOL formed the Intellectual

---

[25] See 'EU ACTA Negotiator Confirms EU Wants Patent Provisions in ACTA', 27 *Inside U.S. Trade* 11, 8 May 2009, at 12 [hereinafter 'EU Wants Patent Provisions in ACTA'] (reporting that Jordan, the United Arab Emirates (UAE), and Uruguay were involved in initial discussions but have dropped out); Michael Geist, 'ACTA Update: New Meetings, New Partners, New Issues', 30 June 2009, available at: http://www.michaelgeist.ca/content/view/4092/408 (reporting that Brazil has approached one ACTA participant about joining the negotiations).

[26] For example, the July 2009 ACTA negotiations were held in Morocco. Press Release, Office of the US Trade Representative, 'Statement from USTR Spokeswoman Carol Guthrie on the Anti-Counterfeiting Trade Agreement (ACTA)', 20 July 2009, available at: http://www.ustr.gov/about-us/press-office/press-releases/2009/july/statement-ustr-spokeswoman-carol-guthrie-anti-counte-0.

[27] INTERPOL, 'Intellectual Property (IP) Crime', available at: http://www.interpol.int/Public/FinancialCrime/IntellectualProperty/Default.asp (last visited 21 July 2011). INTERPOL – the International Criminal Police Organization – is the second largest international organization after the United Nations and focuses on facilitating international police cooperation. See INTERPOL, 'About INTERPOL', available at: http://www.interpol.int/public/icpo/default.asp (last visited 21 July 2011). To maintain its political neutrality, INTERPOL's constitution limits its involvement to cross-border criminal investigations and forbids its involvement in investigations of political, military, religious, or racial crimes. See INTERPOL, *ICPO-INTERPOL Constitution and General Regulations*, available at: http://www.interpol.int/Public/ICPO/LegalMaterials/constitution/constitutionGenReg/constitution.asp (last visited 21 July 2011). INTERPOL has a somewhat checkered history, as it was established in Austria in 1923, but fell under the control of Nazi Germany prior to and during World War II, only to be revived by the victorious Allied Forces and subsequently headquartered in France: Mathieu Deflem, 'The Logic of Nazification: The Case of the International Criminal Police Commission' (2002) 43 *International Journal of Comparative Sociology* 21. In 2008, INTERPOL again became embroiled in controversy, when the President of INTERPOL, Jackie Selebi, National Commissioner of the South African Police

Property Action Group (subsequently renamed the Interpol IP Crime Action Group) as a public/private partnership to combat IP crime.[28] Today, financial and high-tech crime, including IP crime, is listed as one of INTERPOL's six priority crime areas.[29]

In 2005, by way of implementing its new mandate, INTERPOL – together with the World Customs Organization, the national police forces of three South American countries, and representatives from various pharmaceutical, recording, motion picture and tobacco industry organizations – launched Operation Jupiter. This operation focused on the tri-border area of South America at the intersection of Argentina, Brazil and Paraguay, where organized crime involvement in cross-border IP crime was said to represent a particularly challenging environment for law enforcement.[30] In the initial phase of this operation, counterfeit and pirated goods valued at approximately US$15 million were seized, while three subsequent phases of the operation, conducted between 2006 and 2008 in this same tri-border region, netted counterfeit goods valued at US$35 million, US$121 million, and US$132 million, respectively.[31] A common denominator in the first two phases of Operation Jupiter, which was expanded in Phase II to include Chile and Uruguay, was said to be that

> foreign nationals and nationals of Middle Eastern and Asian countries were well represented in these criminal conspiracies. Analysis indicated that typically transnational organized criminals of Arab, Indian and Pakistani origin have a controlling influence in informatics. Typically transnational organized criminals of Chinese origin have a controlling influence over CD/DVD pirate manufacturing and distribution as well as sports clothes and luxury goods.[32]

Service, resigned and was later charged in South Africa on three counts of corruption and one of defeating the course of justice: Chris McGreal, 'SA Police Chief Resigns as Interpol Leader as He Is Charged with Bribery', *The Guardian*, London, 14 January 2008, 17.

28 INTERPOL, Intellectual Property Crimes Action Group, 'Intellectual Property Crimes: Trademark Counterfeiting and Copyright Piracy', 2007, available at: http://www.interpol.int/Public/FinancialCrime/IntellectualProperty/Publications/IIPCAGBrochure.pdf.

29 See INTERPOL, available at: http://www.interpol.int/default.asp (last visited 21 July 2011). The other five priority areas are: (1) drugs and criminal organizations; (2) fugitives; (3) public safety and terrorism; (4) trafficking in human beings; and (5) corruption: ibid.

30 See INTERPOL, 'Operation Jupiter 2004–2010', available at: http://www.interpol.int/public/FinancialCrime/IntellectualProperty/OperationJupiter/Default.asp (last visited 21 July 2011) [hereinafter Operation Jupiter].

31 Ibid.

32 Ibid.

Phase III of Operation Jupiter focused on this same tri-border area in South America, and in particular on the so-called 'Ciudad del Este Piracy Cartel', which had been identified in Phase II as being directed by Lebanese nationals.[33] Phase III of the operation yielded 185 arrests, surpassing the previous phase by 43 percent.[34] In Argentina alone, Phase III yielded seizures of 1 million CDs and DVDs, 8.6 million film and music sleeve jackets, plus 273 burners, together with large amounts of counterfeit brand clothes and machinery for manufacturing the clothing.[35] Operations in Brazil not only detected criminal organizations headed by Lebanese nationals involved in the illegal trade of computer equipment, but also 'disrupted four organizations devoted to the smuggling of pesticides, cigarettes, tires and electronics', and resulted in the seizure of one ton of counterfeit watches, as well as large quantities of marijuana, crack, weapons and ammunition, all said to be directly related to IP crimes.[36] Operations in Paraguay resulted in '[s]eizures of 188,200 counterfeit CDs and DVDs, 2,733,700 sleeve jackets for their commercialization' – an important part of the production of which was managed by the Ciudad del Este Piracy Cartel – as well as 23,000 counterfeit units of medication for treating erectile dysfunction.[37] In Chile, 443 pieces of designer clothing manufactured in Argentina were seized, as well as 2,784 counterfeit books, thus demonstrating the regional nature of IP crime.[38] Finally, in Uruguay, three shipping containers of counterfeit goods (including brand clothing, watches, luxury accessories and computer equipment) valued at US$1.67 million were seized at the port of Montevideo, and other operations netted 23,400 ecstasy tablets, valued at US$800,000.[39]

In Phase IV of Operation Jupiter, two additional countries – Bolivia and Peru – took part, undertaking some of the first enforcement operations of the kind in these two countries.[40] In this phase of Operation Jupiter, officials

---

33 Ibid.; see also Gregory F. Treverton et al., *Film Piracy, Organized Crime, and Terrorism* (Rand Corporation 2009) 75–82, available at: http://www.rand.org/pubs/monographs/2009/RAND_MG742.pdf (describing the connection between organized crime in the tri-border area and Lebanese terrorist organizations).

34 Operation Jupiter, above note 30.

35 Ibid. The city of Ciudad del Este is the capital of the Alto Paraná Department of Paraguay, and is part of a triangle known as the Triple Frontera (Triple border), or Tríplice Fronteira in Portuguese: 'The Americas: Pillars of the Community; Brazil's Arab Diaspora', *The Economist*, 3 November 2001, 64. It is linked to the Brazilian city of Foz do Iguaçu by the Friendship Bridge and is also within just a few miles of the border with Argentina: Treverton et al., above note 33, App. B, 49.

36 Operation Jupiter, above note 30.

37 Ibid.

38 Ibid.

39 Ibid.

40 Ibid.

'carried out 299 coordinated enforcement operations resulting in 311 arrests and the recovery of a range of dangerous products including life-threatening fake medicines, counterfeit foodstuffs, electrical goods and agrochemicals.'[41] In addition, over 34 kilograms of cocaine derivatives and almost 1,500 kilograms of marijuana were seized during the operation.[42] In Argentina, '[c]ustoms and police authorities seized a total of 176,242 units of fake designer clothing, plus 144 bundles with no indication of the number of items', having an estimated value of over US$8 million.[43] Police in Brazil seized 3 tons of counterfeit agrochemicals and disrupted a clandestine agrochemicals factory, seized a shipment of 62 tons, including toys manufactured from hospital waste, and, in the biggest single operation in Sao Paulo State so far, deployed a task force of 1,500 public agents to seize goods valued at over US$11 million.[44] In Chile, 'police authorities seized processed meat products, which were a counterfeit version of a local brand and not manufactured to health or regulatory standards'.[45] In Paraguay, enforcement operations not only yielded 15,000 counterfeit video game DVDs, but also the seizure of a parcel containing 3,190 (apparently authentic) Cytotec abortion pills, 16,000 litres of the agrochemical Glifosato, 3,500 kilograms of Flutrianol, 1,000 kilograms of Imazytapyr, and 23,500 kilograms of Methomil – all of which had apparently been smuggled into the country.[46]

The most recent phase of Operation Jupiter (Phase V), conducted throughout 2010, was a coordinated effort between INTERPOL and the World Customs Organization (WCO)[47] resulting in the seizure of counterfeit goods valued at over US$200 million and close to 1,000 arrests throughout the 13 participating countries.[48] The seizures amounted to more than 8 million coun-

---

41 Press Release, INTERPOL, 'Counterfeiting Networks across South America Targeted in INTERPOL and World Customs Organization Operations', 3 April 2009, available at: http://www.interpol.int/Public/ICPO/PressReleases/PR2009/PR200932.asp.

42 Operation Jupiter, above note 30.

43 Ibid.

44 Ibid.

45 Ibid.

46 Ibid.

47 The World Customs Organization 'is an independent intergovernmental body whose mission is to enhance the effectiveness and efficiency of Customs administrations' which was founded in 1952 and was originally known as the Customs Co-operation Council: World Customs Organization, 'WCO Profile', available at: http://www.wcoomd.org/home_about_us_our_profile.htm (last visited 13 July 2011). The WCO currently represents 177 different customs administrations: ibid.

48 Press Release, INTERPOL, 'INTERPOL-Led Operation in Americas Nets Fakes Worth 200 Million Dollars: Specialist Anti-Counterfeiting Units Established in Region to Boost Police Response', 31 January 2011, available at: http://www.

terfeits, which included counterfeit construction materials, athletic wear, sunglasses, mobile phones, books, car parts, software and alcoholic beverages.[49] An important element of Phase V included increased training for customs officers and police and the creation of intellectual property crime units in Chile and Peru.[50] With the completion of Phase V, close to half a billion counterfeit goods had been seized over the course of Operation Jupiter's existence.[51]

A report by the RAND Corporation stated that the tri-border region of South America that has been the focus of INTERPOL's Operation Jupiter has emerged as 'the most important center for financing Islamic terrorism outside the Middle East'.[52] For example, the report notes that this region channels US$20 million annually to Hezbollah, which included one US$3.5 million transfer from a DVD pirate who received a personal thank you note from the head of Hezbollah.[53]

Data from industrialized countries, such as the United States, likewise reflects a prevalence of counterfeit goods in international trade. US Customs and Border Protection (CBP) and US Immigration and Customs Enforcement (ICE) note, in their report on intellectual property rights seizures statistics for 2010, that seizures of intellectual property 'increased by 34% to 19,959 in [fiscal year] 2010 from 14,841 in [fiscal year] 2009'.[54] The value of these seizures was estimated at $1.4 billion.[55] Significantly, the CBP and ICE report

---

interpol.int/public/icpo/pressreleases/pr2011/pr008.asp. Participating countries included Argentina, Bolivia, Brazil, Chile, Colombia, Ecuador, France (French Guyana), Panama, Paraguay, Peru, Suriname, Uruguay and Venezuela: ibid.

49 Ibid.

50 Ibid.

51 Ibid.

52 Treverton et al., above note 33, 75 (quoting Angel Rabasa et al., *The Outer Rings of the Terrorist Universe* (RAND Corporation 2006) 153). This same report identifies two other cases in which film piracy, organized crime, and terrorism have been linked – one involving the Irish Republican Army in Northern Ireland and the other involving the D-Company, an organized crime group that has been active for generations in India but was transformed into a terrorist organization when it carried out the 1993 'Black Friday' bombings in Mumbai that killed more than 257 people and injured hundreds more: ibid., 82–96, App. A, 116; see also RAND Corporation, Press Release, 'Organized Crime is Increasingly Active in Film Piracy; Three Cases Link Terrorists to Piracy Profits', 3 March 2009, available at: http://www.rand.org/news/press/2009/03/ 03.

53 Treverton et al., above note 33, 77, 80; RAND Corporation, Press Release, ibid.

54 US Customs & Border Protection & US Immigration & Customs Enforcement, Fiscal Year 2010 Seizure Statistics – Final Report 2, 2011, available at: http://www.cbp. gov/xp/cgov/trade/priority_trade/ipr/ipr_communications/seizure/.

55 Ibid. This value was calculated based on the Manufacturer's Suggested Retail Price: ibid., 2. This is distinguishable from the domestic value of seizures – which was

indicated that the vast majority of seized goods – 66 per cent to be precise – originated in China. A significant portion of goods was also traced to Hong Kong and Jordan (14 per cent and 6 per cent respectively).[56]

A second INTERPOL enforcement operation offers a particularly disturbing illustration of the impact that international trade in counterfeit goods can have on the developing world, as this operation specifically involved counterfeit medicines. In 2008, INTERPOL – in the first combined operation with the World Health Organization (WHO), and as a part of the WHO's larger International Medical Products Anti-Counterfeiting Taskforce (IMPACT) – launched Operation Mamba, targeting counterfeit pharmaceutical products in Tanzania and Uganda.[57] In Tanzania, Operation Mamba resulted in inspections of 191 locations, including pharmacies, warehouses and illicit markets, and the seizure of over 100 types of product, including anti-malarial, cardiac, antifungal, multivitamin, hormonal and skin medicines.[58] In Uganda, 45 establishments were raided and a total of 38 shops and pharmacies were subsequently investigated for 'operating illegal businesses without the necessary licenses and controls'.[59] In August 2009, a second operation, Operation Mamba II, included Kenya along with Tanzania and Uganda, which had participated in the first operation.[60] Operation Mamba II targeted more than 270 different premises throughout the three nations and 'resulted in 83 police cases being opened' and the 'seizure of hundreds of fake, unregistered and banned products'.[61]

---

estimated as $188.1 million for 2010 – which the CBP explains is the 'approximate price at which the property will be offered for sale at the first commercial level after importation: ibid., 8.

56 Ibid., 10. The report notes that China has been the 'the top source country for IPR violations as it has been for the last 10 years'. The 4% of seizures originating from Jordan virtually all arose from a large quantity of seized cigarettes: ibid., 16. Rounding out the top five countries was India, where US$1,345,749 worth of illicit pharmaceuticals originated, and Malaysia, which was the source of over US$1 million of illicit footwear: ibid.

57 See INTERPOL, 'Operation Mamba (IMPACT): Targeting Counterfeit Medicines in Tanzania and Uganda', available at: http://www.interpol.int/public/News/2008/mamba20081029.asp (last visited 21 July 2011) [hereinafter Operation Mamba]. For more information on IMPACT, see 'IMPACT: International Medical Products Anti-Counterfeiting Taskforce', World Health Organization, available at: http://www.who.int/impact/en (last visited 22 July 2011).

58 Operation Mamba, above note 57.

59 Ibid.

60 INTERPOL, Press Release, 'East African Counties Crack Down On Counterfeiters In INTERPOL/IMPACT-Supported Operation Mamba II', 2 October 2009, available at: http://www.interpol.int/public/News/2009/OperationMamba II20091002. asp.

61 Ibid. Of particular concern, medicines that had been donated or intended for government distribution only were found in private supply chains: ibid.

Operation Mamba III represents an expanded effort on the part of IMPACT, INTERPOL and WHO to combat counterfeit medicines.[62] This third operation in East Africa – which occurred during July and August 2010 and added Burundi, Rwanda and Zanzibar to its list of participating nations – resulted in the seizure of more than 10 tons of counterfeit medicines and over 80 arrests.[63] Following the completion of the operation, the participants committed, under the Zanzibar Declaration, to 'establish national joint taskforces to fight counterfeit medical products and other pharmaceutical crimes', make 'better use of existing networks to obtain and share information on suspects and suspected companies', and increase 'targeted and intelligence-led operations' and 'public awareness on the dangers posed by counterfeit medical products'.[64] Moreover, participants 'expressed their support for the World Health Organization's (WHO) International Medical Products Anti-Counterfeiting Taskforce (IMPACT), especially its enforcement component'.[65] INTERPOL, IMPACT and WHO have not limited their efforts to Africa, although much of their focus and attention has been directed there, as these three organizations have also led operations to combat counterfeit medicines in South East Asia (Operation Storm).[66]

INTERPOL notes that counterfeit medical products 'pose a major risk to public health and are becoming increasingly prevalent in all parts of the world, particularly in Africa'.[67] Similarly, a 2008 WHO brochure entitled

---

[62] Press Release, INTERPOL, 'East Africa Operation Mamba III Bolsters Fight against Counterfeit Medicines with INTERPOL-IMPACT Support', 26 August 2010, available at: http://www.interpol.int/public/ICPO/PressReleases/PR2010/PR065.asp.

[63] Ibid.

[64] Press Release, INTERPOL, 'East Africa's Declaration to Boost Fight Against Counterfeit Pharmaceutical Crimes', 3 September 2010, available at: http://www.interpol.int/public/ICPO/PressReleases/PR2010/News20100903b.asp.

[65] Ibid. For the full text of the Zanzibar Declaration, see Zanzibar Declaration on Counterfeit Medical Products and Pharmaceutical Crime, available at: https://www.interpol.int/Public/ICPO/PressReleases/PR2010/News20100903b_ZanzibarDec.pdf.

[66] See INTERPOL,'Operation Storm: Final Report', available at: http://www.interpol.int/Public/PharmaceuticalCrime/OperationStormFinalReport.pdf (last visited 14 July 2011). The goal of Operation Storm was to use intelligence gathered during Operation Jupiter to specifically combat counterfeit pharmaceuticals in South East Asia: ibid. The operation took place between 15 April 2008 and September 2008: ibid. According to the final report, a significant number of arrests were made in Thailand, and large quantities of counterfeit erectile dysfunction medications and antibiotics were seized in both Thailand and Vietnam: ibid. For an in-depth discussion of the outcome of Operation Storm and Operation Storm II, see IMPACT, *The Handbook* 100-01 (2011) [hereinafter *The Handbook*] available at: http://www.who.int/impact/resources/handobook/en/index.html.

[67] Operation Mamba, above note 57.

'Counterfeit Drugs Kill!' notes that '[m]any countries in Africa and parts of Asia and Latin America have areas where more than 30% of the medicines on sale can be counterfeit' and that '[i]n many of the countries of the former Soviet Union the proportion of counterfeit medicines is above 20% of market value'.[68] This same brochure notes that medicines that are 'purchased over the Internet from illegal sites that conceal their physical addresses are counterfeit in over 50% of cases'.[69] In July 2010, the World Health Organization reportedly estimated that more than half of medicines bought online are counterfeit.[70] On the other hand, the threat posed by fake drugs is apparently not evenly distributed. According to the US Center for Disease Control and Prevention, while global estimates of drug counterfeits are ambiguous, proportions range from 1 per cent of sales in developed countries to more than 10 per cent in developing countries, while in specific regions in Africa, Asia and Latin America, the chances of purchasing a counterfeit drug may be higher than 30 per cent.[71]

The phenomenon of pharmaceutical counterfeiting and illicit trade in those pharmaceuticals also helps to explain why ACTA seeks to extend IP enforcement mechanisms and remedies to trade that occurs in the digital environment. INTERPOL and IMPACT conducted several operations to combat the illegal online sale of counterfeit drugs. Operation Pangea marked the first coordinated effort among foreign nations to target online sales of pharmaceuticals by so called 'internet pharmacies'.[72] The operation involved a number of developed nations, which included Australia, Canada, Germany, Ireland, Israel, New Zealand, Singapore, Switzerland, the UK and the US.[73] INTERPOL's executive director, Jean-Michael Louboutin, noted that often counterfeits sold by internet pharmacies 'contain little or no active ingredient' and 'have potential long term detrimental consequences on the effectiveness of real medicines'.[74] Furthermore, 'the profits derived from these [medicines] are often

[68] See IMPACT, 'Counterfeit Drugs Kill!', May 2008, available at: http://www.who.int/impact/FinalBrochureWHA2008a.pdf.

[69] Ibid.

[70] See Vidushi Sinha, 'Counterfeit Medicines Grow as Global Threat', *Voice of America*, 9 March 2010, available at: http://www.voanews.com/english/news/Counterfeit-Medicines-Grow-as-Global-Threat-95780054.html.

[71] See Michael D. Green, 'Perspectives: Counterfeit Drugs', Centers for Disease Control & Prevention, available at: http://wwwnc.cdc.gov/travel/ yellowbook/2012/chapter-2-the-pre-travel-consultation/perspectives-counterfeit-drugs.htm.

[72] See INTERPOL, Press Release, 'Illegal Online Medicine Suppliers Targeted in First International Internet Day of Action', 13 November 2008, available at: http://www.interpol.int/public/ICPO/PressReleases/PR2008/PR200863.asp.

[73] Ibid.

[74] Ibid.

directed toward organized crime'.[75] A second and much larger operation involving 25 countries, Operation Pangea II, was conducted in November 2009.[76] This second operation resulted in the identification of over 1,200 websites that trafficked in counterfeit medicines and the inspection of over 21,000 packages, 2,356 of which contained counterfeit or illegal pharmaceuticals.[77] More recently, in October 2010, 45 countries coordinated Operation Pangea III, which resulted in the seizure of illegal and counterfeit medicines valued at US$6.77 million, 297 websites were shut down, and 87 individuals were arrested.[78]

A 2011 study reports that online sales of what it describes as 'counterfeit' goods, including pharmaceuticals, continue to be a pervasive problem.[79] The study, conducted by Mark Monitor,[80] which targeted websites that 'offered "generic" versions of prescription drugs that are not available in generic form in the US, targeted the US market by providing pricing in US currency, and did not require a prescription', found that the most trafficked internet pharmacy averaged 28,000 visits per day, suggesting that the site is visited over 10 million times per year.[81] Data yielded from the 26 sites investigated suggested that the combined traffic for these sites is over 51 million visits per year.[82]

Finally, a 2009 RAND Corporation report, entitled 'Film Piracy, Organized Crime and Terrorism,' offers a cogent illustration of how international trade in pirated goods, like that in counterfeit medicines, can adversely impact upon developing countries.[83] Commentators describe the report as having established that 'film piracy has become a key part of Russian organized crime's illegal business portfolio, along with drugs, money laundering, extortion, and human smuggling'.[84] According to the report itself, the reason for organized

---

75 Ibid.

76 *The Handbook*, above note 66, 110–21.

77 Ibid.

78 Ibid., 108–9. For more details regarding this operation, see ibid., 106–9.

79 See generally Mark Monitor, 'Traffic Report: Online Piracy and Counterfeiting', 2011, available at: https://www.MarkMonitor.com/download/report/MarkMonitor_-_Traffic_Report_110111.pdf. For a critique of the tendency of some companies to make indiscriminate use of the term 'counterfeit' to refer to generic medicines as a class – regardless of whether the medicines are or are not of an acceptable quality – see below note 178 and accompanying text. This loose use of terms seems to afflict the Mark Monitor report, as will be discussed below at 4.1.

80 Mark Monitor is a corporation providing online brand protection. See 'Corporate Overview', Mark Monitor, available at: https://www.MarkMonitor.com/company/overview.php (last visited 19 July 2011).

81 Mark Monitor, above note 79, 8.

82 Ibid., 4.

83 See Treverton et al., above note 33, 6–7.

84 See Nikola Krastev, 'Report Says Film Piracy, Organized Crime Intertwined

crime's embrace of film piracy is easy enough to understand, as the 'profit margins (though not yet the total profits)' are much higher than those for illegal drugs, while the criminal penalties are relatively light in comparison to those for drug trafficking.[85] The report goes on to note that after an upsurge of violence in the 1990s, as Russian organized crime groups scrambled to claim the fruits of privatization resulting from the fall of the USSR, these organizations have since reverted to a pattern closer to that of the 1970s and 1980s, in which political and police corruption is used to create 'protected spaces' for organized crime, free from outside interference.[86] It is thus no accident, as the report goes on to note, that Russia ranked 143 out of 179 countries on Transparency International's 2007 Corruption Perceptions Index.[87]

To round out this tale of IP piracy, organized crime and terrorism, it should also be noted that Dr Moses Nail, Editor in Chief of *Foreign Policy* magazine, published a book in 2005 entitled *Illicit: How Smugglers, Traffickers, and Copycat Are Hijacking the Global Economy*, which documents the link between IP theft and socially destabilizing activities including terrorism, illegal arms trafficking, trafficking in human beings, and trade in illegal drugs.[88] According to Dr Nail, the amounts of money involved are immense: the commercial losses resulting from these criminal networks were said to be US$500 billion (as much as 5 to 10 percent of world trade), and growing eight times faster than legal trade.[89] He also noted that contemporary criminal networks are not like the cartels and mafia of the twentieth century, but are highly decentralized, horizontal and fluid, just as terrorist networks are, and confirms that there is considerable crossover between the two.[90]

Thus, it is hardly surprising that developing countries might be as concerned over international trade in counterfeit and pirated goods as countries (and companies) in the industrialized world. While it is true that three of the developing countries said to have participated in the ACTA negotiations (namely Jordan, Mexico and Morocco) have entered into free trade agree-

in Russia', *Radio Free Europe/Radio Liberty*, 21 March 2009, available at: http://www.rferl.org/content/Report_Says_Film_Piracy_Organized_Crime_Intertwined_In_Russia_/1514434.html.

85 Treverton et al., above note 33, 28–9.

86 Ibid., 98.

87 Ibid., 99.

88 See Moisés Nail, *Illicit: How Smugglers, Traffickers, and Copycat are Hijacking the Global Economy* 217–20 (William Heinemann 2005). Dr Nail is a Venezuelan writer and columnist and the Editor in Chief of *Foreign Policy* magazine: Moses Nail, Carnegie Endowment, available at: http://www.carnegieendowment.org/experts/index.cfm?fa=expert&uscore;view&expert_id=21 (last visited 5 March 2012).

89 See Naím, ibid., 112.

90 Ibid., 127, 226.

ments (FTAs) with the United States,[91] and thus might have particularly strong incentives to support this US-backed plurilateral trade initiative,[92] it is also noteworthy that the first two developing countries to join in the ACTA negotiations – Mexico and Morocco – each border on one of the world's two largest economic markets, and have become conduits for smuggling of all sorts from less developed parts of the world, with all of the attendant adverse consequences thereof; they thus might have their own autonomous reasons for wanting to combat international trade in counterfeit and pirated goods.[93] It is perhaps equally worth noting that three of the four developing countries said to have been involved in the ACTA negotiations are moderate Muslim countries with a track record of trying to combat IP piracy as a part of a larger economic development strategy.[94]

---

[91] See Office of the US Trade Representative,'Free Trade Agreements', available at: http://www.ustr.gov/trade-agreements/free-trade-agreements (last visited 21 November 2009) (listing 18 countries that have signed FTAs with the US); see also 'EU Wants Patent Provisions in ACTA', above note 25, 12 (reporting that Jordan dropped out of the negotiations).

[92] See Margot Kaminski, 'The Origins and Potential Impact of the Anti-Counterfeiting Trade Agreement (ACTA)' (2009) 34 *Yale Journal of International Law* 241, 250.

[93] For example, in Mexico, CD and video piracy are said to have become so rampant that, although Mexico was the eighth largest music market in the world in the year 2000, by 2003 it had fallen out of the top ten: International Federation of the Phonographic Industry, 'Record 16 Million Blank CD-Rs Seized in Mexico', December 2004, 11, available at: http://www.ifpi.org/content/library/enforcement-bulletin-25.pdf. During that same three-year period some 3,500 independent video rental outlets had closed because of competition from pirated videos: International Intellectual Property Alliance, '2009 Special 301 Report on Copyright Protection and Enforcement: Mexico', available at: http://www.iipa.com/rbc/2009/2009 SPEC301MEXICO.pdf. Likewise, although in 2008, Mexico's video game industry was reported to be 'exploding', and likely to be worth $1 billion by the end of the decade, it too has been hampered by piracy, as 75% of games sold in Mexico are reportedly pirated: Press Release, Americas News Intelligence, 'Mexican Video Game Industry Nears $1-Billion Mark', 6 December 2007, available at: http://www.prlog.org/10040808-mexican-video-game-industry-nears-1-billion-mark.pdf; Sarah Coleman and Nick Dyer-Witherford, 'Playing on the Digital Commons: Collectivities, Capital, and Contestation in Videogame Culture' (2007) 29 *Media, Culture & Society* 934, 938. The situation is similar in Morocco, as a 2005 report indicated that software, movie and CD piracy was costing Morocco US$200 million per year: 'Ninety-five Percent of Moroccan Music Products Affected by Piracy', *Middle East News & Information*, 2 June 2005, available at: http://www.menareport.com/en/business/184415.

[94] Office of the US Trade Representative, Press Release, 'ACTA Partners on Recent ACTA Negotiations', 6 November 2009, available at: http://www.ustr.gov/about-us/press-office/press-releases/2009/november/-office-us-trade-representative-

In short, Tale # 1 offers plausible support for the argument that ACTA is indeed responding to legitimate national and international security concerns about the growing link between trade in counterfeit and pirated goods on the one hand and organized crime and terrorism on the other. At the same time, as Tale # 2 below suggests, there are equally strong reasons for concern that the ACTA negotiations were eventually hijacked by private industry representatives whose focus was not limited to combating commercial trade in counterfeit and pirated physical goods, but extended as well to enforcing intellectual property rights in far more controversial contexts (albeit still involving trade in physical goods), as well as combating the far more controversial phenomenon of digital file-sharing.

3. TALE # 2: SEIZURE OF GENERIC DRUGS IN TRANSIT, CRIMINALIZED FILE-SHARING AND LAPTOP BORDER SEARCHES

On 6 April 2009, in an obvious attempt to respond to growing criticisms of the secrecy surrounding the ACTA negotiations and growing suspicions as to ACTA's substantive purpose and scope, governments of a number of the participating countries released a detailed summary of the current state of the ACTA negotiations.[95] Far from quieting concerns over ACTA, however, this

---

releases-statemen; 'Moroccan Piracy Drops against Global Trend', *MIP Week*, 8 July 2001), available at: http://www.managingip.com/Article/1327436/Moroccan-piracy-drops-against-global-trend.html (noting that piracy in Morocco dropped by 5% in 2000); see also 'Arab World Responds to $50bn IP Fraud "Epidemic"', AMEinfo.com, 28 February 2008 at 12:42PM, available at: http://www.ameinfo.com/148378.html (reporting that although software piracy is rampant in the Arab world, the rate of business software piracy in the UAE is no greater than the global average of 35%, and the UAE is the only Arab country on a world list of the top 20 countries with the lowest piracy rates in 2006); Asim El Sheikh et al., 'An Exploratory Study of Software Piracy in Jordan' (2006) 23 *Electronic Journal on Information Systems in Developing Countries* 1, 2, available at: http://www.ejisdc.org/ojs2/index.php/ejisdc/article/viewFile/188/146 (reporting business software piracy rates in Jordan that were said to be comparable to those elsewhere in the Arab world, but also noting that Jordan's developing IT industry employs some 10,000 people and generates some US$167 million in annual revenues; this has stimulated Jordan's government to adopt various IP measures in an effort to encourage foreign investment and promote growth in its fledgling software industry). However, Jordan and the UAE have reportedly dropped out of the negotiations. See 'EU Wants Patent Provisions in ACTA', above note 25, 12.

95 See Summary of Key Elements, above note 1: see also Office of US Trade Representative Releases Summary of Anti-Counterfeiting Trade Agreement (ACTA) Negotiations, above note 1 (announcing the release of the Summary of Key Elements in the US). Identical versions of the Summary released on the same day can be found

'Summary of Key Elements under Discussion' only served to fuel those concerns, and understandably so.[96]

As an initial matter, the Summary of Key Elements made no effort to define 'counterfeiting' and 'piracy', even though both are exceedingly malleable rhetorical terms, as one person's counterfeit may encompass another person's legitimate generic medicine, and one person's piracy may encompass what another person would characterize as simple copyright infringement.[97] Counterfeit goods are arguably mislabeled goods – and thus implicate the law of trademarks and unfair competition – while pirated goods are illicitly copied goods – and thus implicate the law of copyright and related rights.[98] Attacking

---

on government websites in Canada, the EU, Japan, New Zealand and the UK. See 'The Anti-Counterfeiting Trade Agreement: Summary of Key Elements Under Discussion', Dept of Foreign Affairs & International Trade Canada, 6 April 2009, available at: http://www.international.gc.ca/trade-agreements-accords-commerciaux/fo/intellect_property.aspx; European Commission, 'The Anti-Counterfeiting Trade Agreement Summary of Key Elements under Discussion', 6 April 2009, available at: http://trade.ec.europa.eu/doclib/docs/2009/april/tradoc_142745.pdf; Press Release, Ministry of Economy, Trade & Industry of Japan, 'Anti-Counterfeiting Trade Agreement (ACTA) (Summary of Key Elements Under Discussion)', 7 April 2009, available at: http://www.meti.go.jp/english/press/data/20090407_01.html; Press Release, New Zealand Ministry of Economic Development, 'The Anti-Counterfeiting Trade Agreement: Summary of Key Elements Under Discussion', 7 April 2009, available at: http://www.med.govt.nz/upload/67481/883411_1-web.pdf; Intellectual Property Office, 'Anti-Counterfeiting Trade Agreement (ACTA)', available at: http://www.ipo.gov.uk/pro-policy/pro-crime/pro-crime-acta.htm (last visited 21 November 2009).

96 See, e.g., International Centre for Trade & Sustainable Development (ICTSD), 'USTR Releases ACTA "Summary", Civil Society Wants More', *Bridges Weekly Trade News Digest*, 8 April 2009, 3–4, available at: http://ictsd.net/i/news/bridgesweekly/44809 (describing how concerns of public health groups and generic drug makers with the ACTA were not assuaged by the Summary of Key Elements); David Kravets, 'Details Lacking in Counterfeiting Treaty Paper', *Wired*, 6 April 2009, 16:15 EST, available at: http://www.wired.com/ threatlevel/2009/04/details-lacking (explaining that the released Summary of Key Elements did not relieve concerns that the ACTA would criminalize peer-to-peer file-sharing).

97 See Summary of Key Elements, above note 1; ICTSD, 'WHO Executive Board Grapples with IP Issues', *Bridges Weekly Trade News Digest*, 28 January 2009, 3, available at: http://ictsd.net/downloads/bridgesweekly/bridgesweekly13-3.pdf (illustrating the difficulty of defining counterfeiting, particularly in the context of prescription drugs). See also Xavier Seuba, 'Free Trade of Pharmaceutical Products: The Limits of Intellectual Property Enforcement at the Border', ICTSD, March 2010, 30, available at: http://ictsd.org/downloads/2011/12/free-trade-of-pharmaceutical-products.pdf ('companies often refer to generic medicines of guaranteed quality as pirated, counterfeited, substandard or spurious'). For a discussion of the loose use of the term 'piracy,' see below notes 177, 205–209 and accompanying text.

98 See above note 3. While in the US the term 'related rights' refers to such common law rights as the right of publicity, in civil law countries the term 'related

the problem of counterfeiting and piracy without first defining the parameters of the problem to be addressed, however, created a risk of 'policy laundering' – that is, seemingly combating one problem, such as trade in counterfeit or pirated goods, while actually targeting another, more controversial problem, such as generic medicines or digital file-sharing[99] – a 'bait and switch' phenomenon not entirely unknown to international intellectual property negotiations.[100] Although the terms 'counterfeit trademark goods' and 'pirated copyright goods' were eventually defined in the final draft of ACTA,[101] the final draft nevertheless continues to address three conceptually distinct problems – the problem of counterfeit and pirated tangible goods, the problem of intellectual property enforcement in more controversial contexts (albeit still involving physical goods), and the problem of enforcing intellectual property rights in the digital environment.

An equally troubling aspect of the 2009 Summary of Key Elements was its apparent effort to quiet concerns raised by a previously leaked document. The

rights' is generally considered synonymous with 'neighboring rights' – i.e., rights of performers, broadcasters and producers of phonograms – which have no precise counterpart in US copyright law. See International Bureau of WIPO, 'Basic Notions of Copyright and Related Rights', 52–3, available at: http://www.wipo.int/export/sites/www/copyright/en/activities/pdf/basic_notions.pdf (describing the nature of related rights).

[99] See below notes 190–191, 237 and accompanying text (discussing specific examples of how ACTA could be brought to bear on both issues).

[100] For a discussion of policy laundering, see above note 5. For instance, a discrepancy existed between the economic arguments used to justify the protection of database contents and the particular solution adopted in the EU Database Directive. See Directive 96/9/EC of the European Parliament and Council of 11 March 1996 on the Legal Protection of Databases, Arts. 7–8, [1996] OJ L77/20 (EC) [hereinafter EU Database Directive]; Charles R. McManis, 'Database Protection in the Digital Information Age' (2001) 7 *Roger Williams University Law Review* 7, 33 [hereinafter McManis,'Database Protection']. Although the main reason given for the decision to create a sui generis property right in the contents of databases was 'to prevent the potential damage caused by the slavish copying [of data] by competitors; the "economic case for the creation of a right to prevent extraction and re-utilization of unoriginal content by users [in general, non-competitors as well as competitors] has never been satisfactorily explained"': McManis, 'Database Protection', ibid., 33 (quoting Mark Powell, 'The European Union's Database Directive: An International Antidote of the Side Effects of Feist?' (1997) 20 *Fordham International Law Journal* 1215, 1225). The phenomenon of policy laundering was also said to have occurred in the negotiation of the WIPO Copyright Treaty (WET) and Performances and Phonograms Treaty (WPPT) in 1996. Russell McOrmand, 'Copyright Consultations', 5 August 2009, available at: http://www.ic.gc.ca/eic/site/008.nsf/eng/00015.html. For a discussion of these two treaties, see below notes 210–215 and accompanying text.

[101] See ACTA, above note 1, Art. 5(d), (k); see also below notes 183–184, 207–210 and accompanying text (quoting and discussing the definitions of pirated copyright goods and counterfeit trademark goods).

leaked discussion paper indicated that ACTA would not be limited to targeting commercial trade in counterfeit and pirated physical goods but would also extend to 'significant willful infringements without motivation for financial gain to such an extent as to prejudicially affect the copyright owner (e.g., Internet piracy)'.[102] Rather than stating unequivocally that ACTA would focus solely on commercial trade in counterfeit and pirated physical goods, the Summary of Key Elements more ambiguously noted that ACTA's 'intended focus is on counterfeiting and piracy activities that significantly affect commercial interests, rather than on the activities of ordinary citizens'.[103] To the suspicious eye, this carefully crafted wording seemed to amount to a tacit admission that ACTA would not be limited to combating commercial trade in counterfeit and pirated physical goods, but would extend to at least some types of digital file-sharing – namely any file-sharing that significantly affects the commercial interests of digital content providers.

The disclaimer of any intent to focus on the 'activities of ordinary citizens' was further undercut by the subsequent acknowledgement in the Summary that one of the issues being discussed under the heading 'Criminal Enforcement' was 'clarifying the scale of infringement necessary to qualify for criminal sanctions in cases of trademark counterfeiting and copyright and related rights piracy'.[104] As we shall see, the available empirical evidence to date strongly suggests that downloading digital content from unauthorized sources is a widespread and growing global phenomenon among ordinary citizens and – whatever may be its net social welfare effects in the short and long run – is clearly affecting the commercial interests of digital content providers, though it is far from clear that the enforcement measures specified in ACTA will effectively address this concern.[105]

The disclaimer concerning 'activities of ordinary citizens' rang particularly hollow when considered in light of two other statements in the Summary of Key Elements. The first of these was to be found in the sections that identify the issues being addressed relating to Civil Enforcement and Border Measures.[106] In both sections, the Summary acknowledged that one issue under discussion was which intellectual property rights would be covered by the measures under consideration.[107] If commercial trade in counterfeit and

102 Discussion Paper, above note 2, 3.

103 Summary of Key Elements, above note 1.

104 Ibid.

105 See below notes 137–144 and accompanying text (discussing the short and long-term net social welfare effects of digital file-sharing); See also below notes 236–242 and accompanying text (discussing the question of whether ACTA's measures for enforcing IPRs in the digital context will be effective).

106 Summary of Key Elements, above note 1.

107 Ibid.

pirated goods was the sole focus of ACTA, the answer to that question would be obvious. The relevant intellectual property rights would be those created by the law of trademarks – and the associated law of unfair competition – and copyright and related rights, as these two bodies of law collectively comprehend all activities that would fall within the conventional meaning of the terms 'counterfeit' (mislabeled) and 'pirated' (illicitly copied) goods.[108] If, on the other hand, the civil enforcement and border measures mandated by ACTA were drafted so as to extend to patent-protected subject matter, ACTA's reach would effectively extend to goods that are neither mislabeled nor illicitly copied, such as generic drugs unprotected by patents where manufactured or imported but infringing where trans-shipped.[109] The fact that the negotiating parties even considered what intellectual property rights other than trademarks and copyrights might be covered by the civil enforcement and border measures mandated by ACTA again suggested that the ACTA negotiations were ranging well beyond concerns over trade in counterfeit and pirated goods.

A second statement in the Summary of Key Elements that did ostensibly offer reassurance that ACTA would not focus on the activities of ordinary citizens was to be found in the section on border measures, which indicated that one element under discussion is 'a de minimis exception that could permit travelers to bring in goods for personal use'.[110] As it turns out, however, that reassurance was more apparent than real, at least when considered in light of statements made in the course of a 6 April 2009 briefing conducted by Canadian government officials at the time of the Canadian government's release of the Summary of Key Elements. During this briefing, it became clear that a 'big fight' was expected on proposals for a de minimis exception.[111]

---

108 See above note 3 (discussing the meaning of 'counterfeit' and 'pirated' goods and noting that the terms are not defined in the Summary of Key Elements); see also above notes 97–101 for a detailed discussion of the term 'counterfeit' drugs). For the definitions and a discussion of the terms 'counterfeit trademark goods' and 'pirated copyright goods' in ACTA, see below notes182–186, 205–209 and accompanying text.

109 For a discussion of the problem of in-transit seizures of generic drugs, see below notes 189–197 and accompanying text. As discussed below all rights in 'intellectual property' as defined in TRIPS are potentially subject to the civil enforcement provisions of ACTA; however, patents and trade secrets are explicitly excluded from ACTA's border measures and are not included in the criminal enforcement provisions. see below note 188 and accompanying text.

110 Summary of Key Elements, above note 1.

111 Michael Geist, 'Canada's ACTA Briefing, Part Five: The Fight over a De Minimis Exception', Michael Geist Blog, 6 April 2009, available at: http://www.michaelgeist.ca/content/view/3834/99999 (describing the controversy over the inclusion of a de minimis exception in ACTA).

Indeed, this same Canadian government briefing provided a bonanza of other previously undisclosed information about the ACTA negotiations, thus highlighting how little the US government had been willing to disclose.[112] While the Office of the US Trade Representative remained tight-lipped about the ACTA negotiations and was content to limit its comments on the Summary of Key Elements to a brief accompanying press release,[113] the Canadian government adopted a much more open approach to the ACTA negotiations.

According to blogger Michael Geist, who is a law professor at the University of Ottawa where he holds the Canada Research Chair in Internet and E-commerce Law, and who apparently attended the briefing:

> The meeting started with a bang as Don Stephenson, an Assistant Deputy Minister at DFAIT [the Department of Foreign Affairs and International Trade], noted the two sources of ACTA. One was obviously counterfeiting. The other was the stalemate at the World Intellectual Property Organization. With the emergence of the Development Agenda, WIPO now finds itself torn between different views of intellectual property. Canadian officials were clear that [it was the] frustration with WIPO in developing further international IP standards that has led to an attempt to establish a 'plurilateral' treaty rather than the multilateral efforts at WIPO.[114]

Another article described a similar briefing provided by the negotiators for the European Commission's (EC) trade directorate, who were said to be 'very open' in answering questions about the reason for a plurilateral agreement instead of a multilateral agreement, such as the WTO's TRIPS Agreement or the agreements administered by WIPO.[115] 'ACTA is very much about enforcement', one of the negotiators was quoted as saying.[116] 'Speaking on enforcement in WTO, not to

---

112 See Dept of Foreign Affairs & International Trade Canada 'Summary of Discussions: ACTA Roundtable Consultation', 6 April 2009, available at: http://www.international.gc.ca/trade-agreements-accords-commerciaux/fo/discussion_summary-resume.aspx?lang=eng&view=d (summarizing the briefing of a variety of interests groups on Canada's role in the ACTA negotiations).

113 See Office of US Trade Representative Releases Summary of Anti-Counterfeiting Trade Agreement (ACTA) Negotiations, above note 1 (providing general background information about the ACTA negotiations and stating that the summary has been released and is being shared with stakeholders).

114 Michael Geist, 'Canada's ACTA Briefing, Part One: ACTA is a Response to WIPO Gridlock', Michael GeistBlog, 6 April 2009, available at: http://www.michaelgeist.ca/content/view/3830/99999. For both the WIPO and WTO development agendas, See below note 199.

115 Monika Ermert, 'European Commission on ACTA: TRIPS is Floor Not Ceiling', *Intellectual Property Watch*, 22 April 2009 at 7:18 AM, available at: http://www.ip-watch.org/weblog/2009/04/22/european-commission-on-acta-trips-is-floor-not-ceiling.

116 Ibid.

talk about WIPO, is extremely difficult'.[117] There was said to be no intention to duplicate TRIPS; rather, 'we want to go beyond it', the negotiator said, adding, 'TRIPS is the floor, not the ceiling'.[118] These observations by Canadian and EC officials lent considerable weight to the concern that the ACTA negotiations did indeed simply represent the most ambitious effort to date on the part of intellectual property owners to engage in the tactic of forum-shifting, as a part of a larger strategy to ratchet up international protection for private intellectual property rights.[119]

The Canadian briefing also apparently included a PowerPoint presentation (later posted online), which was said to have 'effectively confirmed the substance of many of the leaks online'.[120] Canadian officials were also said to confirm that they favor 'a more transparent approach to ACTA' and that 'there are ongoing discussions among negotiating partners about how to address transparency concerns'.[121] But these officials also apparently 'acknowledged that there is still disagreement on the transparency issue, with some countries favoring release of the draft text sooner rather than later, while others indicat[e] that they typically keep everything secret until completion'.[122] One possibility under consideration, the Canadian officials were said to have noted, was 'releasing the draft with all suggested changes without attribution to the particular delegation'.[123]

According to Professor Geist, one of the most interesting points made during the ACTA briefing concerned 'the possibility of including a de minimus

---

117 Ibid. For a discussion of the stalemate that developed at WTO and WIPO, see below notes 199–201.

118 Ibid. For a discussion of the use of forum-shifting to ratchet up IP standards beyond those mandated by the WTO TRIPS Agreement, see above note 5 and accompanying text.

119 See above note 5 and accompanying text (discussing forum-shifting, nodally coordinated enforcement pyramids and policy laundering as means used to protect private intellectual property rights).

120 See Michael Geist, 'Canada's ACTA Briefing, Part Two: The Treaty Provisions', Michael Geist Blog, 6 April 2009, available at: http://www.michaelgeist.ca/content/view/3831/99999 (noting the substantive points covered in the briefing). The ACTA PowerPoint used for the presentation is available online: Douglas George, Intellectual Property, Information & Technology Trade Policy Division, Presentation at the Roundtable ACTA Consultation, 6 April 2009, available at: http://www.international.gc.ca/trade-agreements-accords-commerciaux/fo/presentation.aspx?lang= eng&view=d.

121 Michael Geist, 'Canada's ACTA Briefing, Part Three: The Official Summary Document', Michael Geist Blog, 6 April 2009, available at: http://www. michaelgeist.ca/content/view/3832/99999.

122 Ibid.

123 Ibid.

[sic] exception within the Border Measures chapter [of ACTA]'.[124] Such an exception, as he noted, presumably would be designed to ensure that tougher border measures will not result in iPods being searched by border guards, for instance – one of the most common concerns raised about ACTA and one that the Canadian government's PowerPoint presentation took pains to refute.[125] Indeed, the Canadian officials were said to have indicated that both they and a number of other participants had put forward de minimis proposals.[126] The Summary of Key Elements document itself acknowledged that one of the elements under discussion with respect to border measures included a 'de minimis exception that could permit travelers to bring in goods for personal use'.[127] On the other hand, it was observed that there would 'be a big fight over this provision, with some groups concerned that it would send a signal that purchasing counterfeit products for personal use is acceptable or that it could lead to the importation of counterfeit medicines'.[128]

The latter statement was of particular concern, as not every generic medicine infringing patents in the country of importation or trans-shipment is necessarily a counterfeit or pirated medicine. Moreover, generic drugs that turned out not to be infringing in either the exporting or the importing country have, in fact, been seized in transit in Europe.[129] Thus, to the suspicious eye, this disagreement over whether to insert a de minimis exception in ACTA's provisions on border measures seemed to underscore the plausibility of concerns that ACTA could indeed be implemented in such a way as to result

---

124 Geist, above note 111.

125 See George, above note 120, slide 7 ('ACTA is NOT about … [s]eizing portable music players and laptops at the border.'). But cf. below note 130 and accompanying text.

126 Geist, above note 111.

127 Summary of Key Elements, above note 1.

128 Geist, above note 111. For a critique of the indiscriminate use of the term 'counterfeit' medicines, see above note 79 and below note 178 and accompanying text.

129 In 2009, it was widely reported that the EU 'has come under fire for seizures by Dutch customs authorities of drugs made outside of patent in India that were headed to South American countries but routed through the Netherlands, where the drugs enjoy patent protection'. 'EU Wants Patent Provisions in ACTA', above note 25, 11; see also 'Developing Countries Attack Dutch Seizure of Generic Medicines', Third World Network, 9 February 2009, available at: http://www.twnside.org.sg/title2/wto.info/2009/twninfo20090203.htm (providing a more detailed discussion of the Dutch drug seizure). For legal analyses of these in-transit seizures, see Frederick M. Abbott, 'Seizure of Generic Pharmaceuticals in Transit Based on Allegations of Patent Infringement: A Threat to International Trade, Development and Public Welfare' [2009] *WIPO Journal* 43; Stephanie H. McAlviney, 'In Transition … When Should In-Transit Goods be Seized for Intellectual Property Infringement in the European Union?' [2010] 12 EIPR 614.

in the in-transit seizure of generic drugs, or for that matter searches of portable music players or laptops, at the border. Both concerns seem to be legitimate – generic drugs have been seized in transit and the current stance of the U.S. Customs and Border Protection is that without cause 'officers may examine documents, books, pamphlets, and other printed materials, as well as computers, disks, hard drives, and other electronic or digital scoring devices'.[130]

For the complaints of India and Brazil filed with the WTO over these seizures, see Request for Consultations by India, *European Union and a Member State – Seizure of Generic Drugs in Transit*, WT/DS408/1, 11 May 2010, available at: http://www.wto.org/english/tratop_e/dispu_e/cases_e/ds408_e.htm [hereinafter DS 408 (India)]; Request for Consultations by Brazil, *European Union and a Member State – Seizure of Generic Drugs in Transit*, WT/DS409/1, 12 May 2010, available at: http://www.wto.org/english/tratop_e/dispu_e/cases_e/ds409_e.htm [hereinafter DS 409 (Brazil)]. For a discussion of these complaints, see Henning Grosse Ruse-Khan, 'A Trade Agreement Creating Barriers to International Trade? ACTA Border Measures and Goods in Transit' (2011) 26 *American University International Law Review* 645, 648–60.

Critics of ACTA were said to fear that 'ACTA would replicate this scenario in other countries': 'EU Wants Patent Provisions in ACTA', above note 25, 11. The Summary of Key Elements acknowledged that one issue under discussion regarding border measures included 'whether border measures should only apply to importations or should equally apply to the export and the transit of goods': Summary of Key Elements, above note 1. Article 13 of the final draft of ACTA contains a footnote stating that the 'Parties agree that patents and protection of undisclosed information do not fall with the scope of this Section'. However, concerns over in-transit seizures of generic drugs persist, for reasons that will be explained in Part 4 of this chapter.

[130] US Customs and Border Protection, 'Policy Regarding Border Search of Information', 16 July 2008, available at:http://www.cbp.gov/linkhandler/cgov/travel/admissibility/search_authority.ctt/search_authority.pdf. In the United States, the legality of border searches is a constitutional issue implicating the IV Amendment of the US Constitution, which governs the legality of government searches and seizures. See US Constitution, amendment IV; Yule Kim, Congressional Research Services, RL34404, Border Searches of Laptop Computers and Other Electronic Storage Devices, 16 November 2009, 1, available at: http://www.fas.org/sgp/crs/homesec/RL34404.pdf. Although the US Supreme Court has not directly commented on the issue of laptop border searches, lower courts interpreting previous Supreme Court precedent have held that laptop searches require 'neither a warrant nor probable cause' for such a search to be legal: ibid., 4. In particular, the Ninth Circuit Court of Appeals held that 'reasonable suspicion is not needed for customs officials to search a laptop or other personal electronic storage devices at the border': *United States v Arnold*, 533 F.3d 1003, 1008 (9th Cir. 2008). See also generally, T. Jesse Goff, 'Regulation of Digital Copyrights and Trademarks at the U.S. Border: How the Proposed Anti-Counterfeiting Trade Agreement and the Enacted U.S. Pro-IP Act Will Destabilize the Current System' (2010) 16 *Southwestern Journal of International Law* 207 (discussing the current state of US border policy and practice regarding IP enforcement and arguing that current US law and ACTA go too far in strengthening IP enforcement at the US border).

The disagreement over the de minimis exception was apparently but one of a number of issues that divided the negotiating parties and slowed down the ACTA negotiations. Professor Geist provided a summary of an article in which Pedro Velasco Martins, an EU official involved in the ACTA negotiations, identified several areas of disagreement, including disagreements over potential internet provisions.[131] These provisions were said to be controversial because 'they may involve liability for Internet service providers that host Internet copyright pirates' or could 'involve requirements that these providers monitor usage by private citizens, [which] could violate EU privacy directives'.[132]

It is worth noting that recent legislation has been introduced in Congress, which would limit the ability of border authorities in the US to search laptops with such ease. See the Securing our Borders and our Data Act of 2009, H.R. 239, 111th Cong. (2009); Border Security Search Accountability Act of 2009, H.R. 1729, 111th Cong. (2009); see also Yule Kim, ibid., 13–14 (summarizing the contents of the aforementioned proposed legislation). However, to date neither of these proposals has been enacted into positive law.

[131] 'EU Wants Patent Provisions in ACTA', above note 25, at 11. Professor Geist summarizes the article by identifying the following areas of disagreement:

1. *The scope of ACTA coverage*: The Europeans would like to extend ACTA to patents. Canadian officials are known to want to limit it to copyright and trademark.
2. *Anti-camcording provisions*: The Europeans are not supportive of a specific anti-camcording provision [prohibiting the recording of films in movie theaters using hand-held devices]. The US obviously is and pressured Canada to enact such a provision in 2007.
3. *Dispute Resolution*: The Europeans prefer a 'peer review' approach to review compliance. Other countries are known to support a judicial process complete with penalties for non-compliance.
4. *Internet provisions*: The Europeans are not prepared to go beyond existing EU law with respect to any of the Internet provisions.

Michael Geist, 'Divisions Between US and EU Begin to Appear Over ACTA', Michael Geist Blog, 18 May 2009, available at: http://www.michaelgeist.ca/content/view/3979/99999. The anti-camcording provision is alluded to in the Summary of Key Elements, which notes that criminal enforcement issues being discussed include 'criminal procedures and penalties ... of camcording motion pictures or other audiovisual works': Summary of Key Elements, above note 1. The internet provisions are contained in a separate section, entitled 'Intellectual Property Rights Enforcement in the Digital Environment', which notes that one issue under discussion is 'the possible role and responsibilities of internet service providers in deterring copyright and related rights piracy over the Internet': ibid. In contrast, the Summary of Key Elements makes no specific reference to issues regarding dispute resolution, other than to indicate that a chapter, entitled Institutional Arrangements, will deal with 'questions related to the implementation of the agreement': ibid.

[132] 'EU Wants Patent Provisions in ACTA', above note 25, 12. For continuing

While the digital content industries – and particularly the music industry – apparently convinced the ACTA negotiating parties that digital file-sharing constituted as much of a threat to the public as trade in counterfeit and pirated goods, the empirical evidence on that point is in fact decidedly mixed, as a comprehensive study commissioned by the Dutch government demonstrates. This report, dated 19 February 2009, entitled 'Ups and Downs: Economic and Cultural Effects of File Sharing on Music, Film and Games', concluded that 'the economic implications of file sharing for welfare in the Netherlands are strongly positive in the short and long terms'.[133] The report found that file-sharing 'provides consumers with access to a broad range of cultural products, which typically raises welfare', even though 'the practice is believed to result in a decline in sales of CDs, DVDs and games'.[134] The report went on to note that '[d]etermining the impact of unlicensed downloading on the purchase of paid content is a tricky exercise', as one track of music downloaded 'does not imply one less track sold'.[135] The study explains that many people download music tracks to get to know new music (sampling), and eventually buy the CD if they like it.[136]

The report noted that 'to the extent that file sharing results in a decline in sales (substitution), [it entails] a transfer of welfare from operators/producers to consumers', who otherwise lack purchasing power (that is, lack the collective power to influence consumer prices, absent the ability to download from unauthorized sources), with no net welfare effect.[137] The reason for this lack of purchasing power is that the music industry, as currently organized, arguably constitutes a functional oligopoly.[138] For that reason, unauthorized music downloading might be serving to encourage innovation and new business models in the music industry. Indeed, it already seems to be doing just that, as evidenced by the runaway success of Apple's iPod and the associated

---

concerns that legislation implementing the internet provisions contained in the final draft of ACTA could make internet service providers liable for infringing acts of users: See below notes 170, 222, and 246 and accompanying text.

133 Annelies Huygen et al., 'Ups and Downs: Economic and Cultural Effects of File Sharing on Music, Film and Games', Ministries of Education, Culture & Science, Economic Affairs & Justice, 18 February 2009 (Willemien Kneppelhout et al., trans), 3, available at: http://www.ivir.nl/publicaties/vaneijk/Ups_And_Downs_authorised_translation.pdf (providing an authorized English translation of the report).

134 Ibid.

135 Ibid.

136 Ibid.

137 Ibid., 120.

138 See Tung Q. Nguyen-Khac, 'The Music Industry in Dilemma: How New Technologies Can Turn an Industry Upside Down', August 2003 (unpublished manuscript, on file with *Houston Law Review*).

iTunes online music store.[139] Of course, organizations such as the International Federation of the Phonographic Industry (IFPI) suggest that, although digital music sales have increased by more than 1,000 per cent since 2004, revenues generated from the sale of recorded music has declined by 31 per cent. Moreover, the IFPI argues that there have been significant losses in terms of employment for creative professionals such as technicians, recording professionals and studio musicians.[140] The IFPI largely attributes such losses to the prevalence of digital piracy. The available empirical evidence on this point, however, is, at best, mixed.

In addition to presenting its own empirical findings, the consortium of organizations involved in producing the Dutch report on the economic and cultural effects of file-sharing on music, films and games also devoted a chapter to evaluating virtually all peer-reviewed academic empirical studies conducted prior to 2009 that had investigated the relationship between downloading and music purchasing. The Dutch report concluded that the results of these studies 'vary widely, ranging from positive to neutral to negative'.[141] The report also noted that these studies 'appear to be methodologically complex and … criticism[s] can be raised about many of them'.[142] A potential problem with many of the studies, for example, was that they focused entirely on the music industry, whereas the Dutch study itself offered a comprehensive examination of the impact of digital file-sharing on the entertainment industry as a whole.[143] The report's overall empirical conclusion was that music file-sharing has had 'only a moderate effect on physical audio format sales',[144] as a variety of other factors appear to have contributed to the downturn in CD sales since the year 2000, including the inevitable end of consumer replacement of obsolete LPs and cassettes (during which the music industry had reaped windfall profits from selling essentially the same music twice to the same consumer), competition from online distribution of music, and – perhaps most importantly – competition with other forms of hand-held entertainment products as well, for example, video games and mobile phones.[145] Indeed, one

---

139 Since 2004, Apple has dominated digital music sales, both in the US and worldwide. See Huygen et al., above note 133, 20. Competition from Apple's iTunes music store and other online distributors has contributed to the decline in CD sales. See below note 146 and accompanying text.

140 Ibid., 17.

141 Huygen et al., above note 133, 83.

142 Ibid., 98.

143 Ibid., 83–102.

144 Ibid., 83, 102.

145 Ibid., 93; accord Felix Oberholzer-Gee and Koleman Strumpf, 'The Effect of File Sharing on Record Sales: An Empirical Analysis' (2007) 115 *Journal of Political Economy* 1, 39 (citing declining patterns of consumer replacement, changing distribution

of the most important insights offered by the Dutch study was that '[w]hereas the size of the entertainment market as a whole is relatively constant, the share of music is declining gradually and the share of games is showing explosive growth'.[146] The study's overall conclusion about the appropriate policy response to digital file-sharing was: 'Don't "criminalise" individual end users – educate them.'[147]

More recent empirical reports on digital piracy and its impact on the entertainment industry continue to be mixed. Indeed, taking two recent and contrasting reports at face value, it would appear that two new tales could be recounted about this particular dimension of ACTA. While the first tale might be called 'The Digital Sky is Falling', the title of the second tale might be (and very nearly is) entitled 'The Digital Sky is Rising'.[148]

In an effort to quantify the extent of online piracy, researchers commissioned by the entertainment industry and intellectual property owners generally have attempted to quantify the amount of pirated materials available online and the amount of internet traffic – that is, the amount of bandwidth – consumed by activities that infringe copyrights.[149] One 2011 study in particular, prepared by a company called Envisional[150] and commissioned by NBC Universal, estimates that 23.76 per cent of all internet traffic globally is used for the purposes of infringing copyrights.[151] The Envisional study examined

---

methods, and substitution of music with other forms of entertainment as all possible reasons for declining CD sales). The latter study has been the subject of detailed methodological criticism: see Stan J. Liebowitz, 'How Reliable is the Oberholzer-Gee and Strumpf Paper on File-Sharing?' 1 September 2007, unpublished manuscript, available at: http://papers.ssrn.com/sol3/papers.cfm?abstract_id=1014399; James Boyle, *The Public Domain: Enclosing the Commons of the Mind* (Yale University Press 2008) 73–4.

146 Huygen et al., above note 133, 6.

147 Ibid., 122.

148 See below note 154 and accompanying text. The phrase 'The sky is falling!' features prominently in the story, Henny Penny (also known as Chicken Little), and has 'passed into the English language as a common idiom indicating a hysterical or mistaken belief that disaster is imminent: see 'Henny Penny', Wikipedia, available at: http://en.wikipedia.org/wiki/Henny_Penny (last visited 18 March 2012).

149 See, e.g., Envisional, 'Technical Report: An Estimate of Infringing Use of the Internet', January 2011, available at: http://documents.envisional.com/docs/Envisional-Internet_Usage-Jan2011.pdf; Mark Monitor, above note 79.

150 Envisional is a corporation providing various products and analyses to 'detect and guard against the threats of counterfeiting, piracy, fraud and online brand abuse': Envisional, 'About Us', available at: http://www.envisional.com/about_us/ (last visited 29 July 2011).

151 Envisional, above note 149, 2. This number is slightly lower in the US, where infringing use is estimated to consume 17.53% of all internet traffic: ibid., 2. Both figures exclude all pornographic material – some of which is undoubtedly pirated –

four different types of online venue, which included BitTorrent, cyberlockers, video streaming, and various peer-to-peer (p2p) networks and file-sharing arenas including eDonkey, Gnutella, and Usenet.[152] The study found that, of the top 10,000 most popular files available on one of the most popular BitTorrent trackers, PublicBT, nearly two-thirds (63.7 per cent) of all content available was copyrighted material and was illegally shared.[153] Because 35.8 per cent was pornographic content, it was difficult to determine the status of the copyright; however, Envisional speculated that the majority of this content

---

because the status of the copyright permissions and licensing is often difficult to determine: ibid., 2–3.

[152] Ibid., 2–3. BitTorrent is a p2p file-sharing protocol estimated by Envisional to be the most widely used worldwide: ibid., 7. Envisional notes that they 'consistently measure over eight million users simultaneously connected to the BitTorrent network': ibid. Moreover, two highly used BitTorrent clients, uTorrent and BitTorrent Mainline, claim they maintain clients exceeding 100 million and have over 20 million users daily: ibid. BitTorrents are accessed via a tracker application that records the IP addresses of users with files they are interested in downloading and makes them available for file sharing at a users request: ibid.

Cyberlockers are 'centralised [sic] file storage services to which individuals can upload material for access by themselves or others': ibid., 15. For users, cyberlockers have a number of advantages over p2p networks: (1) they are accessible with an internet connection and web browser and thus do not require 'dedicated client applications', (2) 'direct downloading from a cyberlocker can be quicker than P2P on high bandwidth connections', (3) they are 'more anonymous', and (4) malware, viruses and spoofing are less prevalent: ibid. However, there are disadvantages for users: cyberlockers do not allow users to search all available content in the way in which a tracker allows BitTorrent users to identify all available IP addresses with desired content: ibid. Cyberlockers are available to both paying and non-paying users – paying users, however, enjoy significant benefits, which include longer storage periods and instant access at high download speeds to *any* content stored with the service: ibid. Popular services include MegaUpload, 4shared, Rapidshare and Hotfile: ibid.

Video streaming is the fastest growing usage of bandwidth worldwide and allows users to watch video content in real-time: ibid., 19. YouTube is perhaps the most well-known example of a video streaming host: ibid.

The study also looked at three 'file-sharing arenas [eDonkey, Gnutella, and Usenet] where copyrighted content is generally distributed': ibid., 24. eDonkey is one of the oldest p2p networks and is most commonly used in Europe: ibid. Gnutella is another p2p network, most prominently used in the US for sharing music: ibid., 25. Gnutella clients include Limewire and other open source derivatives of Limewire: see'Gnutella', Wikipedia, available at: http://en.wikipedia.org/wiki/Gnutella (last visited 20 July 2011). Usenet is a communication network – one of the oldest on the internet – initially intended for use as a text messaging system: Envisional, above note 150, 26. However, users found the network to be useful for transmitting files: ibid. Currently, Envisional estimates only 3.2% of all posts are text messages, with at least 93.4% of posting contained files consisting of copyrighted content.

[153] Ibid., 4.

was also copyrighted and thus illegally shared.[154] Only one file – a list of IP addresses – out of the 10,000 examined files was clearly identified as non-copyrighted content.[155]

Based on these figures, Envisional estimated that infringing BitTorrent use (which excluded pornography) amounted to 11.39 per cent of all internet traffic globally.[156] Similar results were found with regard to cyberlockers and other piracy arenas: 73.15 per cent of content in cyberlockers was copyrighted, accounting to 5.12 per cent of all internet traffic; 69 per cent of files found on Gnutella were infringing, accounting for 1.56 per cent of all internet traffic; 93.4 per cent of all posts on Usenet contained infringing files, accounting for 0.86 per cent of all internet traffic; and 98.9 per cent of all eDonkey content was infringing, accounting for 1.82 per cent of all internet traffic.[157] Although video streaming was determined to account for a significant amount of internet traffic (26 per cent of all traffic), the amount of infringing video streaming was significantly lower than the other three categories – only 5.34 per cent of all video streaming was found to be infringing.[158] Still, the infringing portion, 1.42 per cent, was on a par with the infringing traffic of Gnutella, eDonkey and Usenet.[159] Recent reports by Mark Monitor and the IFPI – entities representing trademark owners and the sound recording industry, respectively – have provided similar results, finding that substantial internet traffic is dedicated to infringement.[160]

With studies such as these in hand, one might well conclude that the digital sky is indeed falling on the entertainment industry, and many have asserted just that.[161] On the other hand, a January 2012 report – entitled 'The Sky is

---

154 Ibid., 5.

155 Ibid.

156 Ibid., 50. These figures were based on four studies that tracked internet usage: ibid., 27–49 (discussing and interpreting the results of studies conducted by Sandvine, Inc., Arbor Networks, Cisco and iPoque).

157 Ibid., 50–5. These figures, like the BitTorrent figures, excluded pornography.

158 Ibid., 52.

159 Ibid.

160 More specifically, the Mark Monitor study estimated that rapidshare.com, megavideo.com and megaupload.com generate over 21 billion visits per year: Mark Monitor, above note 79, 7. In total, the 43 sites which were identified as containing 'digital piracy' were estimated to be frequented over 53 billion times per year: ibid. The IFPI noted that in the UK 76% of all online music obtained by users was unlicensed and that in Brazil and Spain 44% and 45% of users respectively visited sites providing 'unlicensed online services'. IFPI Report, above note 140, 14. Moreover, the report cites studies indicating that 89% of BitTorrent downloads contained infringing content and 98.8% of Limewire downloads were 'copyright protected or highly likely to be copyright protected': ibid.

161 For a particularly readable account asserting that the digital sky is indeed

Rising: A Detailed Look at the State of the Entertainment Industry'[162] – claims that '[c]ontrary to the dire warnings of the legacy entertainment industry players, the market is booming, with ever greater content choices for consumers, more options for creators, and many more opportunities for smart businesses [and] artists to make money'.[163] The report cites US Bureau of Labor Statistics data showing that employment in the entertainment sector grew by nearly 20 per cent in the decade from 1998 to 2008 and that during the same decade the number of independent artists grew at an even faster rate (48 per cent).[164] It also reports that, whereas in 2001 the Gracenote Global Media Database[165] had data showing roughly 11 million sound tracks, in 2010 the number had passed 100 million. The report also notes that, according to UN data, approximately 1,700 films were produced worldwide in 1995, but by 2009 the number was more than 7,000.[166] As we have seen, the 2009 Dutch report had noted that, during this same decade, the video game industry experienced exponential growth, and began competing vigorously with legacy entertainment industry players for a share of the disposable income of consumers, while unauthorized digital file-sharing may have served to encourage innovation and new business models in a music industry that had arguably been operating as a functional oligopoly, thus stifling innovation.[167]

Taking a page from history, the 2012 'Sky is Rising' report notes that this is not the first time that we have heard that the sky is falling on the US entertainment industry:

> [F]or pretty much the entire history of the entertainment industry, there have been complaints about how almost any new technological innovation is a form of 'piracy' that will represent the end of the wider industry. From John Philip Sousa insisting that 'These talking machines are going to ruin the artistic development of music,' to the music industry fearing that radio had similarly destroyed the industry by decreasing the 'life' of a song 'from 18 months to 90 days,' leading radio to

---

falling, see Robert Levine, *Free Ride: How Digital Parasites are Destroying the Culture Business, and How the Culture Business Can Fight Back* (Doubleday 2011).

162 See Michael Masnick and Michael Ho, 'The Sky is Rising: A Detailed Look at the State of the Entertainment Industry', January 2012, available at: http://www.techdirt.com/skyisrising. Masnick is CEO and founder of the weblog Techdirt, which focuses on technology news and tech-related issues: see 'Mike Masnick', Wikipedia, available at: http://en.wikipedia.org/wiki/Mike_Masnick; 'Techdirt', Wikipedia, available at: http://en.wikipedia.org/wiki/Techdirt. The authors are grateful to James Boyle for calling our attention to this report.

163 Masnick and Ho, ibid.

164 Ibid., 3.

165 See 'Gracenote Global Media Database', Gracenote, available at: http://www.gracenote.com/products/global_media_database (last visited 18 March 2012).

166 Masnick and Ho, above note 162, 3.

167 See above notes 138–139 and145–146 and accompanying text.

> 'virtually plug up' the old system, to Jack Valenti's infamous prediction that the VCR would be to the film industry 'what the Boston Strangler was to a woman at home,' the industry has predicted its own demise each and every time a new technology has come along.

The report notes that in each instance these dire predictions proved to be wrong. Far from killing the entertainment industry, each of the innovations in question massively expanded the industry, providing vast new opportunities to create, distribute, promote and monetize creative works.[169]

To be sure, at each of these technological turning points, copyright law in the US and elsewhere eventually established a compromise of sorts between existing content providers and promoters of the new technology in question. In each instance, however, the compromise was structured in such a way as to provide content providers with some form of remuneration, while ensuring that the new technology developed free of content-provider control.[170] That lesson from copyright history proves to be a cautionary one, as we consider the denouement to the two tales of ACTA that we have been examining.

4. THE DENOUEMENT OF THESE TWO TALES

As we have seen, the ACTA negotiations appear to have been driven by three discrete objectives: (i) combating trade in counterfeit and pirated goods; (ii) establishing more robust minimum enforcement standards and practices for intellectual property rights generally; and (iii) combating digital file-sharing.[171] As suggested by Tale # 1 above (IP Piracy, Organized Crime, and Terrorism), the first of these objectives is wholly commendable, given the devastating impact that counterfeit and pirated goods can have in developing

---

168 Masnick and Ho, above note 161, 3.

169 Ibid.

170 The 1909 US Copyright Act, for example, structured a compromise between the then existing music publishing companies, whose revenues from printed sheet music were threatened by the then-new technology (sound recordings), by giving copyright owners of musical compositions the right to make the first sound recording of that composition but providing that thereafter anyone could, upon payment of a statutory license fee, make a recording of the same composition without the authorization of the copyright holder. Sound recordings themselves (and the then-upstart sound recording industry that so upset the music industry in 1909) did not receive federal copyright protection in the US until 1972: see generally L. Ray Patterson and Stanley W. Lindberg, *The Nature of Copyright: A Law of Users' Rights* (University of Georgia Press 1991) 78–81. For recent attempts to control digital technology, as well as ACTA's embrace of that approach, See below notes 215, 218–221 and accompanying text.

171 See above text accompanying note 16.

countries. However, as illustrated by Tale # 2 above ('Seizure of Generic Drugs in Transit, Criminalized File Sharing, and Laptop Border Searches'), ACTA's simultaneous attempt to achieve the other two objectives has mired the agreement in controversy.

Because both the substance of the final draft of ACTA and the process by which it was negotiated have been vigorously critiqued by a host of commentators in a variety of different forums,[172] it is unnecessary to attempt a rehash of all of those critiques here. Rather, this chapter will conclude, as it began, by recounting two contrasting (yet cautionary) tales. Both of these tales illustrate the difficulty of trying to deal appropriately and effectively with three discrete international intellectual property issues in a single plurilateral agreement.

The first cautionary tale takes as its starting point the definition of the term 'counterfeit trademark goods' (as that term is defined in the final draft of ACTA) and focuses on the difficulty of combating international trade in counterfeit goods while, at the same time, fashioning robust IP enforcement measures and procedures that do not themselves become barriers to legitimate trade. At the same time, this first cautionary tale identifies a potentially positive outcome of the ACTA negotiations. The specific focus of this tale will be the controversial in-transit seizures of generic drugs that occurred in 2008 and 2009,[173] prompting India and Brazil to initiate WTO dispute settlement proceedings against the EU and the Netherlands in 2010.[174]

The second cautionary tale takes as its starting point the definition of 'pirated copyright goods' (as that term is defined in the final draft of ACTA), as well as ACTA's provisions governing enforcement of intellectual property rights in the digital environment. This tale focuses on the difficulty of addressing either of these problems in a plurilateral agreement, and offers a more somber assessment of the impact of the final draft of ACTA. The specific focus of this tale will be on digital file-sharing.

4.1 Cautionary Tale #1: Counterfeit Goods, the Problem of Seizures of Generic Drugs in Transit, and a Possible Return to Multilateralism

As noted in this chapter's predecessor, one particularly troubling aspect of the US Trade Representative's 2009 disclosure summarizing the key elements under discussion in the ACTA negotiations was that nowhere in that summary were the terms 'counterfeit' and 'pirated' goods defined.[175] The reason this

---

172 See above note 14.

173 See above note 129.

174 Ibid.

175 See McManis, above note 11, 1247; see also above text accompanying note 97.

was troubling was because it was widely known at the time that industry representatives were being supplied (and presumably supplying) information to the negotiating parties that was not being disseminated to the public,[176] and intellectual property owners and others tend to use these terms quite loosely, often deploying them to refer to any goods that infringe the intellectual property rights of others.[177]

It is a particularly common practice among those associated with the pharmaceutical industry to describe all generic drugs as 'counterfeit', irrespective of whether the drugs in question are or are not of an acceptable quality or do or do not bear a confusingly similar trademark, as the implicit basis for that characterization is that the drug in question infringes a patent on the drug. For example, a 2011 Mark Monitor study, which examined online piracy and counterfeiting, concluded that 'counterfeit' drugs continue to be a pervasive problem, but the criteria Mark Monitor used to determine what constitutes a website dealing in 'counterfeit' goods offered only a rough proxy for distinguishing between generic drugs (that is, drugs that are the functional equivalent of drugs patented in the US but are not authorized for distribution there) and counterfeit (that is, fake) drugs. As we have seen, these criteria focused on

---

[176] see above note 4 and accompanying text.

[177] For loose use of the term 'piracy', see, e.g., Motion Picture Association of America, 'Content Protection FAQs', available at: http://www.mpaa.org/contentprotection/faq (last visited 9 March 2012) ('Piracy is theft and includes the unauthorized copying, distribution, performance or other use of copyrighted materials. With regard to film and television, the term primarily relates to downloading, uploading, linking to, or otherwise providing access to unauthorized copies of movies, television shows or other copyrighted content on the Internet and making and/or selling unauthorized copies of DVDs and Blue Ray discs'). See also below note 206 and accompanying text. One commentator notes a similar confusion regarding the use the term 'counterfeiting' in the pharmaceutical and medical device industry. This commentator explains:

> When commentators refer to pharmaceutical or medical device counterfeiting, they usually mean products palmed off as those of another. *It could be a simple substitution of labels on a cheaper generic product for a branded product. The practice could* also *include the unauthorized sale of generic drugs in a market in which a branded company has exclusive rights.* Most commonly, however, counterfeiting involves the substitution of a substandard or entirely fake product for a legitimate one. The counterfeiter's goal is, obviously, to collect the branded price for what is essentially a worthless good. *While some would include inadvertent source confusion as a form of counterfeiting, it is more useful to apply the label only to intentional acts of deception, with the former designated as simple, common infringement.*

Daniel R. Cahoy, 'Addressing the North-South Divide in Pharmaceutical Counterfeiting' (2008) 8 *Wake Forest Intellectual Property Law Journal* 407, 409 (citations omitted) (emphasis added).

whether the domain (i) offered 'generic' versions of prescription drugs that are not available in generic form in the US, (ii) targeted the US market by providing pricing in US currency, and (iii) did not require a prescription'.[178] Presumably the third criterion (the absence of a prescription requirement) serves as the report's proxy for whether a drug is a fake. While it may be true, as the World Health Organization reportedly warned in 2010, that more than half the drugs bought online are counterfeit, the prevalence of counterfeit goods, as we have seen, varies widely in different regions of the world[179] – and in the developed world, at least, online means exist to verify the safety of online pharmacy practices.[180] Even where no prescription is required for the purchase of online drugs, however, there is not necessarily a one-to-one correspondence between the absence of a prescription and the existence of fake drugs, if for no other reason that at least some of these drugs may be 'grey market goods', also known as parallel imports – that is, products made legally abroad (for example, because the products are not patented where they were manufactured) that are imported without the permission of the intellectual property rights-holder in the country of importation.[181]

Commendably, the final draft of ACTA avoids the problem of distinguishing between counterfeit and generic drugs by defining the term 'counterfeit trademark goods' in relation to the trademarks involved, rather than the goods these marks identify. Article 5 of ACTA specifies that, to be counterfeit, goods must bear without authorization

> a trademark which is identical to the trademark validly registered in respect of such goods, or which cannot be distinguished in its essential aspects from such a trade-

---

178 See above notes 79–81 and accompanying text.

179 See above notes 70–71 and accompanying text.

180 See, e.g., National Association of Boards of Pharmacy (NABP), 'VIPPS: Set Yourself Apart from Rogue Sites!', available at: http://www.nabp.net/programs/accreditation/vipps (last visited 11 March 2012). NABP is a coalition of state and federal regulatory associations, professional associations whose member boards of pharmacy are grouped into eight districts 'that include all 50 United States, the District of Columbia, Guam, Puerto Rico, the Virgin Islands, eight Canadian provinces and New Zealand': NABP, 'About', available at: http://www.nabp.net/about/ (last visited 11 March 2012). To be accredited under the VIPPS program, a site must comply with the licensing and inspection requirements of their state and each state to which they dispense pharmaceuticals. 'VIPPS', ibid. In addition, pharmacies displaying the VIPPS seal have demonstrated to NABP compliance with VIPPS criteria including patient rights to privacy, authentication and security of prescription orders, adherence to a recognized quality assurance policy, and provision of meaningful consultation between patients and pharmacists: ibid.

181 See 'Parallel Imports', OECD Glossary of Statistical Terms, available at: http://stats.oecd.org/glossary/detail.asp?ID=5023 (last visited on 10 March 2012).

> mark, and which thereby infringes the rights of the owner of the trademark in question under the law of the country in which the procedures set forth in Chapter II (Legal Framework for Enforcement of Intellectual Property Rights) are invoked.[182]

To be counterfeit, drugs (or any other counterfeit trademarked goods) must be identified by a trademark that is either identical to or essentially indistinguishable from the registered trademark of another.[183] This is a much stricter test than that governing ordinary trademark infringement, which merely requires a likelihood of confusion.[184]

Given the narrowness of ACTA's definition of 'counterfeit trademark goods', it is not particularly troublesome (at least not on its face) that the definition differs in one important respect from the definition of that term in the TRIPS Agreement. Whereas the TRIPS definition, contained in a footnote to Article 51 (Suspension of Release by Customs Authorities), specifies that the identical or essentially indistinguishable trademark must infringe the rights of the owner of the trademark in question under the law of the country of importation,[185] ACTA's definition explicitly extends the definition so as to permit seizures of counterfeit goods in transit from one country to another via a third country.[186] If the goods in question are indeed counterfeit, however, that extension of the definition is not objectionable, as it merely enhances the ability of customs officials to combat the movement of counterfeit goods in international trade.

The problem, of course, is that, although the definitions of 'counterfeit trademark goods' in both ACTA and TRIPS are narrowly tailored, the actual border measures authorized by TRIPS may be applied to infringements of any

---

182 See ACTA, above note 1, Art. 5.

183 'Counterfeiting is the act of producing or selling a product with a sham trademark that is an intentional and calculated reproduction of the genuine trademark. A "counterfeit mark" is a false mark that is identical with, or substantially indistinguishable from, the genuine mark': J. Thomas McCarthy, 4 *McCarthy on Trademarks and Unfair Competition* § 25.10 (Clark Boardman Callaghan 4th edn 2012). As McCarthy makes clear, this standard 'requires a closer degree of similarity than is required for traditional trademark infringement or unfair competition'. Presumably, these limitations apply also to ACTA's use of a surrogate term, 'trademark counterfeiting'. See below note 208 and accompanying text.

184 '"Likelihood of confusion" is the basic test of both common law trademark infringement and federal statutory trade mark infringement. Infringement of federally registered marks is governed by the test of whether the defendant's use is "likely to cause confusion, or to cause mistake, or to deceive"': 4 *McCarthy*, ibid., § 23.1; see also TRIPS Agreement, above note 3, Art. 16(1) (specifying that the standard for trademark infringement is met where a use 'would result in a likelihood of confusion').

185 See TRIPS Agreement, ibid., Art. 51 n.14.

186 See above text accompanying note 182.

intellectual property rights (as that term is defined in Article 1(2) of TRIPS),[187] while the border measures authorized by ACTA are only slightly more restricted in scope, as that scope is qualified by a footnote to Article 13 stating that '[t]he Parties agree that patents and protection of undisclosed information do not fall within the scope' of Section 3: Border Measures.[188] As one commentator suggests, this restriction in the scope of border measures authorized by the final draft of ACTA is clearly an improvement over earlier drafts, which would have obliged the Parties to impose border measures against any goods in transit suspected of infringing any intellectual property rights, as that term is defined in Article 1(1) of TRIPS.[189] However, this commentator and others continue to be concerned about the possibility that border measures might be aimed at impeding the free trade of medicines, as the authority of customs officials to seize goods is not limited to counterfeit trademark goods but any goods that infringe the trademarks of another, and 'customs authorities are not well-placed to act against "confusingly similar trademark goods" in general'.[190] An illustration of the problem of in-transit seizures (albeit based on alleged infringements of patents, rather than trademarks) occurred in a series of seizures of drugs in transit in the Netherlands in 2008 and 2009, the most notorious of which involved a shipment of a drug manufactured in India and on its way to Nigeria for use as a second-line treatment of HIV/AIDS as a part of a program funded by UNITAID, an international drug purchase facility established in 2006 to facilitate developing-world access to drugs and diagnostics.[191]

---

[187] See TRIPS Agreement, above note 3, Art. 1(2) (defining 'intellectual property' as all categories of intellectual property that are the subject of Sections 1 through 7 of Part II of TRIPS – i.e., copyrights and related rights, trademarks, geographical indications, industrial designs, patents, layout-designs of integrated circuits, and protection of undisclosed information): ibid., Art. 51 (making border measures concerning counterfeit trademark goods and pirated copyright goods mandatory, but authorizing border measures concerning infringements of other 'intellectual property rights').

[188] See ACTA, above note 1, Art. 13 n.6.

[189] Grosse Ruse-Khan, above note 129, 665.

[190] Ibid., 675.

[191] Ibid., 649. As Grosse Ruse-Kahn notes, UNITAID issued a sharp protest, insisting (1) that the shipment contained no counterfeit drugs or any other drugs infringing IP rights; and (2) that the medication was pre-qualified by the World Health Organization and had received tentative approval by the US Food and Drug Administration: ibid., 649–50 (citing 'UNITAID Statement on Dutch Confiscation of Medicines Shipment', UNITAID, available at: http://www.unitaid.eu/en/resources/news/156-unitaid-statement-on-dutch-confiscation-of%20medicines-shipment.html (last visited 1 March 2011)). For other commentators voicing similar concerns, see generally Brook K. Baker, 'ACTA – Risks of Third-Party Enforcement for Access to

As we have seen, these seizures prompted India and Brazil to initiate WTO dispute settlement proceedings against the EU and the Netherlands in 2010.[192] Neither Brazil nor India has requested the establishment of a dispute panel but, as we go to press, neither have they formally notified the WTO that the Parties have reached a mutually agreed solution – though India's Ministry of Industry and Commerce issued a press release on 28 July 2011, announcing an informal resolution of sorts.[193] The announcement makes it clear, however, that India intends to wield the informal agreement and the option to revive the WTO proceedings as a kind of 'sword of Damocles'[194] to pressure the EU into making changes in its customs policy.[195] The mere filing of these two WTO dispute settlement proceedings represents a watershed moment, as it is only the second time in WTO dispute settlement history that a developing country has resorted to the WTO dispute settlement process in an effort to pressure a developed country to revise its intellectual property policy.[196] More fundamentally, it is the first

---

Medicines' (2011) 26 *American University International Law Review* 579; Andrew Rens, 'Collateral Damage: The Impact of ACTA and the Enforcement Agenda on the World's Poorest People' (2011) 26 *American University International Law Review* 783.

[192] See DS 408 (India), above note 129; DS 409 (Brazil), above note 129.

[193] See Government of India, Ministry of Commerce & Industry, Dept of Commerce, Press Release, 'India EU Reach an Understanding on Issue of Seizure of Indian Generic Drugs in Transit', 28 July 2011, available at: http://commerce.nic.in/pressrelease/pressrelease_detail.asp?id=2807 [hereinafter 'India EU Reach an Understanding']. The press release indicated that the parties have reached an Understanding to be adopted by the EU to replace EU Regulation 1383/2003, which permitted customs agents in the EU to detain or suspend the release of goods for a period of three working days if they suspect infringement of an intellectual property right to allow an IP right-holder to submit an application for customs action: ibid.

[194] The phrase 'Sword of Damocles' refers to an anecdote from late classical Greek culture in which a courtier, Damocles, accepted the invitation of his king, Dionysius II of Syracuse, to exchange places, only to discover upon sitting down in the king's throne (which was surrounded by every kind of luxury) that the king had arranged for a huge sword to hang above the throne, held at the pommel by a single hair of a horse's tail: see'Damocles', Wikipedia, available at: http://en.wikipedia.org/wiki/Damocles#The_sword_of_Damocles (last visited 16 March 2012).

[195] The statement announced: '[S]o long as the EU and its Member States adhere to the principles contained in the Understanding with respect to generic drugs in transit through the EU, India has assured the EU that India will not request the establishment of a dispute settlement panel at the WTO. With the exchange of these letters, India and the EU have reached, for the present, an informal settlement of this dispute. India would watch with interest EU's further steps in implementing its commitments. India's options to revive the dispute remain intact in case the EU does not abide by the core principles agreed to in the Understanding': 'India EU Reach an Understanding', above note 193.

[196] Prior to the disputes filed by India and Brazil regarding the aforementioned in-transit seizures, Brazil filed two other requests for consultations pursuant to the WTO dispute resolution mechanism against the United States: see Request for

time in WTO dispute settlement history that 'TRIPS is being used as a benchmark for constraining additional ('TRIPS-plus') IP protection'.[197] One suspects that it will not be the last.

This prospect does not bode particularly well for the future of ACTA, as it suggests that ACTA could become a 'country club' that no one wishes to join.[198] Even so, adoption of the final draft of ACTA could have a positive effect on international negotiations over the enforcement of intellectual property rights, if only because it might help to break an almost decade-long stalemate that has marked the multilateral IP processes of the WTO and WIPO, where developing countries have consistently objected to efforts on the part of developed countries to discuss heightened IP enforcement standards in those multilateral forums, claiming that this issue would distract these international organizations from the development agendas that both have adopted.[199] As a

---

Consultations by Brazil, *United States – US Patent Code*, WT/DS224/1 (31 January 2001) (request by Brazil for consultations with the US concerning allegedly discriminatory provisions in the US Patent Code, particularly those governing patent rights in inventions made with federal assistance, 35 USC §§ 200–212); Request for Consultations by Brazil, *United States – Subsidies on Upland Cotton*, WT/DS267/1 (27 September 2002) (a dispute tentatively settled in a Framework agreement in which the US agreed to review a domestic support program for upland cotton after the WTO Dispute Settlement Body authorized Brazil to impose various countermeasures, including ignoring US IP rights). For a summary of these disputes, see World Trade Organization, 'United States – US Patents Code', available at: http://www.wto.org/english/tratop_e/dispu_e/cases_e/ds224_e.htm (last visited 14 March 2012) (summarizing dispute DS224); World Trade Organization, *United States – Subsidies of Upland Cotton*, available at: http://www.wto.org/english/tratop_e/dispu_e/ cases_e/ds267_e.htm (last visited 14 March 2012) (summarizing dispute DS267); Randy Schnepf, Congressional Research Service, RL 32571, 'Brazil's Case against the US Cotton Program', 30 June 2010, available at:http://www.nationalaglawcenter.org/assets/crs/RL32571.pdf (examining dispute DS267).

[197] See Grosse Ruse-Kahn, above note 129, 655.

[198] See Yu, above note 14, 1074–1094 (discussing ACTA's 'country club' approach and comparing the potential risks of that approach (e.g., forum proliferation and a concomitant erosion in the legitimacy and relevance of both multilateral and plurilateral efforts to protect private intellectual property rights) with one potential offsetting benefit – namely stimulating 'intellectual property coalitions for development' among less-developed countries, enabling those countries 'to shape the negotiating agenda, articulate more coherent positions, or establish a united negotiating front').

[199] See Yu, ibid., 988–98, 1080. For the WIPO's development agenda, see World Trade Organization, 'Intellectual Property for Development', available at: http://www.wipo.int/ip-development/en/ (last visited 18 March 2012). For the WTO's development agenda, including its 2001 Doha Ministerial Declaration, stressing 'the importance we attach to implementation and interpretation of the Agreement on Trade-Related Aspects of Intellectual Property Rights (TRIPS Agreement) in a manner supportive of public health, by promoting both access to existing medicines and research and development into new medicines': see World Trade Organization, 'The

result of the ACTA negotiations, there seems to be a renewed interest among developing countries in discussing IP enforcement at meetings of the TRIPS Council, if only to denounce the ACTA negotiations.[200] As one commentator trenchantly notes, China and India made important interventions at a June 2010 meeting of the TRIPS Council, 'expressing their concerns about the release of the draft ACTA text and the highly disturbing trend concerning TRIPS-plus enforcement standards'.[201] In India's view, although the TRIPS Agreement 'is usually considered to be a minimum levels agreement, enforcement levels cannot be raised to the extent that they contravene TRIPS'.[202]

While the immediate practical significance of India's position should not be overstated,[203] it does highlight a significant long-term shortcoming in ACTA's plurilateral approach to establishing stronger intellectual property enforcement

---

Doha Round', available at: http://www.wto.org/english/tratop_e/dda_e/dda_e.htm (last visited 18 March 2012). For the WTO's December 2005 decision to make permanent an earlier temporary decision to make it easier for poorer countries to obtain cheaper generic versions of patented medicines by setting aside a provision of the TRIPS Agreement that could hinder exports of pharmaceuticals manufactured under compulsory licences to countries that are unable to produce them, see World Trade Organization, Press Release, 'Members OK Amendment to Make Health Flexibility Permanent', 6 December 2005, available at: http://www.wto.org/english/news_e/pres05_e/pr426_e.htm.

[200] See Council for Trade-Related Aspects of Intellectual Property Rights, Minutes of Meeting, IP/C/M/63, 6 October 2010 [hereinafter TRIPS Council Minutes].

[201] Ibid., 996 (citing Catherine Saez, 'Health Waiver, IP Enforcement Discussed at Lively WTO TRIPS Council Meeting', Intellectual Property Watch, 10 June 2010 at 5:48 PM, available at: http://www.ip-watch.org/weblog/2010/06/10/health-waiver-ip-enforcement-discussed-at-lively-wto-trips-council-meeting/). See also Thiru's blog, 'India's Intervention to the WTO TRIPS Council: TRIPS Plus Enforcement Trends', Knowledge Ecology International,10 June 2010 at 8:18 AM, available at: http://keionline.org/node/864 [hereinafter India's Intervention]; Thiru, 'ACTA: Intervention of China to the WTO TRIPS Council', Knowledge Ecology International, 31 October 2010 at 6:30 AM, available at: http://keionline.org/node/1001. My thanks to Professor Yu for pointing out the importance of these interventions to me, as well as for his observation during a presentation at the Spring 2012 IP Colloquium at Washington University School of Law that ACTA may cause developing countries to re-examine their refusal to discuss IP enforcement issues in ongoing deliberations of the TRIPS Council.

[202] Yu, above note 14, 997 n.148 (quoting 'Why "IPR Enforcement" in ACTA and FTAs Harm the South', *S. Bull.*, 28 July 2010, 10) (citing TRIPS Council Minutes, above note 201, 265, 272; Grosse Ruse-Khan, above note 128, 644, 653–7); India intervention, above note 202. For a critique of this position, particularly in relation to ACTA, see Grosse Ruse-Kahn, above note 129, 654–60, 689–725 (concluding that TRIPS can constrain the ability of WTO members to enter into TRIPS-plus agreements but that, in the case of ACTA, most of its TRIPS-plus border measures do not amount to contravention of TRIPS provisions).

[203] See above note 202.

standards. If adoption of the final draft of ACTA does nothing more than help re-activate multilateral negotiations that will focus on balancing the need for effective enforcement of intellectual property rights with the equally important need to ensure developing-country access to essential medicines and other technologies that will promote the WIPO and WTO development agendas in those countries, then the ACTA negotiations could be considered a qualified success.

4.2 Cautionary Tale #2: Pirated Works, the Problem of Combating Digital File-Sharing, and the Spectre of a Superfluous and Ineffective International Agreement

As noted in this chapter's predecessor, a second troubling aspect of the US Trade Representative's 2009 disclosure summarizing the key elements under discussion in the ACTA negotiations was the ambiguous statement that ACTA's 'intended focus is on counterfeiting and piracy activities that significantly affect commercial interests, rather than on the activities of ordinary citizens'.[204] As we have seen, to the suspicious eye this carefully crafted wording seemed to amount to a tacit admission that ACTA would not be limited to combating commercial trade in counterfeit and pirated goods, but would extend to at least some types of digital file-sharing – a suspicion that was reinforced by the more candid statement in a leaked discussion paper that ACTA would extend to 'significant willful infringements without motivation for financial gain to such an extent as to prejudicially affect the copyright owner (e.g., internet piracy)'.

The latter statement offers yet another example of the tendency to make loose use of the term 'piracy',[205] as the leaked discussion document seems to be saying that internet piracy consists of any 'significant' willful infringement of another's copyright, whether the infringement is for the purpose of commercial gain, or embodied in tangible goods, or not. The definition of the term 'pirated copyright goods' in the final draft of ACTA appears on its face to be both narrower and broader than this – narrower because it is limited to 'goods' and broader because it is not limited to 'willful' infringements of copyrights or related rights.[206] As a practical matter, however, ACTA does

204 See McManis, above note 11, 1248; see also above note 103 and accompanying text.

205 For other examples, see above note 177 and accompanying text.

206 Specifically, 'pirated copyright goods' are defined as 'any goods which are copies made without the consent of the right holder or person duly authorized by the right holder in the country of production and which are made directly or indirectly from an article where the making of that copy would have constituted an infringement of a

essentially limit its focus to copyright piracy that is both willful and carried out on a commercial scale for, unlike the term 'trademark counterfeit goods' and its surrogate, 'trademark counterfeiting', which appear in a number of ACTA's civil enforcement provisions,[207] the term 'pirated copyright goods' appears – with but one limited exception[208] – only in the criminal enforcement provisions of ACTA. In addition, the only mandatory criminal enforcement standard imposed on ACTA members is to penalise 'willful trademark counterfeiting or copyright or related rights piracy on a commercial scale'.[209]

The more significant problem in the final draft of ACTA concerns its provisions governing the enforcement of copyrights or related rights in the digital environment. As one commentator puts it, ACTA 'requires participating countries to offer protection against both the circumvention of technological protection measures used to protect copyrighted works and the removal of copyright management information – at times beyond what is required by the WIPO Internet Treaties [that is, the WIPO Copyright Treaty (WET) and the WIPO Performances and Phonograms Treaty (WPPT), both of which were adopted on 20 December 1996]'.[210] To anyone familiar with the processes by

---

copyright or related right under the law of the country in which the procedures set forth in Chapter II (Legal Framework for Enforcement of Intellectual Property Rights) are invoked': see ACTA, above note 1, Art. 5(k). In other words, goods are 'pirated' if they are (1) 'copies' that are (a) made without the consent of the right holder or person authorized by the right holder in the country of production; and (b) made directly or indirectly from an 'article'; where (2) the making of those 'copies' would have constituted an infringement of copyright or a related right in the country where the right is being enforced. The phrase 'copyrights and related rights' is designed to acknowledge a difference in the scope of copyright protection in the US and Europe. In Europe a distinction is drawn between 'authors rights' and 'related rights' (also known as 'neighboring rights') – i.e., the rights of performers, phonogram producers and broadcasters, among others. See above note 98.

[207] See, e.g., ACTA, above note 1, Art 9(2)–(3) (governing civil damages): ibid., Art. 10 (governing other civil remedies); ibid., Art. 12(3) (governing provisional measures); ibid., Art. 20(2) (governing remedies related to ACTA's border measure provisions). It should also be noted, however, that in all of these provisions, the terms 'counterfeit goods' and 'trademark counterfeiting' are being used to limit mandatory civil enforcement measures to instances of trademark counterfeiting, as opposed to trademark (or copyright) infringement more generally.

[208] See ACTA, above note 1, Art. 10(1) (stating that at least with respect to pirated copyright goods and counterfeit trademark goods, 'each Party shall provide that, in civil judicial proceedings, at the right holder's request, its judicial authorities have the authority to order that such infringing goods be destroyed, except in exceptional circumstances, without compensation of any sort').

[209] Ibid., Art. 23 (governing criminal offences).

[210] Yu, above note 14, 1028 (footnotes omitted). For the specific ACTA provisions going beyond the requirements of the WET and WPPT, see below notes 220–222 and accompanying text. For the texts of the WET and WPPT, see WIPO Copyright

which the WET and WPPT were negotiated and subsequently implemented in the United States and Europe,[211] this summary sounds remarkably like a description of the implementing legislation of the US – grandiloquently entitled the Digital Millennium Copyright Act (DMCA) – and the 2001 EU Directive on the Harmonisation of Certain Aspects of Copyright and Related Rights in the Information Society [the EU Copyright Directive].[212]

Whereas the WET and WPPT merely require members to protect against circumvention of effective technology protection measures (TPMs) that protect rights under those treaties and the Berne Convention (that is, copyrights and neighboring rights), thus mandating legal protection for copy control TPMs, the DMCA creates a 'new and unprecedented right'[213] (commonly referred to as 'para-copyright' protection) to control access to copyrighted works. The DMCA also creates two equally controversial 'anti-

---

Treaty, Art. 11, 20 December 1996, S. Treaty Doc. 105-17, 2186 UNTS 121 [hereinafter WTC]; WIPO Performances and Phonograms Treaty, Art. 18, 20 December 1996, S. Treaty Doc. No. 105-17, 2186 UNTS 203 [hereinafter WPPT]. Notably, three of the nations negotiating ACTA – Canada, Korea, and Switzerland – are not contracting members of either of these treaties. For the corresponding US and EU domestic laws implementing the WTC and WPPT, see Digital Millennium Copyright Act of 1998, Pub. L. No. 105-304, 112 Stat. 2860 (codified in various sections of the US Copyright Act, 17 USC §§ 101 et. seq. (2006)); Directive 2001/29/EC of the European Parliament and Counsel of 22 May 2001 on the Harmonisation of Certain Aspects of Copyright and Related Rights in the Information Society, Art 6, [2001] OJ L 167/10, 17 [hereinafter EU Copyright Directive].

211 For readable accounts of this history from a US perspective, see Pamela Samuelson, 'The US Digital Agenda at WIPO' (1997) 37 *Virginia Journal of International Law* 369, 370; Peter K. Yu, 'Digital Piracy and the Copyright Response', in Indrajit Banerjee (ed.), *Internet and Governance in Asia – A Critical Reader* (Asian Media Information and Communication Centre 2007) 340, available at: http://www.peteryu.com/piracy.pdf; Levine, above note 161, 27–34.

212 See above note 210.

213 Dan L. Burk, 'Legal and Technical Standards in Digital Rights Management Technology' (2005) 74 *Fordham Law Review* 537, 558. In a sense, a right to control access to a copyrighted work is implicit in US copyright law, for while federal copyright law has historically focused primarily on protecting those works the copyright owner has chosen to make available to the public, the common law of copyrights, trade secrets, and ideas historically protected a copyright owner's right to choose *not* to disclose a work to the public, and thus provided a potentially unlimited term of protection for unpublished works. However, the US Copyright Act § 301 pre-empts the common law of copyright with respect to all works fixed in a tangible medium of expression and imposed a limited term of copyright protection for unpublished works: see17 USC § 301 (2006). Moreover, Congress has since made it clear that unpublished works are subject to the Act's fair use privilege: see17 USC § 107 (as amended in 1992, adding at the end of § 107's four-factor test the following sentence: 'The fact that a work is unpublished shall not itself bar a finding of fair use if such finding is made upon consideration of all the above factors').

trafficking' provisions, one of which explicitly prohibits trafficking in devices that circumvent access-control technology, while the other prohibits trafficking in devices that circumvent copy-control technology.[214] Since the enactment of the DMCA, every free trade agreement negotiated by the US has included an explicit obligation on the part of US trading partners to provide both forms of anti-circumvention and anti-trafficking protection as well as copyright management information protection.[215]

Likewise, the 2001 EU Copyright Directive,[216] which mandates the harmonized implementation of the WET and WPPT in the 25 member countries of the EU, goes well beyond the requirements of those two treaties, imposing an obligation on its member states to provide legal protection that is basically similar to that provided by the DMCA, albeit with a number of minor differences. Article 6(1), read in conjunction with Article 6(3), seemingly requires anti-circumvention protection to extend to access control as well as to copy control technology protecting either works or other subject matter (databases, for example), while qualifying this obligation with a scienter requirement.[217] Article 6(2), in turn, prohibits possession for commercial purposes, as well as trafficking, in both types of circumvention technology.[218]

---

214 17 USC § 1201(a)(2) (2006) (governing access control); 17 USC § 1201(b) (2006) (governing copy control).

215 See Peter K. Yu, 'Anticircumvention and Anti-Anticircumvention' (2006) 84 *Denver Law Review* 13, 40–4; Anupam Chander, 'Exporting DMCA Lockouts' (2006) 54 *Cleveland State Law Review* 205, 206, 212–16 ; 'U.S. Free Trade Agreements', Export.gov, available at: http://www.export.gov/fta/index.asp. See also Office of the US Trade Representative,'Free Trade Agreements', available at: http://www.ustr.gov/trade-agreements/free-trade-agreements (last visited 17 March 2012) (listing 18 countries that have signed FTAs with the US).

216 See EU Copyright Directive, above note 210.

217 Ibid., Art. 6(1) and (3). Art. 6(1) of the Directive states that 'Member States shall provide adequate legal protection against the circumvention of any effective technological measures'. Art. 6(3) goes on to define 'technological measures' as 'any technology, device or component that, in the normal course of its operation, is designed to prevent or restrict acts, in respect of works *or other subject matter*, which are not authorized by the rightholder of any copyright or any right related to copyright as provided for by law or the sui generis right provided for in [the Database Directive]', and states that technological measures shall be deemed 'effective' where the use of a protected work or other subject-matter is controlled 'through application of an *access* control or protection process, such as encryption, scrambling or other transformation of the work or other subject-matter or a *copy* control mechanism, which achieves the protection objective' (emphasis added). Art. 6(1) limits the obligation of Member States to provide adequate legal protection against circumvention 'which the person concerned carries out in the knowledge, or with reasonable grounds to know, that he or she is pursuing that objective'.

218 Art. 6(2) EU Copyright Directive requires members to provide 'legal protec-

The two ACTA provisions that impose similar requirements are Articles 27(5) and 27(6). The former requires parties to provide adequate legal protection and effective legal remedies against the circumvention of 'effective technological measures' that are used by authors, performers or producers of phonograms in connection with the exercise of their rights in, and that restrict acts in respect of, their works, performances, and phonograms, which are not authorized by the authors, the performers or the producers of phonograms concerned or permitted by law'.[219] A footnote to Article 27(5) specifies that 'technological measures shall be deemed effective where the use of the protected works, performances, or phonograms is controlled by authors, performers or producers of phonograms through the application of a relevant *access control* or protection process, such as encryption or scrambling, or a copy control mechanism, which achieves the objective of protection'.[220] Article 27(6), in turn, requires parties to provide protection not only against the unauthorized circumvention of an effective technological measure carried out knowingly or with reasonable grounds to know, but also against (i) 'offering to the public by marketing of a device or product, including computer programs, or a service, as a means of circumventing an effective technological measure'; and (ii) manufacturing, importing, or distributing a device or product, including computer programs, or provision of a service that is 'primarily designed or produced for the purpose of circumventing an effective technological measure' or 'has only limited commercially significant purpose other than circumventing an effective technological measure'.[221]

The final draft of ACTA backs away from explicitly requiring that parties implement some of the DMCA's more distinctive features,[222] such as the DMCA's complicated safe-harbor provisions for online service providers

---

tion against the manufacture, import, distribution, sale, rental, or advertising [for same], *or possession for commercial purposes* devices, products or components or the provision of services which (a) are promoted, advertised or marketed for the purpose of circumvention, or (b) have only a limited commercially significant use other than to circumvent, or (c) are primarily designed, produced, adapted or performed for the purpose of enabling or facilitating the circumvention of any effective technological measures' (emphasis added). Except for the italicized phrase, the wording of this provision is quite similar to that of 17 USC § 1201(a)(2) (2006) (prohibiting trafficking in devices circumventing *access* controls) and 17 USC § 1201(b) (2006) (prohibiting trafficking in devices circumventing *copy* controls).

[219] See ACTA, above note 1, Art. 27(5).

[220] Ibid., Art. 27(5) n.14 (emphasis added).

[221] Ibid., Art. 27(6)(a)–(b).

[222] See, e.g., Yu, above note 14, 1029 (noting that the absence of these provisions was as a result of the negotiators' inability to agree on 'the adoption of DCMA-style notice and takedown procedure or provide active deterrents against repeat infringement').

(OSPs),[223] the notice-and-takedown procedures that qualify these safe harbors,[224] and the accompanying requirement that OSPs terminate subscribers and account holders who are repeated infringers.[225] Nevertheless, it is clear that either these features of the DMCA or the 'graduated response' approach adopted by other ACTA negotiating parties,[226] or perhaps some privately ordered graduated response regime,[227] serves as a template for what

---

[223] Section 512 of the DCMA provides safe harbors, generally, for businesses who are 'providers of online services or network access': 17 USC § 512(k). Safe harbors include limited liability where infringement takes place via transitory digital network communications (i.e., providing internet service); system cashing; information residing on systems or networks at the direction of users; and use of information location tools (i.e., search engines): 17 USC § 512(a)–(d). Such liability includes the essential elimination of monetary damages and limits injunctive relief in claims for infringement filed against online service providers provided that service provider (1) adopts, reasonably implements, and informs subscribers of the providers system or network of, a policy that provides for termination of repeat infringers, and (2) accommodates and does not interfere with certain measures used to identify and protect copyrighted works: 17 USC § 512(i) (2006).

[224] With respect to infringing information residing on systems or networks at the direction of users (i.e., user generated content), OSPs must comply with a number of requirements which, inter alia, include implementation of a notice and takedown procedure compliant with 17 USC § 512(c)(3). See generally 17 USC § 512(c) (2006).

[225] 17 USC §512(i) (2006) ('The limitations on liability … shall apply to a service provider *only if* the service provider … provides for the termination in appropriate circumstances of subscribers and account holders of the service provider's system *who are repeat infringers*') (emphasis added).

[226] Graduated response is an 'online copyright enforcement regime that requires Internet service providers (ISPs) to terminate Internet access for accused repeat copyright infringers': see Annemarie Bridy, 'ACTA and the Specter of Graduated Response' (2011) 26 *American University International Law Review* 559. To date, a number of nations, including the UK, France, New Zealand, and South Korea (all of whom were involved in the ACTA negotiations) have implemented graduated response legislation. Eldar Haber, 'The French Revolution 2.0: Copyright and the Three Strikes Policy' (2011) 2 *Harvard Journal of Sports & Entertainment Law* 297, 299; see also Bridy, ibid., 560–61 (discussing various countries implementing graduated response legislation); Jeremy de Beer and Christopher E. Clemmer, 'Global Trends in Online Copyright Enforcement: A Non-Neutral Rome for Network Intermediaries?' (2009) 49 *Jurimetrics Journal* 375, 393–6 (discussing the enactment of graduated response legislation in France, New Zealand and South Korea).

[227] See Bridy, ibid., 572–77; see also Margot E. Kaminski, 'An Overview and the Evolution of the Anti-Counterfeiting Trade Agreement (ACTA)' (2011) PIJIP Research Paper No. 17. Bridy notes that ISPs in the US and abroad have engaged in privately arranged and implemented graduated response schemes for some time; however, because of the private nature of such agreements difficulty arose in ascertaining the prevalence of this practice: Bridy, ibid., 572–6. Additionally, Eircom – a major service provider in Ireland – implemented a private graduated response system as a result of the settlement of a law suit brought by EMI, Sony, BMG, Universal and Warner: ibid., 567.

the final draft of ACTA Article 27(1) has in mind in requiring that enforcement procedures 'permit effective action against an act of infringement of intellectual property rights which takes place in the digital environment, including expeditious remedies to prevent infringement and remedies which constitute a deterrent to further infringements'.[228] Privately ordered graduated response regimes also seems to be what ACTA Article 27(3) has in mind when it specifies that parties 'shall endeavor to promote cooperative efforts within the business community' to address copyright and trademark infringement in the digital environment.[229]

The DMCA has particular relevance for understanding the foregoing provisions of ACTA, given the US Trade Representative's stance on US implementation of these provisions. In January of 2010, in an effort to produce greater US transparency regarding the ACTA negotiations, Senator Ron Wyden wrote a three-page letter to the USTR, Ambassador Ron Kirk, requesting more information about the proposed treaty.[230] A number of the questions posed by Senator Wyden centered on how ACTA might affect current US intellectual property law and what types of commitment the US was seeking from the other parties to ACTA.[231] In his response, Ambassador Kirk made it clear that ACTA is not intended to change US law.[232] This stance is congruent with the USTR's insistence that ACTA should be classified as an executive agreement,

---

228 ACTA, above note 1, Art 27(1). During the early stages of the ACTA negotiations, critics worried that ACTA would include specific provisions mandating implementation of the kind of graduated response legislation described above in note 226: see, e.g., Gwen Hinze, 'Leaked ACTA Internet Provisions: Three Strikes and a Global DMCA', Electronic Frontier Foundation, 3 November 2009, available at: https://www.eff.org/deeplinks/2009/11/leaked-acta-internet-provisions-three-strikes-and-; Bridy, above note 226, 562 (noting that ACTA's internet provisions were among the most contested and heavily negotiated, and that references to repeat infringers and account termination were ultimately edited out, as were a DMCA-like safe harbor provision and other provisions requiring secondary liability for online service providers).

229 ACTA, above note 1, Art. 27(3). The full text of Art. 27(3) reads: 'Each Party shall endeavour to promote cooperative efforts within the business community to effectively address trademark and copyright or related rights infringement while preserving legitimate competition and, consistent with that Party's law, preserving fundamental principles such as freedom of expression, fair process, and privacy.'

230 Letter from Senator Ron Wyden, US Senate, to Ambassador Ron Kirk, US Trade Representative, 6 January 2010, available at: http://www.ustr.gov/acta [hereinafter 'Wyden letter'].

231 Ibid.

232 Letter from Ambassador Ron Kirk, US Trade Representative, to Senator Ron Wyden, US Senate, 28 January 2010, available at: http://www.ustr.gov/acta. Ambassador Kirk explained generally that he did 'not view ACTA as a vehicle for changing U.S. Law'.

not a treaty, as the latter would require congressional approval prior to US 'ratification, acceptance or approval' of ACTA.[233] The USTR's position thus seems to confirm that, from a US perspective at least, ACTA is indeed a 'forum-shifting' device designed primarily to ratchet up international intellectual property enforcement standards abroad to a level comparable with that achieved in the DMCA.[234]

However one evaluates the USTR's position that no implementing legislation is needed for the US to comply with its obligations under ACTA,[235] it is clear that the USTR envisions the DMCA as a template for implementing ACTA's digital enforcement obligations. Even though the final draft of ACTA backs away from explicitly mandating DMCA-like enforcement provisions,[236] commentators have expressed continuing concern over the various costs that would be imposed on developing countries in attempting to implement ACTA's digital enforcement obligations, noting in particular the serious implications that implementation would have for the development of system interoperability and free and open source software, as well as the cost of tightening regulation of online service providers.[237] Not surprisingly, these criticisms track those that have already been leveled at the WIPO Internet Treaties and the DMCA itself.[238]

Indeed, with the benefit of over a decade of experience under the DMCA, it must be noted that the DMCA's original proponents and critics now seem to agree that neither the legal innovations produced by the WIPO Internet Treaties and the DMCA nor the digital locks that these legal innovations were intended to protect have been effective in containing widespread digital copying.[239] Thus, while critics of the DMCA have formulated 'damage minimiza-

---

233 See ACTA, above note 1, Art. 40 ('This Agreement shall enter into force thirty days after the deposit of the sixth instrument of ratification, acceptance, or approval'). For a summary discussion of the position of the USTR, see above note 3. For a critique of the USTR's position, see Quinn, above note 3; Katz and Heinz, above note 3; and Yu, above note 14, 1019–21.

234 See above note 5 and accompanying text.

235 For critiques of the USTR's position, see Quinn, above note 3; Katz and Heinz, above note 3; and Yu, above note 14, 1019–21.

236 See above note 222 and accompanying text.

237 See, e.g.,Yu, above note 14, 1028–9.

238 See, e.g., Gwen Hinze, 'Brave New World, Ten Years Later: Reviewing the Impact of Policy Choices in the Implementation of the WIPO Internet Treaties' Technological Protection Measure Provisions' (2007) 57 *Case Western Reserve Law Review* 779; Jennifer M. Urban and Laura Quilter, 'Efficient Process or 'Chilling Effects? Takedown Notices under Section 512 of the Digital Millennium Copyright Act' (2006) 22 *Santa Clara Computer & High Technology Law Journal* 521.

239 Compare Levine, above note 161, 15–16, 33–4 (summarizing the views of Bruce Lehman, who served as the US Under Secretary of Commerce for Intellectual

tion recommendations' for how to structure legal protection for technological protection measures to avoid some of the detrimental consequences allegedly experienced in the United States,[240] digital content providers began lobbying the US Congress in earnest in September 2010 to enact legislation that would more effectively target online 'commercial-scale piracy'.[241] Although the acronyms of the resulting bills are as varied as their specific provisions,[242] the 'watershed event'[243] in this entire lobbying effort proved to be the dramatic reversal in fortunes that occurred on 18 January 2012.

On that day, the prospect of the imminent enactment of two legislative bills backed by the entertainment industry – one a US House of Representatives bill

---

Property and Commissioner of the US Patent and Trademark Office (USPTO) from 1993 to 1998, championed what became the Digital Millennium Copyright Act, and is quoted as admitting in 2007 that '[u]nfortunately, at least in some areas, our policies haven't worked out too well'), with Hinze, above note 238, 781, 783 (noting that the neither the basic policy approach behind the WET and WPPT nor the digital locks they were intended to protect have proven to be effective at containing widespread digital copying and summarizing five 'damage minimization recommendations' for how to structure future technological protection measures 'to avoid some of the detrimental consequences experienced in the United States'). Gwen Hinze is the IP Policy Director of the Electronic Frontier Foundation, one of the major critics of the DMCA: see Gwen Hinze, Electronic Frontier Foundation, available at: https://www.eff.org/about/staff/gwen-hinze (last visited 15 March 2012).

240 See Hinze, above note 238,783, 820–1; see also above note 239.

241 See Levine, above note 161, 249.

242 In September 2010, Senator Patrick Leahy introduced a bill entitled Combating Online Infringements and Counterfeits Act (COICA) which would have authorized the US Attorney General to seize the domain names of sites that are 'dedicated to infringing activities': ibid. Combating Online Infringement and Counterfeits Act, S. 3804, 111th Cong. (2010). COICA, in turn, was eventually reintroduced in May 2011 as the Preventing Real Online Threats to Economic Creativity and Theft of Intellectual Property Act of 2011, or PROTECT IP Act of 2011 (PIPA): Preventing Real Online Threats to Economic Creativity and Theft of Intellectual Property Act of 2011, S. 968, 112th Cong. (2011); see also 'Combating Online Piracy and Counterfeits Act', Wikipedia, available at: http://en.wikipedia.org/wiki/Combating_Online_Infringement_and_Counterfeits_Act (last visited 18 March 2012). The Stop Online Piracy Act (SOPA) was introduced in the House of Representatives in October 2011 and reportedly builds on COICA: Stop Online Piracy Act, H.R. 3261, 112th Cong. (2011); see also 'Stop Online Piracy Act', Wikipedia, available at: http://en.wikipedia.org/wiki/Stop_Online_Piracy_Act (last visited 18 March 2012). [Note, for reasons largely explained below in text accompanying note 245, the neutrality of this article is disputed.] A third bill, the Online Protection and Enforcement of Digital Trade Act (OPEN Act), was introduced in the Senate in December 2011 as an alternative to SOPA: Online Protection and Enforcement of Digital Trade Act, H.R. 3782, 112th Cong. (2012); see also 'Open Protection and Enforcement of Digital Trade Act', Wikipedia, available at: http://en.wikipedia.org/wiki/Online_Protection_and_Enforcement_of_Digital_Trade_Act (last visited 18 March 2012).

243 See below note 249 and accompanying text.

entitled the Stop Online Piracy Act (SOPA) and the other a Senate bill entitled the Protect Intellectual Property Act (PIPA) – which just weeks earlier had overwhelming bipartisan support, provoked an unprecedented online political protest in which Wikipedia temporarily made its English language content unavailable, Google draped its search site trademark in black, and a loose alliance of technology companies, online service providers (OSPs), rival web companies, digital rights groups and social network sites reportedly rallied more than 7 million people to sign an online petition from Google to stop SOPA.[244] Within hours, elected officials began to drop their support for the legislation.[245] Although supporters of the bills claimed that their only intention was to go after foreign websites that distribute unauthorized copies of software, videos and music, opponents claimed that the language of the bills was so broad that it posed a threat to free speech and innovation, and made websites potentially responsible for all content or links posted by their users.[246]

Newspaper accounts gushed that this 'legislative battle over two once-obscure bills to combat the piracy of American movies, music, books and writing on the World Wide Web may prove to be a turning point for the way business is done in Washington' – representing a moment when 'the new economy rose up against the old'.[247] A Pew Research Center poll reportedly found that the antipiracy legislation was the most followed news topic among Americans under the age of 30; even news of the presidential primaries failed to get as much attention in this age group.[248] Even SOPA's backers conceded

---

[244] For news accounts of the events of 18 January 2012, see, e.g., Jenna Wortham, 'With Twitter, Blackouts and Demonstrations, Web Flexes Its Muscle', *New York Times*, 18 January 2012, available at: http://www.nytimes.com/2012/01/19/technology/protests-of-antipiracy-bills-unite-web.html?_r= (estimating the number of people signing Google's online petition to Congress at 4.5 million); Amy Chozick, 'A Clash of Media Worlds (and Generations)', *New York Times*, 22 January 2012, available at: http://www.nytimes.com/2012/01/22/business/in-antipiracy-debate-media-worlds-and-generations-clash.html?pagewanted=all (reporting that more than seven million people had signed an online petition from Google to stop SOPA). See also below notes 246 and 247 and accompanying text.

[245] See Jonathan Weisman, 'In Fight over Piracy Bills, New Economy Rises Against Old', *New York Times*, 18 January 2012, available at: http://www.nytimes.com/2012/01/19/technology/web-protests-piracy-bill-and-2-key-senators-change-course.html?pagewanted=all (noting that on 18 January alone seven senators who were prominent backers of SOPA dropped their support).

[246] See Jenna Wortham, 'Public Outcry over Antipiracy Bills Began as Grass-Roots Grumbling', *New York Times*, 20 January 2012, available at: http://www.nytimes.com/2012/01/20/technology/public-outcry-over-antipiracy-bills-began-as-grass-roots-grumbling.html?pagewanted=all.

[247] See above note 245.

[248] See Chozick, above note 244.

that the one-day protest was a 'watershed event'.[249] Within two weeks, Paramount Pictures sent out what was apparently a mass mailing to intellectual property law professors throughout the United States, confessing that '[o]ver the last few weeks, we at Paramount have been humbled by the strong public opposition to the proposed SOPA and PIPA legislation' and proposing a campus visit 'to exchange ideas about content theft, its challenges and possible ways to address it'.[250]

Nor was this 'watershed event' limited to the United States. The events of 18 January appear to have triggered greater international scrutiny of ACTA. An announcement by Polish officials that Poland intended to sign ACTA on 26 January resulted in a series of petitions, protests, attacks on government websites, and a proposed 'black out' similar to the one that occurred on January 18.[251] Ultimately, this coordinated effort caused Polish Prime Minister, Donald Tusk, to announce that Poland would not sign ACTA and to send a letter to the European Parliament (EP) asking it to reject ACTA.[252] Further protests occurred, starting in Sweden and Slovenia, and eventually culminating on 11 February 2012 with coordinated protests in 200 European

---

249 See Somini Sengupta, 'Big Victory on Internet Buoys Lobby', *New York Times*, 27 January 2012, available at: http://www.nytimes.com/2012/01/27/technology/victory-on-antipiracy-issue-buoys-internet-lobby.html (reporting that Christopher Dodd, a former senator who is now chairman of the Motion Picture Association of America described the events of 18 January 2012 as 'a "watershed event" the likes of which he had not witnessed in his 30 years in politics').

250 Letter from Alfred Clinton Perry, Vice President, Worldwide Content Protection & Outreach, Paramount Pictures, to Professor Charles R. McManis, 2 February 2012 (on file with the author). The letter states that 'Over the last few weeks we at Paramount have been humbled by the strong public opposition to the proposed SOPA and PIPA legislation': ibid. The letter goes on to propose a visit to Washington University Law School 'to exchange ideas about content theft, its challenges and possible ways to address it'.

251 See Mike Masnick, 'Polish Government's Plan to Sign ACTA Gets the SOPA Treatment', *TechDirt*, 23 January 2012 at 2:37 PM, available at: http://www.techdirt.com/articles/20120123/04261617510/polish-governments-plan-to-sign-acta-gets-sopa-treatment.shtml; 'Polish Sites Hit in ACTA Hack Attack', *BBC News*, 23 January 2012 at 2:00PM, available at: http://www.bbc.co.uk/news/technology-16686265; 'Thousands March in Poland over ACTA internet Treaty', *BBC News*, 26 January 2012 at 10:40AM, available at: http://www.bbc.co.uk/news/world-europe-16735219; 'Anti-Counterfeiting Trade Agreement', Wikipedia, available at: http://en.wikipedia.org/wiki/ACTA (last visited 15 March 2012).

252 Quinn Norton, 'How the European Internet Rose up Against ACTA', *Wired*, 21 February 2012 at 4:53 PM, available at: http://www wired.com/threatlevel/2012/02/europe-acta; 'Polish Government Asks European Parliament not to Sign ACTA', *Warsaw Business Journal*, 17 February 2012, available at: http://www.wbj.pl/article-58076-polish-government-asks-european-parliament-not-to-sign-acta.html.

cities.[253] Perhaps the most dramatic event in this entire chain of events was the resignation of the EP Rapporteur (investigator) for ACTA, Kader Arif, who stated that his resignation was intended 'to denounce in the strongest possible manner the entire process that led to the signature of [ACTA]'.[254] Out of these protests grew a petition signed by over 2.5 million people demanding that the EU reject ACTA, prompting the European Parliament to schedule a series of events, beginning with a public workshop on 1 March 2012, aimed at more critically evaluating ACTA in order to determine whether the EU – one of the major players in the ACTA negotiations – should sign the agreement.[255]

Whatever one makes of these 'watershed events', they do not bode particularly well for the future of ACTA. After all, how can ACTA's proponents expect to persuade developing countries to implement legislation modeled on the DMCA or the EU Copyright Directive when it is widely conceded that these measures have been ineffective in containing massive digital file sharing? And how can they persuade developing countries to pass stronger legislative measures in the face of the unprecedented protests at home against precisely such measures? In the words of one ACTA commentator, it is 'difficult to understand how ACTA could induce other countries that are not current parties to the U.S. FTAs or the EU EPAs, especially those that are emerging and quite powerful, to take up new obligations under this agreement'.[256] Thus, even ACTA's proponents have reason to fear that, unless ACTA helps to restart multilateral negotiations over international intellectual property enforcement standards, it may prove to be an ineffective and superfluous treaty.[257]

253 See 'Anti-Counterfeiting Trade Agreement', above note 251; David Lee, 'ACTA Protests: Thousands Take to the Streets Across Europe', *BBC News,* 11 February 2012 at 1:57 PM, available at: http://www.bbc.co.uk/news/technology-16999497.

254 Mike Masnick, 'European Parliament Official in Charge of ACTA Quits, and Denounces the "Masquerade" Behind ACTA', *TechDirt,* 26 January 2012 at 11:55 AM, available at: http://www.techdirt.com/articles/20120126/11014317553/european-parliment-official-charge-acta-quits-denounces-masquerade-behind-acta.shtml.

255 Above notes 22–24 and accompanying text.

256 Yu, above note 14, 1090.

257 Ibid., 1083–93.

10. ACTA, internet service providers and the *acquis communautaire*

Irini Stamatoudi

1. INTRODUCTION

The negotiations for the Anti-Counterfeiting Trade Agreement (ACTA) started unofficially on the basis of Japanese and US initiatives in 2006. Canada, the EU and Switzerland joined later. Official negotiations started in June 2008, which also involved Australia, Mexico, Morocco, New Zealand, the Republic of Korea and Singapore. In essence, these are the countries which account for the vast majority of the world's intellectual property rights. 'Agreement in principle' was reached in October 2010; the text was finalized on 15 April 2011 and was opened for signature on 1 May 2011.

The aim of ACTA was to raise the standards of intellectual property enforcement found in international instruments and, in particular, the TRIPS Agreement. Its aim was enhanced international cooperation and more effective international enforcement. In this light it presents a number of TRIPS-Plus elements. Yet, it chose to create its own governing body outside the World Trade Organization (WTO) and other existing international institutions or fora, such as the World Intellectual Property Organization (WIPO) or the United Nations (UN). The reason for this was that the existing international institutions were thought not to provide procedures that were sufficiently flexible to accommodate the attainment of a fast and effective result. The criticism was that this was achieved to a considerable extent at the expense of transparency.[1]

---

[1] See the 'Joint Motion for a Resolution' on the transparency and state of play of the ACTA negotiations, published on 9 March 2010 by the European Parliament, Document RC/808188EN.doc. See http://www.europarl.europa.eu/sides/getDoc.do?pubRef=-//EP//TEXT+MOTION+P7-RC-2010-0154+0+DOC+XML+V0//EN. On 4 April 2012 the European Commission referred ACTA to the European Court of Justice in order to allow the Court to decide on whether ACTA is compatible with the European Treaties and in particular with the Charter of Fundamental Rights of the European Union, http://europa.eu/rapid/pressReleasesAction.do?reference=IP/12/354.

On 4 July 2012, and before the Court's decision, '[t]he Anti-Counterfeiting Trade Agreement (ACTA), was rejected by the European Parliament [...] and hence cannot

ACTA came at a period where counterfeiting and piracy had reached worrying levels, affecting the economy of all those involved in the production, distribution, marketing and exploitation of intellectual property rights. With this in mind, it has been described as a response to the increase in the global trade of counterfeit goods and pirated copyright protected works.[2] It is worth noting that the text of the Treaty begins with spelling out that 'effective enforcement of intellectual property rights is critical to sustaining economic growth across all industries and globally'. It continues to state that

> proliferation of counterfeit and pirated goods, as well as of services that distribute infringing material, undermines legitimate trade and sustainable development of the world economy, causes significant financial losses for right holders and for legitimate businesses, and, in some cases, provides a source of revenue for organized crime and otherwise poses risks to the public.[3]

ACTA also deals with internet piracy.

This chapter shall explore whether ACTA, and in particular Article 27(4) of ACTA concerning the disclosure by internet service providers (ISPs)[4] to rightholders information identifying an allegedly infringing subscriber, is compatible with the *acquis communautaire*.[5] In this respect it discusses the

---

become law in the EU. This was the first time that Parliament exercised its Lisbon Treaty power to reject an international trade agreement. 478 MEPs voted against ACTA, 39 in favour, and 165 abstained': see http://www.europarl.europa.eu/news/en/pressroom/content/20120703IPR48247/html/European-Parliament-rejects-ACTA.

2 Ministry of Economic Development of New Zealand (2008). 'On Anti-Counterfeiting Trade Agreement', available at: http://www.med.govt.nz/business/intellectual-property/intellectual-property-enforcement/anti-counterfeiting-trade-agreement/.

3 See the Recital to ACTA.

4 Internet service providers (ISPs) are telecommunication companies, which offer access to the internet to their customers. ISPs can themselves host content, which is protected by copyright, act as intermediaries for the transmission of material coming from elsewhere, or they can offer their services as a facilitator for peer-to-peer exchanges.

5 I. Stamatoudi, 'The Role of Internet Service Providers. Ethics, Reality and the Law: The Example of *Promusicae v. Telefonica*', 8th International Conference, *Computer Ethics: Philosophical Enquiry*, Ionio University, Corfu, 26–28 June 2009; (Nomiki Vivliothiki 2009) 750. I. Stamatoudi, 'Data Protection, Secrecy of Communications and Copyright Protection. Conflicts and Convergences. The Example of *Promusicae v Telefonica*', in I. Stamatoudi (ed.), *Copyright Enforcement and the Internet*, Information Law Series (B. Hugenholtz (general ed.), (Kluwer Law International 2010) 199. I. Stamatoudi, 'Ethics, Reality and the Law: The Example of *Promusicae v Telefonica* and *LSG v TELE2*' [2010] 63 *Revue Hellénique de Droit International* 921. I. Stamatoudi, 'Towards an updated EU Enforcement Directive? Selected Topics and Problems', 4th International Seminar on Information Law, 2011,

relevant provisions of EU law and the case law of the Court of Justice of the European Union, and makes reference to national experiences in the area. Conclusions will be drawn at the end as to whether ACTA resolves the problem of internet piracy.

2. COMPATIBILITY WITH THE *ACQUIS COMMUNAUTAIRE*

ACTA deals with the issue of internet piracy in its Section 5. The whole section consists of one article only, i.e. Article 27. Paragraph 4 of this article stipulates that States Parties *may* provide in their laws that a competent authority (that is, a court or other authority) may order an internet service provider to disclose expeditiously to a right holder information sufficient to identify a subscriber whose account was allegedly used for infringement, where that right holder has filed a legally sufficient claim of trademark or copyright or related rights infringement, and where such information is being sought for the purpose of protecting or enforcing those rights.

It also provides that these procedures are to be implemented in a manner that avoids the creation of barriers to legitimate activity, including electronic commerce, and – consistent with that State Party's law – preserves fundamental principles such as freedom of expression, fair process and privacy.[6]

European Union law has been vague and complex on the role of internet service providers with respect to their involvement in the combat of piracy on the internet. And that is so, not because there is no clear EU stance when it comes to the significance of intellectual property rights for the economies of

---

University of Thessaloniki (Aristoteleio), University of Macedonia and Ionio University, Thessaloniki, 19–22 May 2011 (Nomiki Vivliothiki 2011). A. Strowel, 'Liaisons dangereuses et bonnes relations sur Internet: à propos des hyperliens' (1998) A&M 4. A. Strowel/Ide, 'Liability for Linking to Illegal Content (2000) *Computer und Recht International* 91. A. Strowel, *Peer-to-peer File Sharing and Secondary Liability in Copyright Law* (Edward Elgar Publishing 2009).

[6] Section 5: Enforcement of Intellectual Property Rights in the Digital Environment. Art. 27: Enforcement in the Digital Environment: '4. A Party may provide, in accordance with its laws and regulations, its competent authorities with the authority to order an online service provider to disclose expeditiously to a right holder information sufficient to identify a subscriber whose account was allegedly used for infringement, where that right holder has filed a legally sufficient claim of trademark or copyright or related rights infringement, and where such information is being sought for the purpose of protecting or enforcing those rights. These procedures shall be implemented in a manner that avoids the creation of barriers to legitimate activity, including electronic commerce, and, consistent with that Party's law, preserves fundamental principles such as freedom of expression, fair process and privacy'.

the EU and Member States and the importance of their effective enforcement, but because of the multiplicity of EU laws which step in when it comes to providing data concerning individuals. Not all EU legal instruments are compatible with each other and, even where they are (which they should be in any event), their interpretation in order for a balance to be struck creates considerable friction and inconvenience. The role of ISPs with regard to intellectual property infringements is a characteristic example in this respect.

The *acquis communautaire* on this issue is found in a number of EU legal instruments concerning not only intellectual property rights but also privacy, covering data protection and secrecy of communications.

2.1 The Enforcement Directive

The Enforcement Directive[7] provides the only structured set of sanctions in the European Union for intellectual property rights and harmonizes the minimum means available to right holders and public authorities for fighting infringements of intellectual property rights.[8] The European Commission has recently drafted a Report concerning the evaluation of the Enforcement Directive.[9] According to the findings of the Staff Working Paper that accompanies this Report, the available legislative and non-legislative instruments are not powerful enough to combat online infringements of intellectual property rights effectively.[10] The European Commission is currently exploring the possibility of updating the Enforcement Directive to meet the needs of the digital era, with the role of internet service providers being a key issue to the update. The E-commerce Directive is another potential candidate for accommodating this need (see 2.2 below).

---

[7] Directive 2004/48/EC of the European Parliament and of the Council on the enforcement of intellectual property rights, OJ L157/16, 30 April 2004 (Enforcement Directive).

[8] Application of Directive 2004/48/EC of the European Parliament and the Council of 29 April 2004 on the enforcement of intellectual property rights. Report from the Commission to the European Parliament, the Council, the European Economic and Social Committee and the Committee of the Regions. SEC (2010) 1589 final. Brussels, 22 December 2010, COM(2010) 779 final, 2.

[9] Commission Staff Working Document Analysis of the Application of Directive 2004/48/EC of the European Parliament and the Council of 29 April 2004 on the Enforcement of Intellectual Property Rights in the Member States. Accompanying Document to the Report from the Commission to the Council, the European Parliament and the European Social Committee on the Application of Directive 2004/48/EC of the European Parliament and the Council of 29 April 2004 on the Enforcement of Intellectual Property Rights, COM(2010) 779 final, Brussels, 22 December 2010, SEC(2010) 1589 final.

[10] Ibid., 7.

The relevant provision in the Enforcement Directive concerning the right of information is Article 8, according to which:

1. Member States shall ensure that, in the context of proceedings concerning an infringement of an intellectual property right and in response to a justified and proportionate request of the claimant, the competent judicial authorities may order that information on the origin and distribution networks of the goods or services which infringe an intellectual property right be provided by the infringer and/or any other person who:

[…]

(c) was found to be providing on a commercial scale services used in infringing activities:

[…].[11]

What can be derived from this is that Member States need to ensure that *courts* have the discretion to order, if they consider it appropriate, the disclosure by ISPs of information concerning their subscribers with regard to an infringement by a third party. It needs to be noted here that this disclosure of information is irrespective of any ISP liability.[12]

---

11 Art. 8 continues:

2. The information referred to in paragraph 1 shall, as appropriate, comprise:
(a) the names and addresses of the producers, manufacturers, distributors, suppliers and other previous holders of the goods or services, as well as the intended wholesalers and retailers;
(b) information on the quantities produced, manufactured, delivered, received or ordered, as well as the price obtained for the goods or services in question.
3. Paragraphs 1 and 2 shall apply without prejudice to other statutory provisions which:
(a) grant the rightholder rights to receive fuller information;
(b) govern the use in civil or criminal proceedings of the information communicated pursuant to this Article;
(c) govern responsibility for misuse of the right of information;
or
(d) afford an opportunity for refusing to provide information which would force the person referred to in paragraph 1 to admit to his/her own participa tion or that of his/her close relatives in an infringement of an intellectual property right;
or
(e) govern the protection of confidentiality of information sources or the processing of personal data'.

12 See also Art. 3(1) of the Enforcement Directive which provides: '1. Member

If we now compare this provision to the ACTA provision, we can observe the following.

First, the ACTA provision is optional, whilst the Enforcement Directive provision is obligatory, although it is up to the court to decide whether such information should be disclosed. Second, under ACTA information is to be disclosed to rightholders following request by a competent authority, whilst under the Enforcement Directive it is the court that orders the disclosure. In both cases, a judicial procedure should be initiated, which means that a substantiated legal claim should have been filed in both cases. However, disclosure in accordance with the Enforcement Directive takes place with regard to an infringement and not an 'alleged infringement', as is the case with ACTA.

The safeguards of how this right is to be exercised are not spelt out in detail in ACTA but the general framework is there and it is for the States Parties to assess and implement it. The safeguards in the Enforcement Directive are found in the fact that not all information is to be disclosed but only information that is *sufficient* to identify the alleged infringer. At the end of the ACTA provision, reference is made to avoiding the creation of barriers to legitimate activity, including electronic commerce, as well as to the preservation of fundamental principles such as freedom of expression, fair process and privacy. Safeguards in European Union law are also found in other Directives and in the Charter of Fundamental Rights, as these have been interpreted by the Court of Justice of the European Union in relevant cases – for example, in *Promusicae v Telefonica, LSG v TELE2, Scarlet,*[13] *Netlog,*[14] and *Bonnier Audio AB, Earbooks AB, Norstedts Förlagsgrupp AB, Piratförlaget AB, Storyside AB v Perfect Communication Sweden AB.*[15]

On the basis of the above, one can draw the following conclusions. Compared to the Enforcement Directive, ACTA seems to be wider. Competent authorities, and not just courts, order the disclosure of information concerning the infringer. Under ACTA, the disclosure may be ordered in relation to an *alleged* infringement and not just to a proven one. In addition, although one could argue that the provision in ACTA is optional whilst the provision in the

---

States shall provide for the measures, procedures and remedies necessary to ensure the enforcement of the intellectual property rights covered by this Directive.'

[13] Reference for a preliminary ruling from the Cour d'Appel de Bruxelles (Belgium) lodged on 5 February 2010 – Case C-70/10 *Scarlet Extended SA v. Société Belge des auteurs, compositeurs et éditeurs* (*SABAM*), 24 November 2011, [2011] ECR I-0000 (nyr).

[14] Case C-360/10 *Belgische Vereniging van Auteurs, Componisten en Uitgevers CVBA* (*Sabam*) *v Netlog NV*, 16 February 2012, [2012] ECR I-0000 (nyr).

[15] 19 April 2012, [2012] ECR I (nyr).

Enforcement Directive is not, the latter's impact is lessened by the fact that it is up to the court to decide whether or not to issue such an order for disclosure.

2.2 The E-commerce Directive

Apart from the Enforcement Directive, the E-commerce Directive[16] is also relevant to ISPs.

The relevant provision in the E-commerce Directive is Article 15, according to which ISPs have no general obligation to monitor the information which they transmit or store, or to actively seek facts or circumstances that indicate illegal activity.[17]

However, according to paragraph 2 of the same article, Member States may establish obligations for ISPs to promptly inform the *competent public authorities* of *alleged illegal activities* at their request and disclose to them information concerning the identity of their subscribers.

If we now compare this provision with the ACTA provision, we come to the following conclusion. First, both provisions are optional. Second, under ACTA information is disclosed to rightholders following a request by a competent public authority. Under the E-commerce Directive, information is disclosed to the competent public authority that has requested the information, and *not to the rightholder*. As regards safeguards, the comments made in the section for the Enforcement Directive (see 2.1 above) also apply here.

Thus, ACTA in comparison with the E-commerce Directive, ACTA goes further since, under the Directive, information – with regard, this time, to an alleged infringement – is disclosed to the competent public authority, whilst under ACTA information is disclosed to the rightholder.

---

16 Directive 2000/31/EC of 8 June 2000 on certain legal aspects of information society services, in particular electronic commerce, in the Internal Market (E-commerce Directive), OJ L178/1, 17 July 2000.

17 Art. 15 E-commerce Directive provides:

1. Member States shall not impose a general obligation on providers, when providing the services covered by Articles 12, 13 and 14, to monitor the information which they transmit or store, nor a general obligation actively to seek facts or circumstances indicating illegal activity.
2. Member States may establish obligations for information society service providers promptly to inform the competent public authorities of alleged illegal activities undertaken or information provided by recipients of their service or obligations to communicate to the competent authorities, at their request, information enabling the identification of recipients of their service with whom they have storage agreements.

To these two EU Directives should be added Article 8(3) of the Information Society Directive.[18] According to Article 8(3): 'Member States shall ensure that rightholders are in a position to apply for an injunction against intermediaries whose services are used by a third party to infringe a copyright or related right'. This provision does not make clear whether courts may order ISPs to disclose information concerning their subscribers. However, the CJEU in *LSG v Tele2*[19] in paragraph 45 mentions that:

> [t]he protection sought by Directive 2001/29 would be substantially diminished if 'intermediaries', within the meaning of Article 8(3) of that [information society] directive, were to be construed as not covering access providers, which alone are in possession of the data making it possible to identify the users who have infringed those rights.

In any case, however, if information were to be disclosed on the basis of this provision, it would be for the courts only to disclose it.

Summing up, one can draw the following conclusions.

Information may be ordered:

- (according to the Enforcement Directive and the Information Society Directive) by a court for the rightholder with regard to an infringement;
- (according to the E-commerce Directive) by a competent public authority for the competent authority with regard to an alleged infringement; and
- (according to ACTA) by a competent authority for the rightholder with regard to an alleged infringement.

There is therefore one point at which ACTA seems to go further than the above-mentioned EU Directives. *That is the fact that a competent authority orders an ISP to disclose information to the rightholder.* As long as the competent authority is a body other than a court, it is not covered by EU law. The ACTA provision is, of course, optional and it is also true that EU Member States can go further than that provided in the EU Directives and establish their own protection schemes, as France did.

At this point, however, we also need to note that the ACTA provision – although it goes further than the EU Directives – is not entirely alien to EU

18 Directive 2001/29/EC of the European Parliament and of the Council of 22 May 2001 on the harmonisation of certain aspects of copyright and related rights in the information society, OJ L167, 22 June 2001, 10.

19 C-557/07 *LSG-Gesellschaft zur Wahrnehmung von Leistungsschutzrechten GmbH v Tele2Telecommunication*, 19 February 2009, [2009] ECR (nyr), para. 45.

law. This is so if we take into account the Telecom Package,[20] which provides that measures[21] may be imposed with regard to end-users' access to, or use of, services and applications through electronic communications networks; at the same time it does not provide that these measures are necessarily imposed by judicial authorities.

This provision does not directly relate to the right of information, although it may involve it. In any case, it goes a lot further than that by allowing competent authorities other than courts to order ISPs to impose measures on subscribers.

---

[20] Amendment 46 (eh 138) of the Telecom Package, which amends Art. 1(3a) of Directive 2002/22/EC of the European Parliament and of the Council of 7 March 2002 on universal service and users' rights relating to electronic communications networks and services (Universal Service Directive):

> 3a. Measures taken by Member States regarding end-users' access to or use of services and applications through electronic communications networks shall respect the fundamental rights and freedoms of natural persons, as guaranteed by the European Convention for the Protection of Human Rights and Fundamental Freedoms and general principles of Community law. Any of these measures regarding end-users' access to or use of services and applications through electronic communications networks liable to restrict those fundamental rights or freedoms may only be imposed if they are appropriate, proportionate and necessary within a democratic society, and their implementation shall be subject to adequate procedural safeguards in conformity with the European Convention for the Protection of Human Rights and Fundamental Freedoms and with general principles of Community law, including effective judicial protection and due process. Accordingly, these measures may only be taken with due respect for the principle of presumption of innocence and the right to privacy. A prior fair and impartial procedure shall be guaranteed, including the right to be heard of the person or persons concerned, subject to the need for appropriate conditions and procedural arrangements in duly substantiated cases of urgency in conformity with European Convention for the Protection of Human Rights and Fundamental Freedoms. The right to an effective and timely judicial review shall be guaranteed.

The Telecom Package: Directive 2009/140/EC of the European Parliament and of the Council of 25 November 2009 amending Directives 2002/21/EC on a common regulatory framework for electronic communications networks and services, 2002/19/EC on access to, and interconnection of, electronic communications networks and associated facilities, and 2002/20/EC on the authorization of electronic communications networks and services (OJ L337/37).

[21] No measures may be taken unless they are appropriate, proportionate and necessary within a democratic society and never without a prior, fair and impartial procedure that includes the right to be heard and respects the presumption of innocence and the right to privacy.

2.3 Privacy Issues

Although the above-mentioned Directives are quite express concerning the role of internet service providers, they do, however, contain some reservations concerning privacy. Article 1(5) of the E-commerce Directive provides that '[t]his Directive shall not apply to: ... (b) questions relating to information society services covered by Directives 95/46/EC and 97/66/EC'. An equivalent provision is found in the Information Society Directive, Article 9 of which provides that '[t]his Directive shall be without prejudice to provisions concerning in particular [...] data protection and privacy [...]'. Article 2(3) (a) of the Enforcement Directive also provides that '[t]his Directive shall not affect: (a) the Community provisions governing the substantive law on intellectual property, Directive 95/46/EC, Directive 1999/93/EC or Directive 2000/31/EC, in general, and Articles 12 to 15 of Directive 2000/31/EC in particular'.

To these reservations the EU Directives on privacy should be added.[22]

---

[22] Directive 95/46/EC of the European Parliament and of the Council of 24 October 1995 on the protection of individuals with regard to the processing of personal data and on the free movement of such data, OJ L 281, 23 November 1995, 31. Art. 2 provides: 'For the purposes of this Directive: (a) 'personal data' shall mean any information relating to an identified or identifiable natural person ('data subject'); an identifiable person is one who can be identified, directly or indirectly, in particular by reference to an identification number or to one or more factors specific to his physical, physiological, mental, economic, cultural or social identity; (b) 'processing of personal data' ('processing') shall mean any operation or set of operations which is performed upon personal data, whether or not by automatic means, such as collection, recording, organisation, storage, adaptation or alteration, retrieval, consultation, use, disclosure by transmission, dissemination or otherwise making available, alignment or combination, blocking, erasure or destruction'.

According to Art. 3: '1. This Directive shall apply to the processing of personal data wholly or partly by automatic means, and to the processing otherwise than by automatic means of personal data which form part of a filing system or are intended to form part of a filing system'.

Art. 8 provides: '1. Member States shall prohibit the processing of personal data revealing racial or ethnic origin, political opinions, religious or philosophical beliefs, trade-union membership, and the processing of data concerning health or sex life. 2. Paragraph 1 shall not apply where: ... (c) processing is necessary to protect the vital interests of the data subject or of another person where the data subject is physically or legally incapable of giving his consent ...'.

According to Art. 13: '1. Member States may adopt legislative measures to restrict the scope of the obligations and rights provided for in Articles 6(1), 10, 11(1), 12 and 21 when such a restriction constitutes a necessary measure to safeguard: (a) national security; (b) defence; (c) public security; (d) the prevention, investigation, detection and prosecution of criminal offences, or of breaches of ethics for regulated professions; (e) an important economic or financial interest of a Member State or of the European

According to Article 7 of Directive 95/46/EC on data protection:[23]

> Member States shall provide that personal data may be processed only if: … (f) processing is necessary for the purposes of the legitimate interests pursued by the controller or by the third party or parties to whom the data are disclosed, except where such interests are overridden by the interests or fundamental rights and freedoms of the data subject which require protection under Article 1(1).

According to Article 5(1) of Directive 2002/58 on e-privacy,[24] Member States

---

Union, including monetary, budgetary and taxation matters; (f) a monitoring, inspection or regulatory function connected, even occasionally, with the exercise of official authority in cases referred to in (c), (d) and (e); (g) the protection of the data subject or of the rights and freedoms of others'.

23 Even a particular IP address at a particular time of a particular day may constitute personal data within the meaning of Art. 2(a) Directive 95/46. That is so because this information is capable of linking an action to a subscriber: see A. Strowel, 'Security and Privacy on the Internet', WIPO-ESCWA Arab Regional Conference on Intellectual Property and Electronic Commerce, Beirut, 7–8 May 2003. See also A. Fragouli, 'Are IP Addresses Personal Data and What are the Consequences? (in Greek), [2008] DIMEE 198. In Germany (D. Wüstenberg, 'Argumente gegen die Rechtmässigkeit der Vorratsdatenspeicherung', (2006) RDV 102), and Austria (Datenschutzkommission GZ: K213.000/0005-DSK, see http://www. internet4 jurists.at/ entscheidungen/dsk_empfelung061011.pdf) IP addresses are considered personal data. In France (see http://www.legalis.net/jurisprudence-decision.php3?id_article=1954 and http://www.legalis.net/jurisprudence-decision.php3?id_article=1955) and in Hong Kong (see http://www.pcpd.org.hk/english/publications/files/Yahoo_e.pdf) IP addresses are not considered personal data. See 2.5 below for the Opinion of the European Data Protection Supervisor.

24 Directive 2002/58/EC of the European Parliament and of the Council of 12 July 2002 concerning the processing of personal data and the protection of privacy in the electronic communications sector (Directive on privacy and electronic communications), OJ L201, 31 July 2002, 37).

Art. 1 provides: '1. This Directive harmonises the provisions of the Member States required to ensure an equivalent level of protection of fundamental rights and freedoms, and in particular the right to privacy, with respect to the processing of personal data in the electronic communication sector and to ensure the free movement of such data and of electronic communication equipment and services in the Community. 2. The provisions of this Directive particularise and complement Directive 95/46/EC for the purposes mentioned in paragraph 1 … 3. This Directive shall not apply to activities which fall outside the scope of the Treaty establishing the European Community, such as those covered by Titles V and VI of the Treaty on European Union, and in any case to activities concerning public security, defence, State security (including the economic well-being of the State when the activities relate to State security matters) and the activities of the State in areas of criminal law'.

Art. 2 Directive 2002/58 provides: 'Save as otherwise provided, the definitions in Directive 95/46/EC and in Directive 2002/21/EC of the European Parliament and of the Council of 7 March 2002 on a common regulatory framework for electronic communications networks and services (Framework Directive) … shall apply. The following

must ensure the confidentiality of communications by means of a public communications network and publicly available electronic communications services, and of the related traffic data. The same Directive provides for cases where the processing of traffic data is allowed (for example, for billing and marketing services and the provision of value added services). It does not

---

definitions shall also apply: ... (b) 'traffic data' means any data processed for the purpose of the conveyance of a communication on an electronic communications network or for the billing thereof; ... (d) 'communication' means any information exchanged or conveyed between a finite number of parties by means of a publicly available electronic communications service. This does not include any information conveyed as part of a broadcasting service to the public over an electronic communications network except to the extent that the information can be related to the identifiable subscriber or user receiving the information'.

Art. 3 Directive 2002/58 provides: '1. This Directive shall apply to the processing of personal data in connection with the provision of publicly available electronic communications services in public communications networks in the Community'.

Art. 5 Directive 2002/58 provides: '1. Member States shall ensure the confidentiality of communications and the related traffic data by means of a public communications network and publicly available electronic communications services, through national legislation. In particular, they shall prohibit listening, tapping, storage or other kinds of interception or surveillance of communications and the related traffic data by persons other than users, without the consent of the users concerned, except when legally authorised to do so in accordance with Article 15(1). This paragraph shall not prevent technical storage which is necessary for the conveyance of a communication without prejudice to the principle of confidentiality'.

Art. 6 Directive 2002/58 provides: '1. Traffic data relating to subscribers and users processed and stored by the provider of a public communications network or publicly available electronic communications service must be erased or made anonymous when it is no longer needed for the purpose of the transmission of a communication without prejudice to paragraphs 2, 3 and 5 of this Article and Article 15(1). 2. Traffic data necessary for the purposes of subscriber billing and interconnection payments may be processed. Such processing is permissible only up to the end of the period during which the bill may lawfully be challenged or payment pursued. 3. For the purpose of marketing electronic communications services or for the provision of value added services, the provider of a publicly available electronic communications service may process the data referred to in paragraph 1 to the extent and for the duration necessary for such services or marketing, if the subscriber or user to whom the data relate has given his/her consent. Users or subscribers shall be given the possibility to withdraw their consent for the processing of traffic data at any time. ... 5. Processing of traffic data, in accordance with paragraphs 1, 2, 3 and 4, must be restricted to persons acting under the authority of providers of the public communications networks and publicly available electronic communications services handling billing or traffic management, customer enquiries, fraud detection, marketing electronic communications services or providing a value added service, and must be restricted to what is necessary for the purposes of such activities. 6. Paragraphs 1, 2, 3 and 5 shall apply without prejudice to the possibility for competent bodies to be informed of traffic data in conformity with applicable legislation with a view to settling disputes, in particular interconnection or billing disputes'.

concern the communication of that data to persons other than those acting under the authority of the providers of public communications networks and publicly available electronic communications services. Member States may provide for exceptions to the principle of confidentiality of personal data in cases of national security, defence and public security, the prosecution of criminal offences or of unauthorized use of the electronic communications system (as referred to in Article 13(1) of Directive 95/46) as long as these exceptions and restrictions constitute a necessary, appropriate and proportionate measure within a democratic society. On the basis of the reference to 'unauthorised use of the electronic communications system', Member States may take measures to restrict the obligation of confidentiality of personal data where this is necessary for the protection of the rights and freedoms of others.

2.4 The Case Law of the Court of Justice of the European Union

It seems so far that EU law has not taken a clear stance on the role of internet service providers and the disclosure of information concerning their subscribers. It is more a matter of interpretation. There have been some cases before the CJEU which throw some light on this matter as well as an Opinion by the European Data Protection Supervisor concerning the negotiations at the time by the European Union of the Anti-Counterfeiting Trade Agreement.

The first case the CJEU dealt with was *Promusicae v Telefonica*.[25] Promusicae, a Spanish non-profit making organization of producers and publishers of musical and audiovisual recordings, applied to the Madrid Commercial Court No. 5 for preliminary measures against Telefónica, a Spanish internet service provider, in order for the latter to disclose the identities and physical addresses of certain persons to whom it provided internet

Art. 15 Directive 2002/58 provides: '1. Member States may adopt legislative measures to restrict the scope of the rights and obligations provided for in Article 5, Article 6, Article 8(1), (2), (3) and (4), and Article 9 of this Directive when such restriction constitutes a necessary, appropriate and proportionate measure within a democratic society to safeguard national security (i.e. State security), defence, public security, and the prevention, investigation, detection and prosecution of criminal offences or of unauthorised use of the electronic communication system, as referred to in Article 13(1) of Directive 95/46/EC. To this end, Member States may, inter alia, adopt legislative measures providing for the retention of data for a limited period justified on the grounds laid down in this paragraph. All the measures referred to in this paragraph shall be in accordance with the general principles of Community law, including those referred to in Article 6(1) and (2) of the Treaty on European Union'.
Article 19 of Directive 2002/58 provides that 'Directive 97/66/EC is hereby repealed with effect from the date referred to in Article 17(1). References made to the repealed Directive shall be construed as being made to this Directive'.

[25] Case 275/06 [2008] ECR 271.

access services and whose IP address and date and time of connection were known to Promusicae. According to Promusicae, these persons were engaging in peer-to-peer file sharing practices (using the KaZaA file exchange program) and provided access in shared files of personal computers to phonograms in which the members of Promusicae held the exploitation rights. Promusicae requested this information in order to be able to bring civil proceedings against the persons concerned for copyright infringement as well as engagement in unfair competition. The Spanish Court ordered the preliminary measures requested by Promusicae.

Telefónica appealed against the order on the grounds that Spanish law authorized the communication of such data only in a criminal investigation or for the purpose of safeguarding public security and national defence, and not in civil proceedings or as a preliminary measure relating to civil proceedings. The Spanish Court decided to stay the proceedings and ask the CJEU whether Member States should provide that internet service providers are under an obligation to communicate personal data concerning their clients with regard to an exchange of files of protected material, and therefore a copyright infringement (and potentially an infringement of unfair competition law) to third parties (rightholders or others deriving their rights from them) in order for this data to be used in the course of civil proceedings.

The Court of Justice noted that there are provisions in the EU Directives for the protection of personal data which provide that, in cases of infringement of an intellectual property right and in response to a justified and proportionate request of the claimant, the competent judicial authorities may order the infringer to provide information on the origin and distribution networks of the goods or services that infringe the intellectual property right. However, if these provisions are considered in conjunction with Article 8(3)(e) of Directive 2004/48 and Articles 15(2) and 18 of Directive 2000/31 or Article 8(1) and (2) of Directive 2001/29, one comes to the conclusion that Member States are under no obligation to provide for the communication of personal data in the context of civil proceedings. The Court noted also[26] that, although Articles 41, 42 and 47 of the TRIPS Agreement (in the light of which Community law must be interpreted) require the effective protection of intellectual property rights, they do not oblige Member States to provide for an obligation to communicate personal data in the context of civil proceedings.[27]

---

[26] Ibid., para. 60.

[27] Agreement on Trade-Related Aspects of Intellectual Property Rights signed at Marrakesh on 15 April 1994 and approved by Council Decision 94/800/EC of 22 December 1994 concerning the conclusion on behalf of the European Community, as regards matters within its competence, of the agreements reached in the Uruguay

On the basis of the above the CJEU came to the conclusion that Member States are under no obligation to communicate personal data in order to ensure effective protection of copyright in the context of civil proceedings. They may do so, however, if they wish by striking a fair balance between the various fundamental rights protected by the Community legal order and other general principles of EU law, such as the principle of proportionality.

The outcome reached in *Promusicae* has been repeated in another judgment of the Court of Justice, *LSG v Tele2*.[28] LSG, an Austrian collecting society for the rights of performers and phonogram producers had asked the Austrian ISP, Tele2, to communicate to it the names and addresses of persons to whom it provides internet access and whose IP addresses, day and time of connection are known. Tele2 denied the obligation to provide such information on the basis that it was not an intermediary within the scope of Article 8(3) of Directive 2001/29 and did not have the right to store traffic data. The CJEU ruled that the telecommunications company at issue was an intermediary within the meaning of Article 8(3) of Directive 2001/29. According to the Court, Member States should ensure that rightholders are in a position to apply for an injunction against intermediaries whose services are used by a third party to infringe a copyright or related right. An ISP's service, which is limited to internet access, is still a service used by the subscriber for the infringement of IP rights. In many cases such ISPs are best placed to bring such infringing

---

Round multilateral negotiations (1986–94) [1994] OJ L336/1 (TRIPS Agreement). Art. 41(1) and 2 provide:

1. Members shall ensure that enforcement procedures as specified in this Part are available under their law so as to permit effective action against any act of infringement of intellectual property rights covered by this Agreement, including expeditious remedies to prevent infringements and remedies which constitute a deterrent to further infringements. These procedures shall be applied in such a manner as to avoid the creation of barriers to legitimate trade and to provide for safeguards against their abuse.
2. Procedures concerning the enforcement of intellectual property rights shall be fair and equitable. They shall not be unnecessarily complicated or costly, or entail unreasonable time-limits or unwarranted delays'.

Art. 42 provides that 'Members shall make available to right holders civil judicial procedures concerning the enforcement of any intellectual property right covered by this Agreement '.

Art. 47 provides that 'Members may provide that the judicial authorities shall have the authority, unless this would be out of proportion to the seriousness of the infringement, to order the infringer to inform the right holder of the identity of third persons involved in the production and distribution of the infringing goods or services and of their channels of distribution'.

[28] C-557/07 *LSG-Gesellschaft zur Wahrnehmung von Leistungsschutzrechten GmbH v Tele2Telecommunication*, 19 February 2009, [2009] ECR I-1227.

activities to an end. Therefore, without prejudice to any other sanctions and remedies available, rightholders should have the ability to apply for an injunction against an intermediary (ISP) who carries a third party's infringement of a protected work or other subject-matter in a network. So, if such ISPs, being the only holders of such information which allows identification of the users-infringers of IP rights, are excluded from the scope of the Directive, the aim of the Directive (the effective protection of rightholders) will be severely compromised.[29]

The Court also ruled that the Directive on e-privacy does not prohibit Member States from providing in their national laws an obligation for disclosure of personal traffic data to private third parties for the purpose of civil proceedings for alleged infringements of exclusive rights protected by copyright. However, again the principle of proportionality has been referred to as a 'limiting' clause.

Three more cases were recently decided by the CJEU. In the first two cases – *Scarlet*[30] and *Netlog*[31] – the questions brought before the CJEU concerned filtering. The Court was first asked whether under EU law Member States are allowed to authorize a national court to order an ISP to introduce for all its subscribers preventive measures in the form of a filtering system for all electronic communications passing via its services – in particular, those involving the use of peer-to-peer software – in order to identify the sharing of electronic files containing works protected by copyright in respect of which the applicant claims to hold rights, and subsequently to block the transfer of such files. The second issue concerned the principle of proportionality (in the event that the first question was answered in the affirmative) and whether national courts are obliged to apply the principle when they deliver a ruling on an application for an injunction against an intermediary whose services are used by a third party to infringe copyright, and courts are called upon to decide on the effectiveness and dissuasive effect of the measure sought.

In the first case (*Scarlet*) the Court provided that the relevant EU Directives – if read together and construed in the light of the requirements stemming from the protection of the applicable fundamental rights – must be interpreted as precluding the making of an injunction against an internet service provider which requires it to instal a system to filter all electronic communications passing via its services (in particular, those involving the use of peer-to-peer

---

[29] Ibid., paras 42–45. See also Information Society Directive, Recital 59 and Art. 1(1).

[30] *Scarlet Extended SA v Société Belge des auteurs, compositeurs et éditeurs (SABAM)*, above note 13, 20.

[31] *Belgische Vereniging van Auteurs, Componisten en Uitgevers CVBA (Sabam) v Netlog NV*, above note 14, 18.

software), which (i) applies indiscriminately to all its customers, as a preventive measure, exclusively at its expense, and for an unlimited period; (ii) is capable of identifying on that provider's network the movement of electronic files containing a musical, cinematographic or audio-visual work in respect of which the applicant claims to hold intellectual property rights, with a view to blocking the transfer of files the sharing of which infringes copyright. The same outcome was reached in the *Netlog case*.

In the third case, *Bonnier Audio AB, Earbooks AB, Norstedts Förlagsgrupp AB, Piratförlaget AB, Storyside AB v Perfect Communication Sweden AB*,[32] the Court ruled that

> Directive 2006/24/EC [...] on the retention of data generated or processed in connection with the provision of publicly available electronic communications services or of public communications networks [...] must be interpreted as not precluding the application of national legislation based on Article 8 of Directive 2004/48/EC [...] on the enforcement of intellectual property rights which, in order to identify an internet subscriber or user, permits an internet service provider in civil proceedings to be ordered to give a copyright holder or its representative information on the subscriber to whom the internet service provider provided an IP address which was allegedly used in an infringement, since that legislation does not fall within the material scope of Directive 2006/24; It is irrelevant to the main proceedings that the Member State concerned has not yet transposed Directive 2006/24, despite the period for doing so having expired; Directives 2002/58/EC [...] concerning the processing of personal data and the protection of privacy in the electronic communications sector (Directive on privacy and electronic communications) and 2004/48 must be interpreted as not precluding national legislation [...] insofar as that legislation enables the national court seized of an application for an order for disclosure of personal data, made by a person who is entitled to act, to weigh the conflicting interests involved, on the basis of the facts of each case and taking due account of the requirements of the principle of proportionality.

2.5 The Opinion of the European Data Protection Supervisor

The Opinion of the European Data Protection Supervisor (EDPS) on the negotiations by the European Union of an Anti-Counterfeiting Trade Agreement (ACTA) also throws some light on the issues of interest.[33] This Opinion was produced on the EDPS's initiative; it is not binding on the Court. No particular issues were brought to the attention of the EDPS by the European Commission; it is rather a general (albeit structured) discussion of intellectual property rights enforcement in the digital environment.

---

[32] Case C461/10, 19 April 2012, [2012] ECR I-000 (nyr).

[33] EDPS/10/3 Brussels, 22 February 2010, [2010] OJ C147/1 (EDPS Opinion), available at: http://www.edps.europa.eu/EDPSWEB/webdav/site/mySite/shared/Documents/Consultation/Opinions/2010/10-02-22_ACTA_EN.pdf.

Some of its conclusions are very important for the purposes of this chapter: In the view of the EDPS, the monitoring of internet users' behaviour and further collection of their IP addresses amounts to an interference with their rights to respect for private life and correspondence; in other words, there is an interference with their right to private life. According to the EDPS, this view is in line with the case law of the European Court of Human Rights.[34] The EDPS considers IP addresses to be personal data,[35,36] on a par with traf-

---

[34] Ibid., para. 24. It also refers to the ECHR cases of 26 June 2006, *Weber and Saravia v Germany* (dec.), No. 54934/00, para. 77 and 1 July 2008, *Liberty and Others v United Kingdom*, No. 58243/00.

[35] EDPS Opinion, above note 33, paras 25 and 26: 'IP addresses are identifiers which look like a string of numbers separated by dots, such as 122.41.123.45. A subscription to an internet access provider will give the subscriber access to the internet. Every time the subscriber wishes to go onto the internet, he will be attributed an IP address through the device he is using to access the internet (a computer, for example). If a user engages in a given activity, for example, uploads material onto the internet, the user may be identified by third parties through the IP address he/she used. For example, the user holding IP address 122.41.123.45 uploaded allegedly copyright infringing material onto a P2P service at 3 PM on 1 January 2010. The ISP will then be able to connect such IP address to the name of the subscriber to whom it assigned this address and thus ascertain his/her identity'. See also ibid., footnotes 17 and 18: 'The IP address that the ISP attributes to an individual may always be the same for every time he surfs the internet (referred to as static IP addresses). Other IP addresses are dynamic, meaning that the internet access provider attributes a different IP address to its customers every time they connect to the internet. Obviously, the ISP can connect the IP address to the subscriber's account to whom they have assigned the (dynamic or static) IP address' and 'Recital 26 complements this definition: "Whereas the principles of protection must apply to any information concerning an identified or identifiable person; whereas, to determine whether a person is identifiable, account should be taken of all the means likely reasonably to be used either by the controller or by any other person to identify the said person; whereas the principles of protection shall not apply to data rendered anonymous in such a way that the data subject is no longer identifiable; ..."'. It also refers to the *Rundfunk* cases (in footnote 16): 'The Court of Justice takes a wide approach on the applicability of Directive 95/46, which provisions must be interpreted in the light of Article 8 ECHR. The Court of Justice stated in its judgment of 20 May 2003, *Rundfunk*, Joint Cases C-465/00, C-138/01 and C-139/01, ECR [2003], p. I-4989, para 68, that the "provisions of Directive 95/46, in so far as they govern the processing of personal data liable to infringe fundamental freedoms, in particular the right to privacy, must necessarily be interpreted in the light of fundamental rights, which, according to settled case-law, form an integral part of the general principles of law whose observance the Court ensures"'.

[36] Ibid., para 28 and footnote 19: see also the views by the Article 29 Working Party which, in a document on data protection issues related to intellectual property rights stated that IP addresses collected to enforce intellectual property rights, i.e., to identify internet users who are alleged to have infringed intellectual property rights, are personal data insofar as they are used for the enforcement of such rights against a given individual: Article 29 Working Party, Working Document on data protection issues

fic and communication data.[37,38] Any measure that is to be taken should be assessed against the principle of necessity.[39]

In addition, the EDPS does not preclude instances where monitoring of personal data should be available, although this should concern only a limited number of individuals suspected of engaging in non-trivial copyright infringement.[40,41] The data processing operations aimed at gathering evidence for

---

related to intellectual property rights, WP 104, adopted on 18 January 2005. This Working Party was set up under Article 29 of Directive 95/46. It is an independent European advisory body on data protection and privacy. Its tasks are described in Art. 30 of Directive 95/46 and Art. 15 of Directive 2002/58. See also the Working Party's Opinion 4/2007 on the concept of personal data (WP 136), adopted on 20 June 2007, notably at p. 16–17).

[37] EDPS Opinion, above note 33, para. 29: 'Directive 2002/58 is applicable as well, as three strikes internet disconnection policies entail the collection of traffic and communication data. Directive 2002/58 regulates the use of such data and provides for the principle of confidentiality of communications made over public communications networks and of the data inherent in those communications'.

[38] The Data Retention Directive 2006/24/EC27 requires traffic data to be retained for the purpose of combating serious crime. It has to be noted that retention is only allowed for 'serious crime', that the retention is limited to 'traffic data', which in principle excludes information about the content of communications, and that stringent guarantees are adduced. Nevertheless, doubts have been raised on its compatibility with fundamental rights standards; the Romanian Constitutional Court decided that blanket retention is incompatible with fundamental rights (para. 35 and notes 28 and 29): see http://www.legi-internet.ro/english/jurisprudenta-it-romania/decizii-it/romanian-constitutional-court-decision-regarding-data-retention.html. There is currently a case pending before the German Constitutional Court: see http://www.bundesverfassungsgericht.de/pressemitteilungen/bvg09-124.html.

[39] EDPS Opinion, above note 33, para. 30, footnotes 20–22: 'Article 8 ECHR sets forth the principle of necessity pursuant to which any measure that infringes the right to privacy of individuals is only allowed if it constitutes a necessary measure within a democratic society to the legitimate aim it pursues. The principle of necessity can also be found in Articles 7 and 13 of Directive 95/46 and Article 15 of Directive 2002/58. The principle requires an analysis of the proportionality of the measure, which must be assessed on the basis of a balance of the interests involved, which is placed in the context of the democratic society as a whole. It furthermore implies an assessment as to whether alternative measures exist which are less intrusive'.

[40] Ibid., para. 43: 'The IPRE [2004/48/EC of 28 April 2004 on the enforcement of intellectual property rights] Directive provides some guidance in that respect. It sets forth the conditions under which authorities may order that personal data held by internet access providers be disclosed for the purposes of enforcing intellectual property rights. Article 8 provides that ISPs may be ordered by competent judicial authorities to provide personal information that they hold about alleged infringers (e.g., information on the origin and distribution networks of the goods or services which infringe an intellectual property right) in response to a justified and proportionate request in cases of infringements on a "commercial scale"'.

[41] Ibid., para. 45: 'In practice, to make the above effective, copyright holders

alleged copyright infringement should – as an additional guarantee – be checked and authorized by national data protection authorities beforehand.[42,43]

It is evident that the EDPS takes a clear stance which favours privacy over intellectual property protection.[44]

---

might engage in targeted monitoring of certain IP addresses in order to verify the scale of the copyright violation. This would mean that copyright holders would also be allowed to keep track of reports alleging infringement for the same purposes. Such information should only be used after having verified the significance of the infringement. For example, clear cases of major infringements as well as non-significant yet continuous infringements, over a certain period of time, for the purpose of commercial advantage or financial gain'; ibid., para. 46: '... for the purposes of preparing legal proceedings, including litigation'.

42 Ibid., para. 47: 'These views are based on the fact that the data processing operations would present specific risks to the rights and freedoms of individuals in the light of their purposes, i.e., carrying out enforcement actions which could eventually be criminal and in the light of the sensitive nature of the data collected. The fact that the processing involves monitoring of electronic communications is an additional factor that calls for enhanced supervision.

See also para. 52 where the EDPS refers to 'the Article 29 Working Party document mentioned before, which discusses the issue of processing judicial data. The Working Party states that "While any individual obviously has the right to process judicial data in the process of his/her own litigation, the principle does not go as far as permitting in depth investigation, collection and centralisation of personal data by third parties, including in particular, systematic research on a general scale such as the scanning of the internet (...). Such investigation falls within the competence of judicial authorities'. While the collection of targeted, specific evidence, particularly in cases of serious infringements may be necessary to establish and exercise a legal claim, the EDPS fully shares the views of the Article 29 Working Party on the lack of legitimacy of wide scale investigations involving the processing of massive amounts of data of internet users'.

See also ibid., para 85: 'The EDPS takes the view that three strikes internet disconnection policies are not necessary to achieve the purpose of enforcing intellectual property rights. The EDPS is convinced that alternative, less intrusive solutions exist or, at least, that the envisaged policies can be performed in a less intrusive manner or at a more limited scope, notably through the form of targeted ad hoc monitoring'.

43 Other issues are also examined, such as whether the processing carried out by copyright holders by inserting clauses in their customers' contracts allowing the monitoring of their data and the suspension of their access, could be legitimized; the legal difficulties of retaining log files for reasons other than those provided in the 2002/58 Directive; and whether, in case the three strike internet disconnection policies are allowed, they could be a slippery slope towards legitimizing even more massive surveillance of internet users' activities, in different areas and for different purposes. However, these issues are not directly relevant to this chapter.

44 EDPS Opinion, above note 32, para. 83: 'While intellectual property is important to society and must be protected, it should not be placed above individuals' fundamental rights to privacy, data protection, and other rights such as presumption of innocence, effective judicial protection and freedom of expression'. Paragraph 85 is

2.6 National Experiences

In Italy, in *Peppermint Jam v Telecom Italia*,[45] the Italian Court stated that personal data could be acquired without the consent of the rightholder if it was needed to trace a copyright infringement. At that stage no data protection law existed in Italy. However, in a later judgment the Court of Rome[46] decided that identity disclosure requests were unacceptable because of the protection afforded to the secrecy of electronic communications between private parties, which constituted a fundamental right granted by the Italian Constitution.[47]

In the Netherlands, in the *Lycos/Pessers* case,[48] the Dutch Supreme Court ruled that Dutch privacy law does not necessarily prohibit the disclosure of personal data by ISPs to third parties, and whether or not such disclosure is allowed depends on the specific circumstances of the case.

The same approach was followed in *BREIN v UPC/Chello*,[49] in which the Dutch Court decided that an ISP may be obliged to provide the information required by the rightholders in order for them to protect their rights. Nevertheless, it has to be convinced that the copyright infringement has indeed been committed and that the information required relates to the internet users who have committed the infringing acts. In this case copyright protection overrides privacy.

---

also interesting where EDPS takes the view that 'The EDPS takes the view that three strikes internet disconnection policies are not necessary to achieve the purpose of enforcing intellectual property rights. The EDPS is convinced that alternative, less intrusive solutions exist or, at least, that the envisaged policies can be performed in a less intrusive manner or at a more limited scope, notably through the form of targeted ad hoc monitoring'.

[45] See E. Prosperetti, 'The Peppermint "Jam": Peer to Peer Goes to Court in Italy' (2007) *Entertainment Law Review* 280.

[46] *ZO.O. e Peppermint Jam Records GmbH contro Wind Telecomunicazioni SpA,* Tribunale di Roma, Sezione IX civile, ordinanza del 14 luglio 2007 Giudice Costa.

[47] The Italian case of *Mediaset v Google and YouTube* (initiated in 2008 and which has not yet been concluded) should also be of interest. In this case the Italian television network Mediaset sued Google and YouTube for €500 million in damages before the Court of Rome for the illicit use of 4,000 audiovisual clips. Mediaset is also claiming damages for lost advertising revenue for slots in television programmes available on YouTube which were its own property. YouTube has also been sued by Viacom in the US and Telecinco in Spain (the Spanish broadcaster of which Mediaset is the largest shareholder). All cases are ongoing. See http://www. internationallawoffice.com/Newsletters/Detail.aspx?g=cf851402-caac-4eb8-bfb7-0f2facea117f .

[48] Hoge Raad, 25 November 2005, LJN:AU 4019.

[49] Interlocutory Court, Amsterdam, 345291 / KG 06-1112 AB, 24 August 2006.

In *BREIN v Leaseweb*,[50] the ISP Leaseweb was hosting a site ('www.everlasting.nu') that distributed copyrighted material without the rightholders' permission. The Dutch not-for-profit foundation (BREIN) that combats piracy on behalf of holders of copyrights and related rights filed for an interim injunction against Leaseweb, which refused to make the website inaccessible to the public and to disclose to BREIN the contact details of the website owner. The district court ruled in favour of BREIN, finding that this information had to be disclosed because BREIN's interest in disclosure was extensive and more important than the interest of the website owner in preventing his identity from being revealed. This decision was taken on the basis that there was no other way for BREIN to obtain the website owner's contact details other than through the hosting provider, Leaseweb.

In the UK, in a case involving the posting of defamatory material on a website operator's discussion board, *Totalise Plc v Motley Fool Ltd*,[51] the House of Lords held that website operators should disclose the identity of infringers.[52]

In France, following the decision in *SCPP v Anthony G*,[53] a number of authors' and producers' associations applied for permission to CNIL (the French Data Protection Office) to collect the private records of infringers. This application was rejected by CNIL but that decision was later overruled by the Conseil d'Etat on the grounds that providing such information was not disproportionate, given that it was sought only for certain users and given the extent of the piracy problem in France.

---

50 11 September 2008; see http://www.internationallawoffice.com/Newsletters/Detail.aspx?g=c5012adf-9275-4979-817b-7867b886f5a2.

51 [2001] EWCA Civ 1897.

52 On 15 January 2010, again in the UK, the Teesside Crown Court found the Oink website's creator and administrator not guilty of conspiracy to defraud (the offence is committed where two or more people conspire to defraud a victim, so that the victim is deprived of something which is his or hers, or to which he or she is entitled) because he had no money-making motive and the donations he received (£5 from each member) were used to pay rent on the server and eventually to buy a server of his own. His website (with over 200,000 members) did not host music files. It was used to link its members, using torrent software, with a view to sharing their music files. This case tested the criminal side of the matter only. It could also have been brought under section 16(2) of the Copyright, Designs and Patents Act 1988, which provides for a lower burden of proof to establish liability than the 'beyond reasonable doubt' standard in criminal proceedings. See http://www.internationallawoffice.com/Newsletters/Detail.aspx?g=5e4570ac-fe57-46c9-a453-e06a7ff049a4.

53 See Paris Appeal Court decision – *Anthony G. v SCPP* (27 April 2007), available at: http://www.legalis.net/jurisprudence-decision.php3?id_article=1954. See also Paris Appeal Court decision – *Henri S. vs. SCPP* (15 May 2007), available at: http://www.legalis.net/jurisprudence-decision.php3?id_article=1955. See also http://www.edri.org/edrigram/number5.17/ip-personal-data-fr.

In Sweden, in December 2009, the Svea Court of Appeal reversed a district court's decision in the first Swedish case (1 April 2009) involving the Enforcement Directive (2004/38/EC). The district court had previously ordered internet service provider ePhone to provide information to five book publishers regarding the identity of the individual behind a specific internet protocol (IP) address. According to the publishers, the IP address in question had been used for the illegal distribution of 27 audio books over the internet. The appeal court ruled that ePhone should not be obliged to hand over the requested information since no conclusions could be drawn regarding the size of the circle of people with access to the files or regarding the purpose, character or terms of admission to this circle. In fact, it concluded that under these circumstances it should be assumed that the audio books on the server had been made available only to a closed circle of people, and not to the public, and therefore the publishers had not shown probable cause that copyright infringement had been committed.[54]

In Austria, on 14 July 2009, the Supreme Court rejected an Australian collecting society's request to an Austrian ISP to disclose the identity of certain users on the basis of dynamic IP addresses. These users were allegedly culpable of illegal file sharing of copyrighted content. Its decision was based on the fact that Austrian law did not expressly provide for the storage and processing of traffic data with a view to investigate intellectual property infringements.[55]

In Greece, three Opinions of Attorneys General have proved to be very useful for identifying copyright infringers on the internet. Attorney General to the Greek Supreme Court, Georgios Sanidas, delivered Opinion 8/2009 on 29 June 2009 (which was later affirmed by the Opinions of the Attorneys General to the Greek Supreme Court (Ioanni Tente, Opinion 12/2009, 29 September 2009 and Athanassio Katsirodi, Opinion 9/2011, 10 May 2011). This Opinion concerned the ability of the attorney general, the courts and the police under Greek law to request ISPs to disclose data to allow them to identify persons engaging in illegal activities on the internet. According to this Opinion, secrecy of communications applies to those cases only where the parties intended to keep the content of their communication secret and have taken measures to this end (for example, by creating a restricted area on the internet where the two or more communicating parties need to use passwords in order to access it). Secrecy of communications does not cover the situation where a crime is committed and its elements are made public through being posted on

---

54 See http://www.internationallawoffice.com/Newsletters/Detail.aspx?g=5dc41d17-2fb1-4a94-bde4-42b2e6533882.

55 See http://www.internationallawoffice.com/directory/biography.aspx?g=168f6261-58b1-478f-8efa-0See708b3fa79.

a site (such elements may be a defamatory statement, photographs containing scenes of child abuse, and so on). Secrecy of communications also does not cover the external elements of communication (for example, details of the sender and the recipient such as names and subscribers' details, phone numbers, time and date of calls, duration of calls and so on).[56]

Apart from these national cases[57] there has been soft law and legislative activity in many countries, the most notorious of them being the French HADOPI law. This provides for a graduated punishment mechanism for alleged copyright infringements on the internet. Other countries have also enacted legislation or administrative procedures in order to combat internet-based copyright infringement; these include the US,[58] the UK,[59] South Korea,[60] Sweden,[61] Germany,[62] the Netherlands,[63] Italy,[64] Spain,[65] New Zealand,[66] Japan,[67] China[68] and Taiwan.[69]

---

56 For the text of the Opinions in Greek, see http://www.opi.gr. On 16 May 2012 a judgment (No. 4658) was delivered by the Athens Court of First Instance on the basis of a filing for an injunction by a number of collecting societies against the largest Greek ISPs asking them to block particular sites that were offering pirated material. The judgment held in favour of the rightholders.

57 More information can be found on the Hellenic Copyright Organization's website at http:// www.opi.gr.

58 The Digital Millennium Copyright Act (DMCA). Of interest also are the older cases such as *A&M Records v Napster*, 239 F.3d 1004 (9th Cir. 2001) and *MGM v Grokster*, 514 U.S. 913 (2005) in respect of software used for file sharing.

59 See the Digital Economy Act 2010, available at http://www.legislation.gov.uk/ukpga/2010/24/contents.

60 The National Assembly's Committee on Culture, Sports, Tourism, Broadcasting and Communications passed a bill on 1 April 2009 revising its Copyright Law. According to this bill, message boards which allow users to post illegal content may be shut down for up to six months if they fail to clamp down on piracy after two warnings; and users who upload infringing content may also have their internet accounts cancelled. See http://www.ipworld.com/ipwo/doc/view.htm?id=217097&searchCode=H

61 On 1 April 2009, a new law was adopted in Sweden, based on the EU Enforcement Directive. This law allows copyright holders to obtain a court order forcing ISPs to provide the IP addresses identifying which computers have been sharing copyrighted material. See http://news.bbc.co.uk/2/hi/technology/7978853.stm.

62 German legislation was passed in the German Parliament on 18 June 2009. This legislation obliges ISPs to filter websites allegedly containing child abuse material. The secret filtering list is compiled by the German Federal Police and transmitted to ISPs once a day with occasional checks by a five-member monitoring body.

63 The Netherlands has designed a 'Notice-and-Take-Down Code of Conduct', which provides for the role of ISPs in the event of being offered illegal content.

64 On 26 January 2010 the Italian government proposed legislation on the basis of which ISPs are responsible for their audiovisual content and copyright infringements by users.

[65] On 8 January 2010 the Spanish government passed the Law for Sustainable Economy. This law provides, amongst other issues, for the creation of an Intellectual Property Commission (IPC) that, together with a judge, will deal with complaints concerning alleged illegal downloading. This law will give the authorities the power to shut down file-sharing sites within a few days from the date on which the complaint is filed with IPC. The court is to decide within four days from that date whether a certain site is infringing the law or not. See http://www.edri.org/edrigram/number8.1/spain-law-file-sharing.

[66] See the Copyright (Infringing File Sharing) Amendment Act 2011 (for more details see http://www.legislation.govt.nz/act/public/2008/0027/latest/DLM1122643.html), according to which rightholders will be able to report instances of violations of their rights to website owners though ISPs. In addition ISPs will be enabled to take down protected material for which there is no authorization and block access to the internet for up to six months.

[67] Japan has passed new copyright laws which, amongst other matters, also deal with illegal downloading, the sale of pirated materials and storage of documents on search engines. Under the new laws it is now illegal to download copyright-infringing content without it being made a crime; see http://cdnf.tlcollect.com/f1/cl/009/7117/IP%20News%202%20July.pdf.

[68] China uses a system that is equivalent to the US DMCA and its safe harbour provisions, basing it on tort liability. (In fact, the liability of ISPs is derived from the Supreme People's Court Interpretations of Application of the Law in the Trial of Disputes over internet, and from an administrative rule, the Ordinance on the Protection of the Right to Network Dissemination of Information.) According to this, where an internet user takes advantage of online services to carry out infringing activities, the rightholder has the right to require the service provider to remove, block or disable access to infringing material upon notification. If the service provider fails to take necessary measures immediately following receipt of such notification, it will be liable jointly and severally with the user for any extended damage. In addition, if the service provider is aware of the user's infringing behaviour through its online services, but fails to take any necessary countermeasures, it shall be liable jointly and severally with the user. The administrative law (Art. 36 of the Ordinance) also provides for (a) general infringing acts, i.e. cases where the internet user and the ISP are directly responsible for infringement, (b) cases where the ISP bears liability for infringing acts by a user of its online services where the rightholder informs the ISP of the infringing activities that it has identified, but the ISP takes no action to remove the infringing material, and (c) clarifies a key requirement: evidence that the ISP knew of the user's infringements independently of the rightholder's notification, and that its failure to take corrective measures resulted in greater harm. In the second and third instances, the ISP is jointly and severally liable with the infringing internet user by virtue of its knowledge of the infringing activity, regardless of the rights owner's notification. See http://www.internationallawoffice.com/Newsletters/Detail.aspx?g=928a447d-5ca0-4836-8e1c-8bd8a13d0c71&utm_source=ILO+Newsletter&utm_medium=email&utm_ campaign=Intellectual+Property+Newsletter&utm_content=Newsletter+2010-03-15.

[69] The Taiwanese Copyright Act (of November 2009) includes provisions which require ISPs to give rights owners a platform on which to report infringements equivalent to the US DMCA, which provides for procedures of notification and withdrawal of illegal content on the internet. See http://www.cisac.com/CisacPortal/listeArticle.do?numArticle=1269&method=afficherArticleInPortlet.

3. CONCLUSIONS

From the above it can be assumed that the ACTA provisions concerning internet service providers and the disclosure of data relating to their subscribers do not contradict in essence the *acquis communautaire*. They present some additional elements but these elements form more of an interpretation of where the trend within the EU stands rather than a change to this trend or the legal fundamentals on which this trend is based. And the trend is towards the effective protection of intellectual property rights on the internet. If that was not the case the HADOPI solution would not have been 'legitimized' recently through the EU Telecom Package, opening the way to other national initiatives with equivalent effect.

However, the crucial question which arises here is whether ACTA is capable of solving the issue of internet piracy. The answer to this question largely depends on the use that will be made of ACTA. ACTA will by no means change anything in EU law concerning internet piracy as this law stands today. If Member States wanted to adopt more effective provisions in their national laws they could still do that on the basis of the existing EU law. If we also take into account that there is an increased probability that the Enforcement or the E-commerce Directives are updated to accommodate those needs, it becomes clear that ACTA has nothing to add to that.

Yet, the aim of ACTA was to raise the standards of IP protection in developing countries. It reflects the general tendency lobbied by the big economies in favour of the protection of intellectual property rights. Still, however, it will be up to those countries to decide whether or not to implement the particular provisions and, even if they choose to implement them, it depends on how effectively they will do so. In other words, it is more a matter of political will and less a matter of legal provision. From this point of view, there is always the fear that ACTA may prove to be meaningless if it is ever adopted by the EU.

On top of everything the problem of internet piracy cannot be solved solely through the vehicle of law. First, new business models are required, which will allow consumers, first and foremost, to find the content they are looking for on legal platforms. If they cannot find it, they will download it illegally. Second, they need to find it easily and at affordable prices. This means that rightholders have to work thoroughly towards this direction to create new business models, involving in these models ISPs too. If ISPs gain from the distribution of legal content, it will be to their benefit to work together with rightholders to prevent large-scale infringements on the internet. If there are no alternatives or no viable alternatives on the market, law alone cannot be effective.

11. ACTA and access to medicines in the perspective of theory of hard cases

Maciej Barczewski and Sebastian Sykuna

Every year about fourteen million people die from contagious diseases, three million die as a result of complications connected with AIDS, almost two million die from tuberculosis and over one million from malaria. Malaria and tuberculosis can be cured using appropriate pharmaceuticals, while proper antiretroviral therapy (ARV) makes the lives of those infected with human immunodeficiency virus (HIV) similar to their condition prior to the onset of the disease. The high fatality rate of those illnesses results from the fact that the definite majority of patients are not treated effectively. One of the main reasons for this is the high price of drugs fixed by the pharmaceutical industry, which owns the exclusive rights to produce medicines.[1]

It is a cliché to say that increased accessibility to medication could contribute considerably to a reduction in fatal diseases in countries where medicines are unavailable for most of the sick because of either their high price or the lack of interest in their distribution by the pharmaceutical industry. However, in recent years these issues have become the subject of academic debate and literature.[2] Undoubtedly, the key event which led to this situation was the conclusion of the TRIPS Agreement, which provided a strong impetus for legal protection of pharmaceuticals in many countries, but at the same time it raised numerous objections, mostly from the developing states, with

---

[1] M. Barczewski, 'Prawo kontra medycyna', in Jerzy Zajadlo (ed.), Fascynujące ścieżki filozofii prawa (LexisNexis 2008) 145.

[2] See, e.g., K. Gamharter, *Access to Affordable Medicines: Developing Responses under the TRIPS Agreement and EC Law* (Springer 2004); P. Roffe, G. Tansey and D. Vivas-Eugui (eds), *Negotiating Health: Intellectual Property and Access to Medicines* (Earthscan 2006); H. Hestermeyer, *Human Rights and the WTO: The Case of Patents and Access to Medicines* (Oxford University Press 2007); A. Law, *Patents and Public Health* (Nomos-MIPLC 2008); J. Kuanpoth, *Patent Rights in Pharmaceuticals in Developing Countries* (Edward Elgar 2010); F. Abbott and G. Dukes, *Global Pharmaceutical Policy* (Edward Elgar 2009); C.M. Ho, *Access to Medicine in the Global Economy* (Oxford University Press 2011); K.C. Shadlen, G.A. Guzman Chavez, S. Guennif and L. Narayanan (eds), *Intellectual Property, Pharmaceuticals and Public Health* (Edward Elgar 2011).

regard to impediments to access to medicines by those from the poorest states. Thus, as a consequence of the Doha Declaration adopted on 14 November 2001, states have obtained a more flexible interpretation and implementation of the provisions of the TRIPS Agreement that support their right to health protection and improved access to essential medicines. In spite of subsequent concessions in favour of developing countries – resulting from the decision of the TRIPS Council on 30 August 2003 and further modification of the contents of the TRIPS Agreement in the form of a new Article 31 bis – the representatives of the industrialized countries, the United States in particular, wanted more effective enforcement of intellectual property rights, without any concessions for the benefit of developing countries permissible within the World Trade Organization (WTO) system.

However, the need to draw up a new treaty was formally indicated initially not by the US but by Japan in July 2005 during the Group of Eight meeting in Scotland. Japan subsequently presented the proposal to elaborate the so-called Treaty on Non-Proliferation of Counterfeits and Pirated Goods during the Second Global Congress on Combating Counterfeiting and Piracy organized by INTERPOL and the World Customs Organization (WCO) on 14–15 November 2005 in France.[3] The proposal for working out this treaty was repeated by Japan during subsequent congresses dealing with combating piracy and counterfeit goods, which took place in Brussels in 2007 and Geneva in 2008. The idea was approved by the United States, which announced on 23 October 2007 its intention to conclude the Anti-Counterfeiting Trade Agreement (ACTA) with its chief partners, which included Japan and the European Union. As a consequence, formal negotiations involving 11 rounds of discussions started in June 2008 and were concluded in October 2010. The final version of ACTA was adopted on 15 April 2011[4] and is open for signature by the states that participated in the negotiations[5] until 1 May 2013.

In view of the fact that one of the fundamental aims of ACTA, as indicated in its Preamble, was preventing the proliferation of counterfeit goods, the influence of the regulations resulting from this agreement on access to medicines became crucial, particularly when concessions resulting from the Doha

---

3 T.I.S. Gerharden, 'Japan Proposes New IP Enforcement Treaty', Intellectual Property Watch, 15 November 2005, available at: http://www.ip-watch.org/weblog/2005/11/15/japan-proposes-new-ip-enforcement-treaty (accessed 17 November 2011).

4 'Anti-Counterfeiting Trade Agreement', available at: http://www.trade.ec.europa.eu/doclib/docs/2011/may/tradoc_147937.pdf (accessed 17 November 2011).

5 The following parties participated: Australia, Canada, Japan, Republic of Korea, Mexico, Morocco, New Zealand, Singapore, Switzerland, the United States and the European Union.

Round for the benefit of developing countries are taken into consideration. It should be noted that counterfeit medicines constitute 10 per cent of the world's pharmaceuticals trade;[6] on the other hand, it can happen that generics legally produced in one state may be regarded as infringing intellectual property rights in another state.

The most illustrative example of this can be seen in the complications that arose from the transport of generics from India and Brazil to Africa and South America. In 2008 and 2009 deliveries of these medications were retained in Dutch ports during transit on the basis of Council Regulation (EC) No. 1383/2003 of 22 July 2003;[7] customs authorities assumed that these medicinal products were produced in the Netherlands and infringed intellectual property rights. As a consequence, India and Brazil requested WTO consultations with the European Union and the Netherlands regarding repeated seizures, on the ground of patent infringement, of generic drugs transiting through ports and airports in the Netherlands.[8] India and Brazil argued that the Anti-Counterfeiting Trade Agreement, by exceeding the standards embodied in the TRIPS Agreement, undermines the basic principles of the WTO system and disrupts the balance between intellectual property protection and the needs of developing countries.[9]

The draft versions of ACTA contained provisions similar to those in EU Regulation No. 1383/2003, which made it possible to seize goods in transit based on suspicion or an allegation of patent protection infringement. But, under the influence of the opinion that such regulations significantly limit access to inexpensive medicines for citizens of the poorest countries, the issues of patent protection infringement and the protection of undisclosed information were explicitly excluded from the section on border measures.[10] However, ACTA (Article 3) permits the application of these measures with regard to other categories of intellectual property right and, as a consequence,

---

6 'The Anti-Counterfeiting Trade Agreement (ACTA) Fact sheet', 5, available at: http://trade.ec.europa.eu/doclib/docs/2009/january/tradoc_142039.pdf (accessed 17 November 2011).

7 Council Regulation (EC) No. 1383/2003 of 22 July 2003 concerning customs action against goods suspected of infringing certain intellectual property rights and the measures to be taken against goods found to have infringed such rights', [2008] OJ L 196/7, 2 August 2008, 469–76.

8 *India – EU, the Netherlands* (DS408), available at: http://www.wto.org/english/tratop_e/dispu_e/cases_e/ds408_e.htm (accessed 17 November 2011); *Brazil – EU, the Netherlands* (DS409), available at: http://www.wto.org/english/tratop_e/dispu_e/cases_e/ds409_e.htm (accessed 17 November 2011).

9 OUT-LAW.COM, 'ACTA Restricts Developing Economies, India tells WTO', The A-Register, 15 June 2010, available at: http://www.theregister.co.uk/2010/06/15/acta_wto/ (accessed 17 November 2011).

10 See above note 6.

to all types of trademark infringement. Thus, there is a danger that right holders could take advantage of customs measures to delay competitive deliveries of pharmaceuticals based on the allegation of similarity of marks,[11] which may impede the international transit of such products.[12]

Therefore, finding an infringement of rights to a given trademark requires many factors to be taken into consideration, the assessment of which exceeds the competence of customs authorities.[13] The lack of appropriate qualification for such an assessment may become the reason for unjustified obstruction in the transit of medication – in May 2009, for example, the local customs authorities in Frankfurt detained the delivery of amoxicillin (a generic antibiotic) in transit from India to Vanuatu, a state classified among the least developed countries. The shipment was detained on suspicion of infringement of the rights to the 'Amoxil' trademark exercised by GlaxoSmithKline. The delivery was eventually released four weeks later when the company announced that the marking 'amoxicillin' does not infringe its rights, as it is an International Nonproprietary Name (INN) that indicates the active ingredient of the product.[14]

Taking into account the regulations, as well as the provisions referring to third party liability, there are fears that accessibility of medical products will nevertheless be limited and, as a consequence, the implementation of the ACTA standards and any future treaties relating to this agreement may reduce the opportunities for providing treatment for the poorest. In this context the dilemma of law versus health, or rather law versus life, represents an example of what in the theory and philosophy of law is defined as the 'hard case'. The concept of the hard case is connected with complex matters that outrage public

---

[11] Medecins Sans Frontières, 'The Secret Treaty: Anti-Counterfeiting Trade Agreement (ACTA) and its Impact on Access to Medicines', MSF Campaign for Access to Essential Medicines, October 2010, 2, available at: http://www. msfaccess.org/sites/default/files/MSF_assets/Access/Docs/ACCESS_briefing_ACTA_ENG_2010.pdf (accessed 17 November 2011.

[12] In-depth analysis of ACTA in this respect has been carried out by H. Grosse Ruse-Khan, 'A Trade Agreement Creating Barriers to International Trade?: ACTA Border Measures and Goods in Transit' (2011) 26(3) *American University International Law Review* 546–726.

[13] P. Maybarduk, 'ACTA and Public Health', PIJIP Research Paper No. 9, September 2010, 9, American University Washington College of Law, Washington DC, available at: http://digitalcommons.wcl.american.edu/research/9/.

[14] Health Action International, 'Another Seizure of Generic Medicines Destined for a Developing Country, This Time in Frankfurt', 5 June 2009, available at: http://www.haiweb.org/19062009/5%20Jun%202009%20Press%20release%20Seizure%20of%20generic%20medicines%20in%20Frankfurt.pdf (accessed 17 November 2011).

opinion and are of a notorious character.[15] On the other hand, the interest in the concept shown by contemporary theory and the philosophy of law should be emphasized. The theory of hard cases has been dominant for many years; it derives from Anglo-Saxon legal culture and is connected mainly with the integral philosophy of law of Ronald Dworkin.[16] The first of such cases, although not referred to as 'hard cases', appeared in the positivism of John Austin, and later in the sophisticated version proposed by Herbert L.A. Hart.

Dworkin's concept was based on extensive criticism of positivism in general, and of Hart's views in particular. Nevertheless, according to both authors, hard cases appear where law is to be applied. In short, for both philosophers hard cases are situations within the applied law,[17] when we deal with matters for which there is no single correct solution. It can be assumed that the extraordinarity of the case appears in the fact that the authority administering the law has some possible solutions in issuing the final decision, all of which are correct. From another perspective, based on the peculiar *filosofia negativa,* certain criteria may be distinguished when we question the difficult character of a given case. Referring to Bix, the ability to reach a solution quickly should be indicated, together with its certainty – incontrovertibility.[18] Thus, if a conclusive decision can be made quickly when the issue first arises, and it will be upheld – by a higher court, for example – the matter cannot be regarded as a hard case.

Although detailed analysis of traditional concepts of the hard case is not the purpose of this chapter, the views of Herbert L.A. Hart and Ronald Dworkin should be presented. Additionally, for comparative purposes, we should discuss our attitude to the analysed problem. Moreover, in our opinion, the

---

[15] The typical example is proceedings against genocide. See S. Landsman, *Crimes of the Holocaust: The Law Confronts Hard Cases* (Pennsylvania University Press 2005), in which the author describes and analyses the Nuremberg Trial and the renowned cases of Adolf Eichmann, John Demianiuk and Imre Finty. See also, in a different context, D.E. Lee, *Freedom vs. Intervention: Six Tough Cases, Six Hard Cases* (Rowman & Littlefield 2005). For aspects of the use of this notion, see D. Dyzenhaus, *Hard Cases in Wicked Legal Systems: South African Law in the Perspective of Legal Philosophy* (Clarendon Press 1991); L.A. Kloppenberg, *Playing It Safe: How the Supreme Court Sidesteps Hard Cases and Stunts the Development of Law* (New York University Press 2002).

[16] R. Wacks, *Philosophy of Law: A Very Short Introduction* (Oxford University Press 2006) 42 et seq.

[17] B. Wojciechowski, 'Rozstrzyganie tzw. trudnych przypadków poprzez odwolanie się do odpowiedzialności moralnej' (2004) 70 *Studia Prawno-Ekonomiczne* 11; S. Sykuna, 'Trudne przypadki', in Jerzy Zajadlo (ed.), *Leksykon współczesnej teorii i filozofii prawa* (C.H. Beck 2007) 339–40.

[18] B.H. Bix, *A Dictionary of Legal Theory* (Oxford University Press 2004) 81 et seq.

issue of access to medicines cannot be regarded as novel from the point of view of the theory and philosophy of law. In this case, therefore, we encounter conflict of law and morality on the one hand, and conflict of law with law on the other, for this is how we perceive the relationships that arise when the right to life and the right to property collide.

Hart, regarded as the creator of soft positivism, indicated that the system of law consists exclusively of rules. Although it sounds paradoxical, because of his open-texture notions, he looked for solving difficult cases by going beyond the legal system. As it is easy to guess, on the grounds of legal positivism this caused some difficulty, which resulted from the possible rule-making character of the court decision. As a result of the open texture, the judge acquires 'rule-making validity' which allows him or her to issue the ruling while going beyond the legal system.

Dworkin takes up the opposite position. According to Dworkin, in the system of law there are not only rules but also principles and policies. Rules are easily recognizable norms of proceedings, which are applied in the 'all or nothing' fashion. This means that when the circumstances indicated by the rule are fulfilled, then it is either valid and produces acceptance of the resulting solution or it is not, and there is then no influence on the decision of the adjudicating body. When there is a contradiction between the two rules, one of them has to be regarded as invalid by the application of conflicting rules. However, principles can be carried out to varying degrees which, in the event of a contradiction between them, does not cause invalidity. This is so because principles are equipped with the attribute of weight or importance. In the case of conflict between two principles, it comes to weighing, and not eliminating. Principles should be obeyed because of the requirement of justice, honesty or other aspect of morality. Moreover, their role is more to indicate a certain direction in the argument than forcing specific decisions. As indicated by Dworkin the final element in his system of law is made up of policies: they indicate the aim that is to be attained, and are most often connected with development or the political, social or economic protection of the community.

The judge who has no explicit regulation as a rule does not have to go beyond the system of law, as proposed by Hart. Just the opposite: the judge should look for the solution within the system on the grounds of principles and/or guidelines. According to the assumptions of positivism, the judge making a decision in hard cases is obliged to follow legal rules. In this way the judge is bound up with a set of rules which cannot be omitted and is thus looking for an optimal solution rather than a general one, but optimal in the given circumstances. According to Dworkin, who was in favour of the integral philosophy of law, this was insufficient or even incorrect. The legal rule may appear to be unsatisfactory in order to issue the right decision. Hart equips the judge with competence to issue the decision 'freely' in such a situation, while Dworkin proposes to remain within the system of law and demands reference to legal rules. He is of the opinion that the judicial solution of hard cases cannot consist of creating new legal rules. It is necessary to bring out latent standards in the form of principles and guidelines from the legal system.

Regardless of the differences between the two philosophers, they recognize the essence of hard cases by connecting them with the application, or the interpretation of law. Therefore, referring to this phenomenon of law (which, in our view, concerns its five dimensions) the attitudes of Hart and Dworkin to hard cases should be regarded as narrow or classic. Applying the broad approach, which has recently been presented in the literature,[19] it should be assumed that hard cases appear not only in the circumstances indicated by Hart and Dworkin, but can also refer to other 'dimensions' of the phenomenon of law – namely its creation, its binding force and requirement for respect. Thus, a hard case in this sense is not always reserved for the judge seeking a solution in a particular case, where there is no clear rule available. Similar problems may be encountered by the legislator who decides to introduce a regulation or to refrain from regulating specific social relations, or an individual who decides to refer to an institution of civil disobedience.[20] Furthermore, as is assumed by the proponents of the broad approach to hard cases, it is necessary to abandon the absolute acceptance of the above thesis of the necessity of argumentation in direct relation with the law in force because it narrows the notion of the hard case, as it refers only to the application of the law and its interpretation.[21] Regardless of such an opinion, however, the existence of the direct connection with the law will actually occur in the process of legal discourse. However, the extension of hard cases to, for instance, the lawmaking process can make this relation no longer necessary. It happens that the legislator is faced with the decision, which has no direct relationship with the law, as it enters *terra incognita*. At the same time, the lack of the necessary character of this relation does not determine the loss of the name of legal discourse by the practical discourse, and shifting it to the ethical discourse. In addition, supporters of the broad view of the hard case recognize that they occur primarily where there is

---

19 S. Sykuna and J. Zajadlo 'The Theory of Hard Cases and Humanitarian Intervention' (2011) 1 *Polish Review of International and European Law* 1–41; S. Sykuna S. and J. Zajadlo 'Towards a New Theory of Hard Cases', in B Wojciechowski, K. Cern and P. Juchacz (eds), *Legal Rules, Moral Norms and Democratic Principles* (Peter Lang 2012). See also C. Abbt and O. Diggelman (eds), *Zweifelfälle* (Nomos 2007).

20 Sykuna and Zajadlo, 'The Theory of Hard Cases and Humanitarian Intervention', ibid.

21 Ibid.

a conflict between the law and other normative systems.[22] In this respect, of course, relations which may appear between law and morality are most often talked about. Nevertheless, irrespective of the priority of conflict of legal and moral norms,[23] other areas may be identified where this confrontation causes, or may cause, other essential effects.[24] In this context, attention is paid to the relation of law with morality, religion, politics, economy, legal ethics, or as we emphasize in this chapter, with advances in science and medicine.

There are examples of hard cases in each of the above conflicts. It happens because we are faced with the necessity to make a choice between different, rationally justified and right solutions. Thus, there is a choice between different values. It is also seen in our conflict of two values: namely life and property (although it is not possible in this chapter to precisely settle their legal category). Using Dworkin's nomenclature, we should consider whether we are dealing with rules, principles, or even mere guidelines – which would be necessary in the event of a potential conflict between the right to life and the right to property. Moreover, taking the view that hard cases can be considered under the broad approach, the area of conflict should be defined. Without doubt, lawyers' intuition suggests that we are not dealing with simple rules. Furthermore, the simplest answer would refer to the conflict between law and medical science or, adopting the wider approach, to the relationship of law and morality. After deeper analysis, however, one has to reflect whether, by comparing the right to property with the property in an invention, we do not enter the realm of Dworkin's policies? The additional problem appears in the situation of the normative conflict of the right to life and the right to property. One should consider which obligations are connected with the guarantee of the right to life and which subject is burdened with it. Moreover, solving the potential conflict between the right to property and the right to life in the relationships between pharmaceutical companies and people of the poorest countries, one needs to consider whether there is a clash between two legal systems. Then, discarding any moral connotations, we would have to choose the law according to which the potential conflict would be resolved.

We are aware that any claims by least developed countries for access to the blessings of civilization in the field of medicine is not a new-found problem. The same can be said about access to more rudimentary goods – is there a

---

22 Ibid.

23 For instance, David Lyons connects the problem of hard cases with moral decisions: see D. Lyons, *Etyka i rządy prawa* (Dom Wydawniczy ABC 2000) 84 et seq.; for more on the conflict between law and morality, see M.H. Kramer, *Where Law and Morality Meet* (Oxford University Press 2004).

24 See O. Ezra, *Moral Dilemmas in Real Life: Current Issues in Applied Ethics* (Springer 2006).

difference, for example, between recognition of the claim for exceptions to intellectual property and claims to delivery of food in relation to the poorest countries? Such an exception would imply the recognition of primacy of the right to life over the right to property. Without doubt, primacy in the sphere of ethics and morality seems to be justified. Nevertheless, the next question appears: What is the scope of the right to life? It certainly includes the negative element in the form of the prohibition on killing. But what about positive activity in the form of preventing death? It is also relevant to consider which subjects would be covered by this positive activity.

Because of the nature of this book, the answer to the questions posed above go beyond the scope of this chapter. We are aware that it would require a holistic approach, mostly by in-depth dogmatic and legal analysis, and also by theoretical investigation, not omitting the philosophical aspect, in particular in relation to ethics and morality. But, since there is no doubt that ACTA will become the determinant of standards for future bilateral and plurilateral negotiations, the instrument – which will serve to temper norms resulting from this and future trade-related agreements concerning the enforcement of IPRs – would be an attempt to try the broader interpretation of their provisions. What is more, it cannot be ruled out that discussion of this topic may go well beyond a traditional legal discourse and move into the realm of moral argument.

Index